KU-019-317

Invisible Natives

DBS Arts

99010520

Invisible Natives

MYTH AND IDENTITY IN THE AMERICAN WESTERN

DBS ARTS LIBRARY
TEL 648 5475
417 7524

This book is due for return on or before the last date shown below.

0 5 MAY 2005

0 1 MAY 2007

- 7 MAY 2008

2 0 APR 2009

Copyright © 2002 by Cornell University

All rights reserved. Except for brief quotations in a review, this book, or parts thereof, must not be reproduced in any form without permission in writing from the publisher. For information, address Cornell University Press, Sage House, 512 East State Street, Ithaca, New York 14850.

First published 2002 by Cornell University Press

First printing, Cornell Paperbacks, 2002

Printed in the United States of America

Library of Congress Cataloging-in-Publication Data

Prats, A. J.
Invisible natives : myth and identity in the American western / Armando José Prats.
p. cm.
Includes bibliographical references and index.
ISBN 0-8014-3961-2 (cloth : alk. paper)—ISBN 0-8014-8754-4 (pbk. : alk. paper)
1. Western films—History and criticism. 2. Indians in motion pictures.
3. Western stories—History and criticism. 4. Indians in literature.
5. American fiction—History and criticism. 6. Difference (Psychology) in literature. 7. Identity (Psychology) in literature. 8. Group identity in literature. 9. West (U.S.)—literature. 10. Myth in motion pictures. 11. Myth in literature. 12. Race in literature. I. Title.
PN1995.9.I48 P69 2002
791.43'6278—dc21
2001006863

Cornell University Press strives to use environmentally responsible suppliers and materials to the fullest extent possible in the publishing of its books. Such materials include vegetable-based, low-VOC inks, and acid-free papers that are recycled, totally chlorine-free, or partly composed of nonwood fibers. For further information, visit our website at www.cornellpress.cornell.edu.

Cloth printing   10 9 8 7 6 5 4 3 2 1
Paperback printing   10 9 8 7 6 5 4 3 2 1

for

Judy

who blesses my work, my life.

Contents

[vii]

Illustrations

Colonel Thursday: I suggest the Apache has deteriorated, . . . judging
by a few of the specimens I have seen on the way out here.
Captain York: Well, if you saw them, sir, they weren't Apaches.

(*Fort Apache*, 1948)

Preface

When I was growing up in Havana, during the fifties, the Western captured my moral imagination. Even before I thought of Westerns as genre or formula or myth, I responded to their moral force and focus. In the political turmoil that characterized the Cuba of my boyhood, we felt reassured about the inevitable triumph of good: a single explosive moment rid the world of evil, perhaps forever. Since innocence made but small distinction between the Western and America, it followed that—by the unassailable logic of childhood illusions—America was a righteous nation.

My research interests in the Western owe little to my childhood fascination with the gunfighter. Yet they originate in a desire to explore the way in which the Western presented itself as America. How and to what extent was the Western America? Or perhaps more fully articulated: In what ways, if any, could it be said that the Western represented the conqueror's experiences on the frontier? To what extent, if any, was the Western a full and accurate representation of the historical West? Could Hollywood produce, perhaps even despite itself, a culturally significant convergence of the mythic and the historical? And were the West and the Western, then, the essential America—the nation said to have been wrought of the passions and tragedies of the advancing frontier, that America at once heroic and heartless, and as rapacious as it was bold? Similar questions have been recently addressed by Jane Tompkins in *West of Everything* and Lee Clark Mitchell in *Westerns*, though in both cases the emphasis has been on gender rather than on race and culture, which are my principal concerns here. These questions have been most thoroughly considered in Richard Slotkin's great trilogy on the Myth of the Frontier.

The harder I looked at the Western the harder it was to reconcile its moral claims with its image of the Indian. Children growing up in Cuba in the fifties learned about the greatest of all Indians (or so we thought)—the cacique Hatuey. Condemned to burn at the stake for the crime of defending himself and his people, Hatuey was the first martyr in Cuban history. Most vivid of all was the teacher's recitation of the cacique's last moments: already tied to the stake, Hatuey listens to a zealous Franciscan's platitudes about God and Faith. First, the priest proffers the reward: if Hatuey will convert, he will go to glory and everlasting peace. But if the cacique should fail to embrace the Faith, hell's endless torments await. Now the cacique interrogates the Franciscan: Do Christians go to heaven? To the priest's yes, Hatuey replies that he wants to go to hell, where he shall not be among so cruel a people. Here, then, was an Indian far different from the one that we generally saw in the movies, an Indian whose defiant spirit inspired us to play Indian (always dying nobly, of course) as often as we played cowboy. America, I would come to discover, promoted no such heroic vision of its Indian. Of the many Westerns that I saw in Havana, I remember only one whose Indian evoked the spirit of Hatuey—Robert Aldrich's *Apache* (1954). I saw it three times.

I remember only one line out of the whole of my tenth-grade American history text at Miami Beach Senior High School, in 1963. It appears in the brief section on Westward Expansion, specifically as a justifying response to the devastating effects of Manifest Destiny on the indigenous peoples: "The Indians hindered progress." There it is—stark, cruel, absolute in its Darwinian indifference. In the early days of my research into the Indian Western, three decades later, there was hardly an Indian to be seen that did more noble work than that of hindering progress. To be sure, he was ubiquitous, yet he was nearly invisible. He posed a formidable threat to the dreams of civilization, yet he was almost always faceless and voiceless, little more than a stubborn and irrational hindrance to be crushed and swept aside by progress's reckless vanguard. Moreover, it seemed to me, though at first only intuitively rather than systematically, that the claims of the revisionist Indian Westerns, from *Broken Arrow* to *Dances With Wolves*, amounted to little more than an insistence that a white hero could readily become an Indian—that he could become, indeed, the very best of them. In the end, the Indians of the revisionist Western, however refigured, vanished as certainly as did those of the canonical Western. The white hero remained to tell their story—and to claim, if implicitly, sole exception from complicity in their disappearance.

But if the Indian in my history book hindered progress, the Indian in the Western, however oppressed or misrepresented, subverted white America's self-representation as a righteous nation. The heroic tale of a moral vision projected outward on a landscape and thrust upon a savage people managed instead, despite itself, to make clear the nation's moral shortcomings. The Western began to look a good deal like the heaven of the Franciscan priest who tried to convert Hatuey; and so the Indian, a bit like Milton's Satan, might have held it better to burn in hell than serve in a Western.

Let me add that, aside from the occasional ironic remark that I have at times found unavoidable, there is little here that explicitly condemns the Western, either in the name of an ethical system or of a corrective ethnohistory. I could not consider this book less a failure than if it created the impression that it presents itself as an apology for the Indian. For then this book would be no different from those "revisionist" movies in which cultural arrogance overwhelms good intentions and good intentions betray cultural arrogance.

For all that it insists on the Indian's virtual absence, however, the Western *requires* him—not because it needs to depict one more moment in the relentless course of empire, but because the Western functions primarily as a source of national self-identification. Such an idea is hardly new to the study of Indian-white relations, but it is new (or at least fresh) in the study of the Western's Indian. Principally, then, I have wanted to uncover, in the details of the Western considered in the context of American history and culture, the methods and strategies whereby the representation of the Indian contributes to the project of national self-definition even as it undermines it. Most of this book constitutes an effort to respond to the questions that emerged from such a premise. I never hoped for clear answers as much as I did for ever more adventurous questions.

I would not want to proceed without first attending to an important matter of usage. In this book, almost all pronominal references to the Indian appear in the masculine form. The mythology that this book examines has almost always identified "the Indian" as male. The reason, though historically absurd, is nonetheless consistent within the design of the myth's own logic. The male Indian is the "savage" who blocks the white nation's way to the fulfillment of its exalted destiny; the enemy whose powers the hero must appropriate in order to defeat him;

[xv]

the primal sexual force that must be kept from the white woman. His defeat trumpets not only the victory of "civilization" over "savagery," it marks the first moment, prophesied and long-awaited, of the exceptional nation.

How would the New World tell its tales without La Malinche in 1520 or Pocahontas in 1607 or Sacagawea in 1804 or even the lesser known Me-ot-zi in 1868 or Kate Bighead in 1876? Yet, despite the instrumental, even essential, presence of the Indian woman in the chronicles of Contact and Conquest, she features far less prominently in the Western. She can be the exotic bride of a white renegade and, of course, in accord with the myth's penchant for self-flattery, she must be the chief's daughter, the fabled "Indian Princess." She is all too often the object of the hero's sexual and social fantasies: in *Little Big Man*, for example, Jack Crabb's Cheyenne wife, Sunshine, is the beautiful and tender alternative to Olga, Jack's helpless white wife. And when Sunshine's sisters lose their husbands to the white invaders, Jack keeps them sexually satisfied, in exchange for which they attest the wonders of his sexual powers. More often, however, the Indian woman of the white myth is her own father's "donation" to the white hero, perhaps the sexual tribute meant to appease his ever-seething capacity for violence. In the mythology of the frontier, this Indian woman is at least as old as Alfred Jacob Miller's well-known painting *The Trapper's Bride* (1847) and as memorable as *Jeremiah Johnson*'s Swan, given to the hero in exchange for the scalps of warriors from an enemy tribe. At other times she is the bride of the conqueror himself, of Hernando Cortés, of John Smith, of George Custer—the beautiful maiden of divided loyalties, bewitched by a white hero who has no peer among the men of her own tribe. Much too frequently the myth cruelly forces her hand in the destruction of her own people. Or else she simply marks the time—patiently, devotedly, presciently—till the inevitable reappearance of the white virgin in the life of her white lover, even unto consciously sacrificing life or limb so that the destined union can take place. Of such stuff are Magawisca in Catharine Maria Sedgwick's *Hope Leslie* (1827) and Nat-U-Rich in the Edwin Milton Royle play of 1905 that inspired Cecil B. DeMille to film it three different times, *The Squaw Man*. Or she simply dies defending her white husband-hero, as does Sonseeahray in *Broken Arrow*, freeing her Tom Jeffords to declaim on the Indian's "plight" for the rest of his days. Often bartered and as often battered (who will not avert one's eyes in revulsion at the treatment of Look in *The Searchers*?), the Indian bride also serves the myth's skewed sense of comic relief, stands (and falls and even rolls downhill) as the butt of its cruel jokes at the Indian's expense.

Ubiquitous, to be sure, and no less a victim than her male counterpart, yet somehow hardly central to the action: she dies or else she disappears—all in docile compliance to the mythology that so harshly abuses her. For she must often prove nothing so vital as that the white hero is a better man than her own Indian mate. The myth would have its free and easy way with its representations of Indian womanhood because it needs first to destroy the savage warrior. And he is formidable—or must somehow be made to seem so if the myth is to assert the heroic identity of its white protagonist and the exalted destiny of the exceptional nation.

ARMANDO JOSÉ PRATS

Lexington, Kentucky

Acknowledgments

Of all the debts that I have incurred in the writing of this book, the dearest one is owed my wife, Judith Gatton Prats. May the dedication restore some balance to my account.

Thirty years, and I have not yet learned to thank W. R. Robinson fully, even properly. His influence on my work, on my life, is inestimable.

Thanks to all the good people I met during the research and writing—Christine Bold, John Demos, Brian Dippie, Paul Hutton, Lee Mitchell, Susan Sheckel, and Richard Slotkin. I can only hope that my work is in some small measure worthy of theirs.

Some three years ago I received—as it were "unimplor'd, unsought"—an email compliment on one of my essays on the Indian Western. The author was J. Douglas Canfield, who also read the manuscript and greatly enriched it. Although he does not care much for *The Searchers*, his friendship has become a precious thing in my life. *Gracias, hermano, por tu apoyo.*

I have Kentucky colleagues aplenty to thank. Gordon Hutner carried out a vital mission on behalf of this book. Dana D. Nelson read parts of the manuscript and sharpened their focus. John G. Cawelti was the first of my colleagues to read the manuscript. For this I thank him, yet not as much as I do for the thorough delight of a twenty-year friendship. I thank David Durant, who, as chair of my department, most generously supported every aspect of my project, even to the last whimsical (yet ever urgent) request. And I thank colleagues mostly for a quarter century's worth of fellowship—Tom Blues, Joe Gardner, Larry Swingle,

Art Wrobel. I shall miss Bill Campbell—his passionate mind, his poetic soul, and his glorious imitations of John Wayne. I am also grateful for the sustaining friendships of Pat, Ricka, and Darran White. I thank George and Helen G. Frazier for just about everything. Greg Waller was a very dear friend long before, as chair, he had to learn to indulge me. Walter C. Foreman, Jr., was once again, as in the long-ago days, pressed into service as reader, and he is still the champion manuscript annotator and the best of friends. To my brother Pedro M. Fernandez, I am grateful for a lifetime of unstinting loyalty and the most selfless generosity; and to his lovely daughter Kristina Marie I am grateful for the timely rescue that only her father's daughter could have effected.

Thanks to Lucy Combs for so graciously taking care of the innumerable details and to Andy Johnson and Deborah Kirkman, whose kindness and good will enabled my confident neglect of administrative duties.

I owe a debt of gratitude to the following graduate students, who honored my teaching even while I was completing this book: Jeff Birkenstein, Lisa Broome, Ann Ciasullo, Steve Hopkins, David Magill, Jason McEntee, Sean Morris, Michelle Sizemore, and Geoff Weiss.

I also acknowledge the generous help of the staff of the William T. Young and Margaret I. King libraries, especially Shawn Livingston, Kate Black, Gordon Hogg, Paul Willis, Rob Aken, Bill Marshall, and Judy Wiza. I thank Richard and Kay Crist for two years' worth of peace and quiet in a busy library.

This book project was funded time and again by the Office of the Vice-Chancellor for Research and Graduate Studies. Ironically perhaps, the repeated pleas for grant money produced, in time, a fine friendship with Vice-Chancellor David Watt. I also thank his successor, James Boling, for his generous support.

Thanks to the two research assistants who worked so hard on things at which I am so inept: Caren Mulford-Slagel and Ann Ciasullo.

I could never have imagined a more supportive and knowledgeable editor than Cornell University Press's Bernhard Kendler. I thank him for his patience, for the wisdom of his advice, for sharing my anxieties, for caring. Teresa Jesionowski made the copyediting a delight. I will always treasure her graciousness as much as her reassuring expertise. At the Press, I am also grateful to Susan Kuc as well as to Susan Barnett, who generously corrected me on several important details.

I thank James B. Alvord, Jr., and his daughters Megan Jane and Grace Margaret for the wealth of kindnesses, not least of which is the ongoing grand tour of America. To his wife, Ana Prats Alvord, I express my profound admiration and gratitude: she inherited, whole and undiminished, the gift of devotion bequeathed to her by Olga Rodriguez-Cáceres (1922–1991) and Clara Avendaño y Quintero (1899–1997). They live in you.

To Emily Rose and Lily Kathleen . . . What might I more humbly give thanks for than the ineffable joy of your presence?

Invisible Natives

Introduction
Representation and Absence in
Northwest Passage

"For anybody that wants to draw Indians, you haven't taken advantage of your opportunities. Look at 'em!" He waved his big hand toward the sprawled red bodies that lay between us and the [Indians'] houses. . . . "You couldn't draw that, could you?" Rogers asked. "Not and keep your stomach in you, hardly?"

—Kenneth Roberts, *Northwest Passage* (1937)

Passion and talent, no less than dire circumstance, direct Langdon Towne, the enthusiastic young artist in *Northwest Passage*, to paint Indians. Somehow, however, he never shows us even one sketch of an Indian. Yet, long before the ending, he kills more than his share of them: to see Indians—as he eventually does—becomes preliminary not to rendering them on canvas or paper, in oil or watercolor, but to shooting them dead. Had he actually painted them, then, it would have been not because they willingly posed for him, but because they lay dead at his feet. Yet Langdon's sketchbook shows not even dead Indians, for we see none at all, not even the blank page that yet awaits their presence.

Instead of painting Indians, Langdon Towne renders a heroic sketch of the protagonist, Major Robert Rogers, and of one other ranger who, along with Langdon himself, has recently taken part in the destruction of an Abenaki village. And the very sketchbook in which he would have drawn his studies of the natives contains no more exotic images than those of his beloved Elizabeth, who awaits him back home in Portsmouth, New Hampshire. Having killed his share of Indians, Langdon can now hope for happiness ever after in Elizabeth's embrace.

But there are no more Indians in his future: he is off to London (at Elizabeth's insistence) in order to study the craft of the masters (perhaps Sir Joshua Reynolds's himself), his passion and his talent now fully in the service of a triumphant white America and of America's Indian-fighting hero.

Of just such ironies, as cruel as they are unstudied, does the Hollywood Western construct its Indian. These ironies point to a grand source of transformations, of cultural transmutations, a system capable of converting, often past all recognition, the historical encounter with the Indian into that powerful mythology of triumphalist nationhood that I call the *Myth of Conquest*. The Indian Western, not unlike Langdon Towne, would keep the Indian all but invisible, yet it must still "present" him somehow—and with a purpose. It makes him *present* so that it may render him *absent*. Moreover, the conqueror must produce an Other whose destruction is not only assured but justified. The Indian's absence is inevitable, foregone. Even so, the Vanishing American must return (if I may allude to Leslie Fiedler's beautiful and still deeply relevant book), not only to be violently made absent again, but to vindicate—if only in the uneasy interval between triumph and remorse— the "history" that transmutes might into right.

The Myth of Conquest is contained within the larger idea of what Richard Slotkin variously calls, in his monumental trilogy, "the myth of America" or "the Myth of the Frontier."[1] Conquest, even when considered as a nexus of premise, motive, and outcome, defines only one (though important) historical idea in the greater history of America and the frontier. The Myth of Conquest is also contained within the larger history that Patricia Nelson Limerick has documented in her influential book, *The Legacy of Conquest*:[2] the "legacy" may have its mythological ancestry, but it takes other forms beyond those that I consider here.

The Myth of Conquest pretends to supply the "historical" source of the Indian Western. Its confident, if rapacious, appropriations of history tacitly insist that white America's contests with Indian savagery are grounded in the experiences and chronicles of the frontier—that

---

1. These are, in order of publication: *Regeneration through Violence: The Mythology of the American Frontier, 1600–1860* (Middletown: Wesleyan University Press, 1973); *The Fatal Environment: The Myth of the Frontier in the Age of Industrialization, 1800–1890* (Middletown: Wesleyan University Press, 1985); *Gunfighter Nation: The Myth of the Frontier in Twentieth-Century America* (New York: Atheneum, 1992).

2. Patricia Nelson Limerick, *The Legacy of Conquest: The Unbroken Past of the American West* (New York: Norton, 1987).

such conflicts are, indeed, these very experiences and chronicles themselves. Such an insistence is, to me, as compelling as it is disturbing, and at least as instructive as it is deceitful. To be sure, then, we do not make our leap of faith to take such claims in the spirit that Hollywood offers them, but neither should we dismiss the claim out of hand, if only because of the well known historical fondness of nations for invoking their myths as remembered history.

Richard Slotkin clearly explains the relation between history and myth that *Invisible Natives* adopts: "For most Americans—to the perpetual dismay of westerners—the West became a landscape known through, and completely identified with, the fictions created about it. Indeed, once that mythic space was well established in the various genres of mass culture, the fictive or mythic West became the scene in which new acts of mythogenesis would occur—in effect displacing both the real contemporary region and the historical Frontier as factors in shaping the on-going discourse of cultural history."[3] Moreover, the reciprocal relation of myth and history in the Western produces, perhaps inevitably, the hero-centered narrative (and may in part explain why Langdon, intending to paint Indians, ends up painting the white hero instead).

The Myth of Conquest is no less *appropriative* than is Conquest itself. What is Conquest if not omnivorously acquisitive—"just robbery with violence," as Joseph Conrad might have put it, "aggravated murder on a great scale"? And so Conquest's *mythology* presupposes the methodology of historical and cultural appropriation. I am referring to the notion, virtually enjoying the status of a first axiom, that the mythological alterations of historical events—*regardless, and often because, of the resulting distortions*—influence the national character, and that the selfsame alterations, taken as system, structure, and pattern, become not only the major constituents of American culture but also the presumed methodology that articulates it. The relation between myth and history tends to be unequal: if the process of relatedness were to exhibit various temporal phases, then we would see, among the earliest of these phases, the moment when the Myth of Conquest simply *claims* history, without authorization and without remorse. Yet this initial inequality tends to even out when *culture*, begotten of such incompatible parents, influences both history and myth, the one as much as the other.

I do not propose a systematic correction of the immense variety of

---

3. *Gunfighter Nation*, pp. 61–62. Also see pp. 278–312 for a detailed development of the concept that the Western constitutes a coherent appeal to American history.

mythological (mis)representations of the Indian in the Hollywood Western.[4] Neither have I thought it wise to suggest, let alone establish, a critical paradigm—based on other sources, say, native testimony or anthropology—that would explode the basic premises and claims of the Myth of Conquest. What does it avail us that we should contradict a specific event or custom, as mythically rendered, by recourse to historical or ethnological data? How would such a critical strategy not tend to validate the very thing it seeks to discredit? For all that such strategies have identified the need to contest Hollywood's Indian, they have failed in their stated mission to reconfigure the image of the Indian. *Invisible Natives* offers a critique of that image not by recourse to other disciplines or methods but by a detailed and extended descriptive analysis of *modes of representation* that function—simultaneously— as *models of self-subversion*. It seeks to recognize the unsuspected yet pervasive instability within the Myth of Conquest's self-conscious and seemingly static system of representation. Thus, I appeal to the history of the American West not for the sake of correcting the West's mythology or of establishing the authority of historical sources, but for the sake of specifying, so far as this may be clearly done, the intersections of myth and history, that reciprocal and complementary relation that goes so far in identifying American culture. Finally, with regard to methodology, I have taken it as axiomatic that no valid critique of the sort that I am proposing can dispense with the details of the movies under consideration.

The Indian Western demonstrates its inventiveness principally through the fabulous alterations that it can produce in its idea and image of the Indian. It deploys its strategies and methodologies, its historical claims and cultural assumptions, in order to transform its figure of the Indian into the many forms that leave only the Indian's trace. Like Langdon Towne, for example, the Western almost always produces a dead Indian, or else, as if in a more benign transmutation, the Vanishing American. Also like Langdon, the Western will substitute the Indian-fighter for the Indian and ask us, in the bargain, to take the switch as proof that its craft can convert base stuff to something noble. Langdon shows us nothing in the way of a native, yet he will show us, in the native's place, that figure whom we, so well acquainted as we are with the Western and its conventions, would readily take for the native's nemesis. More central to our purposes, however, Hollywood's

4. This task has been nobly attempted by Ralph E. Friar and Natasha Friar, *The Only Good Indian: The Hollywood Gospel* (New York: Drama Book Specialists, 1972).

image of the Indian—*the visual and immediate presence of an Other*—
comes to be itself transmuted, consistently and inevitably, into an *absence.* The same images that would *present* the Indian make him, instead, virtually invisible; similarly, the purported stories of his culture
and his cause sever him from American history and heritage. Accordingly, *Invisible Natives* can be described as a sustained reflection on the
idea that, at least in the Indian Western, *Otherness is absence and absence
Otherness.* I hasten to add, however, that *Invisible Natives,* for all its sub-
versive work, does not pretend to recover an authentic Indian, as if the
Indian's absence in the Western had a proper yet hidden obverse that
can be reconstructed from that absence, as when astronomy infers the
presence of a star from the star's background radiation. Conquest's
alchemy produces white heroic presence out of Indian absence, but this
does not mean that it holds, as if sequestered deep within its arcana,
the essence of a true, elemental, and authentic Indian. Thus the Indian
of the Hollywood Western dramatizes the old Platonic inspiration that
"not-being is a kind of being" (*Sophist* 258b–c), so that he might be said
to belong to the category that Plato designates as ἕτερον ἐκείνου ("the
other of being"), or of what we are more likely to call the Same. Also, the
Indian's very evanescence, what one might more properly describe as
an intermittence, resonates with Macbeth's insight, that "nothing is but
what is not" (I:iii).

   Perhaps my brief account of Langdon Towne's ambiguous talent will
justify my decision to charge *Northwest Passage* with further developing
this introduction.

2

Shortly after the opening of *Northwest Passage* (Vidor, 1940),[5] Langdon
Towne (Robert Young), as outspoken an idealist as he is a talented
painter, returns to his home in Portsmouth, New Hampshire. First in
his family to attend college, Langdon now has to face his parents and
brothers in shame, for he has been expelled from Harvard. His "youth-

   5. The full title of the movie is *Northwest Passage (Book I: Rogers' Rangers).* Vidor was
supposed to make a second part, which "would have dwelt on the flaws evident in
Rogers' heroism when he returns to civilization . . . Rogers would have been seen *promoting* his fame, with a media boost from Towne's heroic paintings, toward the goal of per-
suading King George to finance his search for the Northwest Passage." Raymond
Durgnat, *King Vidor, American* (Berkeley: University of California Press, 1988), p. 192. See
also Joel Greenberg [interviewer], "War, Wheat and Steel," *Sight and Sound* 37, no. 4 (Autumn 1968): 195.

DBS Arts Library

ful folly," as his father puts it, consists of protesting, via a cartoon, a vile-tasting pie that he and his friends have been served in the Commons. Langdon's sketch accords with the description of it in the Roberts novel: "I blocked out a man in Pilgrim dress, holding a dish in his extended hand; and opposite him I lightly sketched a bushy-tailed pole-cat clutching his nose with a paw and shrinking disgustedly from the proffered plate."[6] Langdon's family is quick to forgive and, contrary to the stern sentence that Langdon's father exacts in the novel, in the movie his parents encourage him to follow his "feelings" and fulfill his ambition to paint.

Warmed by his family's blessings, Langdon now heads for the home of Elizabeth Browne (Ruth Hussey), his long-time sweetheart, to ask her parents for her hand in marriage. But the Brownes deny Langdon anything like his own family's full endorsement of his "feelings." No sooner at the Brownes', in fact, than he learns that Hunk Marriner (Walter Brennan), a rebellious rustic whom we first see in the town square pillory, has already told everyone in town about Langdon's expulsion from Harvard. Since Langdon has failed at college, Reverend Browne (Louis Hector) demands to know how he proposes to support his daughter. Langdon, brimming with confidence, responds: "I want to be an artist, an American artist—a painter." But Reverend Browne scorns Langdon's dream. He accounts painters just about as respectable as "actors, mountebanks, [and] drunkards rolling in the gutter." When Langdon retorts that Velázquez and Rubens were "very great gentlemen" and that Sir Joshua Reynolds "is the toast of London," Browne merely scoffs, assuring him that he is not the equal of even the least of those three; and then, somewhat gratuitously, he pronounces Langdon's doom: "I can only say that if you persist in this career [as a painter], then nothing can save you." The beautiful and loving but ineffectual Elizabeth defers to her father's harsh judgment, and Langdon walks out into the street, angry and disillusioned. He heads for Stoodley's Tavern, where he plans to drink himself "out of lovesickness," as his friend Cap Huff (Nat Pendleton) puts it.

In a room at Stoodley's, Langdon's outrage over his treatment at the Brownes' becomes increasingly bold and boisterous. Though not quite "rolling in the gutter," he rails against Reverend Browne, accusing him of caring only for "money and power." More dangerously still, he berates the land-grabbing Wyseman Claggett, the King's attorney, who condemned Hunk Marriner to the pillory because Hunk spoke pub-

6. Kenneth Roberts, *Northwest Passage* (Garden City: Doubleday, 1937), p. 18.

licly against Claggett's theft of his land. As he is telling Cap and Sam Livermore (Lester Matthews) that Claggett is "the biggest thief in this province," the action cuts to the next room, where the surly and pompous Claggett (Montagu Love) is drinking with his henchman, Sheriff Packer (Richard Cramer). Claggett and Packer enter Langdon's room, and Claggett accuses him of slander; then he orders the sheriff to take Langdon away. Here, however, Hunk, fresh off his own punishment at Claggett's hands, shows up at the window of the drinking room, and when Claggett gives the order to have Hunk arrested too, a scuffle breaks out. Cap snuffs out the lights and knocks out both Claggett and Packer. Langdon and Hunk flee.

Young and talented and hopeful, yet also spurned and persecuted, where is Langdon to go? The Western, of course, like the mytho-historical America that it represents, offers its clear and resounding answer: "Go West!" So it makes sense that the dejected young man should now take to the wilderness, as if yielding his very life to a geography of vague yet vigorous hopes. In his decision to go West, of course, Langdon joins the great American throng. Yet Langdon is also a distinctive sort of westering figure: now that he has failed as both scholar and suitor, he proposes to go West (to Albany, in the time of the French and Indian War) with Dutch traders: his mission, to *paint Indians.*

He reveals his intention for the first time shortly after he meets the hero of *Northwest Passage*, Major Robert Rogers (Spencer Tracy), commander of the irregular militia, in the service of the British Crown, known as Rogers's Rangers.[7] At the Flintlock Tavern, where they meet, Hunk tells Major Rogers that Langdon is an accomplished mapmaker. Rogers grabs Langdon's sketchbook and, impressed by what he sees, tries to enlist the two friends under his command, with Langdon as cartographer. In full if devious appreciation of Langdon's talents, Rogers gets Langdon and Hunk drunk enough that they awaken in the shadow of the fort at Crown Point to learn, for the first time, that they have in fact joined Rogers's Rangers. Shortly thereafter, they set off on a campaign—more properly a revenge raid—against the Abenaki Indians in Maine. Still, Langdon insists that he will paint the Indians along

7. Rogers, whose name, Francis Parkman wrote, "was never mentioned but with honor" during the French and Indian War, became a commissioned colonel in the service of the British Crown during the Revolutionary War. "In 1778, he was proscribed and banished." *The Conspiracy of Pontiac and the Indian War after the Conquest of Canada*, 6th ed. (1870; New York: Library of America, 1991), p. 469. Allan Nevins's more detailed account tells us that Rogers died dissolute and all but forgotten. See Allan Nevins, introduction to *Ponteach or the Savages of America: A Tragedy*, by Robert Rogers (New York: Lenox Hill, 1914).

[7]

the way: "I figure as long as we're going," he tells Rogers, "we can paint them as they really are. Nobody's ever done it before." As cartographer, Langdon shall chart the geography of empire, claiming for the nation the regions that come within his perspective, simply *because* they come within his perspective, as if (consistent with the great Columbian tradition) to see were already to discover, and to discover to possess. As artist, Langdon shall record the image of the authentic native, shall "paint them as they really are"; and once he has so precisely rendered the native in the fullness of his being, Langdon will become, as it seems unequivocally, an *American* painter.

3

I studied *Northwest Passage* as only one of many Indian Westerns. In its power to illuminate important aspects of my inquiry, it hardly seemed as remarkable as other movies that, though even more obscure, taught me much—*Arrowhead* (Warren, 1953), for example, or *The Stalking Moon* (Mulligan, 1969). Except perhaps for a certain yet unfulfilled ambition to extol the heroic proto-America begotten of the French and Indian War—an idea that, at least in popular culture, originated with Cooper's *The Last of the Mohicans* (1826)—*Northwest Passage* became just another Indian Western. Moreover, although Vidor was a third-generation Texan,[8] and filmed *Northwest Passage* "in the wilds of Idaho,"[9] the movie's geography (as distinct from its landscape) seemed uninviting for one studying the Western. Furthermore, John Ford's *Drums Along the Mohawk* (1939) had done a more admirable job of locating the nation's birth in the eastern frontier than *Northwest Passage* would a year later. And even *America* (1924), though it may have attested nothing more clearly than the decline of D. W. Griffiths's genius, had brought more passion and drama to the story of the colonial frontier than Vidor had in this one Western. Of the Westerns set in the eastern woodlands, I also studied the major adaptations of Cooper's *Mohicans*, especially Maurice Tourneur's (1920) and George B. Seitz's (1936)—as well as Michael Mann's version (1993); and in many ways these, especially Tourneur's, gave me a much more vivid sense of the Myth of Conquest's role in the reenactment of the great racio-cultural clash than did *Northwest Passage*.

8. Durgnat, *King Vidor, American*, p. 19.
9. King Vidor, *King Vidor on Film Directing* (New York: David McKay, 1972), p. 35.

Still, Vidor's movie, however obliquely, was nothing if not a Western and provided me with a useful version of the type that, in chapter 4, I call the Double Other. Also, it gave us (via the Roberts source novel) Crofton, a character who gnaws on the head of an Indian he has decapitated. In this act I saw as unabashed—and early—an instance of *white* savagery as was to be found until *Ulzana's Raid* (Aldrich, 1972) took up the topic more than three decades after *Northwest Passage*. Perhaps Raymond Durgnat had Crofton in mind when he wrote that *Northwest Passage* is "the single most ferocious prewar film we know."[10]

Now that I find myself having to introduce most of what I have written, *Northwest Passage*—or at least Langdon Towne—seems invaluable: I am struck by the extent to which Langdon—his talents and his passions, certainly, but also his cultural assumptions and claims—can effectively establish the affinity of an individual character with the assumptions, claims, and figural strategies whereby Hollywood represents the white man's historical encounter with the Indian. Langdon's efforts to paint the Indians develops as the story unfolds, and I would like to appeal to them, also, to further my introduction. But to work with what there is so far, let us ask: Why is it that Langdon, who would be an *American* painter, would be so by painting *Indians*? It is true that his models of artistic genius and social respectability— Velázquez, Rubens, Reynolds—never painted Indians, let alone Indians "as they really are." To do so, then, might make of Langdon an original, some proto-Catlin, say, painting his native subjects in their native world.[11] But how would success in painting the real Indians make Langdon an *American painter*? Why would he be most distinctly American who would represent the enemy of Manifest Destiny, of Westward Expansion, of Progress—of all such historical and cultural notions so dear to the Western, so close to the heart of the millennialist genre *par excellence*? Is it because, having painted the Indian, the white hero has in fact performed an *appropriative* deed that amounts to a form of "knowledge," so that he dispossesses the Indian in the act of knowing him, of possessing his image? The native's primal fear of the artist who, in rendering the native's image, would come to capture his soul—was it so unfounded after all (*vide* the absence of attested photographs of the great Lakota warrior, Crazy Horse)? Still, how would painting Indi-

---

10. *King Vidor, American*, p. 190.

11. Edward Countryman notes that Towne is "[l]oosely based on such real eighteenth-century artists as Benjamin West, John Singleton Copley and John Trumbull." See "Colonial Period" in *The BFI Companion to the Western*, ed. Edward Buscombe (New York: Atheneum, 1988), p. 95.

ans make Langdon an American? Is it the uniqueness of the experience? Or we could ask, though more abstractly: Why is it that the Same at once acquires and embodies his national identity only when he contacts—thence to paint or kill—the Other?

These questions, of course, have their source in the complex history of cultural transformations begotten of the contact between Indian and white, and can hardly be said to originate in Langdon's artistic ambitions. Yet Langdon's ambitions crystallize the Western's general assumptions about the representation of the Indian. Chief among these assumptions is that the Indian plays a crucial role in the definition of the American: he is most American, somehow, who knows Indians best—who knows them, we may as well anticipate, principally so that he may destroy them, and who destroys them *even as, if not indeed because, he represents them.*[12] The Western's Indian does not stand in the way of American progress so much as he stands in the way of the coming-to-be of the American. And yet America, the Western also tells us, comes into being when the Indian is out of the way. If the *opposition* is essential to the national self, so too is the *elimination* of it. Perhaps the ambiguity explains why the Indian is the Western's everlasting revenant: the Western had to save the Indian so that it could destroy him. But, of course, American philanthropy told us long ago that it was necessary to "kill the Indian to save the man." Such dilemmas may explain why I have found it impossible to separate white America's representation of the Indian from the issues of national identity that such representations invariably serve.

Invisible Natives also poses questions that the Western would rather sidestep, or at least not raise explicitly, questions about the Western's cultural assumptions and claims, about its figural strategies and motives. Yet, for the most part, these have seemed to me to be fairly obvious questions to ask of the Western. To take a simple one: What cultural assumptions compel Langdon Towne—or the Western in general—to believe without doubt that his art can depict Indians "as they really are"? This anticipates the central question of the first chapter: When the Western, as is its wont, claims to represent the Indian *fully* by recourse to the familiar *fragments* of the Indian's culture, do we take this strategy of representation to betray only the conqueror's arrogance, or can we also explore it for that irony whereby it *presents* the Indian by *making him absent*? During the first moments of the dawn raid on the sleeping

12. Already I am invoking the type that Richard Slotkin has called "the man who knows Indians." See, for example, *Gunfighter Nation*, p. 16.

Abenaki, before anyone is killed or any lodge is set on fire, Langdon and Rogers stealthily make their way to the French fort at the center of the village. They come upon what might best be described as a scalp "tree." "The hairy discs," remarks Langdon Towne in the Roberts novel, "I now saw, were scalps, and there were hundreds of them, moving gently in the dawn breeze."[13] The historical Major Rogers puts it more succinctly (if less poetically): "We found in the town hanging on poles over their doors, 600 scalps, mostly English."[14] Before we see any Abenakis, then, we see this much of them; the scalps tell us who they are, and of course the scalps justify their destruction. How do the scalps, considered as a heavily coded sign of savagery, condition our attitude toward the Abenaki? More important, however, how can the Western represent the Indian *without presenting him*? My attention to these encryptions of isolated cultural images has helped me determine the fundamental form of Indian presence in the Hollywood Western: the Western's Indian appears before us both (and often at once) as an *imminent presence* and a *virtual absence*.

At one point in *Northwest Passage*, before the raid on the Abenaki village, Rogers has Langdon awakened and brought to him. On high ground overlooking Lake Champlain, Rogers asks Langdon: "Want to paint some Indians?" But when Langdon looks at the lake below, he sees no Indians. "Better keep looking," Rogers responds. "If they see you first, you'll lay where they leave you. We don't stop for funerals." Only now does Langdon see Indians and Frenchmen, dwarfed by the distance, in the *bateaux* below. Where, so to say, will Langdon take his perspectival stance? The Indians that he means to paint—like those of the Western—are not just exotic Others but enemies, so he can hardly hope to have them pose as, for instance, Mah-to-toh-pa, the great Mandan chief, did for George Catlin: "[H]e stood," Catlin writes, "until the darkness of night broke upon the solitary stillness."[15]

In the scene from *Northwest Passage* that I have just now described, seeing becomes immediately conditioned by hostility toward the Indian and thus becomes, itself, a hostile act: Rogers, the Indian fighter, mediates Langdon's perspective: Langdon sees the Indians because the Indian fighter makes it possible. *He teaches Langdon to see Indians who shall in time teach him to kill them.* In chapter 2, accordingly, I try to de-

13. *Northwest Passage*, p. 165.
14. Robert Rogers, *Journals of Major Robert Rogers* (Dublin: J. Sheppard and J. Milliken, 1759), p. 140.
15. George Catlin, *Letters and Notes on the Manners, Customs, and Conditions of North American Indians* (1844; New York: Dover, 1973), 1:145–46.

termine how the white representations of the Indian require the demar-
cation of a space, or region, from which the Indian might be beheld, either to confirm his savagery or to endorse his nobility. I refer to these
regions as *the spaces of the Same*. Yet the very designation itself of such a
space already and always identifies its outside—what I call "the spaces
of savage spectacle"—and of course its denizen "outsider." By presupposing the integrity of these cultural geographies, Hollywood and the
representational tradition accomplish no more certain mission than to
identify the *insider* and his spaces by those sites that contain (both hold
and enclose) the Other. Perspective is essentially appropriative, and in
this way it functions as a correlative of the historical dispossession of
the indigenous people. In the Hollywood Western, Otherness often
suggests a compulsorily assigned geography.

Among the strategies of representation that identify the Indian in the
Hollywood Western, the voiceover narration of a white character, often
the protagonist, figures among the most powerful. In recent times,
Dances With Wolves (Costner, 1990) and *Geronimo: An American Legend*
(Walter Hill, 1993) joined those earlier movies, *Broken Arrow* (1950), for
example, or *Little Big Man* (Penn, 1970) that deploy the white character's voiceover in order to praise the virtues of both the natives and the
lone white man who, having befriended them, comes to admire them
and, at times, becomes "one of them." The Western, of course, is un-
daunted by the possibility that its white hero, having become "Indian,"
may be as ephemeral and tenuous a thing as its own "natives" Indian.
The Western, in such cases, tends to value the white hero's appropriation of the Indian's ways, not the authenticity of those ways. *Northwest
Passage* seems at first to dispense with anything resembling the white
hero's voiceover narration, yet it does deploy something like its visual
correlative in the form of the sketchbook that Langdon carries with him
into the wilderness. More important, Langdon shares with these other
narrators a role as *focus* on the Indian: we are led to believe that he will
show us real Indians, just as we are led to believe that the voiceover
narrator will tell us just how different the true Indian—the one he
knows intimately—is from the one *we* know. As I have noted above,
however, we never see a single one of Langdon's sketches of the Indians; and of the few sketches that we do see, none seems more imposing
than that of Major Rogers, who is their worst enemy (the Indians call
him *Wobi madaondo*, which according to the Roberts novel means
"White Devil"). Yet, as I hope to show in chapter 3, the characters who
relate the virtues of the Indians in voiceover form almost always end by
declaring the end of the Indian, his *absence*. What, then, might be the re-

lation between knowing the real Indian and killing him, between appropriating his virtues *and* pronouncing them extinct in all except the white hero? Does the white man's voice relate any story of the Indian that might be really different from that which the movies and their representational tradition have always related?

4

Opposing forces seem to attract Langdon to the Indians: he would paint them "really," or at the very least accurately; yet it is their Otherness—their character both fantastic and exotic, their *strangeness*, then—that draws him to them. Is Langdon's power, conjoined with that of the Euro-American representational tradition, so formidable that he can reasonably hope to capture the very *difference* that defies representation? Does Otherness not, if only by definition, resist, contest, the Same's figure of it? And yet we must ask the complementary question: if Otherness implies full compliance with the representational strategies of the Same, is it not precisely because *no actual and living—no radical—*"Other" was ever involved in the representation? Such a question emerges almost naturally from the basic observation that the Western tends to represent the Indian through the white hero, consistently resorting to him, often as a fully authorized Indian, to teach us all we need to learn about the Indian. In chapter 4, I develop the idea that the Western invests its hero with the power to appropriate the ways of the Indian. Such an investiture, however, suggests not a process of becoming, of "acculturation," but an uncritically held assumption: the Western simply takes it for granted that its hero can be as Indian as the Indian himself and at times even *more* Indian than the Indian. Such an assumption, entertained only by the winner in the great racio-cultural contest, dispenses with an account of the origin of the white hero's Indianness. In fact it must do so, for the Western has as much work to do presenting the white hero's Indianness as it does deploying it as its formidable weapon against the Indian. Because the hero becomes Other while enjoying his status as the preeminent Same, I examine him, in chapter 4, as a *Double Other*. I refer to the unquestioned assumption that the hero can readily become Other and yet retain, undiminished and unaltered, his Sameness, as *the mystique of cultural appropriation*. This mystique functions not only as a tacit endorsement of the hero's authority in matters concerning the Indian but also as a component of his heroic status. Movies such as *Northwest Passage* and *Hombre* (Ritt,

1960), dissimilar though they may be, presuppose some such mystique. That the mystique comes to be presupposed in *Northwest Passage* so as to characterize the genius of the Indian fighter and in *Hombre* so as to underscore the humane Indianness of the white hero—this should indicate not only the "uses" of Indianness or the plasticity of a narrative strategy but also the pervasiveness of this form of cultural self-flattery. Thus, films as dissimilar as *The Searchers* (Ford, 1956) and *Dances With Wolves*, or *Broken Arrow* (Daves, 1950) and *Arrowhead*, uncritically assume that the white hero can readily be Indian—so much so, in fact, that he soon becomes our chief authority in all things concerning Indians.

If the white hero of the Indian Western can so completely incorporate the Indian's culture, what then happens to his whiteness? The Western will not insist on much more than that its hero had to be a *provisional* savage; but it seldom inquires into the problems raised by the transformation. To what extent, then, does Otherness persist in a civilized America if the violent encounter with the Indian really is, as the Western tells us, the crucible in which the American character comes to be wrought? If Langdon Towne stakes his Americanness on his encounter with the Indian, then how much of an Indian is he when he has painted—or killed—the Indian? Even when we see him back in Portsmouth, beside his Elizabeth and ready for London, can we say—can the Western say—that he bears no trace of the very savagery that he is supposed to have erased utterly? And if at last the Western comes to recognize the persistence of the Indian in the white hero, by what strategies does it propose to erase it, or at least to elide it? Chapter 5 constitutes a sustained critique of the idea—again, mostly in the guise of an unquestioned cultural assumption held and promoted by the Myth of Conquest—that neither the hero nor the community that he makes possible bear even a trace of Otherness. The assumption uncovers an illusion, *the illusion of cultural divestment*.

This illusion readily functions as a lead into the *ambivalence* of the white hero: for he would fulfill his heroic mission on behalf of his race by becoming the enemy of his race. Therefore, the racio-culturally compromised hero requires not so much a (re)conversion but a "divestment." That which betokened his racio-cultural sacrifice and his heroism—namely, his having become Indian for his own race's sake—must now, at the end, be suddenly and completely eliminated. Indeed, the national memory itself must be abrogated, for the "history" of white triumph has let loose the demons of guilt and injustice and genocide. And the demons must be silenced, or at least placated. It thus becomes

[14]

necessary to *dehistoricize* the hero and, at least by extension, the national identity that he has brought into being. In chapter 5 I explore one way in which recent so-called revisionist or apologetic Indian Westerns have addressed the problem of history. The heroes in these Westerns, I suggest, embrace Indianness as a way to avoid history, but after they have done so, when the Indian (in compliance with the selfsame history) inevitably vanishes, they remain to inherit the American Paradise. They are therefore not the "only" but the *first*—enjoying the fantasy of the ahistorical, and to that extent therefore guiltless. That nexus of assumption and illusion and desire that makes possible such an American hero evinces a process that I identify with a neologism, *outfirsting*. In this process, the one being "outfirsted"—replaced as original, as "native"—is the Indian.

5

Fleeing Wyseman Claggett and the King's law, Langdon and Hunk come upon the Flintlock Tavern, 54 miles from their next chance to buy rum. Here, as I mentioned earlier, they meet Major Rogers, though they also meet the first Indian in *Northwest Passage*. He is, Major Rogers tells us, a Stockbridge Indian, and his name is John Konkapot (Andrew Pena). Konkapot is drunk, sitting at a table, his head buried in his arms. All this, his origin, his name, his drunkenness, and still more, we learn from Rogers, even though Konkapot is, himself, present before us. Rogers explains to Langdon and Hunk: "This Konkapot's a [psalm-] singing Indian, and he wants to sing. We can't sing to suit him, so he's dissatisfied. Whenever he's dissatisfied, he won't drink anything but rum. Unless we can get him to drink some beer so he'll get sick, he won't be fit to travel, and he's got to travel with me. So come on, we'll sing some beer into him." The four white men stand above the unconscious Indian and now burst into Ben Jonson's "Song to Celia." Slowly, Konkapot stirs and, now in close-up, lifts his head to reveal a hideously idiotic grin on his face. He provides bass accompaniments (chanting "boom, boom, boom") to the white men's song while the innkeeper plies him with one beer after the other. The beer foam rings Konkapot's idiot's grin. At last he gets up from his chair, saying to Langdon, "You my sweet bludda [brother]," and begins to stagger about the room, raising his feet high and grasping before him. Rogers interprets (and so again alerts us to the Indian's dependence on the white man): "He's

[15]

DBS Arts Library

climbing a mountain, now. When he gets to the top he'll fall off the other side. [*Konkapot staggers against the door and out of the tavern*] There he goes, right down into the valley. When he comes to, he'll be sober enough to travel."

The movies endowed the image with an unprecedented degree of specificity, releasing it into time and change and narrative; they culti- vated an unsurpassed ability to evoke a humanity at once individual and universal (*vide* Chaplin) through their capacity to render visual de- tail; and they learned to draw the very soul itself from the moving image. Yet these same movies, in the form of the Western, denied such dignity and distinction to the Indian, and so an old cultural history (one that William Faulkner might have cast among "the gnawed bones of the old world's worthless evening") victimized a new aesthetic. Rogers presents to us as degraded an Indian as Hollywood ever pro- duced. Konkapot is, of course, contemptibly drunk and stereotypically inarticulate. He is also simple-minded and, as Sergeant McNott (Don- ald McBride) informs us later, he reeks—so that he becomes, if only by an oversight on the part of the filmmakers, the embodiment of the foul- smelling pie that Langdon's painted polecat found so revolting. Per- haps more than anything else, however, Konkapot's Otherness be- comes most clear in his utter and abject *dependence* on the white man who represents him. His dependence itself defines the form of his pres- ence, the extent of his reality; it at once foreshadows and explains his absence. Moreover, in the very moment of his introduction, Konkapot comes to be known by some strange, even unlikely, admixture of su- perfluity and lack. The same hero who claims to need Konkapot refers to him as if Konkapot were already absent. Konkapot is at once essen- tial and expendable. We learn all we need to know about him even be- fore we see his face.

Although Konkapot exits, the scene continues, with Rogers now try- ing to get Langdon and Hunk drunk because he needs Langdon's map- making skills on his expedition. Langdon reveals for the first time that he is off to Albany to paint Indians because there he can find "tame" In- dians, not the ones that he is likely to encounter in Rogers's expedition. If he is to paint "tame" Indians, why did he pass up the opportunity to paint Konkapot? How could an Indian be any tamer? Or is it that Konkapot, tame to the point of being almost comatose, is not *exotic* enough for Langdon? Would Langdon have taken to his sketchbook if Konkapot had not lacked the accoutrements and regalia with which the Western invests the Indian and through which it almost invariably identifies him? All these, are, of course, plausible rhetorical questions,

[16]

and they hardly seem mutually exclusive. But I would like to offer a more radical answer to the question why Langdon never painted Konkapot at the Flintlock Tavern: he never did because he is, instead, listening to Rogers's description of Konkapot. Rogers's description— reductive, tendentious, demeaning—becomes the "true" picture of the Indian; and Langdon will not see the Indian for himself. It is of no small significance that Langdon and Hunk wake up at Crown Point, drunk, next to John Konkapot, himself still under the effects of the force-fed beer. One shot shows the three of them, each the other's equal, and not just in drunkenness but as living images and as brothers in arms. (Yet the two white men go off to glory and, at least one of them, romance.) Sergeant McNott wakes up the men and, as I mentioned above, orders Konkapot to change his shirt because he stinks. At this point, the supposedly indispensable Indian all but disappears from the story. Yet we shall hear from him again.

Much later, Rangers already seasoned enough to be among the advance party, Langdon and Hunk find themselves within the palisades of the French fort in the St. Francis Indian village. Having made their way to the ramparts, they look into the block house and see, only a few feet away, three drunk Frenchmen and two attendant Indians. As Rogers climbs to a rooftop and calls the rest of the Rangers to attack, Langdon and Hunk swivel a cannon around and aim it point-blank at these five men. Langdon lights the fuse and blows up the block house and the men in it. As the fight reaches its fevered pitch, Langdon shoots at the Indians from behind the ramparts. Rogers runs by and asks him, "Getting any pretty pictures?" Langdon looks away from his rifle sights only long enough to smile at Rogers, then he returns to his grim art. On the ground outside the fort; now fighting *mano a mano*, Langdon, out of ammunition, assaults an Indian with his rifle, and then, in an act of humanity clearly calculated to temper the delight that he has so far taken in killing Indians, he saves an Indian boy from the cannibalistic Crofton.

The Indians that Langdon might have painted now lie dead before him. But of course he does not paint these, either, though he might have sketched one or two, if only in anticipation of that formula that, a century after the historical setting of the action, would insist that only a dead Indian could be a good Indian. He paints none that we ever see, though he killed plenty. And so, in a turn of events perfectly illustrative of the ironies that we will pursue in this book, the man who would paint Indians becomes an Indian killer; who would render them in their native humanity renders them, instead, absent; who would be an

Northwest Passage (1940, MGM). The "American artist" as Indian fighter. Courtesy of MGM/Museum of Modern Art Film Stills Archive.

American for painting them becomes an American for destroying them; who would get his "pretty pictures" by obeying his calling, his passion, his talent, gets them, instead, by an acquiescence in, indeed a perverse connivance with, the blind and implacable drive of Conquest. His brush a rifle, his palette the Indian's blood—what more efficient method could the Myth of Conquest want of representing the Indian?

After the raid on St. Francis, the Rangers suffer greatly from hunger on their way to Fort Wentworth. Langdon, returning from a scouting foray to meet Rogers on Eagle Mountain, as previously agreed, reports that Lieutenant Dunbar's entire detachment, of which he is the lone survivor, has been wiped out. He further reports that the Indians cut up Dunbar (John Merton) while he was still alive, and that they "were playing ball with [the] heads" of Dunbar's men. Indians were not worth painting after all. As the young Mark Twain, who claims to have revered Indians before he actually saw them, so Langdon Towne. Like the very myth that empowers him, Langdon comes to "see" Indians as worthless artistic subjects, savage and degraded brutes. Dead before him, they already take "shape" as a "represented" absence. Here is no

[18]

nice and dainty metaphor to equate painting the Indians with killing them, with robbing them of their native being for the sake of importing them into an alien art. The decree is harsh and unequivocal; the artistic afflatus must yield to the exterminationist animus. Thus, once the cannibal Crofton commits suicide, the white race is rid of its own last "savage," and savagery can safely become the Indian's exclusive and defining trait. It is in the context of Langdon's report of Indian cruelty that the following crucial scene takes place.

In what appears to be only a moment of idle reflection, Rogers once again reaches for Langdon's sketchbook. In the transcription below, the bracketed insertions are as important as the dialogue.

> *Rogers*: When did you make these pictures?
> *Langdon*: On the way to St. Francis, about a hundred years ago.
> *Rogers*: [*Turning to the first page; CUT. Close-up of a charcoal sketch of McNott; CUT. Rogers, smiling*] McNott. [*Turning the page*] Konkapot! [*No corresponding CUT to a sketch of Konkapot*] Ugh! I can smell him! [*CUT. Close-up of sketchbook: on the recto page, opposite the unseen sketch of Konkapot, which is in the verso page*] Major Robert Rogers. [*CUT. Close-up of a white-black-and-red chalk study of Rogers*] No flattery, either. My boy, you're quite an artist.

I wrote a moment ago that Langdon never paints an Indian that we ever see. He does, however, paint one, or at least sketches him—John Konkapot. But we never see the rendering, though it lies next to Rogers's own. The sketch of the Major lies fully before us, while the verso page lies almost entirely outside the screen, showing not one line of the sketch of Konkapot. The page that contains Konkapot is not, therefore, a blank page but *an absent one*, a page lost beyond the edge of the screen; at once a showing forth and a withholding, a *claim* to have represented and a *failure* to show the representation. Therefore, *the representation is the absence*. The image that, if shown, might have somehow—by simple physical adjacency, if not by moral propinquity—bound Rogers to Konkapot—the Indian fighter to the living source of his gifts—this image has been cast into darkness, denied, and gratuitously vilified.

Recall now that earlier moment when we saw Langdon, Hunk, and Konkapot in close-up in one shot. They were sleeping peacefully, and their hangovers (and perhaps also their innocence) held them gently in their shared space. But McNott awakened the men, and white and Indian went their separate ways. The separation of that moment returns in the scene that I have just now described. Open Langdon's sketchbook, and you will find Indian and Indian-fighter together in the same folio—opposites, perhaps, one verso and one recto, but also complements each of the other. Yet *Northwest Passage* shows only the Indian fighter. And the Indian—it will do to know him by his smell! At this moment, at least, there is a convergence of "artist," hero, narrative, genre, myth: the artist who would have painted Indians has rendered, instead, the white hero; the story that would have shown the artist painting the Indian shows us, instead, his sketch of the hero while denying us a look at the Indian; the genre that would show the Indian as he "really" was, accounts it a sufficiently accurate representation of the Indian to show him by that which *fails* to show him fully—by fragments of his culture, by such pictures of him as demonstrate only his failings, and by producing, first and last, a white enemy of the Indian whose knowledge of the Indian enables the genre to dispense with the Indian even as it pretends to represent him. All of which redounds upon the Myth of Conquest, upon that tale, 500 years in the making, that so resolutely and confidently insisted—nay, yet insists—on representing him whom it will not see.

Part I
Strategies of Figuration

[1]

"By All the Truth of Signs"

The Indian in Synecdoche

"There they are, by all the truth of signs!" whispered the scout; "two ca-noes and a smoke!"
>   —James Fenimore Cooper, *The Last of the Mohicans*

I had often during an Indian campaign seen these signal smokes, on my front, on my right and left—everywhere, in fact—but could never catch a glimpse of the Indians who were engaged in making them . . .
>   —George Armstrong Custer, *My Life on the Plains*

Indian hater: *I ain't seen no Indians.*
Johnny Hawks: *It depends on how you look. I've counted 39 so far.*
>   —*The Indian Fighter* (1956)

1

The Hollywood Western never produced an Indian antagonist more memorable, or more familiar, than the one whom we never quite see. He can be formidable enough, this near-invisible Indian foe, in the great mythic tale of "the winning of the West": the disquieting antici-pation of an encounter (armed or sexual) with him often pervades the action; and (when at last he comes into view) the climactic battle against him specifies the crucial moment in the destined emergence of white America's national identity. Yet, imposing as such an Indian may be in his capacity to arouse the consternation of the white settlers or to challenge the white hero's powers, he tends to appear before us as a loose collection of fragments, at once hinting at and concealing a com-plete human identity. Smoke signals and feathered bonnets, arrows and lances, faces in war paint, painted ponies and frenzied dances, the reeking scalp (more often inferred than seen), the obligatory row of warriors on the distant ridge, the bloody aftermath of the massacre—such are the familiar images whereby Hollywood announces the Indian's inauspicious presence. When at last he appears before us, he is most often the misrepresented agent of an indigenous culture so muddled, fudged, and falsified that it seldom admits of reference except through those contrivances that configure Hollywood's idea of frontier savagery.

Perhaps such fragments of Indian culture disclose merely the frivolous archaeology of a fantasied primitive; or perhaps they do little more than enact that age-old and serviceable expedient whereby we come to fear most whom we see least. Certainly, however, these fragments unfailingly identify the Indian in his limited role as savage antagonist. At once reductive and recurrent—and quite beyond their status as indifferent tokens of a clichéd ethnicity—they purport to stand for the Indian.

But so easy an identification of the place of these fragments in the ranks of generic convention hardly explains their function as *figures* of the Indian, or exhausts their possibilities for a critique of the strategies whereby Hollywood represents the Indian Other. Because he appears in such broken and partial forms, the Indian remains allusive, often little more than part of an inferred and deferred whole. And yet—lest we forget the obvious—though these bits and pieces may show the Indian imperfectly, they are clear about his role as threat to America's national hopes. To see him thus is to know *of* him without ever knowing him. These culturally disconnected images therefore establish the Indian's *imminent presence* even as they enforce his *virtual absence*. The Indian's imminent presence, his appearance as the sign of an impending threat, already implies his virtual absence, that is, his emergence only as cultural *least* and human *lack*. In the most general way, then, these tropes of Indianness obey a pattern of representation in which, as Gerald Vizenor notes, "simulations of the other are instances of the absence of the real."[1] It is precisely in their capacity to designate the absence of a cultural "reality" that these presences derive their own cultural power. For it is, indeed, an unmistakable indication of cultural power to make the Other absent in the very act that purports to present him. This study does not—and cannot—aspire to produce a cultural or tribal

1. Gerald Vizenor, *Manifest Manners: Postindian Warriors of Survivance* (Hanover, N.H.: Wesleyan University Press, 1994), p. 1. And again: "Simulations are the absence of the tribal real," p. 4.

"real" out of the nexus of signs and images through which Hollywood has pretended to represent its Indian. Yet it can, by an appeal to the representation itself, generate a critique of both the assumptions and methods, of the image as well as of the idea, that the Western so often asks us to take as "real." To put it another way, the Indian Western *falsifies* the Indian not so much because it deliberately lies—since this would presuppose that Hollywood knows the Indian truly—but by making the Indian absent.

In their general ability to indicate a complete image of the Indian, these fragments tend to behave as *synecdoches*. I propose to adopt—but mostly to *adapt*—the term throughout this chapter, keeping in mind the modifications called for by the particular nature of the inquiry at hand, while exercising an earnest skepticism toward any term that would claim to be more than merely useful. Traditionally, *synecdoche* refers to the trope through which the part suggests the whole (as "hand" does "laborer") and, though less frequently, the whole the part (as "the law" does the "policeman"). Murfin and Ray write: "In synecdoche, the *vehicle* (the *image* used to represent something else) of the figure of speech is part of the *tenor* (the thing being represented)."[2] Thus, as Frank Beaver explains, "the use of a close shot of synchronized marching feet is a synecdoche for military power," as in the famous example of Sergei Eisenstein's *The Battleship Potemkin*.[3] So considered, then, *synecdoche* holds the advantage over "image," "symbol," or "signifier," because it readily evokes the strategy whereby the part implies the whole. The structure, action, and ideology of the Indian Western dictate the first of my modifications to the term: traditionally, synecdoche enables us to know the whole by the part, but in the Indian Western it also *contextualizes* that whole and assigns it its measure of relevance to the tale of Conquest.

Now, strictly speaking, an arrow or a feathered bonnet does not function synecdochically for the whole Indian, since these objects are not a part of the Indian's physical being. "A cave man coming suddenly upon his enemy," writes the poet John Frederick Nims, "perhaps a more primitive type with snarling teeth bared, might later report to his cave wife, 'Guess what I saw today! The Fang!' "[4] "The Fang" functions synecdochically for the whole of this toothy cave man. Arrow and

2. Ross Murfin and Supryia M. Ray, *The Bedford Glossary of Critical and Literary Terms* (Boston: Bedford Books, 1997), p. 395.
3. Frank E. Beaver, *Dictionary of Film Terms*, s.v. "synecdoche."
4. John Frederick Nims, *Western Wind: An Introduction to Poetry*, 3d ed. (New York: Mc-Graw-Hill, 1992), p. 50.

[25]

feathered bonnet are not to the Hollywood Indian as bared teeth are to Nims's cave man. I therefore adapt the term to include both the Indian and *Indianness*, the reference to both the being and the culture that the Myth of Conquest pretends to represent. I have little doubt that the Western can show itself remarkably unconcerned with the identity of any specific Indian, or that even when it would identify an individual Indian through these familiar fragments it means primarily to identify *savagery*, to announce its presence for the white community that must protect itself from it. In thus modifying the term, I am, to some extent, using a figure figuratively: Hollywood presents the Indian *as if* the arrows, the burning farm houses, the smoke signals, and so forth were fully empowered to stand for the whole Indian, who in his turn appears before us only as the representative of Otherness. It is crucial, then, to anticipate the effects of such a modification of the term: in this study, though it may *imply* some vague whole, synecdoche functions not only as image but as irony, for the image comes to specify the fundamental irony whereby the fragment of the Indian or of his culture is in fact deployed as a way of *dispensing* with that whole. The "part" can often be *all* the Indian that we ever see—the spurious, not to say the specious, "whole." Even when he appears at last in recognizable human form, he tends to remain inhuman, known to be "whole" only because he has now fully embodied the savagery betokened by the fragments that presented him. Accordingly, all references to a "whole" Indian are to be taken with a good measure of skepticism, and though the term will hereafter appear without quotes, it is to be understood throughout in this limited and all too ironic sense.

For our purposes, the distinction between synecdoche and metonymy answers roughly to that between image and name. "If our cave man," Nims writes, "had run into a more advanced type of enemy, he might have been especially impressed by something the stranger was carrying: a sharp rock fastened with deer hide thongs to a stout stick. If he had had a second escape, he might have reported later, 'I saw the Axe today!' A metonymy—the cave man is referring to one thing by using the name of something associated with it."[5] The second significant adaptation that I will make to the term *synecdoche* is to let it mingle more or less freely with *metonymy*—to take it, that is to say, as the visual fragment that "names" the Indian. Hence metonymy: "A figure of speech which consists in substituting for the name of a thing the name of an attribute of it or of something closely related. [ad. late L.*met*

5. Ibid.

ōnymi -a, a. Gr. μετωνυμία, lit. 'change of name', f. μετ(α)-META—+ὄνομα, Aeol. ὄνυμα name]."[6] We should note, however, that the Western is perfectly capable of invoking the name of the Indian in full correspondence with the traditional use of *metonymy*, as a portent of unrestrained savagery, for example, as when the name "Geronimo" resonates throughout the early sequences of John Ford's *Stagecoach* and clearly announces savagery's imminent presence.

2

Often, the first Indian synecdoche in a given Western effectively preempts the emergence of an Indian in more complete or complex form. To this initial synecdoche I will give the name *defining synecdoche*, since it presents the Indian in such a way as to already secure his defeat and guarantee his disappearance.[7] Thus the defining synecdoche tends to determine the Indian's *representational destiny*: it *originates* his presence even as it *foretokens* his doom. At the end, he is what he was at the beginning—absent still, present but to confirm his own inevitable passing in movie after movie. The defining synecdoche becomes, accordingly, a strategy whereby the Western denies the Indian participation in those processes said to constitute the source of American virtues—expansion, progress, the high and exalted pursuit of happiness. If he consistently struggles against the forms that represent him, it is only in the end to affirm their power over him, if only by proving to be as consistently and as hopelessly their victim.

Let us consider John Ford's *She Wore a Yellow Ribbon* (1949) in terms of its relation between the defining synecdoche and the Indian's representational destiny. The economy of Ford's tropes will serve as the clear

6. *Oxford English Dictionary* (New Edition), s.v. "metonymy."
7. The Indian synecdoche is coeval with Contact: already on 9 December 1492 the distant Indians appeared before Columbus as a threatening presence: "He [Columbus himself] thought that the settlements were probably far from the sea, from which settlements they saw when he arrived, and so all fled and took with them all that they had and made smoke signals [*ahumadas*] like people at war." *The* Diario *of Christopher Columbus's First Voyage to America, 1492–1493*, trans. Oliver Dunn and James E. Kelley, Jr. (Norman: University of Oklahoma Press, 1989), p. 213. I also refer the historically-minded reader to Moffitt and Sebastián's analysis of early images of the American Indian in the miniature paintings in *The Triumph of Maximilian I* of 1519 (Albrecht Dürer was one of the contributors), wherein the "ethnicity" of the male Tupinangas of Brazil "derives from their distinctive weapons, to which a few lances are now added, and of course by their routinely featured feathered apparel and headgear." John F. Moffitt and Santiago Sebastián, *O Brave New People: The European Invention of the American Indian* (Albuquerque: University of New Mexico Press, 1996), p. 166.

starting point for further study of the Indian in synecdoche. Early in the action, Sergeant Tyree (Ben Johnson) shows to his superiors at Fort Starke the feathered half of an arrow that he has taken from the side of the paymaster's stagecoach, which galloped driverless, pursued by Tyree and another trooper, during the opening montage. Sergeant Quincannon (Victor McLaglen), Major Allshard (George O'Brien), and Captain Nathan Brittles (John Wayne) examine it in silence. All but Quincannon offer their interpretations:

> *Allshard*: It's not Kiowa.
> *Brittles*: No, and it's not Comanche nor Arapahos either, with those color bands.
> *Tyree*: Sir.
> *Brittles*: All right, Sergeant, put in your two cents worth.
> *Tyree*: Sir, these arrows with the yellow, white, and red bands are sign of the Southern Cheyennes.
> *Brittles*: Well, I've seen Bannocks and Snakes use the same colors.
> *Tyree*: That's very true, sir, but look at the clan mark on this arrow. It's a sign of the dog. That arrow came from the bow of a Southern Cheyenne Dog Soldier.
> *Brittles*: What in blazes would the Cheyennes be doing this far South, Sergeant?[8]

The authority of the Indian fighters, as derived from the broken arrow, generates (and elaborates upon) the paradox whereby the Indian, however great the perceived threat that he poses, comes to be known through his virtual absence. Such "presence" as is the Indian's emerges here from the dubious ethnology that would identify the tribal origin of the arrow only for the sake of determining the extent of the Indian threat to Fort Starke. More important, however, the authority of the white men increases as they define the arrow's origin. The understanding of the signs is a privilege enjoyed by the white hero or the heroic white group, a racial gift only to the extent that the hero may represent his race's best. The *identification* of the Indian sign identifies the Indian fighter himself—at least as much as it identifies the Indian. The Indian synecdoche requires the white Indian fighter as much as it requires the fragment itself.

Over the course of the action, the vague yet insistent Indian danger signaled by the broken arrow comes to be embodied in the villain Red Shirt (Noble Johnson), an Arapaho chief who tries to unite the many tribes in a war against white encroachment. Once war seems inevitable,

---

8. For a similar scene establishing the presence of Indians by the white man's ability to "read" the arrow, see the synecdochically titled film, *War Arrow* (Sherman, 1953).

the voiceover narrator (at the very beginning he delivered the urgent news, "Custer is dead!" over the guidon of the defeated Seventh Cavalry) now reemerges over the familiar image of Indians riding single file on a ridge:

> Signal smokes, war drums, feathered bonnets against the Western sky, new messiahs, young leaders are ready to hurl the finest light cavalry in the world against Fort Starke. In the Kiowa village, the beat of the drums echoes in the pulse beat of the young braves. Fighters under a common banner, old quarrels forgotten, Comanche rides with Arapaho, Apache with Cheyenne. All chant of war, war to drive the white man forever from the red man's hunting grounds.

Although the voiceover narrator tells us that the Indians are now united, he presents them mostly by recourse to the familiar tokens of Indianness. The Indian need be only the portent of terror to fulfill his role in the epic of Anglo-American nationhood. Thus the Indian synecdoche becomes a way of insisting on the Indian *menace* as the Indian of greatest interest to and importance in the Myth of Conquest.

Toward the end of the action Brittles and Tyree, still hoping to avert an all-out war, ride into the Indian camp to appeal to an old friend, Pony That Walks (Chief John Big Tree). As Brittles, now on foot, makes his way through the camp, Red Shirt gallops close to him and shoots an arrow between his feet. Brittles picks it up, breaks it in two, spits on it with contempt, and throws the pieces at the startled and clearly intimidated Red Shirt. After this scene, Red Shirt all but disappears—as if the breaking of the arrow could so conclusively signal the beginning of savagery's fated end on the western frontier. Both early and late in *She Wore a Yellow Ribbon* the arrow betokens not so much a hostile Indian as the white man's power over the Indian.[9] This power has its principal source not in the hero or in the director (however undeniably these may influence the action) but in the discourse of Conquest itself—that is to say, in the rhetoric of its values and the economy of its representations, and also in the capacity of this discourse to produce the *Indian*

---

9. Brian W. Dippie relates the droll ritual whereby Native Americans became citizens of the United States early in the twentieth century: "The Secretary of the Interior called each applicant forward by his white name, asked him for his Indian name, handed him a bow, and instructed him to shoot an arrow. Addressing him by his Indian name, the secretary said: 'You have shot your last arrow. That means that you are no longer to live the life of an Indian. You are from this day forward to live the life of the white man. But you may keep that arrow; it will be to you a symbol of your noble race and of the pride you feel that you come from the first of all Americans.' " *The Vanishing American: White Attitudes and U.S. Indian Policy* (Lawrence: University of Kansas Press, 1982), p. 193. All Indian arrows would be henceforth shot on the white man's command.

DBS Arts Library

out of its own mytho-cultural assumptions and requirements. The Myth of Conquest assumes uncritically that the Indian's Otherness can be properly objectified, and it demands that it appear not only as difference but as opposition to its values and its virtues. Thus it creates the Indian type that Marsden and Nachbar have named "the Savage Reactionary." This Indian, they write, "is a killer because he detests the proper and manifest advancement of a White culture clearly superior to his own and often because of his own primal impulses. He must be annihilated for the good of civilization."[10] The Myth of Conquest defines the Indian's historical and cultural reality by postulating his *reaction* to white America. In this way, the Indian Other becomes the ironic agent of the Same: by insisting that the Savage Reactionary is the essential Indian, the Myth of Conquest transforms the Indian's historical and cultural reality into a strategy of American self-definition. The new nation comes to affirm its civilized being through persistent—and persistently passionate—tributes to the destruction of the "savage" native peoples. America's representations of the triumph over savagery reveal its own genocidal animus, the cultural brutality that at once supports and subverts the new "civilized" order.

Tyree and Brittles's knowledge of Indians originates not so much in individual experience (how often, really, do we learn just how the white hero came by his knowledge of the Indian?) but in their presupposed and unchallenged *agency* on behalf of the Myth of Conquest. To define the Indian synecdoche is to attest to this discursive power that makes the synecdoche possible in the first place, that enables and promotes just such an incomplete Indian as if he were in fact all that there is to the Indian. Discourse about the Indian thus places itself *before* the Indian, postulates a beginning that predates the defining synecdoche. And thus it also places itself ever *after* the Indian, posing as the repository of his memory, prescribing the rule and measure of his character— at once the augury, the method, and the proclamation of his end.

3

If the Indian synecdoche designates the form and function of the antagonist in the great struggle for mastery of the West, it also identifies the

---

10. Michael T. Marsden and Jack Nachbar, "The Indian in the Movies," *Handbook of North American Indians,* ed. William C. Sturtevant (Washington, D.C.: Smithsonian Institution, 1988), 4: 609.

dynamics of discursive power through which such an Indian comes into being. Indeed, Indian synecdoches may at times betoken nothing with greater clarity than the power of the Myth of Conquest to ironically appropriate Indian culture for its own purposes. The fact itself of the Indian's virtual absence, as denoted by these synecdoches, suggests their status as *indices of power over the Indian.* When Brittles breaks Red Shirt's arrow in two, he in effect returns the Indian to his initial condition, to the virtual absence specified by the defining synecdoche. By enforcing the Indian's virtual absence, the synecdoche, which had seemed to produce or at least to anticipate something like a complete Indian, instead keeps the Indian from developing. It exists not so much to indicate the Indian as *to suppress* him. The artifacts of a presumed culture derive their significance from the discourse the values of which the Indian is supposed to threaten.[11]

The status and function of the defining synecdoche as index of power can be clearly confirmed in instances of enforced *reversion*: in such cases the Indian appears first as a whole image, but a white character, usually the hero, identifies him through the familiar fragment, which appears *after* the Indian does. Thus, the Indian in full corporeal form, appearing before the defining synecdoche, confirms rather than negates the minimalized Indian of *She Wore a Yellow Ribbon*. For example, Raoul Walsh's *Distant Drums* (1951) opens with a head-on shot of three Seminoles in war paint and feathered headdress, each beating on a war drum. Yet, even before the opening credits begin, Walsh cuts to a close-up of a single drum, so that the Indian beating it is now offscreen.

Immediately after its opening credits, André de Toth's *The Indian Fighter* (1956) cuts to a shot of Onahti (Elsa Martinelli), the daughter of Chief Red Cloud, undressing for a plunge in the river. A cut shows the white hero, Johnny Hawks (Kirk Douglas), making his way through the woods, and a subsequent cut shows Grey Wolf (Harry Landers), the Indian antagonist, also riding through the woods. Moments later in

11. At the time of King Philip's War (1675–77), the synecdoche, as Indian menace, seems to have been well established in Puritan lore. At a particularly difficult time during the war, reports the Puritan historian William Hubbard, some soldiers take counsel with an eclipse of the moon: "Some melancholy Fancies would not be perswaded, but that the Eclipse falling out at that Instant of Time was ominous, conceiving also that in the Centre of the Moon they discerned an unusual black Spot, not a little resembling the Scalp of an *Indian*: As some others not long before, imagined they saw the Form of an *Indian Bow*, accounting that likewise ominous." (William Hubbard, *The History of the Indian Wars in New England* [1677; Bowie, Md.: Heritage Books, 1990] 1:67.) The scalp (if it is an Indian's, why does it bode ill?) and the bow (why could it not be an English longbow?) stand for all the Indian that the despondent Puritans would ever wish to encounter. The Indian may as well be, himself, the Man on the Moon, what with the forms of presence that he takes and the utter Otherness that such synecdoches denote.

this sequence, Johnny reins in his horse behind a tree and gazes at On-ahti as she steps into the river. Suddenly, an arrow strikes the tree; Johnny smiles, turns, and says: "My friend Grey Wolf likes to play games." The arrow, by itself, evidences the Indian threat more effectively than the shot of the Indian himself does. Indeed, the synecdoche, and not the Indian's full image, is the source of the Indian's identity. We did not see Grey Wolf shoot the arrow, yet we know that he did so, and know therefore that the arrow presents him already as the hero's presumed arch-enemy. To Johnny's gibe, the sullen Grey Wolf responds: "Next time I kill you." He therefore only confirms what the arrow has already established—not only the portent of a deadly encounter with an Indian but also the process whereby the Indian enemy need be identified by an image no more complex than an arrow shot in anger at the white hero. If the arrow betokens the Indian menace, then the hero's recognition of his enemy by even such an indifferent glance at it appoints him already the victor in the racial struggle for mastery of the West. To be sure, the reversion to defining synecdoche does not have to refer to the overall narrative process: Grey Wolf does not disappear from the action for being identified through his arrow. But the arrow already limits his development as a character; it confines his potential humanity. He is the surly, envious, skulking Indian, and all with but a word from the hero who "interprets" the arrow. Synecdoche designates the white hero's power to present the Indian as a foredoomed Otherness. The white hero who identifies the Indian by the fragments of his culture executes the dual demand to vilify and reduce him, to announce his mastery over him by representing him as nothing but Savage Reactionary.

In *Jeremiah Johnson* (Pollack, 1972) the Indian also precedes his own synecdochical form. Here, however, the Indian fighter does not come ready-made, and he endures a rugged, if droll (and thus reassuring), apprenticeship in the Rocky Mountain wilderness. As the starving Jeremiah (Robert Redford) struggles in freezing water after a trout, a magnificent looking Crow whom we shall come to know as Paints His Shirt Red (Joaquín Martínez), appears suddenly before him, a string of trout dangling from his saddle. Paints His Shirt Red looks gravely at the white oaf and slowly rides away. In time, Jeremiah improves his chances of survival in the mountains because he meets Bear Claw (Will Geer), the grizzled mountain man who teaches him the necessary wilderness skills. Following a successful elk hunt, the two white men sense that there are Indians nearby (they already know that they are trespassing in Crow territory), and as they move stealthily about, an

[32]

arrow flies before them and sticks in a tree. "Yep, Crow," an unruffled Bear Claw remarks after only a casual glance at the arrow. Over the close-up of the arrow with its red markings on the shaft, he adds: "Fellow by the name of Paints His Shirt Red. That's his sign." From behind trees and snow banks, a small band of Crows now appears, led by Paints His Shirt Red. The encounter ends amiably enough, since Jeremiah placates Paints His Shirt Red by giving him some of the hides on his pack mule. But in the context of Jeremiah's continuing apprenticeship, the moment discloses the still superior wisdom of Bear Claw: the wilderness curriculum, at least as the Myth of Conquest would have it, requires the white man to identify the Indian by the tokens of Indian danger. In the very next scene, where the two men part ways, Bear Claw certifies Jeremiah's newly gotten wilderness wisdom: "You've learned well, pilgrim." He sends Jeremiah forth not merely as a man capable of surviving in a harsh land but also of becoming a mythic Indian fighter. To read and report aright the signs of imminent presence is to enjoy already the power to demand that the Indian be known through no more complete measure or mode than his defining synecdochical form. It is to remand him ever to his first form, to reduce him to a loose collection of cultural shards that disclose no destiny so certain as the absence begotten of the token of presence.

Perhaps the most radical instance of reversion to defining synecdoche appears in Charles Marquis Warren's *Arrowhead* (1953). The action opens with two mounted Apaches looking out from atop a hill into a vast expanse of land. A slow pan right from this shot eventually ends with a long shot of two tired riders crossing a shallow stream. These are Ed Bannon (Charlton Heston), who serves the army as Chief of Scouts, and his companion, Sandy Mackinnon (Milburn Stone). When Bannon makes an indistinct grunt in response to the possibility of Apache tracks, Mackinnon remarks: "Two weeks scouting, no signs. Now [that we are] fifteen miles from the fort, that inner sense of yours has gotta act up." In almost immediate validation of Sandy's remark, Bannon dismounts and concludes that the Apaches have covered their tracks with the cut branches that he finds nearby. A new shot of the two Apache sentinels shows them watching intently as a cavalry column crosses the stream. Bannon and Mackinnon now sneak up on the two Apaches and shoot them; then they kill two more who charge them. When Colonel Weybright (Lewis Martin), who commands the column, arrives atop the hill, he reprimands Bannon. "Today," Weybright explains, "Chief Ozuni was supposed to bring his people into the post. These men Bannon murdered were to lead me to him." Bannon, confident of his actions and contemptuous of Weybright for his credulous trust of the Apaches, asserts what strikes him as only too obvious: "Colonel, these are *Apaches* you're dealing with"—by which he no doubt means that they are malevolent and deceitful. But Weybright fires Bannon and, compelled now to prove him wrong, says: "These Apaches were here for peace. Do you see any paint on their faces?" Seeing no war paint on the dead Apaches, Weybright reasons that they must have been peaceful and friendly. Yet, in thus determining that the Indian without war paint can never be hostile, it is Weybright who, if unsuspectingly, confirms what Bannon already knows: the hostile Indian is always the Indian in synecdoche. Thus a still unshaken Bannon retorts: "They don't have to have it on their faces, but they can't fight without paint. They've got to have it on them somewhere." Here he walks up to one of the dead Apaches, opens his shirt front, then looks up high on the back of his arm, and finally finds three white stripes on the back of his neck, as does Mackinnon on the Indian he searches. Bannon returns the Indian to his condition as defining synecdoche—and thus gives early testimony of his power to overcome the self-proclaimed Apache messiah, Toriano (Jack Palance), who will try to unite all the Indians against the whites. Surely, then, Bannon's intimate knowledge of the Indians guarantees that evil will befall those who do not listen to him.

No doubt these early scenes from *The Indian Fighter* and *Arrowhead* obey the convention that at once determines and certifies the white hero's credentials. *Jeremiah Johnson* initially invests Bear Claw with the wisdom that eventually devolves to the white hero; it documents the manner in which Jeremiah learns what Johnny Hawks and Bannon and Bear Claw already know. Authority on matters concerning Indians falls to him who identifies them by their signs, who presents them—and by so doing also absents them—in their synecdochical forms. Even when we have seen him before, often in grand and stately form (as we do Paints His Shirt Red), we are to know him best by what he is in his first form, an icon of savage Otherness whose disappearance signals the augured instauration of the Anglo-American millennium.

To be sure, an Indian can appear first without the mediation of synecdoche and never suffer the sort of radical reversion that the white hero can inflict upon him. Yet, more often than not, this exception introduces us to an Indian who, however reluctantly, accepts white control. This Indian belongs to the type of faithful companion that Cooper gave us in Chingachgook, and is most familiar in the form of Tonto. One memorable appearance of this sort occurs in John Ford's *Drums Along the Mohawk* (1939): shortly after newlyweds Gil and Lana Martin

[34]

arrive at their rude and bare cabin in Deerfield, Gil (Henry Fonda) goes out in a violent storm to stable his mare. Lana (Claudette Colbert), already dismayed by so sudden a change from the sumptuous surroundings of her home in colonial Albany, now turns from the hearth fire to see, where she expected Gil, an Indian, impassive in the lurid light, framed by her door. As if deaf to Lana's frantic screams, the Indian advances slowly toward the fire. Gil returns and explains that this is his friend Blue Back (Chief John Big Tree). Earlier in 1939, the same actor, Chief John Big Tree, played the first Indian that we see in Ford's *Stagecoach*. He rides furiously alongside a white scout to deliver the news of Apache raids and then stands in close-up, somber and mute, while Captain Sickels casts a suspicious glance at him and the white scout speaks for him: "No, he's a Cheyenne," he says to reassure Sickels, "They hate Apaches worse than we do." Yet even in these two Westerns, where each of the first Indians that we see is a trusted friend, Ford gives us mistaken looks, Lana's and Sickels's, that accord with the genre's dominant representation of the Indian as savage Other. Eventually, both *Drums Along the Mohawk* and *Stagecoach* resort to the Indian synecdoche to identify the Indian threat. In the former, we see a close-up of the one-eyed Caldwell (John Carradine), the dastardly Tory, summoning a small band of hostile Indians to fire Gil and Lana's haystacks and cabin. In *Stagecoach*, the fragments of Indian culture are many, as we will see, but perhaps none more striking than the smoke signals that stop Ringo in his tracks at Apache Wells, as he tries to make his escape from Marshal Curley Wilcox (George Bancroft). Thus, as Edward Buscombe notes, "smoke signals can be more frightening than the actual appearance of the Indians they foreshadow. Fear of the Other and the unknown feeds on this simultaneous presence and absence."[12] These synecdoches show that Lana and Captain Sickels were not so far wrong in their initial perceptions, only that they misplaced them: they may have mistaken the Indian ally for an enemy, but in fact they merely failed to make an exception of him.

4

Reversion to synecdoche underscores the tendency of the Myth of Conquest to remove the Indian from the flow of time and narration. It functions as a conspicuous instance of the imperative to *detemporalize* the

---

12. See the topic "smoke signals" in *The BFI Companion to the Western*, ed. Edward Buscombe (New York: Atheneum, 1988), p. 221.

Indian. Or if the Indian here is not quite atemporal (reversion, after all, requires a duration of its own) then his temporality is so far the opposite of that reserved for white America that he appears before us as if outside time—the opponent of all processes, of the white visions of bright racial destinies and everlasting progress. The Myth of Conquest defines the Indian's antagonism itself as an opposition to "history." Thus "history"—here conceived of as the teleology of racial and cultural triumph—reveals the Indian's doom as it unfolds Conquest's foreordained mastery. Robert Berkhofer has noted the "curious timelessness" that characterizes "the white man's Indian": "Since Whites primarily understood the Indian as an antithesis to themselves, then civilization and Indianness as they defined them would forever be opposites. Only civilization had history and dynamism in this view, so therefore Indianness must be conceived of as ahistorical and static."[13] Not only does the Indian recede as white America carries out its foreordained advance, but he remains unchanging, "iconic." He is history's discard, an exile from the Western paradise. To exclude the Indian from temporality has become an inherent feature of mythic "history," a fundamental strategy of figuration. History becomes tableau, and nothing happens that is not therein prefigured. The Myth of Conquest "emplots" the Indian only to *dis*emplot him. Otherness implies timelessness.

The Indian synecdoche specifies dominion over the Indian's temporality. It is a trope whose immediacy denotes *distance*, a strategy, accordingly, that announces imminence yet portends absence. It discloses the curious alchemy whereby the "native" becomes the alien. Thus it can defer and postpone and even entirely withhold the image of the Indian. From the very first scene of John Ford's *Stagecoach* (1939) the mere name Geronimo stands for savage menace itself. Yet Geronimo's actual appearance in the story occurs quite late, and only after the values and virtues of civilization have claimed preeminence. The synecdoche that seems to alert us to the presence of the Indian functions principally to withhold his appearance until the triumph of civilization is no longer in question. The Indian appears at last only to confirm the inevitability of his defeat. The early scenes of *Stagecoach* rely more properly on metonymy than on synecdoche to establish the Indian's imminent presence. The name "Geronimo"—though disconnected alike from action or intention—nonetheless ripples through the first scene to strike

---

13. Robert Berkhofer, Jr., *The White Man's Indian: Images of the American Indian from Columbus to the Present* (New York: Vintage, 1978), pp. 28, 29.

terror in the hearts of the white characters. The white scout, who has the first spoken lines in *Stagecoach*, tells Captain Sickels that the Cheyenne scout "had a brush with [the Apaches] last night; [he] says they're being stirred up by Geronimo." "Geronimo!" Sickles exclaims. Just then an urgent telegraph message from Lordsburg to the army post cuts off abruptly after just one word, "Geronimo," and the faces of the white men register the requisite alarm, just as the shot dissolves to the town of Tonto where the name of "Geronimo" evokes the horrors to be visited on a frail and vulnerable citizenry.

In Tonto, where we meet most of the passengers of the stagecoach, Ford establishes the mettle of his characters by specifying their response to the threat implied by the dreaded name. For example, the whiskey drummer Peacock (Donald Meek), for all his timorousness, asserts his devotion to his family in the face of this threat; and Lucy Mallory (Louise Platt), for all her superciliousness, risks her life and that of her unborn child to be with her husband, a U.S. Cavalry captain, who awaits her at Apache Wells. The threat implied by the name also allows Ford indirectly to pass judgment on a mean and spiteful America gone mad with self-righteousness and social respectability. Both Dallas (Claire Trevor) and Doc Boone (Thomas Mitchell) account their fate at the hands of Geronimo preferable to the zealous scorn of Tonto's ladies of the Law and Order League. All these different responses—fear, defiance, resignation—as well as the specified humanity of those who embody them, succeed in delaying the actual presence of Geronimo; they postpone the embodiment of the name. Furthermore, the malignant Indian serves as the common focus of all the whites, and thus becomes, by a process as implausible as it is compelling, the ironic agent of Conquest's cause in the West. If the Indian were to appear early, then society would not be possible; neither, however, would that society be possible were the Indian not to appear at all, for civilization defines itself by its opposition to savagery: the trick, then, is to produce the Indian in such forms as may delay his presence until the one propitious moment that guarantees his defeat.

Eventually, the images of savagery appear as if to materialize the dreaded name; synecdoche underscores metonymy.[14] The change from an Indian in metonymy to one in synecdoche occurs almost as soon as the stagecoach leaves Lordsburg, that is, once it enters what should be

14. To be precise, the first scene has produced something like a synecdoche even before the mention of the name "Geronimo." Pointing at the map on Captain Sickels's desk, the white scout reports: "These hills here are full of Apaches. They've burned every ranch building in sight."

the Indian's domain. Yet these wide-open spaces in which the Western typically locates the Indian reveal the white hero before they do the Indian himself. Ringo (John Wayne), self-assured and unafraid, implicitly claims the Indian's space and thus appears before us as the promise of deliverance from savagery. On his way to Lordsburg to avenge his brother and father, Ringo's horse has pulled up lame. Now that Ringo is about to step on the stagecoach, Marshal Curley Wilcox demands his rifle. "You may need me and this Winchester, Curley," Ringo replies. "I saw a ranch house burning last night." He verifies what the white scout reports earlier; but only Ringo has witnessed the image of what, for the rest of the passengers, remains only a dreaded name. Thus we know the Indian not through any actual appearance before us, but through the hero's own self-presentation as indispensable Indian fighter.

The strategic deployment of the Indian synecdoche defers the Indian's presence for the sake of defining the American nation. The "timing" of the deployment allows the fledgling society to identify and articulate its own central values and then have them consecrated in a climactic Indian fight. At Apache Wells, Dallas—resplendent and content—appears at the door of the saloon with Lucy Mallory's baby, in whose delivery she has helped the other social outcast, Doc Boone. The moment unites the white community. All the male passengers except Doc Boone, who is still busy tending to Mrs. Mallory, and Gatewood (surely because he is a crooked banker), now gather around Dallas and the child in adoration. Out of this event, Ford confirms the identity of Ringo and Dallas as America's Edenic couple, an identity that had begun to form earlier through the nuances of politeness and civility between these two outcasts. Moments after the adoration scene, Hatfield (John Carradine), the murderous Confederate gambler, toasts the health of Doc Boone, the dissolute pro-Union drunk; and Peacock earns the respect of the other men for the first time when he demands silence for the baby and the mother. The Indian may lurk about, but he will continue only to lurk until this new America is ready to hand him his defeat.

Late in the Apache Wells sequence, Ringo tries to escape from Curley so that he can fulfill his promise to kill the Plummer brothers, but almost as soon as his horse jumps over the fence, he reins it in. Pointing at the smoke signals in the distance, he says to Curley (who has caught up with him), "Look at them hills." "Apaches?" Curley asks. Ringo nods yes: "War signals." The new America has not yet formed itself so completely that it can dispense with the hero. Ringo, who was alone in the desert when we first saw him, now belongs in the community. Even

[38]

the revenge against the Plummers becomes subordinate to the hopes of the anointed couple in a post-Indian America.

At Lee's Ferry, the passengers arrive at the site of savagery, and their presence there seems to reduce the distance between them and the Indians. The burning ranch houses and smoke signals of earlier reports now acquire their frightful immediacy. A dead (and by implication raped) woman—so far as we can see she is the only victim—lies half naked among the smoldering ruins. The woman has suffered the fate which Lucy Mallory, during the attack on the stage itself, shall fervently pray to be delivered from, even as Hatfield aims his pistol, with its one remaining round, at her unsuspecting head. Thus the dead woman at Lee's Ferry provides the cautionary synecdoche; the aftermath of the massacre reveals the dreaded consequences of the encounter with the Indian. This is what happens when savagery at last overtakes white womanhood. For all the urgency of the moment, however, the pontooned stagecoach crosses the river, leaving Lee's Ferry behind, and the passengers believe that they are safe—as if by quitting the site of the massacre they have avoided the encounter with the Indian. There follows a reconciliation of sorts: Gatewood, if only stiffly, apologizes for his boorishness; and Doc Boone, convinced that the "danger's passed," toasts the health of all the passengers. The mobile community has achieved its moment of greatest unity. All the evil intent that the Indian may bring against this society can only strengthen it the more.

Moments before the passengers exchanged these latest pleasantries, however, we saw the stagecoach in an extreme long shot, dwarfed by Monument Valley, and a quick pan left came to rest on a medium shot of a large band of Apaches looking on from above. Geronimo, we are to assume, is one of the two in the group that now appear in individual close-ups. But neither of these close-ups gives a clear sense of just which one of these Apaches might be Geronimo. Geronimo is most likely the first of the two, but we have only this specific precedence to distinguish between them, so that "Geronimo" remains mostly a generic Indian. He is not so much a character, or even a historical reference, as a threat embodied, a mere expedient whereby the promised encounter—and the fated disappearance—can be brought about. The presence of the Indian in this form, in the close-up just before the attack, stands for the "whole" Indian in *Stagecoach*. And so, as destiny will have it, he reverts. When the Apaches attack the stagecoach, we do not see them immediately. Instead, Ford gives us a sudden swoosh and then the arrow that strikes Peacock in the chest. The fragment that would represent the whole Indian reemerges as if to supplant him. We see not one distinct Indian face during the attack. The passengers, however, all get close-ups: theirs is the ordeal, the achievement, and inevitably the close-up. The Apache who jumps on the lead horse never appears in a shot so close that allows us to see his face, but the heroic Ringo, who jumps on the lead horse after Buck (Andy Devine), drops the reins, fills up the screen, and is the embodiment itself of unconquerable resolve. Inside, Hatfield's pistol with its last shot in the chamber intrudes upon a close-up of Lucy Mallory, who is lost in desperate prayer. But an instant later the same close-up reveals her mad joy, for she can hear the distant bugle blow of the cavalry charge. The Apaches fade in a cloud of dust, fated to extinction more by discursive strategy than by force of arms. Sometimes the cavalry is superfluous.

If the Indian synecdoche in *Stagecoach* defers the Indian's presence until the moment of society's greatest cohesion, it defers it in *The Stalking Moon* (Mulligan, 1968) until the hero and his mate are assured of their American paradise. The paradisal garden in *Stagecoach* is as distant from "the blessings of civilization" as it is from the savage wilderness—more an ideal yet to be lived than a place to occupy, more vision than instituted geography. In *The Stalking Moon*, however, place circumscribes hope, and paradise has its precise locale. Early in the action, after what he takes to be his last campaign in the Apache Wars, Sam Varner (Gregory Peck), an army scout, proposes to retire to a New Mexico ranch that he has bought some time before, though he has seen it only once. "The skirmish was finished," we read in the T. V. Olsen source novel, "the last skirmish for him, and he could grin at his misgivings; he was alive and free for the new life."[15] But Varner's retirement plans are complicated by the plight of a white woman, Sarah Carver (Eva Marie Saint), whom the soldiers find, along with her young son (Noland Clay), among the Apaches. A captive for ten years, Sarah now importunes the major in command for an escort to the railhead at Silverton, but since she claims that she cannot wait the necessary five days for the escort, she turns to Varner, whom she knows is leaving the next morning. Varner, after the useless expostulations, agrees to escort her to Silverton; but it shall be a long while till he learns that the boy's father is Salvaje (Nathaniel Narcisco), the dreaded Apache.

Once Salvaje appears on the outskirts of Varner's paradise—indeed, even during the climactic fight itself—Mulligan gives us only the most

15. T. V. Olsen, *The Stalking Moon* (1967; New York: Leisure Books, 1997), p. 26.

fleeting glimpses of him. Whenever the camera has an opportunity to see Salvaje in detail, it cuts away from him, or otherwise fails to produce a visually defined individual. Mulligan deliberately trims the duration of the shots of Salvaje, or settles for brief profile shots, intentionally avoiding the full-face close-ups that Varner abundantly enjoys, even when both men appear in the same scene. In this way, Salvaje is *any* Indian, *all* Indians. And yet we see him often enough: though he is faceless, he has a body—a body feral, truculent, unappeased. He is now a shadow, now a rustle, now a distant flitting form, then a sudden and unimpeded manifestation, and at last only a rush to certain defeat. In this way, Salvaje's body suggests how the discourse of the Western presents the Indian by suppressing other possibilities for representation. The Indian's body itself becomes a synecdoche, identifying Indianness as elemental physical menace.[16] Indeed, the glimpses of Salvaje show nothing more clearly than the bear skin that covers him from the shoulders to the knees.

Moreover, the Indian, for being so named, need not be shown. For the name itself of the character—Salvaje (Spanish for "savage")—though unimaginative and offensive, nonetheless predicates the essential quality of the Hollywood Indian, indicating, in the name itself, all the heartlessness that we encountered in Ford's Geronimo while candidly (or crassly) dispensing with the pretense of the Indian's personal or historical identity. The name replicates a generically assigned essence: it designates the Indian's proper role in the contest between savagery and civilization. The name—the utterance that, as in *Stagecoach*, marks the time to the inevitable encounter—becomes a strategy to promote the *persistence* of the Indian threat, all the while postponing, until one auspicious moment, the actual physical encounter where savagery, in compliance with the old irrevocable decrees, vanishes.

The *defining* synecdoche is the aftermath of the massacre. Early in the story, Varner, his "half-breed" sidekick Nick Tana (Robert Forster), and a small cavalry detachment come upon three dead troopers. "One set of tracks and a buffalo rifle," Varner observes, meaning that only Salvaje could have done the deed alone. Here Sergeant Rudabaugh confirms Varner's assessment: "Last I heard of Salvaje, he was clear down to Window Rock. . . . Took on ten troopers down there, killed four of

16. When Salvaje first appears in the Olsen novel, about two thirds of the way into it, we see him from the perspective of Sam Vetch, as the hero is named there: "This man was as gaunt as a great timber wolf, and the sense of something free and fierce, something that had never been tamed and would never be, reached out from his motionless stance and prickled along Vetch's spine." *The Stalking Moon*, p. 170.

'em, and not one of 'em got a look at him." Some time later, Varner and Sarah return to Hennesey station with the boy, who fled in a windstorm in hopes of finding his father. Salvaje has killed all the people at the station—all but one, the stationmaster, who lives just long enough to say, "Never seen nothing like him." All that the Indian can ever be in this Western is given in the images of his helpless victims. Invisible, Salvaje is yet the image of savagery.

In time, then, the massacre as synecdoche charts Salvaje's approach to Varner's place. Now that Varner, Sarah, and the boy have settled in New Mexico, Nick arrives to warn them that Salvaje has followed them from Arizona. On his way, Nick has come upon the massacre at the station in Hennesey. "I dig up that grave in Hennesey," Nick tells Varner in the butchered English assigned to his generic type: "I figure maybe you really go by, Sam, huh? Then I ride Silverton. Silverton they're all dead, too. Even your horse dead Silverton. Then I hear he stops a wagon at Oakley. Two days later he's at Columbia Pass. I figure it out. I come tell you. He's on his way." So sustained a threat becomes, itself, the full measure of the Indian. Presence collapses into absence: the Indian's absence presents him. One may wish that Mulligan had worked Olsen's other name for the savage Indian into the film. In the novel, Nick reveals that Salvaje is known among his own people as *"Ya-ik-tee,"* a name that "nearest you can put it in English is, 'He is not present.' "[17] For all his obvious importance to the action, Salvaje remains bound to—and rendered inhuman by—his synecdochical form. The massacre consigns him, as individual antagonist, to the synecdoche that is his name. He is but an *epithet*—the superadded and disparaging name that specifies his one individual characteristic even as it reduces him to the generic attribute of all male Indianness.

The aftermath of the massacre is to white civilization what the Indian's fearsome body is to the white woman—the initial defeat, the ensuing martyrdom, and the assurance of eventual triumph. Indeed, the massacre implies the savage body, not only because the one body wreaks such havoc against civilization's forces, or even because Sarah herself was taken captive after a massacre ten years before the action begins, but because the trail of massacres announces the inexorable approach of the one menacing body. In obedience to the Myth of Conquest, *The Stalking Moon* demands two prerequisites for the fulfillment of the paradisal hope: first, that the white woman return, as if untouched, to her racio-cultural origin—that is, then, that she should be

17. *The Stalking Moon*, p. 65.

worthy of the Adamic hero even after sexual contact, perhaps even *consensual* contact, with the Indian; and second, that the Indian child find his own place in paradise by the civilizing influence that washes him clean of savagery. Both conditions, of course, presuppose the elimination of the Savage Reactionary. In *The Stalking Moon*, as in the Myth generally, the demand for racial purity in the woman takes precedence over the racial makeup of paradise's progeny. The first condition is essential: when the white woman has lived with the Indian, she must somehow repudiate him, as if the rebuke of the Indian somehow invested her with a sort of retroactive virginity. The second condition, though it reveals much about the fantasies of the Myth, can be easily enough met by lavishing generous portions of paternalism on the compliant child: when the savage Indian is good and dead, the only good Indian shall be a child.

Sarah Carver's redemption begins with acquiescence in Varner's Edenic dream: already in New Mexico, overwhelmed by Varner's well-intentioned effort to engage her and the boy in familiar dinner-table chit-chat, she explains, "It's not easy for me to talk. It's been a long time since I have talked. But I would like to say this, that it pleases me to be here, and I think it is a beautiful place to be." At this point in the story, Varner knows that the boy is Salvaje's son, but not that Sarah yielded to Salvaje so that he would spare her life (this, which is her darkest secret, she reveals a good deal later). Earlier, as Varner buried the dead at Hennesey station, Sarah abruptly announced: "He'll come back."

> *Varner*: Not here.
> *Sarah*: We should go now. He'll come.
> *Varner*: We're not going anywhere. He's finished here; he did what he came to do.
> *Sarah*: He is not finished. He came for his son. He'll come back for his son.

She knows the signs of imminent presence because she has "known" the Indian's carnal presence, and this massacre now is as if a recrudescence of it, a revelation of unregenerate savagery that Varner, however much *he* may know about Indians, cannot yet fully comprehend. He mistakes the aftermath of the massacre for the Indian's absence; Sarah knows it to be the portent of his presence. Sarah has been savagery's intimate: only thus can the white woman know more about the Indian than the Indian fighter himself does. And only thus, in virtue of such a dreadful knowing, can her Edenic aspiration demand from her a sacrifice that will make her Varner's worthy mate.

[43]

When Salvaje reappears before her, Sarah shall have renounced her knowledge, yet not without first explaining her failure at the time of her captivity to resist the Indian, to avoid at all costs that moral ruin known in the euphemism of frontier America as "a fate worse than death." Now that Salvaje prowls about, the ranch house, especially at night, becomes more like a fort (and for the boy, who still yearns for his father, more like a prison). Varner tells Sarah to stay inside, but Sarah, visibly dejected—perhaps despairing of deliverance from the Indian—goes out in the dark nonetheless. Her brief presence, alone, in the darkness suggests her willingness to expose herself to savagery as a way of removing its threat from Varner's place. Varner, not quite understanding the gesture, goes out after her and innocently assures her: "This has nothing to do with you." As if in compliance with a demand that she explain her very existence, Sarah states: "It *has* to do with me. I didn't have the courage to die. I knew what I had to do to stay alive. I chose to be with him. Tomorrow I'm going to take my boy away, and Salvaje will find us, and maybe that will be enough for him." Thus the massacre as synecdoche alerts Varner and Sarah not only of the approach of Salvaje but also of the possibility (however remote it may seem in the end) that Sarah will again yield before the savage and implacable body. Yet this willingness to die unto savagery already proves Sarah's worth. The scene ends with an embrace, a tear in Sarah's eye, caresses and relevant musical strains, and above all with Varner's blessing: "You and the boy aren't leaving here. I want you to stay here. It's right that you're here." The hero remythifies the fallen woman. As if his reassurance were restoration enough, Sarah goes back in, out of the darkness. His validation of her right to be in his world shall enable her to perform the necessary act of resistance.

That she obeys Varner and returns to the house virtually guarantees that Salvaje will somehow accost her precisely there and not in the dark, wild spaces beyond. In the morning, while Varner rides off to warn a neighboring rancher and Nick teaches the boy how to play poker, Salvaje appears in the bedroom before Sarah, who is busy with her domestic duties. When Varner returns (having found his neighbor dead), Salvaje has taken Sarah away into the wilderness. Salvaje's presence before Sarah, ominous as it may seem, prefigures her deliverance. Now she can behave as she should have then: she can pray as hard as Lucy Mallory did or die the martyred death of the nameless woman at Lee's Ferry.

When Varner and Nick find her, she is unconscious and beaten, but she is not "ruined." Her bruises are the outward and immediate marks of redemptive triumph in the contest with savagery.[18] In her resistance itself is already the defeat of savagery. Still, skeptics might call for proof. After Varner and Nick bring her back to the house, wash her facial wounds, and assure the boy that she is alive, they wait for her recovery. Soon enough she emerges, composed if not quite healed, while the three men—Varner, Nick, and Ned (an old man in Varner's employ)—gaze upon her much as the men did upon Dallas when she came into the saloon with Lucy Mallory's baby. Varner asks if she is all right, and she answers with a clear and hearty yes. The social (and sexual) gaze, no less than Sarah's own testimony, confirms her triumph.

The affirmation places her, as if by destiny ordered, precisely here. Yet it is not in this image of recovered innocence, but in that earlier one of the mauled yet triumphant body, that she exalts mythic white womanhood. The image of heroic resistance transmutes the synecdoche of savagery: Sarah's defiance specifies not only her own redemption but also that of the defeated America, as given in the aftermath of the massacre. The battered body, itself now synecdochical, betokens not savagery but civilization's ascendancy over it. This synecdoche delays the Indian's last presence with supreme purpose. When Salvaje appears for the final showdown, the restoration of Sarah Carver shall already be beyond doubt, and so too the end of the Indian.

The old man Ned, enraged because Salvaje has killed his guard dog, tries to track the Apache on his own, and for his troubles he is killed and scalped. Later, when Nick shouts to warn Varner, he draws Salvaje's fire and dies. Then, before Varner goes out alone after Salvaje, he gives Nick's playing cards to the boy—as if the gesture should not only endear the boy to Nick's memory, which is to say, to the loyal Indian now martyred in the cause of the American paradise, but turn him decisively against his father. The boy never again tries to escape into the wilderness, and for all practical purposes this is the last we see of him—pensive, perhaps contrite, presumably civilized. Thus, even before Salvaje dies, this is the remnant of the Indian—the bestial body now made docile and dependent, tamed by the first glimmer of emergent conscience. If the body of the mother came to be transformed into

---

18. In the Olsen novel, Salvaje does attack Sara (so spelled there) in the house, but does not kill her, promising to do that later. Vetch finds her unconscious, lying on the floor, a huge welt along the side of her face. When she awakens, Sara says: " 'Sam—he was here.' 'I know,' Sam replies. 'What did he do?' " Sara does not answer immediately; she is concerned that the boy now knows that Salvaje has come for him. But Vetch returns her to what is crucial to him: "Vetch shook her. 'What did he do?' 'He—nothing. Just this.' " *The Stalking Moon*, p. 176.

the synecdoche of virtuous, even virginal American womanhood, the body of the boy specifies an Indian divested of autonomy, made ready to receive the blessings of civilization in the form of paternalism. He remains nameless throughout—this, as Sarah explains, in accordance with the Apache custom that withholds the child's name until he performs a deed that names him; but now that savagery—even to its name, Salvaje—is about to be forever eradicated, the boy shall *remain* nameless: when Salvaje dies, the boy shall be baptized in the non-identity that follows the end of mythology's Indian, his but the name of absence.

Wounded yet victorious in the dubious and long-drawn-out battle (wherein we never catch a single clear and sustained shot of Salvaje's face), Varner stumbles within sight of his place. Sarah rushes out of the house to help him, but the boy is nowhere to be seen. His father's death and his mother's restoration leave him an orphan of sorts, without even an identity as Other. More important, however, the boy's absence clearly obeys the mythic injunction—operative already in the various massacres and more immediately in Nick's and Ned's and the neighbor's deaths—that the hero and his mate be first, unprecedented, ahistorical. In truth, then, the contest with savagery unfolded not (or at least not primarily) for possession of the boy but for the enactment of restitution and recovery, both of which at once required the savage Indian even as they negated him.

The Indian synecdoche never threatens the hero, or for that matter the westering white community, quite as much as it does the hero's potential mate—the white woman destined to become Eve to his Adam. The function of the synecdoche as a power to defer the Indian already suggests the need to shift the focus of the present chapter—from an emphasis on the way in which the synecdoche absents the Indian by "presenting" him to an inquiry into its role in the relation between the Indian and the white maiden. Our study of *Stagecoach* and *The Stalking Moon* has of course already introduced this relation, but it underscored the strategies of representation rather than the cultural—and sexual—codes made possible by those strategies.

5

Late in James Cruze's *The Covered Wagon* (1923), the heroine, Molly Wingate (Lois Wilson), seems resigned to marry the villain, Sam Woodhull (Alan Hale). Woodhull has calumnied Molly's other suitor, the heroic Will Banion (J. Warren Kerrigan), identifying him as a deserter and horse thief in the Mexican War. Although Molly's trust in Banion wavers, her love for him remains undiminished. But some time earlier Woodhull's malice has worked chaos in the train, and at the suggestion of Molly's father Jesse (Charles Ogle), who captains the whole train, Banion and his contingent from Liberty, Missouri, split up from the Wingate-led folk. As Molly, already in bridal white, makes ready to appear before the expectant emigrant throng, Jim Bridger (Tully Marshall), Banion's friend, sneaks in her wagon and tells her not to marry Woodhull. Later in the scene, having consumed all the contents of the Wingate family jug, Bridger remembers to tell Molly that Banion was in fact a hero in the war. Before she rides out to Banion, Molly appears before the celebrants to announce that the wedding to Woodhull is off.

Meantime the Indians, whose presence has long been anticipated, have stealthily surrounded the wagon train. No sooner does the determined Molly make clear her intentions to parents, rejected groom, and fellow emigrants than Cruze cuts to a medium shot of an Indian in silhouette at the edge of the screen firing an arrow into the camp below.[19] The arrow strikes Molly high in the chest. The presence of the Indian—especially in the stark contrast between Indian arrow and bridal gown (concentrating in one image the separate shots of the dark savage and the white maiden in white)—endangers Molly's promised union to Banion by introducing the dread of miscegenation. Even when the arrow strikes Molly, the Indian synecdoche continues to designate an imminent presence, for this form of the Indian's appearance betokens an impending threat to Molly's virginity, and thus to the mission of American womanhood in the mythic West. The image of the arrow impaled in the bride's chest makes little distinction between the risk to life and the risk of racial mixture. The arrow spreads not one drop of blood over the white bridal gown, but the implication of the image is unmistakable: now that she has courageously rebuffed the villain, in the moment *before the hero reclaims her and she is without a white mate*, the presence of the savage Indian threatens the vision of the agrarian paradise. In his synecdochical form the Indian claims the fissure created by absent white manhood.

When we first meet Molly, in only the second shot of *The Covered Wagon*, she is alone, idly sewing on the seat of the prairie schooner. In

19. For a critique of the image of the Indians in *The Covered Wagon*, see Virginia Wright Wexman, "The Family on the Land: Race and Nationhood in Silent Westerns," in *The Birth of Whiteness: Race and the Emergence of U.S. Cinema* (New Brunswick: Rutgers University Press, 1996), pp. 129–69.

[47]

DBS Arts Library

The Covered Wagon (1923, Paramount). Pioneering madonna. Courtesy of
Paramount/Museum of Modern Art Film Stills Archive.

this medium close-up, the arch of canvas behind her creates the effect
of a halo, of the nimbus that sanctions and sanctifies. The design of the
shot inevitably recalls the painting by W. H. D. Koerner, *Madonna of the
Prairie*, completed only two years before the release of *The Covered
Wagon*. In Koerner, as in Cruze, the wagon cover surrounds the
madonna's head in a radiance that extends to the edges of the frame,
the deceptively unassuming variant of the venerable hagiography.
Moreover, the arching canvas also sets the madonna in place and time
even as it excludes all visual reference to a historical dialectic—to the
relation between East and West, for example, or to the tension between
her enterprise and the Indian's way of life. Neither does it present her
as a member of a larger social group. And yet she seems the essence itself of any possible community, the source of an unassailable teleology:
her engagement in westward migration seems to cast her not as a participant but as the very distillation of the process itself. Her gaze un-
perturbed, the reins firmly yet gently in hand (in contrast to Molly's
gender-specific needle and thread), Koerner's madonna is the apotheo-

[48]

sis of American womanhood—at once tender and determined, virginal though she bears the very seeds of empire.

In *The Covered Wagon*, however, the first shot of Molly soon gives way to the mystified image of the plow, establishing thereby the proper ideological context of Molly's maidenhood, and subordinating her virginity to male power. Specifically, Cruze cuts from the shot of Molly in the seat of the wagon to a group of emigrants, who argue about waiting for Banion's people or starting without him; but once he convinces them that they should wait, Jesse, with reverent hands on the plow handles, reassures them: "I'm just as anxious to git my plow in Oregon soil as anybody." The plow that shall furrow the virgin land—and that in so doing shall be the instrument that fulfills the nation's high moral destiny—belongs in the capable and manly hands of some such Moses of the Prairie; and in time his dream and his daughter, both, shall be the inheritance of the white hero. The cut from Molly to the plow establishes not only the affinity between the fruitful land and the fertile woman, but also their shared dependency on the white male.[20] Molly sews, Jesse plows. If the first shot of Molly seems to cast her as Koerner's self-reliant and ahistorical madonna, the cut to Jesse's reverie of the virgin land presents her as an object of the man's jealous and adoring gaze, of a look that confirms her dependence even as it invests her with the necessary awe. As the dreamed-of land shall be made to grow by the plow, so the virgin shall bear the fruits of her union with the chosen man. And as the Indian endangers the dream of agrarian ascension (huddling around a captured plow, the Indians have earlier vowed to destroy the "monster weapon that will bury the buffalo, uproot the forest, and level the mountain"), so, too, he threatens this other vital source of national identity, the pure and virtuous American woman. And now the phallic arrow challenges the phallic plow. The contending synecdoches bring into focus the racial struggle for the woman and the land.

In the first of its many triumphalist intertitles, *The Covered Wagon* affirms: "The blood of America is the blood of pioneers—the blood of

20. I am thinking of the oil by Alexander Hogue, *Erosion No. 2. Mother Earth Laid Bare*, 1938. Hogue, as William Cronon notes, "discovers a nude female figure in the eroded gullies of an abandoned Great Plains farm. In front of this raped figure he places an all too phallic plow, thereby turning the traditional symbol of pastoral progress into a demonic instrument." "Telling Tales on Canvas: Landscapes of Frontier Change," in *Discovered Lands, Invented Pasts: Transforming Visions of the American West* (New Haven: Yale University Press, 1992), p. 83.

[49]

lion-hearted men and women who carved a splendid civilization out of an uncharted wilderness." The mythic affirmation unfolds an exultant epic of sacrifice and mastery lived by the privilege of race and divine decree. But the mythic virgin, like the virgin land itself, seems far removed from even so mystified a history, as if by unsurpassed importance exempt from time and process, and thus from toil and sacrifice—ordained, then, not to bleed but be. If Molly should be lost, Oregon itself may as well be lost. When she bleeds, then, it had better be in due fulfillment of her mission as matriarch of the westering nation—not in the howling wilderness, surrounded by dusky savages, but in Oregon and in the arms of Will Banion. And this last, of course, since it was foretold, comes to pass. Banion and his Liberty men save the Wingate train from the Indians; Molly recovers and makes it to Oregon; and after striking gold in California, Banion darkens her door, ready no doubt to take up the plow.

If the Indian synecdoche tends to obey the presiding racio-cultural mythos of the Western, it also deploys it, becoming at once its focus and its form, both its immediate disclosure and its validation. The synecdoche's power of immediacy could be enlisted as both an agent in the temporal unfolding of the action *and* a nexus of recurrent signs that revealed the concerns of the Myth of Conquest, the latest versions of its eternal verities. To note merely that a synecdoche falsifies the Indian amounts to a case of picking up the stick by the wrong end. That the culture and the history thereby rendered are false can hardly yield a critique of the logic whereby loose and scattered fragments of an indigenous culture can somehow prop up the popular mythology of Anglo-American national origins. Principally, then, the Indian synecdoche suggests the power of transformation, the alchemy whereby the presence of the Other—ever supervised by the Same—identifies, defines, and authorizes nothing more clearly than his own absence. The Indian synecdoche constructs the outcome of the epic of Conquest—for example, the identity of the mythic hero, the geography of the American paradise, and the illusional demographics of the America that is said to emerge after the postulated disappearance of the Indian. But it also defines the elemental conditions under which the triumph over savagery must take place.

The role of the Indian synecdoche in the construction of the imperiled maiden can be seen succinctly in *Red River* (Hawks, 1948). Chiefly, of course, *Red River* narrates the epic tale of the first cattle drive on the Chisholm Trail. Although the Indian here is incidental to the action as a whole, his synecdochical presence contributes to the identification of the mythic requirements for the restoration of the woman. It is 1851. As *Red River* opens, Tom Dunson (John Wayne) and his companion Nadine Groot (Walter Brennan) are parting ways with a wagon train headed for California.[21] Before they turn south to Texas, Dunson takes leave of Fen (Colleen Gray), his betrothed. She begs him to take her along, but he has made up his mind, and he promises to send for her, once he has made his fortune. In token of his fidelity he gives her a bracelet that once belonged to his mother. He and Groot then point horse and wagon south. Later that day, they see a column of smoke rising from the far off spot where the wagon train should be. "It's too big for a signal smoke, ain't it?" Groot remarks. They know by the form of the smoke alone that Comanches have wiped out the wagon train, and that all efforts at rescue would be in vain. Groot sighs the futile regret: "We should've took her along." Dunson's own "reading" of the smoke rising from the site of the massacre—his tacit assent to Groot's fatalism—determines that Fen is now lost forever. His vast cattle empire will be meager compensation for the paradise lost when the Indian overwhelms the white woman.

That night the Comanches attack Dunson and Groot's camp. In this scene we first "see" the Indian in the form of a flaming arrow. Moreover, three of the Indians that rush at Dunson and Groot become mere blurs in brief medium shots. Most of them (a total of seven) die offscreen, and even the one that Dunson fights hand-to-hand in the river lacks a distinct face. The most clearly visible detail about this Indian is the bracelet that he wears, the one that Dunson had given to Fen just before he left the wagon train. The beloved one herself is now reduced to a sort of Indian synecdoche: she has fallen to them, and American destiny lies in doubt. And so *Red River* awaits another opportunity to deliver the white woman from the Indian, to include her, untainted, in its vision of America.

Fourteen years pass, and Dunson, isolated by his irrational insistence on taking the cattle herd through Missouri, loses control of the drive to his adoptive son Matthew Garth (Montgomery Clift), who leads it to Kansas in hopes that rumors of a railhead at Abilene turn out to be true. Out on the trail, Matthew's cowboys pull an arrow from a dead cow and take it to Quo (Chief Yowlachie), a comical Cherokee who accompanies the cattle drive as assistant cook. Quo verifies that the arrow is

21. This is the action immediately following the journal that introduces us to time, place, and character. In this version the journal functions as do the intertitles of silent movies. In an alternative version of *Red River*, Groot's voiceover narration substitutes for the journal.

[51]

Comanche. Thus, as Matthew reenacts Dunson's early struggles in the western wilderness, the Indian menace appears before him in synecdoche (the deadly arrow), as it did for Dunson (the smoke from the massacre, the flaming arrow). Although a fight with the Comanches follows, we never see a single Indian in close-up, or even in medium shot. Instead of showing the different aspects of the fight, Hawks concentrates on the first encounter—during the fight itself, inside the circle of wagons—between Matthew and Tess Millay (Joanne Dru). To be sure, Tess's virginity is questionable: she has been traveling in the company of the Donegal, a New Orleans tough who, as Buster (Noah Beery, Jr.) reports, is moving his outfit—women and all—to Nevada. And though Hawks never gives us the Donegal as an actual character in the story (Borden Chase's *Saturday Evening Post* source story makes much of him) we have little doubt that the Donegal is as much pimp as he is gambler. Because we never see him, however, we may be even more inclined to spare Tess our self-righteous cynicism. Besides, the Western never blushed for presenting women of dubious reputations as potential virgin-mothers: Tess is in this way similar to Dallas in *Stagecoach*, minus the strong maternal impulse, perhaps, but mercifully unencumbered by a Law and Order League to remind us of her origins. More important, however, Tess's encounter with Matthew—as well as her fidelity to him, later, in the face of Dunson's perverse attempt to buy her reproductive powers to assure himself of an heir—amounts to that of the virgin with her true intended.

Within the circle of wagons, Tess has been shooting too high to hit any Comanches, and Matthew gets her to reload for him; but she now turns to him, her back to the wagon, and asks him repeatedly what makes him so mad at her. As she talks, an arrow hits her high on the shoulder, pinning her to the wagon (and still, ever voluble, ever Hawksian, she would talk). When Matthew sees that she has been hit, he stops shooting and cuts the shaft from the arrowhead; and after he and the other men rush from the circle of wagons to rout the Comanches, he comes back to Tess, cuts the dress around the arrow, pulls the arrow out and, tearing yet more of the dress so that he bares her whole shoulder, sucks the "poison" from her wound, his mouth coming away bloody.

In *The Covered Wagon*, Molly Wingate languished uncertainly from her arrow wound, and the convalescence delayed the final meeting of the lovers with a succession of desultory episodes. And working with much the same sense of distance between hero and virgin—the absence wherein the Indian presents himself—Hawks earlier allowed Dunson's Fen to suffer a "fate worse than death." Now, however, the white hero

appears within the circle of racial identity, a defender of the race because a rescuer of the white woman. The arrow in Tess's shoulder becomes an immediate reason to bring Matthew close—familiarly so—to
her, thus allowing him (and Hawks) to dispense with the awkward romantic preliminaries. What possible threat can a mere Comanche
arrow (even one so suggestively phallic) be then to the white woman
when the man of destiny appears before her? Where Dunson's decision
put an everlasting distance between himself and his betrothed,
Matthew's resolve collapses a similar distance almost at once. Such an
elimination of distance between the hero and the woman assures us
that the Indian shall be made absent in the very next moment. Matthew
pulls out the arrow and sucks out the poison immediately after the Indians have been driven away, as if in confirmation of his power to deliver Tess from Fen's fate. Not only does the moment produce the
timely deliverance of the new—or rather the reincarnated—American
virgin-mother, it also anoints Matthew as Dunson's worthy son—wor-
thier, by far, than the father, in fact, since Matthew loses neither the cattle nor the woman. Principally, however, Matthew claims the mythic
birthright by virtue of his power to erase the taint of miscegenation
from white womanhood. No mere epigone, then, Matthew becomes
the guarantor of Dunson's millennial dream, abrogating time and tragedy in the consummation of his own Adamic mission.

Although hardly an Indian Western, then, *Red River* recommends itself to a study such as this one mostly on the strength of the almost par-
odic economy with which it invokes the iconography of the Indian
Western. Surely Cupid flies among the raiding Comanches, that an "Indian" arrow should have so fortunate an effect. Urgency is not without
its drolleries: we are assured of a romantic happy-ever-after in the
midst of an Indian attack. Wondrous synecdoche that so adroitly transforms the sign of a dreaded miscegenation by finding its mark in the
promised partner!

In *Fort Apache* (Ford, 1948), the romantic encounter seems so much
more demure, always willing to affirm the courtly conventions, even in
the howling wilderness that subverts them. After many awkward preliminaries in a courtship whose outcome is never in question, Lt.
Michael—"Mickey"—O'Rourke (John Agar) escorts the newly arrived
Philadelphia—"Phil"—Thursday (Shirley Temple) on a riding tour of
the vast open land surrounding Fort Apache. Following an exhilarating
ride, the lovers rein in their horses to survey the land before them. Earlier in the scene, Phil looked out into the Western vastness and exclaimed: "Isn't it wonderful?" thus responding to the land as she did

[53]

when she first saw Mickey (at the stagecoach station) and blurted out an unabashed "Wonderful!" When she first saw him he was half-naked (washing himself in preparation for his arrival at Fort Apache); and later, in the stagecoach to the fort, as Mickey rides gallantly behind, she flips open the lid of her double hat box to look at him in the mirror. Seen so innocently and early on, the new man appears before her as the measure of the new land. But now, as she looks in the distance, where Mickey says the telegraph station should be, Phil notices smoke. "Is it an Indian signal?" she innocently asks. Mickey, still looking away in the distance, immediately responds that it is not; but even as he says so he slowly undoes the flap of his revolver holster. Though the distant smoke is not "an Indian signal," it does designate an Indian menace. The smoke rises from the site of a massacre, and Mickey, guided by military duty, rides to the source of the smoke. Phil follows.

The Indian synecdoche in *Fort Apache* therefore specifies a more complex relation between the Indian and the virgin than it does in *Red River*. By identifying a *region* of savagery, the synecdoche designates *space as proscribed spectacle*. The white maiden, however gallantly escorted, intrudes upon a threatening racial environment. She must not see the savagery therein; and yet she must see enough to learn certain essential lessons. The site of the massacre does not merely indicate the Indian's imminent presence in that particular *there;* it determines that the moment of the American couple has not yet arrived. The synecdoche that creates a space also therefore specifies a time. Moreover, it identifies the site of a confrontation that must be avoided at all costs, even as it thrusts upon Phil a West more appalling, and yet eventually far more marvelous, than the one of her romantic suspirations. The Indian synecdoche appears in the Western landscape in order to subvert the romantic response. She comes to know, then, and knowing to value "how the West was won." Thus, the boundaries of the Indian's region *require* the trespass. They exist for and even invite the intrusion. The precincts of savagery, demarcated by the Indian synecdoche, exist principally as a strategy for identifying and affirming the mythic entitlement of the couple, while only *appearing* to threaten it.

Now close enough to see enough, Mickey shouts at Phil, "Get back!" The camera pans left, staying with her a while after she turns her horse and rides away, but she has already entered the space of proscribed spectacle. With Phil offscreen, Mickey now takes us as if on a tour of the site—the two dead troopers, their wagon wrecked and burned, the downed telegraph poles and cut wires. Then he picks up an Apache's bloody headband, evidence (as Captain York [John Wayne] later determines) that Diablo and his band perpetrated the massacre. When they return to the fort, Mickey reports to the fort commander (and Phil's father), Col. Owen Thursday (Henry Fonda), that troopers Berry and Williams are dead—"spread-eagled on the wheels [of the wagon], roasted." "And my daughter saw all this?" asks the irate Thursday. "Yes," Mickey answers. Phil has confronted the Indian in his radical Otherness by confronting him in his virtual absence. Not a face, not a voice, identifies the Indian in her encounter with the aftermath of the massacre. And yet, having witnessed "all this"—having seen the *entire* spectacle of savagery that includes not one single "savage"—she stands as if validated, by Indian and wilderness alike, as the essential western woman: as she who shall inherit, and by that legacy tame, the very land that now drives her back to the fort.

Out there the formidable enemy dwells, unseen to innocent white eyes; and out there Phil has ventured, and she has seen, in the one sight, both what she should not (the unspeakable horror) and what she must (for the unspeakable horror disabuses her of her romantic illusions and introduces her to the West where triumph and tragedy mingle freely). Hence the beguiling efficiency, the narrative parsimony even, whereby the pure eyes of the young white maiden, only belatedly averted, register the completely savage Indian *through*—and not just despite—his virtual absence; and hence, too, the fearful dialectics whereby she comes to know such unspeakable horrors as she can now conjure up out of just such an absence. And thus the name of the savage antagonist—Diablo, "devil"—though it might lend an apocalyptic air to these proceedings, becomes in fact redundant (as does the name of Salvaje in *The Stalking Moon*): the synecdoches already present the diabolical Indian through his savage work against an imperiled virginity and a fragile American paradise.

Phil never leaves the fort again. Indeed, the last time that we see her look outward to the land beyond, she has joined the wives in the "widow's walk" to see the men off on their campaign against Cochise. Hers is the somber and stoic look that binds her to the other, much older women, who themselves look out after husbands and sons as Phil looks out after both her father (to whom she has played wife) and her sweetheart. The woman looks at the savage spaces beyond and sees not the romantic sublime but heroic sacrifice—her own no less than the men's. However moving the moment, it specifies the woman's proper space. So long as the Indian lurks about, Phil shall venture out no more. Phil now belongs to time, to a West—and therefore to an America—still in the making. The Indian's presence in the wide open spaces annuls her innocent perception of an atemporal, ready-made West. Her possession of it lies in the future, and she must wait.

It seems both proper and necessary to sketch the way that the Indian Western deploys synecdoches to claim the contested spaces. The process is most instructive in *Fort Apache*, which deftly, subtly, transmutes the synecdoche of imminent presence into that of virtual absence. The process begins shortly after Phil's encounter with the aftermath of the massacre, when York and Sergeant Beaufort (Pedro Armendariz) ride out to convince Cochise to cross the Rio Grande and present his grievances against the Indian Bureau to Colonel Thursday. Face to face with Cochise, York sees what neither Mickey nor Phil see—an Indian at once noble and defiant, most noble, indeed, in his defiance of culturally hostile intrusions upon his land. York's respect for the Apaches—complemented by his contempt for the corrupt Indian agent Meacham (Grant Withers)—keeps him from the climactic fight (Thursday, taking him for a coward, assigns him to take care of the supply wagons). The rest of the momentous events in *Fort Apache* tend to unfold out of this incursion of York's into the spaces of savage spectacle: the easterner, Thursday, his eye on professional advancement, insults the proud Cochise, giving him no choice but to fight; the ensuing annihilation of Thursday's command ensures the martyrdom of the fallen (and especially of the commanding officer) as well as the elimination of the Indian; Thursday's eastern prejudices about class and race are dissolved in the new heroic identity given him by York in the last scene when he declares that the painting of Thursday's heroic "charge" in Washington, D.C., is "correct in every detail." By mere fact of his birth, Phil and Mickey's young son sanctions the union of region, ethnicity, and class, even as his name—Michael Thursday York O'Rourke—brings together the different influences that determine his—and the nation's—new identity.

Victorious now (following the climactic battle), Cochise and the Apaches ride up to York and his men, as if to attack; but then, out of a swirl of dust created by the many horses on the dry land, only Cochise appears, bearing the guidon of Thursday's annihilated Company B. Already standing some distance ahead of his men, York walks out into the cloud of dust to face Cochise. Through the thick film of dust we see Cochise drive the guidon in the ground, whirl his pony, and ride off. Then the dust clears enough to let us see York looking after the vanished Indians. Cochise, once honorable and lordly, reverts to a swirl of dust in the distance, to an impending absence, already the Vanishing American. Tag Gallagher has noted the pervasiveness of the cloud of

[56]

dust that designates the Indian in *Fort Apache*: "[D]ust is their constant ally: dust thrown by Cochise as sign he will engage the cavalry (conveying sorrow at having to fight, in contrast to Thursday's elation, and telling us also that the soldiers are already dead); dust clouds warning York the Apache are near; dust clouds squaws create to fool Thursday; dust engulfing the trapped regiment; dust into which the Apache disappear after planting the destroyed regiment's banner in front of York and which then rolls over York's men."[22]

The very moment of the Indian's victory produces his defeat. Richard Maltby observes that "the threat vanishes as soon as it becomes visible. This encapsulates a condition of the Western: the Indian constitutes an immediate physical threat to the hero and his charges, yet he cannot but be vanquished, wiped out by the vanguard of civilization."[23] The Indian synecdoche reappears to mark the "historical" inevitability of the Indian's vanishment—to announce, if not indeed to help determine, a "historical" event through the strategies of figuration so dear to the Myth of Conquest. No doubt the Indian in synecdoche contributes to the transformation of Thursday from ill-humored martinet to mythic hero. Paul A. Hutton's description of Thursday's "last stand" takes into account the role of the Indian synecdoche as agent of the Myth of Conquest: "A distant rumble of hooves builds to a crescendo as the Apaches suddenly burst onto the scene, ride over the soldiers, and just as quickly vanish into the swirling dust. Their appearance is only fleeting as they claim their victory and affirm both Thursday's dishonor and his heroism."[24] If the swirl of dust in the "last stand" scene forms part of the total image that enshrines Thursday in the lists of American martyrdom, then in its final version (when Cochise turns from York) it indicates that the Edenic space shall soon be inhabited by its destined occupants. The aftermath of the massacre, which drove Phil away, comes to be transmuted into the sign of the Indian's impending dispossession, into the glimpse of the beckoning Eden.

The Indian synecdoche marks the boundaries of a space wherein the white virgin may suffer racial contamination. Yet the ready interventions of the hero prevent the dreaded fate. Rescue comes without much sustained effort on the part of the hero, as if the effective disposal of the perceived racial emergency required little more than the white hero's

22. *John Ford: The Man and His Films*, p. 249.
23. Richard Maltby, "A Better Sense of History," in *The Book of Westerns* (New York: Continuum, 1996), p. 34.
24. Paul A. Hutton, "Correct in Every Detail: General Custer in Hollywood," in *The Custer Reader*, ed. Paul A. Hutton (Lincoln: University of Nebraska Press, 1992), p. 505.

awareness of the woman's danger. The hero's sacrifice on her behalf seems an almost casual gesture by comparison to the terrifying urgency that calls him to action. Perhaps, then, heroic sacrifice can be estimated by the white woman's presence in the regions of savagery—that is, not only by her position relative to that space but also by the duration of such a presence—and thus by the concomitant racial taint that a prolonged captivity implies. In *The Stalking Moon*, for example, Sam Varner's epic contest with Salvaje seems justly proportional to Sarah's ten-year captivity. Accordingly, it becomes possible to measure his struggle in terms of Sarah's implied lapse, for she has known the savage and begotten his progeny. The duration of the woman's captivity tends to function as an index of loss, and thus of the degree to which the white woman has ceased to be, culturally if not racially, white. No Western incorporates this ethos into the plot of Conquest as integrally as does *The Searchers*.

6

Ethan Edwards (John Wayne) and his adoptive nephew Martin Pawley (Jeffrey Hunter) arrive too late to save their family from a raid led by the Comanche chief Scar (Henry Brandon). Ethan's brother Aaron (Walter Coy) and nephew Ben (Robert Lyden) are dead. Dead also, and for Ethan most tragically, is Aaron's wife Martha (Dorothy Jordan), for whom Ethan has earlier shown such tender affection as to make it clear that he is in love with her. A niece of marrying age, Lucy (Pippa Scott), has been taken captive, and Ethan shall soon enough find her (most likely raped and mutilated) in a canyon: we never know if he found her dead or if he finished her off to spare her further agony. Also captured is the much younger Debbie (Lana Wood; later in the action played by the older Natalie Wood); the search for Debbie lasts over five years. When they find her, Debbie is one of Scar's wives.

If the Western identifies one form of the heroic with the power to remove the white woman's racio-cultural taint, then *The Searchers* would seem to narrate an exalted heroism. Yet in the very effort to deliver the two girls from the Comanches, racism and heroism mingle freely, often indistinctly. Indeed, Ethan's sacrifice identifies racism itself among the forces that animate his heroic labors. Tag Gallagher assures us that his "kindnesses . . . explain Ethan's unbridled hate as a form of terror, a terror he can only control by exteriorizing it into the search for Debbie."[25] And so it may well be; but his "kindnesses" come to be vested in the animus that compels him to shoot Debbie once he finds her among the Comanches. If his struggle is so great, his self-denial so complete, and his fortitude so impressive, still these virtues—at least to the extent that they are deployed against both the Indian and the "Indian" Debbie—indicate just how loathsome a thing many of the white characters in *The Searchers* hold miscegenation to be. Peter Lehman notes this particular racist revulsion that often drives the search. "[A]t the most explicit level Ethan's mania is fueled by the knowledge that after being kidnapped, Debbie would have been subjected to sex with Indians. Brad [Harry Carey, Jr.], upon hearing that Lucy had been raped before being killed, loses all control and rushes wildly to his death. Although distraught by the news of her death, his awareness that she was first raped is too much for him."[26]

If Ethan could merely wink at Debbie's long captivity among the Comanches, he would not have tried to shoot her shortly after he finds her in Scar's camp. The sentiment that compels him to kill Debbie has deep roots in the American psyche, and forms, indeed, an important part of the Myth of Conquest. Early in his brilliant narrative of the Williams family of Massachusetts, John Demos describes the fundamental *cultural* irony arising from the possibility that the Puritans, who accounted themselves clearly superior to the Indians, would find their faith eroded, even dissolved, by the New World wilderness:

> Instead of their civilizing the wilderness (and its savage inhabitants), the wilderness might change, might *uncivilize, them*. This they will feel as an appalling prospect, a nightmare to resist and suppress by every means possible. . . .
>
> Moreover, in the continuing struggles with Indians, certain colonists will be captured and physically removed from the "abodes of civilized life." Reduced thereby to the status of prisoners, they will have to adjust to the "brutish ways" of their "masters." (Indians as *masters*: another, deeply shocking inversion.)[27]

Long before they find Debbie, Ethan declares just how racially and culturally lost he holds a captive of the Comanches to be. When Ethan and

25. *John Ford*, p. 328.
26. "Texas 1868 / America 1956: *The Searchers*," in *Close Viewings: An Anthology of New Film Criticism*, ed. Peter Lehman (Tallahassee: Florida State University Press, 1990), p. 403.
27. John Demos, *The Unredeemed Captive: A Family Story from Early America* (New York: Random House, Vintage Books, 1994), p. 4.

Martin come upon a Comanche village recently devastated by the U.S. Cavalry, they follow the trail to the army post. An army doctor shows them to the post's chapel, where the recovered white captives are sheltered. Martin shows Debbie's doll "Topsy" to two of the younger captives, but neither one responds to it, or to the name "Debbie"; one cowers and cringes, the other shows only vacant astonishment and a skewed simper. Suddenly, as Martin turns from these two, an older captive (Ruth Clifford) shrieks and snatches the doll from him. She coos plaintively over it, rocking it as if it were a child returned. The doctor remarks: "It's hard to believe they're white." But Ethan is not so incredulous: "They ain't white, anymore," he declares. "They're Comanch'."[28] Of the close-up of Ethan that ends the scene, Scott Eyman writes: "the rapid track-in to Ethan's face, contorted with hate as he looks at a group of Indian captives, stands as an especially poignant reminder of the same track-in that Ford had used to introduce a boyish, optimistic John Wayne seventeen years before in *Stagecoach*. Same shot, but both actor and director had deepened over the years."[29]

Well before this scene, however, it has become clear that the rescue and restoration of Debbie does not constitute Ethan's primary motive for the search: how else are we to interpret Ethan's repeated assurances to Martin and Brad that he will find *them*, even after Lucy's death? He wants revenge for Martha, and the "them" refers to the Comanches, or perhaps more precisely to that frightful plurality implicit in the union of Scar and Debbie. That he will find "them" gives no assurance that he will rescue Debbie. Of course Ethan saves Debbie; and to the extent that he delivers her to the tender mercies of the Jorgensen home—to what Mrs. Jorgensen (Olive Carey) wistfully foresees as the "fine good place to be"—he redeems her as well. Yet Ethan saves Debbie in no more profound way than by saving her *from himself*, from his own racial hatred.

---

28. In the source novel, this sentiment of racial perdition is expressed quite early. "At the start Amos [the novel's Ethan] had led them at a horse-killing pace, . . . That was because of Lucy, of course. . . . [G]rown white women were raped unceasingly by every captor in turn until either they died or were 'thrown away' to die by the satiated." Alan LeMay, *The Searchers* (New York: Harper and Brothers, 1954), p. 29. Yet Ethan's sentiments are grounded in cultural responses to Otherness. In 1872 General Phil Sheridan refused to authorize the payment of five ponies to ransom a white woman, Mary Jordan. 'I cannot give my approval to any reward for the delivery of this white woman,' declared Sheridan. 'After having her husband and friends murdered, and her own person subjected to the fearful bestiality of perhaps the whole tribe, it is mock humanity to secure what is left of her for the consideration of five ponies.' " Paul A. Hutton, *Phil Sheridan and His Army* (Lincoln: University of Nebraska Press, 1985), p. 144.

29. Scott Eyman, *Print the Legend: The Life and Times of John Ford* (New York: Simon and Schuster, 1999), p. 447.

The Searchers (1956, Warner Bros.). "They ain't white anymore . . ." Encounter with the returned captives. Courtesy of Warner Bros./Museum of Modern Art Film Stills Archive.

Earlier, when she stood before him, he tried to kill her, and seemingly would have but for Martin 's intervention. Only moments before this, they had at last seen her, in Scar's lodge, the one wife out of four whom Scar orders to show Ethan and Martin the white scalps that Scar has taken in revenge for the death of his sons. She brings to them a lance upon which hang several scalps (including one which Ethan later declares to be Martin's mother's). Thus, as Ethan sees it, her presence before him as the bearer of the tokens of savagery renders her "Comanch' "—as much so as the captive women at the army post.

And so, as I mentioned above, when Debbie comes to warn them that Scar means to attack them, Ethan tries to shoot her. Yet later, after he scalps Scar (whom Martin has just shot dead), now that he could easily enough shoot her, he saves her instead and takes her to the Jorgensen place. How is such a reversal possible? "Much has been made," writes Geoffrey O'Brien, "of Ethan's abrupt turnaround, encapsulated in the single image of Wayne lifting the rescued Debbie . . . into his

The Searchers (1956, Warner Bros.). Fruits of the long quest. Debbie, bearing scalp pole, appears before Ethan and Martin. Courtesy of Warner Bros./ Museum of Modern Art Film Stills Archive.

arms, but moving though it is, it is also the most Hollywoodish moment in the film. . . . [O]ne can't make too much of it; it's a sudden reversal of everything else we know about the character, perhaps even a momentary weakening of purpose he might come to regret."[30] Fortunate is the critic who can make in all sincerity so disarming an affirmation of faith.

Certainly the ending of *The Searchers*—or more properly its resolution, the Aristotelian *lusis*—seems to take place not *because* of an event (as the *Poetics* prescribes for the best plot) but merely *after* it. The causal efficacy of the moment when Ethan tries to kill Debbie demands that he kill her now—or else that the action produce a plausible reversal. I agree, then, that it would be presumptuous to propose anything like a solution to this puzzle, not because the ending seems to me as simple a thing as it does to O'Brien, but because any "solution" would deny *The*

30. Geoffrey O'Brien, "The Movie of the Century," *American Heritage* 47, no. 7 (November 1998): 16–22.

[62]

Searchers its irrepressible cross-currents of motive and passion. Within the scope and context of the present chapter, however, one possibility suggests itself—not as a *cause* for the reversal but as a *code* that articulates it, not as an explanation, quite, but as a disclosure.

To begin, then, with a hypothesis. There must be more to the rescue of Debbie than a sudden burst of avuncular affection, and certainly more than a whimsical change of mind. It is true that when Ethan lifts Debbie up and says, "Let's go home, Debbie," we are reminded of the first scene, when he arrived at Aaron and Martha's and lifted her up in the same way but mistook her for the older Lucy. Now he no longer mistakes her. This gesture affirms her personal identity, even as it reconnects her to the white home. Moreover, the gesture implicitly accepts Debbie's captivity as part of her personal and cultural identity. All this, then, is true enough. The gesture confirms and affirms, but it neither causes nor explains, the reversal. If, as Ethan holds, the years among the Indians can so completely claim Debbie for the savage Other, then he can only rescue her at the expense of his own racial identity. Hence the following proposition: the deliverance of Debbie Edwards requires a forfeiture on Ethan's part. She may cross the threshold of the Edenic "fine good place to be"; yet such a dispensation has its price, and in *The Searchers* that price is paid in the coin of a relinquished racio-cultural identity. When Ethan, toward the end, scalps Scar, he restores Debbie's "whiteness" by surrendering his own. Her Indianness is not so much *removed* as *displaced*. Ethan transfers it to himself. In *The Searchers* the Indian synecdoche functions as the currency of this fearful transaction that balances at last the reckoning of things racial.[31]

IN PURSUIT of the unknown riders who have run off cattle belonging to Lars Jorgensen (John Qualen), Ethan, Martin, and the hastily deputized Texas Rangers come upon two prize bulls, each killed by a lance. The image itself of the impaled bulls settles the question, raised earlier, whether the raiders were Indians or rustlers; but alone of all these white men it is Ethan who determines the Indians' tribal identity. The lovable fool, Mose Harper (Hank Worden), predicted that the raiders would be Caddoes or Kiowas. In response, Ethan advised his brother Aaron to stay in the house and protect his family: "Might be this is rustlers," he says, "might be that this doddering old idiot ain't so far

31. James J. Clauss suggests that the scalping of Scar "leads one to believe that the director saw this brutal desecration as an act of self-immolation," but Clauss does not make clear Ethan's reason for "self-immolation." See "Descent into Hell: Mythic Paradigms in *The Searchers*," *Journal of Popular Film and Television* 27, no. 3 (fall 1999): 2–17.

The Searchers (1956, Warner Bros.). "Ain't but one tribe makes a lance like
that." Courtesy of Warner Bros./Museum of Modern Art Film Stills Archive.

wrong. Could be Comanch'." Now standing with one leg propped on
the dead bull, Ethan pulls out the lance and contemptuously says to
Mose: "Caddoes or Kiowas, huh?" He hurls the lance just in front of
Captain Sam Clayton (Ward Bond) and the other three Rangers: "Ain't
but one tribe uses a lance like that."

In some respects it seems of slight consequence that the lance should
be specifically Comanche. For Comanches, as far as Hollywood is concerned, are Indians (or, more to the point, generic Others). In the scene
in question, the lance, as defining synecdoche, designates not an ethnicity but the impending menace of the virtually absent Other. Even
more important, however, the scene commands our attention because it
establishes Ethan's uncontested power to define that which the .West-
ern asks us to accept as authentically Indian. Henceforth, almost all
that we learn about the Indians we learn from Ethan. And Ethan knows
Indians because he hates them. His hatred authorizes his knowledge;
and it is his knowledge, here as evidenced in the identification of the
lance, that foreshadows an emergent Indianness of his own, and that
thus prefigures the irony whereby he shall come to subvert his own

[64]

heroic purposes. "Ethan's most profound source of power," Slotkin writes, "is his mastery of the most terrible and magical of the Comanche's powers—their capacity to imagine and create 'the horror,' which enables them to destroy the souls of White men and women by driving them mad."[32] No wonder that so many have noted the irony that Ethan and Scar, though they may be mortal enemies, should yet have so much in common.[33]

As defining synecdoche, the lance that Ethan identifies as Comanche seems to enforce the Indian's virtual absence, the way the Cheyenne arrow does in *She Wore a Yellow Ribbon*. Yet the cut from this scene subverts the synecdoche's traditional function as a sign of the hero's power to define the Indian as a virtual absence. Immediately after Ethan identifies the lance, the action shifts to the first scene in which we see the Indian fully. Scar casts his ominous shadow over the cowering Debbie Edwards, whose parents have sent her to hide in the family cemetery. Now engulfed by the shadow, the terrified child looks up helplessly, and an eyeline match shows Scar's lowering look, the gaze that damns. Then he blows the horn, signaling the attack on the Edwards place. The Indian is present here—a fearful portent now made fearfully corporeal—because *Ethan* is absent, and thus powerless to rescue his family. Here is a case of ironic dominion over the traditional images of the Indian: Ethan is right about the lance; yet the assertion of his authority— "Ain't but one tribe uses a lance like that"—fails to enforce the Indian's absence *from the threatened place. The synecdoche that should establish the Indian's absence signals the hero's instead.* The Indian fighter fails to mediate the presence of the Indian menace. Where there should be only an imminent presence, there is instead an Indian overwhelming, superabundant, implacable.

Rather than enforce the Indian's absence by virtue of Ethan's identification of it, the lance anticipates the rape of Martha during the Comanche raid. And yet, as phallus still, the lance seems also to reflect a double irony: not only does Ethan's possession of the lance fail to emasculate the Indian, it fails to empower Ethan himself. Moments after Ethan identifies the lance, Ford underscores the fatal consequences of Ethan's absence by giving us the memorable terror-fraught

32. *Gunfighter Nation*, p. 465.

33. See, for example: *Gunfighter Nation*, pp. 468–69; John Caughie, "Teaching through Authorship," in *Screen Education, The Searchers: Materials and Approaches*, no. 17 (winter 1975/76): 3–13; Lehman, "Texas 1868/America 1956," p. 397; Alan Lovell, "*The Searchers* and the Pleasure Principle," *Screen Education, The Searchers: Materials and Approaches*, no. 17 (winter 1975/76): 53–57; Joseph McBride and Michael Wilmington, *John Ford* (New York: Da Capo Press, 1975), pp. 151, 163.

[65]

scream of Lucy Edwards once she realizes that her parents anticipate an Indian attack. More subtly, perhaps, he produces, earlier in the same scene, the adolescent Ben Edwards at the door, just after his brief foray for signs of Indians (he sees none). In this shot, Ben carries the Confederate saber that Ethan has given him earlier, and that Ethan wore when we first saw him coming to the Edwards place, three years after the end of the Civil War. Now Martha opens the door for Ben, just as she did for Ethan at the beginning. When Ben says to his mother, "I wish Uncle Ethan was here, don't you, Ma?" we realize that the boy can be present before Martha in just this way—saber and all—and at just this instant, because Ethan, though he should be here, is not. The saber doubles the ironic impotence evoked by the phallic lance. The boy's possession of it, and most especially in the presence of his mother, hints at Ethan's own forbidden love for Martha. Thus, much later, when we see Debbie bearing the lance with the scalps on it, the synecdoches confirm Ethan's notion that Debbie is now lost for so "knowing" the Indian. If the lance once intimated Ethan's impotence, it now designates Scar's potency, at once reminding Ethan of Scar's rape of Martha and of Scar's present union with Debbie. By the lance and the scalps Ethan confirms not the Indian's identity this time but the Indianness of Debbie; he verifies his earlier judgment of the white captives: "They ain't white, anymore. They're Comanch'."

Toward the end of *The Searchers*, however, Ethan enforces the Indian's absence, but his way of doing so only compounds the ambivalence of his racio-cultural identity. He scalps Scar. After Martin kills Scar and takes Debbie from the lodge, Ethan rides into it, pulls Scar up by the hair, and scalps him. Moments later he rides out bearing the scalp in his right hand. He sees Debbie running away and gallops after her, and when he catches up to her, just before the mouth of a cave, he lifts her up high and says to her, "Let's go home, Debbie."[34]

A disturbing image of white heroism, to see Ethan take a scalp; and an image, certainly, in which we may easily confirm the persistent critical observation that *The Searchers* subverts the white ideal of the frontier by compromising the values of its hero.[35] The sight of a scalp is rare

34. "The sequence of events," writes Clauss, "suggests that in desecrating Scar . . . [Ethan] rid himself of the emotional scar caused by his painful loss and bitter anger, perhaps even his unspoken desire for his brother's wife." "Descent into Hell," p. 11.

35. See, for example, McBride and Wilmington, p. 148. The scene in which Ethan scalps Scar was censored in England. See Douglas Pye, "*The Searchers* and Teaching the Industry," *Screen Education*, no. 17 (winter 1975/76): 34–48. Pye also reports that "The film's American League of Decency rating was A2–Unobjectionable for Adult audiences," p. 40.

The Searchers (1956, Warner Bros.). With Scar's scalp in hand. Courtesy of Warner Bros./Museum of Modern Art Film Stills Archive.

in the Western, and rarer still when it is the hero who takes it, since the reeking scalp has long memorialized Indian savagery. Historically, whites no doubt practiced scalping; they also promoted it among tribes to whom it was originally unknown. But as a *culturally coded* act it has always been Indian, so that, as Edward Buscombe writes, "When whites do resort to scalping it . . . has a shock effect."[36] One early version of that shock is recorded in Cotton Mather's famous account of Hannah Dustan, a white captive who, with her accomplices Mary Neff and Samuel Lenorson, killed and scalped ten of the twelve Christian Indians (including two women and six children), that were leading her to Canada. A century and a half later, Hawthorne, revolted by the cultural shame of the deed that Mather had praised, condemned Mrs. Dustan in a story titled "The Duston Family": "Would that the bloody old hag," Hawthorne writes toward the end, "had gone astray and been starved to death in the forest, and nothing ever seen of her again, save her skeleton, with the ten scalps twisted round it for a girdle!"

36. See the topic "scalping" in *The BFI Companion to the Western*, p. 215.

Thoreau, attracted by the same event, framed a pithy parable of the American soul lost in the wilderness.[37] In Cooper's *The Deerslayer* (1841), scalping functions throughout as a culture-specific practice that distinguishes whites from Indians, "white gifts" from "red," so that a white scalp-hunter is the forest's most debased creature. God, Deerslayer explains to one such creature, "Hurry" Harry March, "'made us, in the main, much the same in feelin's; though I'll not deny that he gave each race its gifts. A white man's gifts are christianized, while a red skin's are more for the wilderness. Thus it would be a great offence for a white man to scalp the dead, whereas it's a signal vartue in an Indian.'" And only a paragraph later he produces evidence as damning to the white scalp-hunter: "'Ay, and a bad business it is, Hurry. Even the Indians, themselves, cry shame on it, seeing it's ag'in a white man's gifts.'"[38]

That a white *hero* should take a scalp is hardly uncommon in the historical record. Theodore Roosevelt, for one, tells with unrestrained relish of a hand-to-hand fight in which the Kentucky hero Simon Kenton lifts an Indian's scalp as a trophy. Later in the same volume of *The Winning of the West*, he serenely reports that George Rogers Clark and his men harvested ten scalps following a foray into Indian territory. And the Indian fighter William Campbell told his wife, in a letter filled with otherwise tender and exalted sentiments, that he would be bringing home an Indian scalp. "Evidently," Roosevelt remarks, "it was as natural for him to bring home to his wife and children the scalp of a slain Indian as the skin of a slain deer."[39]

Perhaps so. But in the Hollywood Western the white hero almost never scalps.[40] In the rare instances that scalping is associated with the

37. See Cotton Mather, "A Narrative of Hannah Dustan's Notable Deliverance from Captivity," in *Puritans among the Indians: Accounts of Captivity and Redemption, 1676–1724,* ed. Alden T. Vaughn and Edward W. Clark (Cambridge: Harvard University Press, Belknap Press, 1981), pp. 161–64; Nathaniel Hawthorne, "The Duston Family," in *The Complete Writings of Nathaniel Hawthorne* (New York: Houghton, Mifflin, 1903), 17: 238; Henry David Thoreau, *A Week on the Concord and Merrimack Rivers* (New York: Library of America, 1985), pp. 262–64.
38. *The Deerslayer or, The First War-Path. The Leatherstocking Tales,* vol.2 (New York: State University of New York Press, Library of America, 1985), p. 528.
39. Theodore Roosevelt, *From the Alleghanies to the Mississippi, 1777–1783,* vol. 2 of *The Winning of the West,* 4 vols. (Lincoln: University of Nebraska Press, 1995), pp. 26, 230-31.
40. Edward Buscombe identifies *The Scalphunters* and Ford's own *Cheyenne Autumn* as films where scalping by whites also appears. See *The BFI Companion,* s.v. "Scalping." In Howard Hawk's *The Big Sky* (1952) the Indian-hating hero Boone Caudill carries with him into the Western wilderness a sack containing the scalp of a Blackfoot Indian. Long before, in Kentucky, Boone's uncle Zeb Calloway has given him the scalp and has made him believe that it belonged to the Indian that killed Boone's brother Ben. Much later, as if in acknowledgement that his love for the Blackfoot maiden Teal Eye cancels his hatred

white hero, the act betokens a soul in a state of savagery. When he scalps Scar, Ethan surrenders to such a savagery, and he does so through the same image in which he earlier confirms Debbie's own savagery. He has avenged Martha, so that the scalping can be seen as the emasculation of Scar, and even perhaps (to the extent that Scar is his double) as the final suppression of his own illicit desires, even as these might have been indicated by the lance. But in performing a deed so consistently and exclusively charged to the Indian, he becomes as "Comanch' " as the white captives at the army post—or as Debbie. In this context, Andrew Sarris's insight seems especially apt: "the dramatic struggle of *The Searchers* is not waged between a protagonist and an antagonist, or indeed between two protagonists as antagonists, but rather within the protagonist himself."[41] *For the same sign of savagery also betokens Ethan's heroism.* Ethan's deliberate erasure of his racio-cultural identity, far more than the time that he invests in revenge and rescue, stands as evidence of his sacrifice. Yet the scalping of Scar also makes possible Debbie's deliverance, for it removes the stigma of Indianness that was immediately hers when she showed Ethan and Martin the Comanche lance adorned with the scalps.

I am not arguing that Ethan becomes a savage only now. He has been one, for all we know, since the movie's first moments. Certainly he has long before made it easy for us to suspect him of having appropriated "red gifts," for example, early during the pursuit of the Comanches (shortly after he identifies the Comanche lance), when he shoots out the eyes of the dead warrior, so to damn him "to wander forever between the winds." But the scalping of Scar confirms him irrevocably in his savagery. Scar's scalp becomes the outward and visible mark of the indelibly Indian Ethan. The hero appropriates—and becomes known by—the trope meant to identify the Indian. Scar's scalp becomes Ethan's "scar," the outward form of that culturally determined sign of Indianness so far hidden from full view by Ethan's own rabidly overt Indian-hating. Yet it is in and through this act of savagery that he can hope, however unconsciously, to deliver Debbie from her Indianness.

---

of Indians, Boone burns the scalp. In *Jeremiah Johnson*, the hero refuses scalps that his friend Del Gue offers him after a battle with the Blackfoot. When the Pawnees in *Dances With Wolves* take the muleskinner Timmons's scalp, they are confirmed as irredeemable. Tristan Ludlow, the hero of *Legends of the Fall* (1994), who has been taught wilderness skills by the Indian One Stab, makes forays into a World War I battlefield to take German scalps in revenge for his brother's death.

41. Andrew Sarris, *The John Ford Movie Mystery* (Bloomington: Indiana University Press, 1975), 173.

The appropriative act suggests the true meaning of Ethan's "search"—a search that, while it may be motivated by either revenge or deliverance, issues at last into a fearful manifestation of an unsought, perhaps even unwelcome, self-discovery: that which he had so long held buried deep within has now surfaced to give the lie to his "cultural" values.

In a way, then, I am suggesting that this act of scalping remains ambivalent enough to suggest, in the end, Ethan's common humanity with the Indian, and therefore with Debbie—a humanity beyond ethnic and racial categories, beyond ethical "universals." His is the true *sympathy*, urging us not so much to forgive as to yield to that transcendent humility—selfless, profound, unassailable—that often graces the ending of the world's darkest tales. Made Debbie's equal through the shared token of savagery, Ethan can recognize her as a savage and still save her—which is not to say that Ethan is likely to find a place that would honor his sacrifice.

Having delivered Debbie safely over, he turns from the Jorgensen door and returns to the wide open and windswept spaces.[42] As he had earlier shot the eyes out of the dead Comanche in hatred, thus condemning him "to wander forever between the winds," so now he stands condemned, by hatred and heroic sacrifice alike, to the selfsame fate. True to the pattern long before established by the Western, the hero has helped to create the new order of the ages only to be, if implicitly, that order's worst enemy. He is America's last remaining savage—Indian not by descent—as the eighth-Cherokee Martin is, or by force, as Debbie was—but by the terribly ironic consent whereby he becomes Other to his own race and culture. He turns from the threshold of the Jorgensen home as its door closes on him. There, in the wild spaces beyond, Ethan, at once accursed and heroic, affirms his wild and tragic presence—outcast of the "fine good place to be," both the Indian's nemesis and the sole remnant of his being, ambiguous testament to the Indian's insistent presence, unequivocal decree of his absence.

---

42. Charles B. Pierce's *Grayeagle* (1978), though clearly a conscious reworking of *The Searchers*, alters the ending—to say nothing of generic expectation—and allows the *Indian* hero, Grayeagle, entrance into its version of the "fine good place to be." For all its roughness, *Grayeagle* seems a compelling effort to integrate the Indian in the new American Eden. Perhaps, however, its most interesting feature is that Lana Wood, who played little Debbie in *The Searchers*, plays Beth Colter, the maiden (begotten illegitimately of fully Indian parents) who eventually marries the eponymous hero.

[2]

Prospects from the Spaces of the Same
The Indian, the Land, and the "Civilized Eye"

The surrounding group of savages offered no very attractive spectacle to a civilized eye.
> —Francis Parkman, *The Oregon Trail*

Mama let her lip tremble, now that it was over. She whimpered, "I only wish those people would stay away."
Ben said, "There weren't any people here, Mama. Those were Indians."
> —Alan LeMay, *The Unforgiven*

1

The Myth of Conquest intones its paean to the white hero in phrases as confident and cheerful as they are familiar. When the hero moves about the Western landscape, he leads the vanguard of civilization; he follows the setting sun; he maps the course of empire; he fulfills the manifest destiny of his race. When the Indian moves in the same spaces, however, he threatens, he lurks, he skulks—ever the serpent in the American Eden. He blazes no trail; neither does he grow up with the country. He has no future, for he is the apostate of the Cult of Progress; yet he has a destiny, manifestly foredoomed to vanish as he is. That which is familiar about his image is also fragmentary, or else distant: the lance and the arrow, the shield and the feathered bonnet, the faceless figures on the faraway ridge, the aftermath of the massacre. By contrast to this Indian, who so rarely amounts to more than the sum of his meager parts, the Indian fighter moves about as if enfolded by an aura of promised triumph, complete in his humanity and clear in his purpose—unfettered, privileged, self-determined. Emerging in full-formed manhood, the great Western vastness his abiding home, he embodies the foreordained mastery of his race. The famous zoom-in shot that instantly identifies *Stagecoach*'s Ringo as the deliverer of a vulnerable and beleaguered white America; the solitary sunset ride of Nathan Brittles at the end of *She Wore a Yellow Ribbon;* the persistently fabulous presence of Ethan Edwards in a land of which he seems to be the very substance—even if he is also the agent of its profanation—recount, as if for the first time, the enduring moment that both contains and projects an American ethos. Such an ethos includes the sentiment of archaic heroism, the allure of the timeless wilderness, the comfort of dreams entrusted to a hero who overcomes the undreamed-of hardships that fulfill them. Formidable as the Indian may seem to be in these same Westerns, where does he appear in form more memorable than that of the reverberant name "Geronimo," or of Red Shirt cowering before Brittles, or of Scar's shadow spreading ominously over the helpless child Debbie Edwards? The exigencies of American racio-cultural self-definition produce such an Indian, so that his presence always betrays a paradox of representation: he is the *image* (i.e., the presence) of the *absent* Other. Perspective becomes the essential instrument of representation. Perspective enforces the Indian's virtual absence and defines the limits of Indian identity.

For our purposes, *perspective denotes the ideological inflection of the visible.* The Western's Indian always appears before us as a *projection* of a perspective over which the Myth of Conquest exercises virtually absolute control. Richard Maltby's fine insight into a scene from *Two Rode Together* (Ford, 1961) enables us to develop the complex relation between perspective, the Indian, and the contested western spaces—the relation that this chapter explores. In this scene, the hero, Guthrie McCabe (James Stewart), and the recently rescued Elena de la Madriaga (Linda Cristal) are sitting around a campfire when Stone Calf (Woody Strode), Elena's Comanche husband, appears before them out of the darkness, a lurid presence at the edges of the firelight, knife in hand. At this moment, Stone Calf, as Maltby accurately notes,

> embodies the magnificent, threatening, ignoble animal of savagism, his intentions violence, rapine and despoliation. Calmly, belying the dramatic potential of the confrontation, the hero shoots him.
>
> In this archetypal confrontation between savage Indian and frontiersman over the fate of feminine civilisation, we witness a paradox: the divergence between the terrifying image of the Indian and his actual impotence in the sights of the White hero's gun—*the threat vanishes as soon as it becomes visible.* (Italics mine.)[1]

1. "A Better Sense of History: John Ford and the Indians," p. 34.

Two Rode Together (1961, Columbia). Guthrie McCabe shoots Stone Calf.
Courtesy of Columbia Pictures/Museum of Modern Art Film Stills Archive.

Perhaps such a moment—the threatening presence of an Indian at the edges of the space that contains the hero—has its source in the familiar row of mounted and warbonneted Indians appearing suddenly on the faraway ridge. So abused by convention has become the image of the Indian at the physical margins of a space dominated by white Americans, that movies as different as *The Searchers* and *Thunderheart* (Apted, 1992) resort to it, each for opposite purposes—the one to announce the Indian menace, the other to announce the deliverance of the beleaguered part-Indian hero.[2] Yet long before *The Searchers* it had become common practice to represent the Indian at the edges of the world itself—an Indian fast running out of Western ground to avoid the white man. Of the many representations of such an Indian, by far the most well known is James Earl Fraser's *End of the Trail*. One need but look at the horse's feet, all gathered together, unable to take one more step, so to recognize the inevitability of the Indian's disappearance from the land that he might call his own. The Western, perhaps typically, turned his-

2. The latest version of this tired convention—a parody—appears, twice no less, in *Shanghai Noon* (Dey, 2000), starring Jackie Chan as Chon Wang. In one of the two instances the Indians appear magically, horses and all, on the roof of a church.

tory into cliché by placing the victim of Westward Expansion on the far horizon of the white hero's view.

The moment that Maltby describes may readily recall Salvaje's invasion of Sam Varner's Eden, as well as his motive for doing so, since in both movies the white hero takes the captive woman from her Indian husband. But McCabe disposes of his Indian enemy much more efficiently than Varner does his own: his fight with Stone Calf is hardly a fight at all; certainly it is a mismatch, since Stone Calf has no firearm of his own. More important, the camera unambiguously sides with McCabe and Elena. It becomes an agent of perspectival projection, its view of the Indian clearly aligned with that of the deadly six-gun. Perspective is lethal, and projection becomes projectile.

Two Rode Together makes clear the tendency of the Myth of Conquest to locate its Indian at the periphery of the contested terrain, out where he is least visible, less discernibly human—always as if the Indian, not the white hero, were the trespasser, an unwelcome interloper disrupting the smooth course of empire. It makes no difference that McCabe and Elena are still in Comanche territory, or that Elena is Stone Calf's wife. Without any ambiguity, the moment presents the Indian as the intruder, and no sooner does Stone Calf make his move toward the center of that space than McCabe shoots him dead, as if the defense of the physical space and that of the woman (and perhaps even that of his own manhood) were all one and the same thing. The Myth of Conquest demands the *cultural* integrity of these spaces, even when these spaces remain *geographically* vague, debatable ground. Indeed the primary purpose of spatial thinking, at least of this variety, is unmistakably cultural: space, whether conquered or yet to be so, confers racio-cultural identity.

Because the Western never accords the Indian anything like a perspective of his own, all reference to perspective here shall be to the view *of* the Indian and the land—of the Indian *in* the coveted land. Perspective casts the *native* as an alien within its ideal spaces. Accordingly, narrative action only confirms what perspective has already assumed, and all dramatic resolutions are prefigured. Roy Harvey Pearce has given us a characteristically subtle insight into that convergence of the visual and the ideological that I am calling "perspective": "Already [the colonial Englishman] had God and civilization and rejoiced in the power they gave him. Looking at the Indian in his lack of such power, the Englishman could be sure of what he himself was; looking at himself, he could be sure of what the Indian should be. In America, from the very beginning the history of the savage is the history of the civilized."[3] The view of the Indian, disclosing the inevitable *visual* difference, revealed at the same time his *cultural* limitations, the insurmountable deficiencies that would vindicate white civilization. The fundamental paradox reappears: the Indian's *distinguishing* mark is his *lack*.

The Indian, of course, looks—Geronimo at the tiny stagecoach below, Red Shirt at Brittles, Scar at Debbie; but he is almost always an *image* looking with intent to harm, looking in fear at the white hero, looking mournfully at his own inescapable fate. His "gaze" itself derives from the dominant perspective. In *Stagecoach*, for example, Geronimo's gaze is governed completely by the requirements of the Myth of Conquest. His is the ravenous and predacious look that casts him unmistakably as civilization's nemesis. Ironically, then, his visual position, which would appear to grant him great advantage over the vulnerable stage below, in fact determines already his inevitable defeat. Thus, the Indian's *derivative gaze*, if I may so call it, functions always as a portent of its own rescission, of its repossession by the "original" owner. He may look, but he has no perspective of his own. His gaze is only reflective—mirroring as it does the evil projected upon him. His own perspective projects no ideal, and it extends in space and time only to confirm the prospect of his impending disappearance.

When it is not casting the Indian as the serpent at the margins of the Western Eden, perspective identifies the point from which the action tends to unfold and toward which it tends to move. Perspective—considered as prospect—belongs to an America ever "realizing westward," to use Robert Frost's striking phrase. It claims the West as the site of a national patrimony. The hero looks upon the land adoringly and hopefully and, looking, already possesses it—at least enough to tell himself that he is *defending* it rather than *invading* it.

Westward lies the encounter with America's own beginnings: in space if not in time, the Western (re)invents the original American moment, the instant when desire, perhaps guiltless still, reconceives the Garden and invests the idea (and thus the place and its impending occupation) with the power to reinstate the prelapsarian order. The prospect consecrates the site where possession—with its intimations of blood and blame—becomes redemption. Depth, therefore, the extended and extensive look, projects American ideals that sustain the hero in his continual quest for the spaces that his vision already consecrates. Inevitably, almost logically, the projection extends beyond the

3. Roy Harvey Pearce, *Savagism and Civilization: A Study of the Indian and the American Mind* (Berkeley: University of California Press, 1988), p. 8.

present margins of territories already conquered: perspective comes to constitute—and indeed to institute—an assault against the Indian. When the patriarchal Jesse Wingate, in *The Covered Wagon*, envisions Oregon as an agrarian paradise, and when the innocent Philadelphia Thursday, in *Fort Apache*, sighs the wonders of the West, they project a culturally conditioned ideal. It seems appropriate that scenes foregrounding such yearnings should be soon followed by some form of Indian presence. From Jesse Wingate's agrarian reverie, as we saw in chapter 1, the action cuts to the Indians, far away, who have captured the "monster" plow belonging to a nameless predecessor of Jesse. As we have also seen, Philadelphia ventures out of the fort's safety only to find unmediated savagery in the form of the massacre's aftermath. In both cases, the projected perspective produces the enemy that blocks it; yet the same perspective foreshadows the elimination of the obstacle. Perspective becomes as predictive as it is appropriative. A bit like Lady Macbeth, it feels "the future in the instant"—perhaps, in the end, with no less tragic a result.

2

Mary Louise Pratt's influential book—a book as much about perspective as about "travel writing and transculturation"—underscores the ways in which "subjugated" cultures have influenced their colonizing (or "metropolitan") masters.

> Borders and all, the entity called Europe was constructed from the outside in as much as from the inside out. Can this be said of its modes of representation? While the imperial metropolis tends to understand itself as determining the periphery (in the emanating glow of the civilizing mission or the cash flow of development, for example), it habitually blinds itself to the ways in which the periphery determines the metropolis—beginning, perhaps, with the latter's obsessive need to present and re-present its peripheries and its others continually to itself.[4]

In a later chapter, I will undertake a critique of the assumption (or the illusion), so pervasive in the Indian Western, that the encounter with the Indian alters neither the white hero nor the perspective that he represents nor the society that his labors make possible. But here, where we are discussing perspective as a strategy of "othering," the passage

4. Mary Louise Pratt, *Imperial Eyes: Travel Writing and Transculturation* (London: Routledge, 1992), p. 6.

from Pratt's *Imperial Eyes* precisely describes the operations of perspective, however unconscious and uncritical these operations may be. Perspective in the Western is utterly indifferent to the potentially self-transformative power of its *own* representations of the Indian. It therefore projects a racio-cultural consensus, upholds what might be called, in a sort of pleonasm, an ethos of Sameness. It premises (and privileges) the uniformity of outlook that Edward Said calls *vision*—namely, the belief that the Other "can be seen panoptically."[5] The view of the Indian as "alien" has remained "panoptic," which is to say atemporal, through half a millennium, and his "character" indelible, regardless of the many contradictory traits that are said to compose it. The same outward glance that covets and possesses must generate—as much for its triumph as for its vindication—an Indian whose very presence in the land requires his removal even as it justifies it.

Even on first contact, the view of the Indian revealed more about white Europeans than about the American native himself. "The white man," as Bernard Sheehan notes, "dealt with the Indian as he perceived him."[6]

> According to the Lockean position, the way men saw the world was at least as important as what they saw. The manner of seeing influenced profoundly the nature of the object seen. In consequence, the locus of identity moved from the object to the eye of the subjective viewer. The essences of things were unknowable; men knew the sense impressions in their own minds. Without the stability of the Linnean construction, Locke's interpretation of how mankind perceived its surroundings transferred the center of initiative from the external world to the human mind.[7]

It was not, therefore, for the sake of the Indian that the white man looked at him. Nor—or at least not primarily—did he look so that he might establish a bond of common humanity with one so seemingly different; or that he might take delight in the varieties of human culture; or even that he might satisfy an idle curiosity. Nor, looking, did the white man merely misreport what he saw. His image of the Indian was no mere perceptual error but a determined mode of miscasting him, if only because the viewer's unacknowledged aim was to identify and vindicate—and at the last absolve—himself.

As an instrument of the Myth of Conquest, perspective articulates

5. Edward Said, *Orientalism* (New York: Random House, 1978; Vintage Books, 1979) p. 240.
6. Bernard Sheehan, *Seeds of Extinction: Jeffersonian Philanthropy and the American Indian* (Chapel Hill: University of North Carolina Press, 1973; New York: Norton, 1974), pp. 26–27.
7. Ibid., p. 26.

[77]

and validates the racio-culturally defined region that I would like to call *the spaces of the Same*. Both claim and possession, dream and dominion, configure the spaces of the Same. The expansion of present geographical boundaries presupposes a hope at once projected and fulfilled, and the present hoping and the future having, both, endow the new nation with its "exceptional" character. The land belongs not to him who inhabits it but to him who beholds it—or so would the Myth of Conquest have it. He inherits it who gazes longingly upon it, who sees it as his patrimony deeded time out of mind, and who thus invokes the sentiment of America as "gift outright": "The land was ours before we were the land's. / She was our land more than a hundred years / Before we were her people." These mythic chronologies of inclusion replicate the historical chronicles of exclusion: the Western configures the landscape of a homogeneous *us*—"ours" ever, but "theirs" only till the title is extinguished, till the trust expires, by destiny's irrevocable decree.

One early example of the geography of cultural self-definition appears in William Bradford's *Of Plymouth Plantation*. Late in the colony's first winter (1621), Bradford writes: "All this while the Indians came skulking about them, and would sometimes show themselves aloof off, but when any approached near them, they would run away."[8] The Indians appear at the edges of Plymouth colony as Stone Calf appears at the edge of McCabe's campfire. To be sure, the colonists do not shoot these Indians that come "skulking about," but the Indians here seem no less frozen in time and space than Stone Calf is in the sights of McCabe's six-gun. Indeed, we know the dominant perspective by the claim itself, by the persistent fact of its inscription as well as by the absence of an inscribed counterclaim. The inscription identifies the spaces of the Same even as it invents the Other both as imminent presence and virtual absence. Not surprisingly, then, as Jill Lepore relates: "supposed Indian violations of the laws of war produced some of the colonists' most vitriolic prose. In the colonists' words, enemy Algonquians fought like beasts, marauders, and fiends, or even like women, not truly fighting but 'skulking': 'creeping: & cruching: behinde any bush, tree, rock, or hill.'"[9] The violation of the "laws" of war, and therefore the Otherness that such a violation confirmed, presupposed the Same's power to demarcate not only its own inviolable space but also

8. William Bradford, *Of Plymouth Plantation*, ed. Samuel Eliot Morison (New York: Modern Library, 1981), p. 87.

9. Jill Lepore, *The Name of War: King Philip's War and the Origins of American Identity* (New York: Vintage Books, 1998), pp. 112–13.

to specify the boundary beyond—the margin that located the habitations of the Indian even as it determined the very regions yet within savagery's hold.

Perspective comprises both the scene *and* itself, projects the scene as an extension of itself (of *the* "point of view"). It affirms the site and source of power even as it projects it: in the case of the skulking Indian, perspectival projection takes the form of the power to *emplace* the Other (hence, historically, Removal and the reservation system). The Indian, placed in the region beyond as a skulker, helps to identify the spaces of the Same: the inscribed outward look that detects the Indians tells us that these spaces—and thus this story, this "master narrative"—belong to the English colonists as if by right of discourse. Discourse creates the spaces of the Same before might and triumph do; it augurs both, in fact, since it is coeval with the divine apportionment of the "gift outright."

When the chronicles of early New England became so engrafted in the stuff of the new nation as to become the well-worn material of sentimental fiction, Helen Hunt Jackson could produce a poignant image of the Indian as "skulker" just outside his very own home, now forcefully taken over by rude American settlers. Alessandro, fleeing during the night with Ramona, passes by his home in Temecula and, seeing a light within, decides to have a look: "He would see the new home-life already begun on the grave of his. Stealthily creeping under the window from which the light shone, he listened. He heard children's voices; a woman's voice; at intervals the voice of a man, gruff and surly; various household sounds also. . . . Cautiously raising himself till his eyes were on a level with the lowest panes in the window, he looked in."[10] When one of the children catches a quick glimpse of Alessandro, the father rushes outside to shoot him, firing wildly in the night.

In Bradford, the Same looks at the Other; in Jackson, the Other (so cast by his Indianness, by his having to flee so that he can marry Ramona) looks at these that were recently his haunts and beholds an Other. Indian dispossession could be confirmed not only by the loss of place but by the loss of the perspective that distinguishes Other from Same. Perhaps the most significant difference between Jackson and Ford is that the gruff American settler misses and McCabe does not. But Alessandro is no less a threat to the American settler than Stone Calf is to McCabe and Elena.

However separated by time, each from the other, the images from *Two Rode Together*, *Of Plymouth Plantation*, and *Ramona* share a specific

10. Helen Hunt Jackson, *Ramona* (1884; New York: New American Library, Signet Classic, 1988), p. 215.

method of configuring the opposition between the Same and the Other. More often than not, it is true, conflict can be represented by the fine line (in all respects as metaphorical as it is physical) that divides the contestants; and surely the Western offers numerous examples of such a configuration, for as surely does it presuppose the existence of a "frontier line" dividing civilization from savagery. But another image, not as common or as clear yet just as fundamental as the line, designates the concept of racio-cultural space that I am trying to elucidate. There is, then, a space; and there is, at or near its implied center, the white man or woman (or both) looking out from it. In the brief scene from *Two Rode Together*, McCabe and Elena sit by the generous campfire, whose light illuminates all the space that there is, as if there could be nothing beyond it. So, too, in the implied space beyond which Bradford sees the skulking Indians: when "any approached near them," the Indians run away, and the implication is that the motion of the colonists across the spaces and toward the edges where the Indians skulk only reaffirms their possession of these spaces, while the Indian, instead of returning to his own spaces, vanishes in the darkness beyond the margins. In neither case, then, do the Indians quite have their own space; instead they have only (and always) the edges of the spaces of the Same. And if the Indian were to move toward the center of that space, as Stone Calf does (or in a more complex way, as Bradford eventually accuses the Wampanoag Squanto of doing), it would be as an invader. Moreover, if the white man should move beyond the boundaries where the Indian skulks, he shall transform them into yet more of his own spaces. The Indian of the Myth of Conquest lives but to recede, to remain forever at the periphery of paradise. *Such space as there is, exists as perspective's power to possess that which it beholds, to make of looking the very source of possessing.* Virginia Wright Wexman has noted that the "modest, egalitarian implications" of the Western's agrarian ideal "are typically countered by the genre's predilection for grandiose views of scenic panoramas and expansive vistas. The implications of such visions of vast territories embraced in a single possessive gaze is far from egalitarian; they rather suggest the more hierarchical, dominating dimension of American imperialist aspirations."[11] In the New World the "possessive" or appropriative gaze is as old as the moment when Columbus stepped off the caravel and claimed the land, however narrow the stretch of beach or the man's own outlook might have been

11. "The Family on the Land," pp. 129–69.

then. To take possession of the land was to claim it not only as property but as birthright; and it was this idea of land that came to be inscribed in the discourse of culture, and thus enabled Europeans to claim it *all already and at once*, to transform the appropriation of it into a mission, so that the puny island and the rickety ships and the weary sailors fore-tokened vast continents and mighty armies and far-famed *conquistadores*. What McCabe sees within his spaces—woman and all—belongs to him by virtue of the gaze itself, and the Indian can never appear at the periphery of those spaces but as an enemy, as a skulker with evil intent.

The Puritans in John Demos's *The Unredeemed Captive* nurture the hope of Eunice Williams's return by a sustained appeal to this vague and yet insistent geography of ethnic Sameness. Long after she has lost her English, has married the Kahnawake Mohawk François Xavier Arosen, and has borne his children—long, indeed, after she has openly refused permanent residence in New England—we continue to encounter the white family's piteous hopes that Eunice "may yet return & dwell with us," that she "may long to return to us," "that she will now be persuaded to stay with" her English family.[12] It is hard to pinpoint the sentiment, if such it is, that allows the family to continue to claim Eunice for a space and a culture that she has long since renounced. Yet the family persists in registering the stubborn hope; and the hope, inscribed and promulgated for decades after Eunice's captivity, delineates the spaces of the Same and identifies thereby the racio-cultural region beyond, the site of Otherness where, surely (as they believe), Eunice continues to abide as *captive*. And so returning and dwelling and staying are all racially and culturally defined; and the curse of Eunice's continued stay with "them" identifies her not so much as Other but as would-be Same. Only such a discursively defined concept of space could continue to account her an "unredeemed captive."

As the New England Williamses vaguely hoped that Eunice's physical "return" would wash her clean of her Indianness and restore her to Puritan society, so the hopes for the return of the Western's female captives—Debbie Edwards, for example—tend to equate return with restoration: presence in a culturally defined space revalidates the fallen woman's status as potential mate of the white hero. However indistinct or inchoate, then, and however demarcated more by the discourse that establishes, authorizes, and enforces them than by physical bound-

12. *Unredeemed Captive*, pp. 206, 207.

aries, the spaces of the Same promote the work of redemption, for they are, themselves, products of mythology's ideal geography.

The Myth of Conquest never lacks for specific disclosures of an underlying ambivalence that beholds the land in two contradictory ways: the domains that are always and already "ours" in union coeternal of deed, vision, and possession are also the *spaces of the Other*—the land was *theirs*, so to say, *before* it was "ours." The young nation may look out into the unconquered districts and behold its birthright, but it also encounters the troubling presence of the Indian. The Myth of Conquest proposes to solve the historical problem of Indian presence by simultaneously simplifying it and compounding it: the spaces of the Other become what we knew in the previous chapter as "the spaces of savage spectacle." Seldom, then, do such spaces specify mere difference. The conquering gaze identifies them as abodes of savagery.

Small wonder that whites so often enter the Indian's native world only to register revulsion. A romantic yearning for the simple life drove the young Francis Parkman west, that he might observe Indians at first hand.[13] Yet, throughout his sojourn, Parkman never relinquishes his perspective, or leaves it outside when he enters the spaces of the Other. The Lakota have killed a buffalo and Parkman, ever the splenetic, follows behind at his own incurious pace. As the side of a hill comes into view, Parkman notes the Indians already at work on the carcass. "The surrounding group of savages," he notes, "offered no very attractive spectacle to a civilized eye. . . . The faces of most of them, besmeared with blood from ear to ear, looked grim and horrible enough. My friend the White Shield proffered me a marrow-bone, so skillfully laid open, that all the rich substance within was exposed to view at once. Another Indian held out a large piece of the delicate lining of the paunch; but these courteous offerings I begged leave to decline."[14]

The spaces of the Other enable white viewers to define themselves

13. Francis Parkman, *The Oregon Trail* (1849; New York: Library of America, 1991), p. 111.
14. Ibid., p. 191. The literature of contact is awash with similar moments. Shortly after making contact with the Shoshones (who had seemed so essential to their expedition only a few days before), Meriwether Lewis comes across a spectacle much like that which Parkman would witness more than four decades later. Here is Lewis's gloss on the scene (in all its orthographic freedom): "I really did not untill now think that human nature ever presented itself in a shape so nearly allyed to the brute creation. I viewed these poor starved divils with pity and compassion." *The Journals of Lewis and Clark*, ed. Frank Bergon (New York: Penguin Books, 1989), p. 236. Herman Melville, whose *Typee* appeared in the year of Parkman's sojourn in the West, registers a revulsion of his own to the way in which the Typees eat their fish. The disgust does not exempt Melville's lovely Fayaway, though he does note that she eats the raw fish as daintily as any savage can. In his infamous chapter on the "Goshoot" Indians in *Roughing It*, published in 1872, Twain

by and through *aversion*—by a culturally cultivated repugnance that affirms the virtues of the "civilized eye" and through the withheld gaze that so often intimates the dread of becoming the thing beheld. The spaces of the Other never quite exist independently of the spaces of the Same. To the extent, at least, that they enable the white viewer's censure, the spaces of the Other function as a construction of the Myth of Conquest. The nearer, physically, to the Indian, the greater, culturally, the gap. Pity for the Indian becomes a function of distance. Yet, as Pearce instructs, such pity implies "censure":

> We can say that the American, as the self-consciously civilized and civilizing man, could envision the possibilities of a life free from what he somehow felt to be the complexities of civilization. Envisioning that life, he might very well yearn for it. But seeing it, as he thought, in disturbing actuality to the west, he hated himself for his yearning. He was tempted, as we might say; and he felt driven to destroy the temptation and likewise the tempters. He pitied the tempters, because in his yearning for a simpler life, he could identify with them. He censured them, because he was ashamed to be tempted, and he refused to deny his higher nature.[15]

A century and a half after Parkman, *Dances With Wolves* (Costner, 1990) would take much the same moment and invert the white hero's response to it. However revolted Lieutenant Dunbar (Kevin Costner) may be when Wind In His Hair (Rodney Grant) offers him the piece of raw buffalo liver, he never shrinks from the spaces of the Other, never proclaims his friends' "besmeared" faces a spectacle too savage for his "civilized eye." Yet in the longer version of *Dances With Wolves*, in a scene that just precedes the buffalo hunt (but excised from the 1990 theatrical release) Dunbar arrives at the Lakota camp and sees his friends, including his mentor Kicking Bird (Graham Greene), dancing around a fire over which hang a blond scalp and a severed hand. These belong to the white buffalo hunters that defiled the buffalo herd some days be-

could scorn the Indians, because he had now come among them, into their space: "It was curious to see how quickly the paint and tinsel fell away from [the Indian] and left him treacherous, filthy and repulsive—and how quickly the evidences accumulated that *wherever one finds an Indian tribe* he has only found Goshoots more or less modified by circumstances and surroundings—but Goshoots, after all. They deserve pity, poor creatures; and they can have mine—*at this distance*. Nearer by, they never get anybody's" [italics mine]. Mark Twain, *Roughing It*, vol. 2 of *The Works of Mark Twain*, ed. Paul Baender (1872; Berkeley: University of California Press for the Iowa Center for Textual Studies, 1972), p. 146. Leslie Fiedler calls attention to a similar passage from Twain's *Innocents Abroad*. See *The Return of the Vanishing American* (New York: Stein and Day, 1968), pp. 122–24.

15. *Savagism and Civilization*, p. 74.

fore. Dunbar reins in his horse and rides around the periphery of the circle, looking on aghast. Then, over the tight close-ups of his appalled look (intercut with the images of the hand, the scalp, and his friends), he comments in voiceover on his own version of the savage spectacle: "It was suddenly clear now, what had happened, and my heart sank as I tried to convince myself that the white men who had been killed were white people and deserved to die. But it was no use. I tried to believe that Wind In His Hair and Kicking Bird and all the other people who shared the killing were not so happy for having done it, but they were. As I looked at familiar faces, I realized that the gap between us was greater than I could ever have imagined."[16] Order the raw to be cooked, decline the Indian's offering, or look at the Other and then look away in disgust and censure. Know, then, and by all means affirm, the immense cultural abyss that, no doubt mercifully, separates "us" from "them." In this way, perspective already possesses the spaces of the Other, for it claims them, in consequence of the distance and the demurral, for civilization. It is instructive to consider one more detail in the contrast between the moment from *Dances With Wolves* and that from *Two Rode Together*. In the former movie, it is the white man, not the Indian, who appears at the edges of the firelight. Yet, regardless of relative position, perspective enforces the Otherness of the Indian. To see the Indian is to censure, and the perspective that projects its deadly reproach seems less important for its position than for its power to cast the Indian as the outsider in the spaces of the Same.

The "civilized eye" recognizes the spaces of the Other only insofar as it identifies them as the spaces of savage spectacle. The simple Manichaean calculus unfolds its own complexities, its inevitable ironies. The spaces of savage spectacle belong to the perspective of the Myth of Conquest, for they exist as a requisite mirror construction of the spaces of the Same. Hence the problem compounded since, disturbingly enough, savagery has its source not in the "seen" but in the "seeing." The spaces of the Same *require* the savage borders. Perspective locates the Indian in the spaces of the Same that it may thereby rescue these regions for civilization's exalted mission: it projects the regions in which it is to perform its "errand into the wilderness." Thus it

---

16. The scene first aired in the United States when ABC Television broadcast the four-hour version of *Dances With Wolves* in the fall of 1993. This version, minus the commercials and the slightly bowdlerized ABC print, appeared on laserdisc a year or so later. For the differences between the two versions and their treatment of the relation between the white man and the Indians, see Armando José Prats, "The Image of the Other and the Other *Dances With Wolves*," *Journal of Film and Video*, 50 (Spring 1998): 3–20.

charts and expands, but it also *redeems* the spaces of savage spectacle, transmutes their desolate sweeps into the mythic geographies of hope and triumph and self-vindication.

3

The Indian Western inherits from frontier literature the discursive distinction between the seeing and the seen, appropriating the historical conflict with the Indian over the land so that it may define, highlight, and extol Conquest's own values and virtues. This is another way of drawing attention to the American tendency to *spatialize* its history, to define itself continually in terms of the land or of reference to the struggle for the land. "The Western landscape," writes Howard Mumford Jones, "dims . . . our eastward vision; the immigrant coming hither came to escape history, despite the injunction that escape from history is impossible. He put the past behind him, with the result over decades, whether radicalism or conservatism reign, that the American people are a people in space rather than a people in time."[17] At its noblest, the spatial perspective liberated from history finds its expression in the greatest American spokesman "for absolute freedom and wildness," Thoreau, in the endearing declaration, "Eastward I go only by force; but westward I go free."[18] Meaner, if no less American, the Indian Western recognizes the history of westward expansion, indeed appeals to it continually; but it views it through a teleological prism, rearranging it thereby into recurrent cycles of vision, contest, and triumph. The ideological refractions of mythic tales disturb and distort the claims of other narrative disciplines: perspective usurps such spaces as an alternate temporality might designate the Indian's by precedent claim. Beyond the light of McCabe's campfire; beyond Phil Thursday's encounter with the aftermath of the massacre; in the ambiguous zones just beyond Varner's New Mexico paradise—there dwells the Indian, not as Other merely but as savage utterly. The dark regions, as if in moral chiaroscuro, highlight the heroic and the civilized. No other moment in the Indian Western gives such poetic expression to the devastation that the "savage" wreaks upon Edenic aspirations as does *The Searchers* just after Ethan and Martin arrive at the

17. Howard Mumford Jones, *O Strange New World: American Culture: The Formative Years* (New York: Viking Press, 1964), p. 388.
18. Henry David Thoreau, *Walking* (Boston: Applewood Books, 1987), n.p. [16].

DBS Arts Library

Jorgensen place following the first year of their quest. Recall that the Comanches killed Brad Jorgensen, who suicidally charged their village, having lost his mind at the news (delivered by Ethan) of his fiancée Lucy Edwards's rape and death. As the scene opens, the three remaining Jorgensens (mother, father, Laurie) come out to greet the two searchers. Now facing the father, Lars (John Qualen), and behind him the house, Ethan dismounts and asks him if he received the letter telling him about Brad's death. Lars faces Ethan, and beyond him the hard and hard-hearted stretches, thinly bespattered with scrub and scrag cattle, and far beyond them the impassive buttes. He acknowledges receipt of the letter and then, with an awkward and pained sweep of the hand over the mean hardscrabble, he utters the simple and touching plaint: "Oh, Ethan, this country!" Here perspective identifies the land as the regions of savagery: the look outward reveals only the cruel betrayal of noble hopes.

Only moments later, however, Mrs. Jorgensen appears on the porch while Lars and Ethan are talking. Ethan has just claimed responsibility for Brad's death ("I got your boy killed"), but Lars remains obstinate: "It's this country killed my boy! Yes, by golly! I tell you, Ethan, it's . . ." Mrs. Jorgensen interrupts: "Now, Lars, it just so happens we be Texicans. [A] Texican is nothing but a human man way out on a limb—this year and next and maybe for a hundred more. But I don't think it'll be forever. Some day this country's going to be a fine good place to be. Maybe it needs our bones in the ground before that time can come." There is hardly a more genuine moment in the Western, and it is precisely the cultural refulgence of such moments that blasts the Indian into absence. Mrs. Jorgensen does not so much contravene her husband's perspective as she extends it, projects it far beyond even the memory of heartbreak and defeat. The conflict between the savage "country" and the "fine good place to be" culminates in the millennial instauration of the American Canaan. Perspective thus augurs the Edenic dispensation: out of the savage desert rises the garden, focus and center of the new order of the ages. In the Western, temporality emerges out of the dialectical play between the perspective of defeat and the perspective of triumph, so that the savage Indian appears merely as a requirement of that conflict—an Indian as formidably cruel as he is logically necessary. In its vision of the imperial embrace of the whole continent, the Myth of Conquest forces the Indian into oblivion, and American "history" yields to the millennialist, ahistorical, mode: "For the Indian," Roy Harvey Pearce writes, "was the remnant of a savage past away from which civilized men had struggled to grow. To

[86]

study him was to study the past. To civilize him was to triumph over the past. To kill him was to kill the past."[19]

Perspective implies the action's concern with the *boundaries* that separate the contested spaces. For on the existence of that boundary depends the racio-cultural identity of the Same: boundaries indicate the Indian Western's underlying preoccupation with separate identities. Indeed, the exclusion itself of "savagery" from the contested spaces requires that civilization redefine itself anew, that any historical idea of American nationhood recast itself in the mold of the conflict in the wilderness. Thus, it seems as if the new identity wrought of the clash of cultures subverts the vision of a racially unmixed people enjoying exclusive dominion over the western landscape.

The emplacement of the Indian at the edges of the reconfigured landscape makes him, curiously no doubt, central to it. The Myth of Conquest compelled the Indian's central presence only to confine it to the outskirts. Then it demanded and enforced his absence even from the margins. Hence the dubious national status of the emergent American Garden: the Indian demon had enabled and empowered the identity of the Same, so that the redeemed spaces were to be known not only by what they newly contained, or by the felt absence of the Indian from what had been the edges of the land, but also by the transformation that the exorcism of savagery had wrought, in the national identity no less than in the land itself. Historically, no doubt, the Indian's presence precedes his absence (or if not quite this, then at least his decline). But in the mythology of the West the two are virtually simultaneous, since the presence already foretokens the absence, and the absence in turn proclaims the birth of the new nation; so that if that nation's identity would ever come into question, the Indian would again return from his vanishment to occupy his accustomed haunts.

Perspective, of course, did not place its Indian at the threshold so that he might pass through and be thereby "assimilated," but rather so that he might pass *away*. Only gunfire greets Stone Calf when he appears at the edge of McCabe's campfire. And yet, for our purposes at least, the more important fact about perspective is that it *required the sustained presence of the Indian at the threshold*. The Indian was a skulker before he was a threat to the hero and his maiden—as was the Serpent. The Western grandeur that so inspires Philadelphia Thursday becomes, only moments later, the site of savage spectacle, when she unexpectedly rides into the aftermath of the massacre. But in the end, those spaces

19. *Savagism and Civilization*, p. 50.

have been won over for the new nation. Yet at the end of *Fort Apache,* Captain York and Mickey O'Rourke go off to fight Geronimo. Not all of the West is yet won—is it ever so?—and if the outcome of the fight against the last Apache holdout is too clear even to need foreshadowing, still perspective reaffirms its reliance on the Indian, projects the space that contains him as unregenerate savage, and thus promotes and renews the Myth of Conquest.

Mere vastness, one might add, plays no crucial role in this process of claim, redefinition, and dispossession. The installation of the humble garden in *The Searchers* or in *The Stalking Moon* proclaims the elimination of the Indian from *all* the imaginable spaces beyond just such a site: the consecration of the "fine good place to be" at the conclusion of *The Searchers,* the securing of the house at the end of *The Stalking Moon* (or, as we shall see, of the cabin in *The Battle at Elderbush Gulch* or the soddy in *The Unforgiven*) postulate the end of the Indian no less than does the implied appropriation of huge amounts of Indian land, for example, at the end of *She Wore a Yellow Ribbon,* or of *Arrowhead.* Thus the Westerns that, like *Fort Apache,* end with the promise of a new clash, still all too readily posit the end of the Indian—indeed do so all the more convincingly because they seem so much more willing to make universal the conflict that so many other Westerns are happy to make merely local.

All the newly realized American dreams presuppose the elimination of the Indian. The spaces of the Same cease to have boundaries only when the Indian dies or vanishes; or if they include the Indian still—as *The Searchers* does Debbie and Martin, *The Stalking Moon* the unnamed Indian boy, and *The Unforgiven* (as we shall see) the Kiowa-born sister / bride of the white hero—it is only in the various postures and figures of submission and "assimilation." And in the story of boisterous mastery and mute loss, these spaces, small or large, are alike consecrated as the fields of American mythology, the exclusive cultural property of the Same. Yet, though seldom acknowledged as such, the spaces of the Same form the site of the white man's union with the Indian; it is the only place where the blood of the races commingles without boast and without censure.

4

The Indian of the classic (as opposed to the revisionist) Western may look at the land or at the woman of the white man's desires, but his gaze never envisions anything so exalted as the racio-cultural legacy that the Myth of Conquest bequeaths to its hero. Even less does the Indian's gaze suggest adventure or romance; and the possibility that the Indian may look kindly upon the white man's imperial design seems unlikely indeed. He looks upon the landscape only with intent to deprive white America of its dream. He seldom looks, therefore, without meaning thereby to obstruct the course of empire. Inevitably, however, the Indian's way of looking indicates his doom: if he looks to destroy, he also looks that he may himself be destroyed, and so his gaze itself affirms his savage character and enacts the ironic agency whereby his elimination comes to be justified. In *Stagecoach*, for example, when Geronimo finally appears, he looks threateningly from atop the ridge at the vulnerable stagecoach below. Moreover, he appears at the edges of the screen, already an outsider to the spaces of the Same, the invader of those newly consecrated territories of the American sublime that mirror the social concord that the passengers have just affirmed. Geronimo's scowl becomes the correlative of the dreaded name that echoed throughout the early scenes, and thus invests upon him the menacing gaze that only seemed to belong to the Cheyenne ally in the movie's first interior scene. Poised as he is upon the perimeter of paradise, ready to pounce upon the unsuspecting passengers below, Geronimo recalls no less formidable a figure than Milton's Satan, for instance, at that moment when the archfiend first sees Adam and Eve in the recently created Eden:

> O Hell! what do mine eyes with grief behold,
> Into our room of bliss thus high advanc't
> Creatures of other mould, earth-born perhaps,
> Not spirits, yet to heav'nly Spirits bright
> Little inferior.
>
> (*Paradise Lost*, 4:358–62)

The visual intrusion of the Indian in the American paradise vindicates the Indian fighter. Indeed, this looking down at the defenseless stagecoach identifies not cultural resistance but mere envy as the source of Geronimo's hostility. Yet, though the motive behind the Indian's gaze may always be simple, its *function* is less often so: for the gaze of the Indian intransigent tends to split intention and effect. It means to subvert the new America—its hopes and its labors—yet it invariably succeeds in doing the very opposite, for it highlights American values and virtues: nothing could animate the Indian to destroy such enlightened social consonance except rancor.

There are, to be sure, other important variants of this gazing that identifies the Indian "look" as the one to be eliminated—principal among them the Indian's look at the white woman. No doubt such a gaze links him to the lecherous villain of melodrama, but with the following difference—that the threat of rape is coded and qualified by the attendant fear of miscegenation. Early in *The Searchers*, for example, Scar's shadow, spreading ominously over the cringing Debbie Edwards, anticipates the threatening scowl that transfixes her into utter submission only moments later. Even earlier, in fact, Lucy Edwards's shriek (upon her realization that an Indian attack is imminent) implies an evil Indian lurking just beyond, looking at her with just such a leer. Thus, when Ethan, much later, finds her raped and mutilated, we are supposed to realize that Lucy's terror was well-founded. Indeed, more than a decade before *The Searchers*, the Indian Western had already adopted the convention of the Other's concupiscent ogle, a convention evident in some of the Indian films of D. W. Griffith before *The Birth of a Nation* (1915), as well as in his later *America* (1924), so that Ford's *Drums Along the Mohawk* could comfortably invoke that gaze and parody it in the memorable early scene when Blue Back enters the cabin and Lana screams in terror as the impassive Indian moves toward the hearth.

The Myth of Conquest tends to specify the threat of rape through the possibility of miscegenation, as if the sexual union of the two races could not happen but through violence. The white hero's woman has to be rescued from the violation stamped on the Indian's look; and so it seems valid to suggest that the Myth of Conquest equates the rescue of the white woman with the preservation of her racial identity. Ethan Edwards can look at the white captives in the army post and declare them no longer white but "Comanch'." Their return to white society, he insists, does not imply *restoration*. Ethan's own look at the white captives affirms the deprivation that the Myth of Conquest assigns to the white woman who survives Indian captivity—and thus Ethan, by so looking at the returned captives (and later at Debbie), evinces his ambiguous affinities with the Indian even as he articulates, bluntly if not indeed aphoristically, the dread pronouncement of his culture on the unclaimed (the irreclaimable) captive.

The Stalking Moon suggests the extent to which the hero's—indeed the narrative's—energies come to be deployed in the interest of denying the Indian his look at the white woman. It seems as if the central action of Mulligan's film stands description in terms of the hero's effort to

[90]

keep Salvaje outside the staked-out New Mexico paradise, to keep him, specifically, from looking at Sarah Carver, as if his seeing her would be itself a violation, as if it would rescind her fragile restoration. Salvaje does of course penetrate the forbidden spaces of Sam Varner's paradise. The spaces that separate the covetous look from the sexual act seem to collapse when, in Sam's absence, Salvaje enters Sarah's room and carries her off into the wilderness, where Sam finds her later, bruised, as I put it in the first chapter, but not "ruined." Sarah's bruises may in fact indicate that the reenacted captivity shows her no longer willing to surrender her womanhood to mere survival; and they may also indicate that she has come to share her white man's dream so intimately and passionately that it now acts as her talisman against the "fate worse than death." But it seems equally valid to suggest that Varner's perspective, his own earlier looks at Sarah as an integral part of his paradisal dream, blunts the force of Salvaje's own look, abrogates his claim on both the woman and the land.

As the Indian surveys the spaces of the Same, the white man comes into view always as an interloper; yet the Indian's *assigned* position as outsider belies his own claims on the land. This malicious Indian resistance unfolds its own narrative possibilities in *Arrowhead*, which I would now like to consider as an example of the Western's treatment of the Indian's look.

To recall the opening: from the top of a hill, two mounted Apache warriors look out at the vast expanse of land before them; but theirs is no Mosaic vision of a future paradise. The hero, Will Bannon, and his sidekick, Sandy Mackinnon, soon come into their field of view, yet we soon realize that the Apaches are not stalking the two white scouts, but rather awaiting the appearance of the cavalry column, which rides out into Indian territory to escort Chief Ozuni and his people to the fort. Bannon and Mackinnon sneak up on these two warriors, as well as two others that charge at them from another side of the hill. Once Bannon uncovers the dead Apaches' war paint and shows it to the skeptical Colonel Weybright (in command of the cavalry), he confirms the intent of the Other's gaze: the Indian never looks without evil purpose, and the white hero's mission is, in part, to expose and eliminate that gaze and replace it with his own.

Maligned and misunderstood though Bannon may be at first, he in time acquires the status of American Adam—for example, when he tells his future mate, Lee (Mary Sinclair), the tale of how he came to hate Indians. In his youth, when Bannon was living among the Apaches, the evil Toriano put his own baby brother to death. The baby had been "born sickly," and Apache custom, Bannon explains, required that he be put to death. Bannon tried to stop Toriano, but "Toriano fought better Apache than I did. So I had to run, keep on running, nearly ten years now." At one time, Bannon had a ranch near White Sands, but the Apaches burned it. "I never could set up again." Here the crucial cut to Lee's reaction shows that she is moved by this sudden disclosure of Bannon's tender side, the one defined by his vision of the American paradise. "I had to keep on moving," Bannon continues, "trying to settle down, just live; but they were always one step behind. A man gets selfish living that way; scared, too." Though the scene fairly drips with mawkish inanity, it also makes a crucial revelation: *Bannon's Indian-hating is itself the source of his humanity*, while the Apache's own hatred of Bannon amounts to the sustained perversity that would deny him his place in the Western paradise.

All too banal, perhaps, but only in its details; for in its general and all too generic outlines Bannon's story narrates the perspective whereby the Myth of Conquest justifies the dispossession of the Indian. Toriano, by this account, seems not as evil, when taken as an individual, as when taken as a representative of his nation and his race. As Bannon explains to Lee, Toriano killed the sickly baby in accordance with Apache practice: "like a good Apache he took him out and bashed his head against a rock." Thus the entire race must be exterminated—not for its threat to any one white man or woman, but because of its inherent perversity. The white hero labors to eradicate this dreadful view of life, and as he does so he toils to install his own benevolent perspective. The future partner understands all too well: "[I] wish I could have been with you in all those places you had to run away from," says Lee only a few moments after Bannon ends his sad tale. "You never told me you just wanted your—what you said—[to] settle down and live."

All that the white hero ever wants to do is "settle down and live," but the Indian appears before him as an obstacle. In the conflict that invariably follows, we discover an America that defines itself not only by this Edenic hope—or even by its fulfillment—but by the resolve with which it meets the Indian's opposition to it. Nor did the Western have to wait for sound that it might "tell" of the American passion to settle down and live in the Indian's land. By their second decade (and in the first year usually accorded to the birth of Hollywood—1914), the movies had learned to fashion images out of racial ideology. Though it had its sources in history, literature, and the business of everyday life, the cinematic perspective developed a strategy of representation that had been only latent in America's triumphalist tradition: according to this strategy, the Indian would appear as a byproduct of the projection of heroic beings and ideal geographies. Thus perspective erases the Indian from the account of American nationhood while presenting him as its historical enemy. Perspective does not turn its gaze from the Indian; rather, it looks at him so as not to see him. It presents him as the product of an *omitted gaze*.

No silent short Western clarifies the role of perspective as a power of racio-cultural self-definition as D. W. Griffith's *The Battle at Elderbush Gulch* (1914). I now turn to a detailed analysis of this movie, hopeful that its combination of visual intricacy and racial ideology justify both the space that I devote to it and the historical and cultural contexts in which my analysis places it. An analysis of *The Unforgiven* (1960) follows that of *Elderbush Gulch*, and though equally lengthy, develops mostly as a special case of the inferences and insights into the earlier movie.

5

According to Virginia Wright Wexman, one benefit of studying the silent Western "is that our temporal and cultural distance from these films renders their rhetorical contrivances more transparent."[20] To complement that proposition, I offer this other: if we could narrow, so far as it is possible, this temporal and cultural distance, we might acquire a heightened sense of the narrative strategies and cultural assumptions whereby the Western—both silent and sound, old and new—configures the Indian. Distance distorts these strategies, often making them appear cumbersome, heavy-handed—"contrivances," in short. The same distance, of course, compels us to recast the ideological stances of the past, to account them not only "transparent" but also crudely, almost laughably, biased. But these Westerns were made when moving images did virtually all of the mythopoeic work; and if they seem at times too simple or too rough—and they do—they as often surprise us by the complexity and subtlety that they bring to the visual articulation of the Myth of Conquest.

Aside from its formal accomplishments and from whatever importance it may have had in the development of D. W. Griffith's career, *The Battle at Elderbush Gulch* merits close attention for the way in which it

20. "The Family on the Land," p. 131.

charts the direction of the Indian Western.[21] Perhaps more than any other single silent short, it determines and develops the dominant perspective of the Myth of Conquest—narrative function begotten of ideology—projecting it in recognizable variants well into the century's second half.

By an intricate construction of visual space in one of its early scenes—the arrival of the stagecoach at the frontier town—*Elderbush Gulch* establishes the racio-cultural preeminence of its white characters. The scene would be conventional enough, even prosaic, as a transition scene, were it not for the presence, if at times barely noticeable, of Indians at the edges of the screen space that the new arrivals come to occupy. The stagecoach carries the most important characters—two "waifs," sisters of considerable difference in age—the older one played by Mae Marsh (and hereafter the Waif) and the younger by Leslie Loveridge[22]—whose guardians look none too sad to see them go out West to live with their uncle, as well as a young couple (Lillian Gish and Robert Harron) with their infant. In the first interior shot of the stagecoach, two small puppies pop out of the large basket that sits on the Waif's lap, and they, too, will play a significant role in the action. A crusty old man sits next to the Waif. He hurts her feelings because he disapproves of her sleeve bows. He dies, perhaps condignly, during the Indian attack on the cabin. A trooper escorts the stagecoach, and the obligatory shotgun rider accompanies the driver, but these three are only minor figures. From the stagecoach out on the dusty road, the action cuts to the ranch, where we meet the Uncle (Alfred Paget) and the "Community Ranch Boss" (Charles Hill Mailes). Soon the Uncle, accompanied by the Mexican ranch hand (William Carroll), leaves on a buckboard to greet his new charges.

The arrival scene consists mostly of a single shot, a long take without any camera movement (and with cuts only to brief intertitles and to the Uncle's arrival). In the opening moments of the shot, two white men—a tall one wearing a gunbelt and another at first almost entirely off-screen—occupy the extreme left foreground. Men and women line up along both sides of the street in anticipation of the stagecoach's arrival, and at the end of the street, near the farthest point of focus, two other

---

21. The movie, a two-reeler, was the last of the Griffith Biographs to be released. Completed in July of 1913, it was not released until 28 March 1914. Often referred to as *The Battle of Elderbush Gulch*, it also goes, erroneously, by the title "The Battle of Elderberry Gulch." It was reissued by Biograph on 30 July 1915 and again on 24 October 1916. See Cooper C. Graham et al., *D. W. Griffith and the Biograph Company* (Metuchen: Scarecrow Press, 1985), pp. 210–11.

22. The credits for *The Battle at Elderbush Gulch* are from *D. W. Griffith and the Biograph Company*, pp. 210–11.

white men talk animatedly. Almost immediately the stagecoach appears from the left background and rushes toward the foreground, stopping only when it is almost entirely out of the frame, so that when the passengers get out they occupy both center and right foreground. But to go back only a few seconds, before the stagecoach came into view: in the middle ground, walking by the townspeople that line the left side of the street, two Indians appear. They seem to have no interest in the arrival of the stagecoach, or even to know about it, since they walk toward the foreground, whereas everyone else's attention is drawn to the opposite direction, where the stagecoach is about to appear. After the stagecoach rushes by them, the Indians still walk slowly toward the foreground; but it is easy to lose them from sight, since the white townspeople run past them to the foreground and get between them and the passengers.

Although the scene has hardly completed its work of "othering," it has already succeeded in placing the two Indians at its margins, so that this virtual exclusion functions as an early index of their stubborn resistance to the hopeful dynamics of civilized life. As the passengers file out of the stagecoach and occupy the foreground, they form what might be described as overlapping human *layers*, so that on more than one occasion in this short scene as many as five such "layers" extend in almost perfect diagonal from the extreme right foreground to the middle ground. Beyond the last such "layer," we can see the Indians, but only partially, and only if we tear ourselves from the effervescence of the moment—from this jubilee of the Chosen. The teeming and impossibly congested foreground anoints even as it envelops. The spatial privilege of the white characters functions as a correlative of the culturally determined values already announced in the interior scenes in the stagecoach—family, innocence, community. We see the Indians only as the movement of the whites allows. Sullen signposts of western geography, they stand outside the nimbus of purposeful humanity, an isolated tableau set apart from the great American commotion. Though the scene affords them many opportunities to do so, *the white characters never notice the Indians*. At one point, for instance, the Mother has an unobstructed view of the Indians, who stand only a few feet away; yet she gives no evidence of noticing them. Soon the exuberant characters leave the frame, eager to get on with the task of civilizing the West. The Indians remain in place, however, and as the scene closes, now that our view of them is no longer obstructed, we see them cast baleful looks at the whites.

Back at the ranch, the Boss sees the puppies and orders them out, and the Waif dutifully, if sadly, places the basket just outside the cabin. With only an intertitle to mediate, the action cuts to an Indian "Dog Feast" in full swing. In a brief cover shot that fails to reveal a single distinct Indian face, the wildly emoting braves, several in war-bonnets, dance feverishly around a fire where a dog (presumably) roasts. Indians do not merit a close-up. We know them by their wild gyrations and by the synecdochical dance and warbonnets. As incurious about the Indians as it is scandalized by their outburst, the camera retreats hastily to the cabin, where the waifs sing sweetly for the men before going to bed. An intertitle now reads: "The chief's son and his friend return too late for the feast." Again in a cover shot that refuses to enter the spaces of savage spectacle, dozens of surfeited braves lie scattered about, dulled by savage excess. Surely whole kennels have been ransacked that such a multitude of Indians should so glut on dog! In conspicuous contrast with the harmony in the cabin, Indian communal life exhibits only so much consensual debauchery.

As the two disgruntled Indians leave in search of a dog of their own, the action cuts to the girls in bed, and then to the intertitle, spoken by the Waif: "The puppies will die outside"; but a brief exterior shot shows the puppies climbing out of the basket and running away. Outside, the Waif searches frantically for them, but a cut shows that they have fallen into the hands of the chief's son (Henry B. Walthall) and his friend. The friend holds one between his teeth by the scruff of the neck, and he is about to stab the other one. Coming upon this scene of savagery, the Waif rushes into the frame, pushes the Indian down, and takes the puppies. The chief's son grabs her, however, and as she struggles the Uncle arrives and shoots him dead. Soon two other Indians join the friend of the chief's son and shoot back at the Uncle, who is himself now joined by four of the ranchers, including the Mexican ranch hand. Throughout the fight, the camera is "with" the Uncle, just behind him as he fires at the Indians. When the Indians shoot back, however, the camera never cuts to the Uncle, and thus denies the Indians' "look."[23] The camera also promotes the perspective of the Myth of Conquest by linking humanity to the face—to the details, in close-

---

23. This pattern reappears later. Alarmed by the sound of gunfire in the distance, the Mother and the Old Man rush out of the cabin seeking protection in the forest. The Indians pursue, and the Old Man shoots at them while the Mother attempts her escape. The camera takes the same position that it took earlier, when the Uncle shot at the Indians. The Indians kill the Old Man and scalp him. The cut to a reaction shot of the Mother suggests that she witnesses the scalping. For a detailed description of the images of Indian savagery in *Elderbush Gulch*, see Michael Hilger, *From Savage to Nobleman: Images of Native Americans in Film* (Lanham, Md.: Scarecrow Press, 1995), p. 24.

up, that register the emotional range of a complete and complex human being: devotion and distress, resolve and heroism. By contrast, the chief's son and his friend, seen first in full shot and later in a brief medium shot, have no significant facial identity. Indeed, the most prominent feature of the friend's face is the puppy that dangles precariously between his teeth. It is true, then, as John Hawkridge writes, that "the film's melodramatic plot makes a sharp distinction in its depiction of whites and Indians. The white settlement," he explains, "is sentimentally portrayed, with a dramatic emphasis on babies, children, and puppies, whilst the Indians, eaters of dogs and murderers of children, are shown as wholly savage."[24] All this is true enough, though I would like to add that these cultural determinations constitute the *active*—I wish it were possible to say "deliberate"—representations of Otherness that at once require and confirm an *omitted gaze*. The omitted gaze enforces the Indian's virtual absence; it is therefore to be understood in its dual (and therefore paradoxical) function as *omission* and *acknowledgment*—and thus as the active (re)presentation of absence. Perspective did not suffer a lapse of sorts for so presenting the Indian; nor did it merely neglect to look at the Indian in the fullness of his representational possibilities. It cast so uncertain a glance in his direction because it needed just such an Other that it might extol just such a Same.

In this way, the omitted gaze tends to explain the hopelessness of that recurrent lament, that the Western never produces an authentic Indian. The "clarity" of the Western's perspective extends no further than its image of a fully realized white America somewhere in the future of the action. In such a cultural cosmology, the Indian need not be seen any more "clearly" or "authentically" than he already is in *Elderbush Gulch*: hence the enduring need to contest the Western not for its image of the Indian but for the *pretense* of representation itself, for the looking without seeing—*for the looking so as not to see*. Before elaborating on the omitted gaze as a strategy of figuration, it is useful to consider the particular ideological context that demands it.

In the puppy rescue scene, as in the opening scenes, *Elderbush Gulch* reaffirms its concern with family; but the later scene introduces miscegenation, with its inevitable intimation of rape, as a related theme. Nick Browne has noted the threat that miscegenation poses to the emergence of the white family in Griffith's films. Referring in particular to *Broken Blossoms* (1919), Browne writes:

---

24. John Hawkridge, "*The Battle at Elderbush Gulch*," in *The BFI Companion to the Western*, p. 249.

[T]he true subject of these films, I suggest, is the interpersonal drama of the family within its social and historical setting. From within or from without, the family is under attack. This attack is always represented, however, by a generalized moral weakness or aggressivity and not by a sociological or institutional condition. But nevertheless, the structure of the drama is usually an attack on and defense of the integrity, should I say the virtue, of the woman, and on the social codes and prohibitions which enable her to maintain her place.[25]

In the first scene, the guardians had dispatched the waifs out West without ceremony or regret. In this later one, the Uncle fills the parental void in the life of the two girls when he shoots at the Indians, killing the chief's son. When the other white men join in the shooting, they confirm their identity as part of the girls' "extended" family. It has been suggested that the shooting of the chief's son justifies the Indian attack on the settlement.[26] Perhaps so; but the Uncle shoots the Indian when— need one write *because*?—the chief's son grabs the Waif. He delivers her from the dreaded touch. Thus the Indian contributes to the definition of the white American family by serving as would-be rapist, and he thus ironically endorses America's finest aspirations by *provoking* his own death. Each theme, family and miscegenation, forms in fact the other's obverse: not only does the family emerge in consequence of its resistance to the threat of miscegenation, it defines itself precisely in terms of that resistance and thus *requires* it even as it *condemns* it.

In town to show off his baby, the Father slips away for a quick drink with a friend, leaving the newborn with doting admirers. Before he can reclaim the baby, however, the Indians overrun the town. The newborn's four admirers (three men and a woman) join in the general panic, carrying the baby with them. Almost as soon as the Father runs out on the street, he is wounded. He staggers to the edge of the forest, falls unconscious, and spends much of the rest of the action in the same place and condition. Meanwhile, the death of the chief's son has fanned "the ever ready spark of hatred to revenge," as an intertitle indicates. When the warriors bring the dead son into the camp, the Indian Father (Frank Opperman), still in his postprandial torpor, awakens and is instantly moved to revenge. Only the inveterate Indian propensity for vengeance, that essential "red gift" and indelible trait of the "Indian character," could bring the Indian Father so suddenly out

25. Nick Browne, "Griffith's Family Discourse: Griffith and Freud," *Quarterly Review of Film Studies* 6, no. 1 (Winter 1981): 67–80.
26. See, for example, Michael T. Marsden and Jack Nachbar, "The Indian in the Movies," p. 609; Kevin Brownlow, *The War, the West, and the Wilderness* (New York: Alfred A. Knopf, 1978), p. 330.

of his stupor. The Indians "emote" much, but they are emotionless. The overwrought sensibilities that allow the Waif to weep so for her lost puppies and the Mother to fret so over her misplaced child find no counterpart in the Indian. Otherness specifies emotional retardation.

Distraught, the Mother wanders into the vicinity of the cabin and gets caught in the crossfire, but the Uncle brings her in and the Boss leads her out of harm's way. She sits on the floor, between the foot of a rude staircase (leading, it seems, to a loft) and a large wooden chest, and here she spends most of the action, dutifully (and heavily) emoting her anxiety. Only moments before, while the Mexican ranch hand pleaded with the Boss to be allowed to ride for the cavalry, we saw, briefly and in the background, a man take his place about halfway up the staircase and make ready to fire at the Indians (presumably from a window in the loft). So brief are the two different shots of this man, however, and so distantly is he photographed on both occasions, that he may as well be faceless. Yet as we will see, he plays a crucial role in the action. With the exception of the second time that we get a glimpse of his face (in the background, over the Mother's head just before she sits down) we know of his continued presence by the boots propped on the third and fourth rungs of the staircase. He serves one function—to shoot the Mother the instant before the Indians overrun the cabin.

Moments before the Mother found refuge in the cabin, the Waif brought the puppies into the cabin through a trapdoor (fashioned for her earlier by the ranch carpenter) that leads from the outside to her tiny room, a sort of lean-to. Now she sees the Mother in despair and comforts her. As if frightened by the Mother's terror and grief, she dashes into the room, grabs her sister and the puppies, and hides them in the large wooden chest; then she scurries off to another part of the cabin. By this time, the Mexican ranch hand, over the objections of the Boss and the Uncle, has galloped away to alert the cavalry. The "nation" shall owe the Mexican a double debt of gratitude: not only does he ride for the cavalry, he dies almost as soon as he finds it. The Indians, meanwhile, fire the outbuilding near the cabin, and all the white people there, including the tall gunslinger and the crusty old man (from the early scenes), run out, only to be shot dead. The infant, however, survives. It lies nestled in the arms of a dying white man, just outside the cabin. Looking out through a knothole, the Waif sees the man fall and recognizes the baby. She rushes out through the trapdoor and, after a brief scuffle with an Indian, darts back in, baby in tow, and hides in the same chest where the puppies and the little sister hide.[27]

---

27. The Mother, moments earlier sitting between the staircase and the chest, is now mysteriously away from it, so that she fails to see the Waif and the baby getting in. Nor

Perspective registers all the grit and devotion of the whites in the cabin, and so humanizes them; but it also humanizes them by *preempting* the Indian's image. It therefore exercises as much power by *refusing* its look as by entrusting it entirely to white heroism. Glimpsed through the gunsmoke outside the cabin, or in high-angle iris shots, the Indians are only spectral portents of defeat and doom for the whites. Perspective's omitted gaze configures the Indian as the savagery that vindicates the emergent nation. Yet it must be understood that the omitted gaze neither originates in nor confirms mere indifference; it is, instead, the consequence of an *active* engagement of the Indian within the ideological and iconographic context of the Myth of Conquest. The Indian's absence itself—his virtual invisibility paradoxically coupled with his ubiquity—accounts for his principal contribution to the Myth of Conquest and the cinematic iconography of nationhood.

In a compelling precedent for *Elderbush Gulch* entitled *Firing the Cabin* (McCutcheon, 1903), two Indians barge into a lonely cabin, kill the two adults, and take a young woman captive.[28] Thus, the filmed Indian assault on the cabin appears in the same year of the acknowledged first Western, Edwin S. Porter's *The Great Train Robbery* (1903); and so the assault on the cabin would engraft itself on the Western from its inception. Of course, the origins of the desperate defense of the cabin predate the movies.

Richard Slotkin has noted that the defense of the cabin was a basic feature of the dime novel and the Wild West shows;[29] and even more recently L. G. Moses reports that in November of 1886 Buffalo Bill Cody staged a grand spectacle in Madison Square Garden entitled "The

does it seem to occur to the Waif to find the Mother and show her the baby. If the tiny cabin is large enough to contain "America" itself, then surely it is large enough to misplace a character or two for a while.

28. The total running length of *Firing the Cabin* is 76 feet. Within this given length, the outcome differs from that of Griffith's movie. According to Karen C. Lund, however, *Firing the Cabin* may be only the first part of a longer (if still quite short) film entitled *The Pioneers* (1904), consisting of three other parts, *Discovery of Bodies, Rescue of Child from Indians,* and *Settler's Home Life.* If Lund is right, then the outcome of *The Pioneers* seems less different from that of *Elderbush Gulch,* and the cabin becomes not only a ready cinematic icon of humble national origins but an elemental figure of the spaces of the Same. The film is catalogued FLA 4624 in Karen C. Lund, *American Indians in Silent Film: Motion Pictures in the Library of Congress* (August 1992). I am grateful to Rosemary Hanes of the Library of Congress Motion Picture, Broadcasting and Recording Sound Division for arranging the screening of this and many other silent Westerns featuring Indians.

29. In *The Birth of a Nation,* Slotkin writes, "Griffith emphasized the connection [with the Western] by setting the climactic struggle as a Reconstruction version of the 'Attack on the Settlers' Cabin' scene that had been a staple of dime-novel illustration, Buffalo Bill's Wild West, and Griffith's own early Westerns." *Gunfighter Nation,* p. 241.

The Battle at Elderbush Gulch (1914, Biograph). Siege of the cabin. Courtesy of Museum of Modern Art Film Stills Archive.

Drama of Civilization." The "drama," written by Steele Mackaye, originally consisted of four acts, each corresponding to a different "epoch" in the history of the West. The second of these "epochs," in which Cody starred, was entitled "Cattle Ranch": "The action centered on 'The Attack on the Settler's Cabin,' which had been borrowed as a set piece from the arena show. Gunfire and screaming Indians provided the danger, Cody's timely rescue the drama. The masterful shooting of Buffalo Bill and Annie Oakley followed the third act."[30]

30. L. G. Moses, *Wild West Shows and the Images of American Indians, 1883–1933* (Albuquerque: University of New Mexico Press, 1996), p. 34. Nor is it hard to imagine that the fictional event may have its historical counterparts—and this as much in its narrative methods and assumptions as in the terms and contexts of the conflict. Deep into his loose and baggy *History of the Indian Wars* (1677), William Hubbard relates the ordeal of Major William Phillips and his defense of his "garrison" (as often referred to as the "house") on Saco River on 18 September 1675, during King Philip's War. Hubbard constructs his narration as if he were shoulder to shoulder with the defenders. From this vantage the Indians, not surprisingly, appear either in synecdoche (a sentinel notices a burning house on the opposite side of the river) or at a distance (the same sentinel "saw an *Indian* by the Fence-side, near a Corn-field"). William Hubbard, *The History of the Indian Wars in New England,* ed. Samuel G. Drake (1677; Bowie, Md.: Heritage Books, 1990) 2:106.

In *The Massacre* (1912), Griffith presented the coming-to-be of a nation even more pluralistic than the one in *Elderbush Gulch*—with devoted Mother (Blanche Sweet) and infant, repentant gamblers and rugged preachers, cowboys and ex-Confederates, soldiers and scouts all huddled together in desperate battle against the savage foe.[31] The spaces of the Same become the site of reconciliation—between North and South, saints and sinners, past and future (*Stagecoach* before *Stagecoach*, then). But reconciliation never cuts across racial boundaries, surely because the movies had even then proved inept at overcoming racism, but also because the configuration of the American *ethnos* had long before the movies insisted on an irredeemable Other. The nation, that it might be "born" united, demanded racial division. To be sure, *The Massacre*, far more so than *Elderbush Gulch*, knows how to lament the passing of the Indian. Nor does unabashed empathy make for much of an exception in the Griffith corpus. *The Call of the Wild* (1908), *The Red Man and the Child* (1908), *Comata, the Sioux* (1909), *The Mended Lute* (1909), *Ramona* (1910), *Iola's Promise* (1912), *The Yaqui Cur* (1913), and, most especially for the purposes of this chapter, *The Redman's View* (1909), deployed the sort of *counter-perspective* that later times might well have called "revisionist." In the first battle of *The Massacre*, the camera registers the distress of the Indians; and in its aftermath it follows the dejected survivors in their exodus, staying with the Indian family—man, woman, child—and placing them in the foreground as they die, as if of terminal historical irrelevance, and become enshrined as Vanishing Americans.

At the end of the second massacre (of whites by Indians), the young father arrives on the scene of defeat and desolation only to see his wife and child come out, unharmed, from under the pile of dead bodies.

---

31. Even before *Elderbush Gulch*, the movies incorporated the "last stand" tableau of the paintings, lithographs, and Wild West shows that burst on the American consciousness after Custer's defeat in 1876. Perhaps most stirring of the early cinematic representations was Thomas Ince and Francis Ford's *Custer's Last Fight* (1912). But the "last stand" is inherently an all-male event, and the heroic moment chiefly marks the apotheosis of white American manhood. In Thomas Ince's *The Invaders* (1912) there are two women in the fort during the desperate hours before the cavalry arrives—one is the daughter of the commanding officer, Colonel Bryson; the other is Sky Star, the daughter of the Sioux chief, who, for love of one of the white surveyors (the original "invaders") sent into Sioux land by the railroad, rides to alert the fort of the impending Indian attack. On her way to the fort she falls headlong off her pony and sustains injuries that later prove fatal, thus leaving the Colonel's daughter as the only woman. As the defense of the fort reaches its critical moment, she acquiesces in her father's attempt to shoot her with his last bullet. The cavalry arrives just before the Colonel pulls the trigger.

America's innocents outlive its guilty dead, and these last atone for their crime against the Indian by dying for mother and child. The surviving trinity embodies at once the millennial mission of the new nation and the pathos of the unfortunate Indian family. All is in its place, then: the new dispensation vested in the white family, American mythology grounded in the martyrdom of the common man turned Indian-fighter, the lament that alone rescues a "vanished" race from oblivion.

Far less generous than *The Massacre, The Battle at Elderbush Gulch* refuses the privilege of family to its Indians. A harmless puppy hangs between the teeth of the chief's son's friend, the chief's son grapples with the helpless Waif, the besotted chief awakens not to grieve but to avenge.[32] Even so, the Indians' absence has less to do with the lack of distinctiveness than with his exclusion from perspective's ideal view of white America. The graphic force of such images of the Indian gives the clearest evidence of perspective's omitted gaze. We see them thus, and thus know them for their inhumanity. Accordingly, the deadlier forms of invisibility are not those that hide the Indian from view—indeed, one would think this a blessing to the Indian, for whom being seen ("discovered") marked the beginning of endless woes. Not the hiding of *him* from view, then, but the concealment of his humanity, the ideologically predetermined separation of that humanity from his image is the cinematic variant of the curse begotten of "discovery." This separation of humanity from image, then, renders paradoxical forms of human invisibility that envision Otherness only for the sake of reproaching it.

The pioneers have all but run out of cartridges; the Indians have slithered up to the cabin like so many serpents and are now battering the door; and the cuts to long iris shots of the cavalry seem to establish only the impossibility of rescue. In the critical moments of the defense, the imminent violation of the spaces of the Same seems concentrated on the impending capture and rape of the Mother. Together with an older woman (one of the infant's admirers in that earlier scene), the Mother sits on the floor between the staircase and the wooden chest, staring bug-eyed at the door, expecting the Indians to burst in at any moment.

32. In all of *Elderbush Gulch* we see only one Indian woman and one Indian child (the chief's son being, of course, a grown man). They appear briefly when the warriors ride against the settlement. Their backs to the camera in a single brief shot, they cheer and dance as the warriors ride out—faceless as ever the men are, and as excited as they by the prospect of revenge.

She who in the stagecoach arrival scene did not see the two Indians standing at arm's length, now "sees" the invading horde in all the vivid terror that her mind summons up. At this moment a hand gripping a long-barreled Colt's revolver appears from the top of the screen; the man on the staircase, still minus head or torso, cocks the six-gun and holds it at point-blank range over the head of the unsuspecting Mother.

Of course the cavalry arrives in time, and the Indians disperse; but the ready six-shooter over the Mother's head has already claimed a deadly priority in her deliverance. The gesture betokens the triumph of the Myth of Conquest even at the moment of impending defeat, reaffirming the sacred pledge to perish pure rather than live mixed. Any number of white men in the cabin might have done the deed before firing the last round; yet the duty fell to a virtually faceless figure that lives only for this moment—to an agent, moreover, that descends from above—his hand an appendage of the six-gun rather than the reverse, in the Western's own version of the ancient deities of the machine.[33] As American an image as the frontier cabin may be—humble icon of promised greatness, traditional emblem of the beleaguered but stalwart nation—it becomes here only an extension of the one and essential configuration of the spaces of the Same—*the white woman's body*. The white woman is thus, so to say *in extremis*, ordained and confirmed as source and origin of destiny's favored race, the female space *of*—that is, *belonging to*—the male Same. Thus ready to annihilate the very object of its desire, the hand that holds the pistol also indicates the racial jealousy of the Same. Perspective's omitted gaze becomes an ironic projection of this jealousy, denying the Indian a competing sexuality by denying him the image/body of the white woman.

The momentary confusion over the fate of the infant gives way to unrestrained joy once the Waif, her sister, the infant, and the puppies all burst out of the wooden chest. In this image of the children and the puppies, the nation marks an increase in the power of innocence. The children lead a new America to the sweet oblivion of dark and guilty deeds. And the Indians? They scatter to the edges of the screen, indicating not only their destined disappearance but the emergence of cinema itself as the spaces of the Same—the cinematic "nation" begotten of perspective triumphant.

33. Ford's *Stagecoach* and *The Searchers* reserve much the same sort of "deliverance" for the white woman, as does of course *The Birth of a Nation* when Dr. Cameron makes ready to strike his daughter Margaret's head with the empty revolver. But all three movies assign the attempted deed to *characters*—Hatfield, Ethan, Dr. Cameron—not to a figure with half its body above the screen.

The Battle at Elderbush Gulch (1914, Biograph). Reunion of the Chosen. Courtesy of Museum of Modern Art Film Stills Archive.

6

The failed defense of the cabin generates the plot of revenge and rescue of the white captive in *The Searchers,* and of revenge and final reconciliation with the Indian in *Jeremiah Johnson.* Both Ethan Edwards and Jeremiah are absent from the cabin at the time of the Indian raid, and in both movies the collapse of the cabin de-centers the heroes' lives, so that much of the subsequent conflict with the Indians unfolds out of the loss of place, of the potential paradise. *The Stalking Moon,* by contrast, narrates the triumph of that defense, even if Varner has to carry the fight well beyond the cabin in order that he may keep Salvaje from it. All three of these more recent movies complicate the defense of the spaces of the Same: whereas *Elderbush Gulch* insists on the absolute racial homogeneity of the group in the cabin (even to the death of the heroic Mexican), these other Westerns locate an Indian, or at least someone not quite "all" white, *within* the cabin. No doubt these later movies feel compelled to explain the presence of the ambiguous ethnic in the spaces of the Same. When Martin Pawley, early in *The Searchers,* reveals that he is "eighth Cherokee," he is responding to Ethan's near-shock upon seeing him for the first time after so many years: "A fellow could mistake you for a half-breed." And in some ways, of course, *The Searchers* narrates the justification of Debbie's presence, at the end, in the "fine good place to be," so that Ethan and Martin's search negotiates the passage of the Other—of the captive earlier held to be no longer white—back into the spaces of the Same.

In *Jeremiah Johnson* the Flathead chief Two Tongues Lebeaux (Richard Angarola) gives his daughter Swan (Delle Bolton) to the hero in appreciation for the Blackfoot scalps that, as the chief mistakenly believes, Jeremiah has taken in battle and now brings to him as tokens of respect. Reluctant as he is at first to accept Swan, Jeremiah learns to love her, and together with the adopted boy Caleb (Josh Albee) they build a cabin: "This'll do," says Jeremiah once the cabin is finished. "River in front, cliffs behind. Good water. Not much wind. This'll be a good place to live." Soon thereafter, Jeremiah agrees to lead the arrogant Reverend Lindquist (Paul Benedict) and a small cavalry escort through treacherous mountain passes to the stranded wagons of the preacher's congregation. The cutoff leads through Crow burial ground, and by the time that Jeremiah returns, the Crows have killed Swan and Caleb. Jeremiah burns the cabin. The rest of the action is taken up with the *mano a mano* combats between the vengeful Jeremiah and the Crow warriors. The concluding freeze-frame shows Jeremiah acknowledging Paints His Shirt Red's gesture of peace and reconciliation; but Jeremiah, long placeless, seems doomed, like Ethan, to "wander forever"—unless the concluding freeze-frame itself signals an even more severe and abrupt end to his story.

That Sam Varner should protect the Apache boy, or that the "half-breed" Nick Tana should join him against Salvaje, seems not quite as out of step with *Elderbush Gulch* as does the presence of Sarah Carver in the cabin. For Sarah, as we saw, confesses to Sam that she "knew what [she] had to do to stay alive." Had some disembodied hand tendered her a six-shooter with only one cartridge left, Sarah would likely have turned it down: "I chose to be with him." If in *Elderbush Gulch* the woman's body became the essence of the spaces of the Same, then in *The Stalking Moon* that same "space" has already become *the space of the Other*. By the standards of *Elderbush Gulch* at least, Sarah would have deserved the "fate worse than death."

Regardless of motive or cue, however, the post-World War II Indian Western seems generally more willing than its prewar counterpart to place an Indian within the spaces of the Same. Where can we find such an Indian in the stagecoach to Lordsburg, or even in the Indian Western of the immediate postwar, for instance, in Ford's cavalry trilogy?

In 1976, Clint Eastwood's *The Outlaw Josey Wales* included Indians in the community of outcasts that followed the hero from the ruins of the Civil War to the Texas paradise. Josey's America includes two Indians, Lone Watie (Chief Dan George) and Little Moonlight (Geraldine Keams). While Lone Watie recalls the archetypal Chingachgook in his intimacy with the white hero, his defiance of civilization (symbolically enacted by the burning of his frock coat and stovepipe hat) rather parallels Josey's than mimics it. There is even less precedent for the Indian *woman* in the cabin; and indeed, we can measure the presence of Little Moonlight in the cabin against the shameful opprobrium heaped upon the Indian woman "Look" (Beulah Archuletta), in *The Searchers*, when Martin Pawley kicks her from his camp bed. Nor does Little Moonlight pine after the white hero, as the Indian maidens of early Westerns had done at least since Cecil B. DeMille's two silent versions of *The Squaw Man* (1914 and 1918), based on the play by Edwin Milton Royle. Thus, when Josey goes to Little Moonlight for sexual favors, he discovers that she has chosen Lone Watie already. And if this pairing along racial lines is mostly a way of saving the hero for the white maiden, still *Josey Wales* finds a way of diffusing the threatened Indian fight when Josey and the Comanche chief Ten Bears (Will Sampson) pledge brotherhood. Thus the *Union* soldiers become the enemy of the new "nation,"[34] and the fiendish Terrill (Bill McKinney) finds himself leading an all-white regiment against an America composed of whites, Indians, and Hispanics; of middle-class folk, former prostitutes, and adulterers; of outlaws and gamblers; of men and women both old and young—all with their assigned posts at the loopholes or else entrusted with reloading. Here American diversity exercises the power of perspective, appropriating the strategy of the Myth of Conquest while repudiating its ideology.

Even so, the Western constructed yet another variant of the defense of the cabin. This version complicates the racial identity of a central

---

34. D. W. Griffith had portrayed the Union as the enemy in 1915, when the all-black Union soldiers, whom Griffith presents as an unruly mob, assault the cabin where the Camerons, the faithful black slaves, and the two white Union veterans and their little girl hold them off. But in *Josey Wales* the *white* soldiers invade the cabin, and of course there is no timely rescue, as in *Birth of a Nation*, by the Ku Klux Klan. It is necessary to note, however, that Forrest Carter, the author of *Gone to Texas*, the source novel for *Josey Wales* (originally entitled *The Rebel Outlaw: Josey Wales*), has been exposed as a rabid klansman and racist. For a fine analysis of the role of the Indian in *Gone to Texas* (and Carter's fraudulently autobiographical *The Education of Little Tree*) see Shari M. Huhndorf, *Going Native: Indians in the American Cultural Imagination* (Ithaca: Cornell University Press, 2001), pp. 129–61.

character by assigning her two equally valid, though conflicting, ethnicities, and thus places her—as much culturally as physically—at once
inside and outside the spaces of the Same. John Huston's *The Unforgiven* (1960), not unlike *The Searchers*, develops to a great extent out of
the question whether the spaces of the Same can include a character of
ambiguous ethnicity. Does Ethan shoot Debbie, or does he rescue her
from the Comanches and deliver her to the Jorgensen home? So similarly: do the Zacharys in *The Unforgiven* keep their sister Rachel (Audrey Hepburn) within the soddy and away from the Indians, even after
her Kiowa lineage is no longer in doubt? Edward Buscombe has noted
that *The Unforgiven* reverses the meaning of "captivity" that *The
Searchers* gives to the term: if Debbie is a white captive of the Indians,
Rachel is an Indian captive of the whites.[35] Buscombe's observation implies that the Kiowa warriors who come to the soddy for Rachel have at
least as legitimate a claim to her as Ethan has to Debbie. Rachel's
Kiowa brother, Lost Bird (Carlos Rivas), however brief his scenes and
notwithstanding his inarticulate English, seems genuine in his wish to
be reunited with his sister. Of course, Rachel's white family claims her
as well; nor should we be surprised that they do so with far more
touching—or at least familiar—expressions of love and devotion than
Lost Bird and the Kiowas ever display. The passionate and desperate
effort to keep Rachel within the spaces of the Same suggests an affinity
with the maternal anxiety over the misplaced infant in *Elderbush Gulch*.
For our purposes, then, I would like to claim license to treat *The Unforgiven* as a dialogical play on possibilities left unnarrated in *Elderbush
Gulch*—somewhat as if the young Mother in *Elderbush Gulch*, rather
than being reunited with her baby, had lost it after all. In time she bore
three boys, as does Mattilda Zachary (perhaps not coincidentally
played by Lillian Gish) in *The Unforgiven*. Then one day her husband
returned from a raid on a Kiowa village bearing a newborn Kiowa girl,
and Mattilda, having so recently lost a newborn, takes to the Kiowa
baby as though she were her own.

Many years later, when Mattilda reveals to her children that Rachel
was in fact born of Kiowa parents, her son Cash (Audie Murphy), a
self-professed Indian-hater, comes out of the soddy disgusted (and
drunk), as if gasping for a racially pure air, refusing to share the physical space with this sister now so suddenly certified as Other. He tells
his oldest brother Ben (Burt Lancaster) that the *white* Zacharys, including the youngest, Andy (Doug McClure), must either "pull up stakes"

35. Edward Buscombe, *The BFI Companion to the Western*, s.v. *The Unforgiven*, p. 307.

or send Rachel away to the Kiowas. This last alternative, presumably, will preempt any Indian attacks on the whites. Then, with Rachel out of the way, Cash now proposes, they could "at least get the cattle to market." Ben refuses to send Rachel away and offers Cash the entire cattle herd. When Cash again insists that Rachel be sent away, Ben, growing steadily angry, offers him an image of Rachel alone, dispossessed, in the squalor of an Indian camp, or maybe squatting "outside the garrison at Wichita and pick[ing] up silver dollars from the troopers." Then, enraged, he challenges Cash to reveal his real motive for wanting Rachel to go away:

> *Ben*: Why don't you say it, Cash? Damn you, why don't you say it? It's not the Kiowas or the cattle, it's the red Injun in the house!
> *Cash*: [*No longer veiling his racism*] Get her outta here! I don't care how you do it! Get her outta here, I'm telling you!
> *Ben*: I'm stayin', Cash. She's stayin'. We're all stayin'.
> *Cash*: I'm not stayin'. Not with a red-hide nigger!

Cash leaves, himself now an outcast from the outcast family.

My critique develops out of the strategies that *The Unforgiven* deploys in response to this relation between space and ethnicity. All too predictably, perhaps, *The Unforgiven* spins out a romantic resolution to this racial conflict: Rachel can continue to dwell within the spaces of the Same only because Ben, heretofore her brother, suddenly claims her for his bride. Ben does not so much accept Rachel's Indianness as he *abrogates* it; and Rachel's transformation does not so much legitimate her whiteness as it does Ben's power to erase her native racial identity for the sake of possessing her sexually. In this respect the resolution becomes rather an evasion. Yet this uncertain alchemy, whereby an individual's own ethnicity dissolves before the demands of sexuality and romance, hardly precludes an appeal to the specific events and strategies that produce both Rachel's racial conversion and the reconfiguration of the spaces of the Same—even if the specter of incest comes of a sudden to loom large over the proposed "resolution."[36]

The play of three events following the angry exchange, quoted

36. Hepburn biographer Barry Paris describes *The Unforgiven* as the story of "an adopted Indian girl entangled not only in the violence and racial nightmares of frontier Texas but, simultaneously, in an incestuous relationship with her brother (Lancaster)." *Audrey Hepburn* (New York: G. P. Putnam's Sons, 1996), p. 162. That *The Unforgiven* itself is aware of its own flirtations with incest may perhaps be best illustrated by recalling that Mattilda lies dead offscreen when Ben tells Rachel of the grand wedding they will have in Wichita, and that Andy, be he ever so close, does not see Ben and Rachel kiss.

above, between Ben and Cash, produces Rachel's "metamorphosis": Rachel "others" herself; Ben redeems her; Rachel shoots Lost Bird. Some useful terms—"the othering gaze," "the counter-gaze," and "the redemptive gaze"—help in the analysis of the relation between these three events. Now briefly to place each term in its context. Gazing at herself in a mirror only moments after Cash's expression of revulsion, Rachel endorses what I would like to call the *othering gaze*, the look, that is, whereby the Same cast her as Other. She tries to leave the soddy to join the Kiowas outside. But Ben keeps her from leaving. Ben's *counter-gaze* cleanses Rachel of her Indianness and validates her presence in the soddy. Since this form of the appropriating gaze presumably delivers her from the fallen condition to which her Indian descent condemns her, I shall refer to it as *the redemptive gaze* (for so it functions, regardless of our skepticism toward the benefits that it is meant to confer). Before I elaborate on the resolution to the racial crisis, it will be useful to provide an account of the events that bring it about.

Led by Ben since the violent death of the patriarch William ("killed on this place in defense of his family and stock by red Indian devils," as his rude grave marker reads), the Zacharys now find themselves on the verge of great wealth. After years of struggle with the land and against the Indians, the Zachary cattle herd, owned in partnership with the Rawlinses, has grown fat—"fat as ever I've seem 'em in all my long days," exults the patriarchal Zeb Rawlins (Charles Bickford)—and is now ready for market in Wichita. With good times only a cattle drive away, the oldest of the two Rawlins boys, Charlie (Albert Salmi), asks Ben for permission to court Rachel. The proposed union augurs a dynastic cattle empire, a Western paradise to realize a fabulous construction of the American promise—even if the comely Rachel finds the oafish Charlie little more than amusing.

But almost from the start an aura of calamity darkens the hopes of the Zacharys and the Rawlinses. A demon out of the Zachary past, Abe Kelsey (Joseph Wiseman), returns to haunt them after a seven years' absence. In the first scene following the opening credits, Rachel, who is out riding her spirited horse, comes upon a ghost rider and his gaunt mount. The rider asks her name.

Rachel: Rachel.
Kelsey: Rachel what?
Rachel: Why, Rachel Zachary.
Kelsey: You're no Zachary.

Rachel: Why, not a Zachary born, but Ma says it's no different than if I were flesh and blood. How do you know who I am, mister? I've never seen you before.
Kelsey: [*Bringing his hand to his sword's hilt*] I am the sword of God, the fire and the vengeance whereby wrong shall be righted and the truth be told.
Rachel: [*In a whisper, backing the horse while staring at Kelsey*] Well, I declare!

Kelsey, the Texas Tiresias doubling as Aeschylean Fury, throws Rachel's ethnicity into question. He knows what the Zacharys deny, even though they know it to be true—Rachel is Kiowa. Decades before, we eventually learn, the Kiowas took Kelsey's young boy captive, and when he asked Will Zachary to "swap" the Kiowa foundling for the boy, Zachary refused. Ever since, he has persecuted the Zacharys, chasing them from one place to the other, and counting on widespread frontier racism as his unfailing ally. The Zacharys always surrender to this racist blackmail, and when they do not move away, they resort to mere denials of Kelsey's claims. But in denying Rachel's Indian birth they seek to hide the mark of her difference, and so to deny the difference that is *their own* for loving one so unlike themselves. Hence their transgression, their *hamartia*: Rachel *is* different, and though the Zacharys' love for her transcends that difference, it also seeks to hide it, to make her "no different than if [she] were flesh and blood." Kelsey, however ill-omened his reappearance, only enforces the punishment; their own perpetuation of the lie holds the Zacharys "unforgiven."

Yet we should also remember that this deception which the Zacharys so desperately practice amounts to an alternative construction of Rachel's ethnicity. As Werner Sollors writes:

It is when Americans speak of generations, numbered or unnumbered, that they easily leave history and enter "the myth of America." Apparently talking about lineage, they are actually inventing not only a sense of communal descendants—the coming generation so much worried about—but also a metaphoric ancestry in order to authenticate their own identity. Even supposedly pure descent definitions are far from natural, being largely based on a consent construction.[37]

37. Werner Sollors, *Beyond Ethnicity: Consent and Descent in American Culture* (New York: Oxford University Press, 1986), p. 234. A basic definition of Sollors's central terms may be found much earlier in the book: "Consent and descent are terms which allow me to approach and question the whole maze of American ethnicity and culture. They are relatively neutral though by no means natural terms. Descent relations are those defined

The Zacharys, we might say, seek the authority of descent to validate their consent. Yet their stubborn distortion of Rachel's origins accounts for only one source of Rachel's victimization. For the construction of Rachel's ethnicity depends on almost everyone else but herself, and almost entirely on *men*—both Indian and white—who impose their othering gaze on her—who view her therefore as Ethan Edwards views the white captives at that moment when he peremptorily nullifies their membership in the white race and pronounces them "Comanch'." It depends, then, on Kelsey: "You're no Zachary"; on Lost Bird, who says to Ben: "You have in your house woman, one of *our* woman"; on Zeb Rawlins, who later demands that Rachel strip so that he may determine her race, and thus her fate, by the color of her skin; on Cash, whose own othering gaze becomes more like a glare of repugnance and rebuke once he learns of her descent; as well as on Ben, who in the end must turn against his own (earlier) othering gaze, disclaiming her as Indian sister to "redeem" her as bride. In *The Unforgiven*, then, both descent and consent are bound to perspective, and so correspondingly is Rachel. When she looks at herself in the mirror and brands herself an Indian, she is not so much exercising the freedom to choose her ethnicity as she is seeing herself with an othering gaze of her own. In the face of the impending Kiowa attack, shortly after Ben reconfigures her relation to the Zacharys, he counsels: "When they get close enough so you want to scream, don't scream, just shoot." Rachel complains: "What if I can't do it, Ben?"

> *Ben*: You can.
> *Rachel*: I've never killed anybody before.
> *Ben*: The gun does the killing.
> *Rachel*: My own kind?
> *Ben*: By blood, yes, but not by anything else.

Once the redemptive gaze abrogates the imperatives of descent, Rachel can look out of the soddy to kill Indians (she knocks three off their horses), to "other" *them* as she herself had been "othered"—namely, as intruders in the spaces of the Same.

The events that lead to the Indian assault on the soddy, and thus to the purported resolution of the racial conflict, unfold with considerable

---

by anthropologists as relations of 'substance' (by blood or by nature); consent relations describe those of 'law' or 'marriage,'" (p. 6). Unfortunately, Sollors's sole reference to *The Unforgiven*, only a few pages before the passage cited in the text, contains so many inaccuracies that I could not use it in my analysis.

economy. Prompted by Kelsey, Lost Bird and the Kiowas come to the soddy to claim Rachel. Ben refuses. Charlie Rawlins dies in a Kiowa ambush after visiting Rachel. Kelsey witnesses—and no doubt incites—the Kiowa attack on Charlie. At the funeral, Charlie's mother Hagar (June Walker), comes out of a grief-induced trance to curse Rachel, who has come to offer her sincere sympathies. "Squaw!" she yells. "Kiowa squaw! Red nigger as ever was! . . . You killed 'im! You killed 'im! You killed 'im!" Pressured by Zeb Rawlins to bring the moment to its crisis, Ben leads a large posse—all of them in funeral black—to ride after Kelsey. After he is captured, Kelsey, oblivious of the hangman's noose around his neck, wistfully recalls the day that he and Will Zachary found Rachel. Long ago, in retaliation for a massacre, the settlers raided a Kiowa village. "We killed and we killed, and we had to lay down tired of the killing. I heard a baby cry. I went and found her, a little baby strapped to a Kiowa cradle board. She had Injun paint on her belly, on the flat of her hands and the soles of her feet. I had my hand on her throat when Will Zachary said to me, 'There'll be no more killin'. No more killin' today.' And he took her from me. . . . And he took her to Mattilda, and they kept her as theirn." Though Ben now interrupts to offer another version of Rachel's origin (Will Zachary "found Rachel in a settler's wagon, wrapped in a Boston blanket"—as if Rachel could be saved by reference to such tokens of whiteness), and though he blames Kelsey for spreading false rumors that caused the Zacharys to move away, he fails to sway the crowd, least of all the embittered Rawlinses. "And that old man [Kelsey himself] made you run," Kelsey now counters sardonically: "That poor old man chased you from town to town. That poor old man with his lies. No, you run from the truth. [*Sneering at Mattilda*] She knows. She that washed off that Kiowa paint, washed it all off, though she [Rachel] still be as brown as the bark of the tree." Even before Kelsey ends the sentence, Mattilda rushes at his horse from behind and whacks it on the rump with a firebrand; the horse bolts, and the old man hangs, silent at last. But Kelsey has done his work, and the Zacharys are once again pariahs, especially after Ben resists Zeb and Hagar's demand that Rachel strip and show the color of her skin.

Back in the soddy, the Zacharys find a Kiowa winter count impaled on the loose plank floor: "It's Kiowa," Ben says, "a page out of their bible, like. Like chronicles. . . . Thirty-odd years recorded here, winter by winter." As the camera pans over the pictograph, Ben "reads" of a "baby girl strapped to a cradle," born in "the year of the falling stars." Then, over Mattilda's protests (and over an extreme close-up of the pictograph): "Kiowa baby girl stolen from their camp by white men with rifles." Cash snatches the winter count and holds it before Mattilda, who recoils in horror at both her son's anger and the emerging truth: "Did Abe Kelsey paint this, Mama? Did he do this? Did he put these lies down year by year? Did he, Mama? Did he? That man you hanged last night in Rawlins's yard? You tell me, Mama!" Ben, downcast, softly exhorts: "Answer him, Mama."

Heaving off the oppressive weight at last, Mattilda relents: "All right!" she screams. "It's the truth!" (Cash looks at Rachel in disgust: "My sister's an Injun?") As Mattilda, offscreen, brings the story of Rachel's origins to a close (the story that confirms Kelsey's own story), Ben stands opposite Rachel, looking at her in silence and then, despondent, walks out of the soddy, himself no more able to share a space with her than the Indian-hating Cash was moments earlier. Shrinking before Ben's gaze, Rachel retreats to her bedroom. She lights a kerosene lamp, sets it on a shelf and, unbuttoning the top part of her dress, stands before a mirror examining the color of her skin. She then raises her head, and the mirror faithfully registers the mixture of disgust and resignation in her face. Still standing before the mirror, she runs a finger over the soot on the lamp and smudges her forehead with it, leaving a horizontal black mark across it—the brand, at least as she understands it, of her Indianness. On the soundtrack we hear the slow drumbeat that confirms her racial descent.

Inevitably the three Kiowa warriors reappear and claim Rachel. Rachel has braided her hair and smudged her forehead and, instead of wearing the white dress of the previous scene, wears a drab homespun—as if Indianness implied lost virginity. She dashes to the door to join the Kiowas. While he holds Rachel back, Ben calmly orders Andy to kill one of the three Kiowas. Rachel protests and tries to stop Andy (who also protests, since the Kiowas have come under the sign of peace); but the shot goes off and an Indian falls: "Ain't much point in going out now, is there?" Ben caustically remarks. But now Rachel, at once ashamed and outraged, confused about the way that her own brothers have treated her, identifies the othering gaze as both the source of her anguish and their guilt. "Why didn't you let me go? Why did you stop me? When Mama told the truth this morning, I wanted to die. And you wanted to die, too. *I could see it in your faces.* You had to turn away."

When Ben keeps Rachel from going out, he effectively reclaims her for the spaces of the Same. He responds to her lament by looking closely into her eyes, caressing her face tenderly, embracing her, and

[114]

consoling her: "Little Injun, little red-hide Injun." The over-the-shoulder shot of Rachel in Ben's arms shows her delight at this restoration of her self—her *Zachary* self, I would call it, Indian or white, sister or bride. To be sure, the gesture and the gaze hardly mask the inevitable infantilization of Rachel, in any of its several forms—baby sister, dependent bride, or just simply "Little red-hide Injun." Does Ben *accept* her as Indian? Perhaps, but if he does so then his acquiescence, rather than endorse her Indianness, *erases* it: the redemptive gaze, confirmed by the appropriative embrace, nullifies the claims of descent and removes the stigma that the othering gaze has imposed on her. The embrace of Ben and Rachel dissolves to a "Kiowa moon," the image that announces the impending attack. We now see the Kiowas preparing for the assault; but when the camera returns to the interior shots of the soddy, we see Rachel by her loophole, rifle at the ready, her perspective on the Indians "no different than if [she] were flesh and blood" of the Zacharys. And then we also notice, perhaps, that the braids and the face paint have disappeared.

During the full-force assault against the soddy, generic convention rules: the desperate fight against superior numbers, the heroic resolve in the faces of the Zacharys, the virtually faceless savages without, the ammunition running low, and the dire provision made for Rachel and Mattilda—one pistol each with one shot each—"Just in case," as Ben tells Rachel. Mattilda is spared the decision when she suffers a wound that proves to be fatal, but then the battle was not fought for possession of her body, as it may have been fought for the Mother's in *Elderbush Gulch*, as it is fought for Rachel's.

The outcome of the fight seemed decided in the Kiowas' favor even before they herded the Zachary cattle onto the soddy's roof, and seems utterly lost when Ben sets the roof on fire to drive the herd away and rushes Rachel and Andy into the root cellar. But the sound of a six-gun tells the Zacharys that Cash has ridden to the rescue; and in a short while Ben charges out of the soddy and joins Cash in routing the Kiowas. With Mattilda already dead and Andy unconscious, Rachel is alone in the soddy when Lost Bird appears within. Here, it would seem, is the dreaded moment at last. Yet such menace as there might be in Lost Bird's presence seems muted by an unexpectedly disconsolate expression, as if he has come to the soddy not to harm but to implore. Earlier during the assault, Rachel looked out her loophole as Lost Bird rode up close enough to see her and shout at her (first in Kiowa, then in English): "Sister!" Though he came close, Rachel did not scream. Neither, however, did she shoot. Even earlier, when the Kiowas first came to claim her, Rachel looked out the window, and after they rode off she exclaimed about Lost Bird: "The one in the white buckskin, I'll never forget him. He was beautiful!" As Lost Bird stands before her, sharing the same space for the first and last time, Rachel's identity seems to be thrown again into ambiguity: by dint of mere presence (he never speaks to her), he demands the irrevocable decision, and Rachel, though she still grips her six-gun, hesitates. Even as her vacillation before Lost Bird humanizes her, reawakens for a moment her kinship with this "beautiful" warrior, the redemptive gaze has already delivered her from her Indianness, not to make her white but *Zachary*; and that seems somehow better, more exalted, than being white or Indian.

Since Rachel is now a Zachary again, Lost Bird is the only "red Injun in the house." Staring at her from the very moment that he stood at the soddy's threshold, he walks to within arm's length; he then takes one more step toward her. To harm her? To embrace her as Ben had earlier? Would his own gaze not carry redemptive powers of its own? It does not really matter: the harm would not subject Rachel any less to the "fate worse than death" than would the tender gesture. She shoots him. As well may she be raped than be sister to this Indian, now that Ben's gaze has restored her. Even as he falls to his knees, Lost Bird continues to look up at her, pleading, victim of Rachel's own counter-gaze, of this fatal look that redeems *her* for damning her own biological brother. The last shot fired at once kills the last Indian and signals the birth of Rachel's uncontested ethnicity, triumphant over savagery's vanished gaze. There is no one left to contest the new configuration of the Zachary *ethnos*. The only "red Injun in the house" lies good and dead at their feet.

In the millennialist context of *The Unforgiven*—announced early by dynastic hopes whose fulfillment seemed imminent—Rachel's identity transcends even her status as Zachary: she is now an *American*—by which I mean that she has been *dehistoricized*—in a way that neither the white Zacharys nor the Indian Lost Bird could ever be, bound as they were to the obstinate demands of descent. *The Unforgiven*, I suggested above, deflects attention from its own complex racial problems by offering a resolution based on the romantic attraction between the white hero and the Indian maiden. Such a resolution trivializes the conflict itself: a loving glance, a ready embrace, magically transform the ethnicity of one so unremittingly made to suffer for the color of her skin. And yet the romance that binds Ben and Rachel seems but part of a greater "romance," of the overarching fiction by which the frontier experience delivers America from history and begets the exceptional—indeed, the

The Unforgiven (1960, United Artists). Rachel shoots her Indian brother.
Courtesy of United Artists/Museum of Modern Art Film Stills Archive.

exempted—nation itself. So, correspondingly, the redemptive gaze releases Rachel from ethnicity—from Indianness or whiteness—and renders her American. Thus the soddy, however battered, functions as the
very center of the spaces of the Same—source of an unbounded American empire, at once the origin of an Adamic inheritance and its fulfillment, the new beginning of American history and the mystification of
it—timeless, abiding, mythic.

Yet history plays midwife to Rachel's dehistoricization, as well as to
this birth of the ahistorical America out of the "resolved" racial conflict.
In the brief instant before they leave the soddy, while Rachel and the
three brothers stand over the dead Lost Bird, *The Unforgiven* becomes a
tableau of westward expansion. At the level of the individual character
herself, then, Rachel's own history mostly recapitulates the general
scene, since the tableau also suggests itself as the conclusion of the winter count narrative: the "baby girl strapped to a cradle" grew up, and
again—this time forever, since there are no more Indians to claim her—
she has been taken from the Kiowas "by men with rifles." History, both

national and personal, becomes the source of the ahistorical illusion. Is Rachel aware of such an irony? Does she doubt that her transformation had to be purchased in Lost Bird's blood, or that it was worth it to shed his blood because he was kin to her, as Ben said, "by blood . . . but not by anything else"? Now that Ben reenters the soddy he smiles gently at Rachel for her resolve in killing the Indian, but she retains a doleful expression, and can barely look at Ben and Cash as she walks past them out of the soddy. Before long, however, Ben and Andy join Rachel outside. At their feet lie yet more dead Indians, as if stretching to doom's own crack, the tableau of the Myth of Conquest reenacted and expanded far beyond the soddy's boundaries. But then the lilting airs of flutes direct their eyes up to a flock of geese high overhead. The geese, especially since we saw them in the opening scene, may suggest, among other things, a symbolic renewal. But their most immediate function is to lead the eyes of the Zacharys away from the devastation so uncomfortably close at hand. The Zacharys then look back at the soddy to Cash, last to emerge. They look warily at him, Rachel most so, as if uncertain still of his reaction to his once-white, once-Indian sister now become American sister-in-law. Cash manages a smile at Rachel— his version of the redemptive gaze—and only then do the four Zacharys, smiling up in wonder, return their collective gaze to the geese above, though very dead Indians still lie at their feet. The gaze seems now liberated from history, and the geese high overhead complement the unfettered eye itself, an eye that is now free to roam over— and claim—the spaces of the Same. History itself can be overcome by looking away from the Indian. Thus is America born righteous, transracial, Edenic—forgiven only by its inexhaustible capacity to forget.

7

D. W. Griffith's *The Redman's View* (1909) opens with an idyll of the wilderness. A proud young chief in a feathered bonnet and full-length blanket stands just off center screen, his back to the camera, while his people sit contentedly nearby.[38] The young chief seems to take in the far distant mountains, his view unimpeded by clamor or strife. He belongs

38. *The Redman's View* premiered December 11, 1909. The running length is approximately 14 and a half minutes (about 400 feet). I first saw it at the Museum of Modern Art, and have since had the opportunity to re-screen it in a video entitled *"The Female of the Species" & Selected Biograph Shorts of Social Commentary*, included in *Griffith Masterworks*, vol. 2 (1996), produced for video by David Shepard.

to all he surveys, and nowhere within this limitless vista is he a stranger. To the right of this chief and a bit behind him stands a young maiden, Minnewanna, just at the entrance of her lodge.[39] Soon, however, she steals away to the river to meet her suitor, Silver Eagle (Owen Moore). After some awkward preliminaries, Minnewanna happily consents to be Silver Eagle's bride, and the couple returns to the village scene, which but for the presence of Silver Eagle in it remains virtually unchanged. All is serenity and unanimity with the aboriginal soul, and the passion of young lovers, often so great a threat to the social fabric in civilized societies, only perpetuates the elemental equipoise. The camera does not so much see an action as it beholds the enduring scene. The people are happy; the land abides. At once, then, we recognize the exhortations of this *perspectival shift* whereby the Indian, who had heretofore provided the "savage spectacle" to the "civilized eye," now suddenly finds himself in possession of a perspective. No cultural difference is so radically Other that it cannot be transformed into an incipient Sameness by perspective. And if the Indian has a view of his own, he has, simultaneously and equally, a soul. And all this did the white conqueror fail to see; yet now he sees, he knows, he acknowledges: the Indian is his fellow human, bound to him by a tie stronger than race or culture.

In these early scenes, we encounter not only the two presiding (and complementary) assumptions of *The Redman's View* but their implied subversion as well. The first of these assumptions is evident in the title, and the opening images of arcadian bliss confirm it: the Indian, in possession now of his own view, produces an authentic self-representation. His view warrants his authenticity; and the camera, present among those who thus see the world, acts as witness to this pastoral dispensation so far safe from the violence of racio-cultural conflict. Yet the assumption of authentic self-representation, however basic, derives from another, even more fundamental one: the very idea of an indigenous view originates in the assumption that perspective can be readily transferred, even to an inveterate Other, without thereby drawing attention to the *transfer itself* as an indication of ascendancy—of the power to empower, let us say. A view that must be specified as the Indian's own is a view that already designates a prior and supervisory perspective. It is the conqueror's to give to the Indian, and the con-

---

39. The authors of *D. W. Griffith and the Biograph Company* identify the *character* as Minnewanna, but they provide no name (only a question mark) next to the actor's name. The Internet Movie Database (http://us.imdb.com) identifies the actor as Lottie Pickford, Mary's younger and less famous sister.

DBS Arts Library

queror's, one assumes, to take away. After all, the Myth of Conquest never identifies itself as "the white man's view"; its perspective inheres in the discourse of Conquest and resists separation from the ideology that it articulates. Thus the Indian's view is not so much an alternative as a derivative. His having a perspective endows him with one more mark of his narrative dependence.

The perspectival shift does not identify the integral native before contact, or even the one who resisted Conquest and its Myth. Instead it designates, even highlights, *perspective itself*, what I called at the beginning of this chapter an ideological inflection of the visible. The Indian—with or without a view—appears only as a projection of such a perspective. That the historical outrage against him (and not his reputed savagery) should now define him hardly makes this view his own. He remains the extension of the one who sees, as is evident in the following passage from Alberti's famous treatise, *On Painting* (1486):

> Among these rays [imaginary lines in pyramidal arrangement that extend from the eye and create the illusion of depth] there are differences in strength and function which must be recognized. Some of these rays strike the outline of the plane and measure its quantity. Since they touch the ultimate and extreme parts of the plane, we can call them the extreme or, if you prefer, extrinsic. Other rays which depart from the surface of the plane for the eye fill the pyramid . . . with the colours and brilliant lights with which the plane gleams; these are called median rays. Among these visual rays there is one which is called centric. Where this one touches the plane, it makes equal and right angles all around it.[40]

In the Myth of Conquest the white hero occupies this "centric point," at once seer and vision, "the observed of all observers," as Ophelia says of Hamlet. The white hero projects himself out of this latest center to yet others, vanishing only to reappear further westward, at a new center. If, in *The Redman's View*, it is the Indian who now appears at the "centric point," we nonetheless see him as a projection of a revised (or at least reversed) mythology, and thus as its product still. He appears at the

---

40. Leon Battista Alberti, *On Painting* [*Della pittura*], trans. John R. Spencer (New Haven: Yale University Press, 1966), p. 46. Alberti's "centric point" is Leonardo's "single point": "Perspective is a rational demonstration by which experience confirms that every object sends its image to the eye by a pyramid of lines; and bodies of equal size will result in a pyramid of larger or smaller size, according to the difference in their distance, one from the other. By a pyramid of lines I mean those which start from the surface and edges of bodies, and, converging from a distance meet in a single point." *The Notebooks of Leonardo da Vinci*, comp. and ed. Jean Paul Richter (New York: Dover Publications, 1970), 1: 30.

"centric point," but he is not there, as is the white hero, to begin again but rather to end, to be seen always and already receding, not so much at the "centric" as at the *vanishing point*.

The opening romance of Indian life cuts to an intertitle that reads, simply, "The Conquerors," and which in turn gives way to a shot of some dozen or so white men, every one of them with guns drawn, as they reach a rise that places them near the Indian camp.[41] These conquerors on the march embody the inheritance which, as nineteenth-century racial theory would have it, drove the "Aryan" peoples relentlessly westward. History, by which I mean here *the ideology of purposive temporality*, had generously bestowed these paradisal guarantees on Anglo-America, but the same history vouchsafed to the Indian only his extinction. The Indian knew nothing of the theory of "natural selection," already fermenting two decades before Darwin's *Origin of Species* (1859), a theory which, so easily abused and perverted, could sanction the disappearance of an entire race in the name of scientific fact. Nor did the Indian know about Hegelian notions of historical inevitability, or about the utilitarian variant of these ideas christened Manifest Destiny in 1845. The Indian stood still, awaiting his doom, ever about to be trampled by the course of empire.

This contrast between the two cultures, as *The Redman's View* presents it, finds a vivid precedent in a scene witnessed by the young Francis Parkman in the trans-Mississippi West at the very time that racialist thought formulated its curious theories:

> Not far from the chief, stood a group of stately figures, their white buffalo robes thrown over their shoulders, gazing coldly upon us; and in the rear, for several acres, the ground was covered with a temporary encampment; men, women, and children swarmed like bees; hundreds of dogs, of all sizes and colors, ran restlessly about; and close at hand, the wide shallow stream was alive with boys, girls and young squaws, splashing, screaming, and laughing in the water. At the same time a long train of emigrant wagons were crossing the creek, and dragging on in their slow, heavy procession, passed the encampment of the people whom they and their descendants, in the space of a century, are to sweep from the face of the earth.[42]

As portent of Indian vanishment, moreover, the contrast seems to have enjoyed some popularity at the very time that Parkman constructed it.

41. Most of the plot elements of Griffith's film can be found in the decisive chapter 24 of Helen Hunt Jackson's *Ramona*, pp. 163–82. Griffith's own *Ramona* appeared in 1910, after *The Redman's View*.

42. *The Oregon Trail*, p. 90.

Angela Miller notes that William Louis Sonntag's now lost series of paintings, *Progress of Civilization* (1847) comes to exemplify "the celebratory vision of republican destiny." An 1864 description of the second painting of the series notes "a group of Indians, scattered in their single shabby tent, some indolently basking in the sunshine, and others seeking a precarious livelihood by catching the fish of an adjoining river. In the third [painting], a party of pioneers are pressing westward, through a country which is gemmed on all sides by countless, thriving log-cabins." Miller notes that the 1864 description "reflects an iconographic tradition rooted in Genesis and in the prophetic books of the Old Testament: the mandate to transform the landscape into a fruitful garden through human labor."[43] In blind obedience to such a "mandate" the Myth of Conquest constructed its perspective on the Indian.

When *The Redman's View* produces its first shot of the conquerors, it transforms the significance of the opening scenes (the Indian idyll) to produce something like Parkman's image of an unsuspecting culture about to be crushed by empire's relentless march. Thus "the red man's view" designates not a scene from a culturally independent way of life but a *dialectical response* to history's intrusion in the ahistorical scene. The camera, it turns out, though it witnessed the opening idyll, never gave us the Indian's "view" but rather the view *of* the Indian, and its presence in the village initiated the dialectical process whereby Conquest could be introduced only so that it might be thereafter condemned.

As the white men threaten and cajole the Indians—firing over their heads, jostling Minnewanna, manhandling both the young chief and the old one (Silver Eagle's father [James Kirkwood]), and generally terrifying the women and children—the Indians become victims of "history." Yet *The Redman's View* neither restores nor re-creates an Indian perspective. We know this to be so not by claiming to know what the Indian's perspective truly is, since (for all we know) an Indian "perspective" may well establish its integrity and authenticity through a difference so radical as not to be even recognized as a perspective. We know this, rather, by the film's ethical tone, by the conspicuous rebuke aimed at the conqueror rather than by any manifest effort that it might have made to know the Indian. Consider therefore the obvious: the "view" outlasts the Indian; it endures past his purported vanishment, to take its place in a culture fated *to remember* him whom it *never really*

---

43. Angela Miller, *The Empire of the Eye*: *Landscape Representations and American Cultural Politics, 1825–1875* (Ithaca: Cornell University Press, 1993), pp. 138, 139.

knew. If the Indian has a "view," then, it is only so that he may condemn Conquest on behalf of the very civilization that Conquest made possible. There is something scandalous, obscene, in having *the Indian* enable Conquest's heirs to claim exemption from "the legacy of Conquest."

After some futile remonstrances, the young chief agrees to lead his people in the exodus. The white men, however, keep Minnewanna from joining the band. Torn between duty to his aged father and his love for Minnewanna, Silver Eagle decides to go along with the band. Minnewanna, the only member of the band who stays with the white men, becomes, perhaps, the white men's sex slave, certainly their drudge. Now that the Indians have left, the white men celebrate their possession of the land, while an intertitle introduces us to the Indians' suffering and also to their hope: "Oh morning sun, light us on to a better land." The Indians move out of the enduring space of the opening shots into the vanishing point, into that infinitesimal and all-too-ironic space where alone the primordial idyll can be recovered. At the vanishing point, where perspective last sees them, they shall at last become anointed as Vanishing Americans. Hence, as it seems inevitably, the intertitle that confirms the movement of the Indian not only westward, in space, but into oblivion, in time, following a brief shot of the arduous trek: "The West sea before us[.] Is there no land where we may rest our heads?" No sooner do the Indians agree on a spot to settle down than the conquerors reappear, again truculent and boisterous, allegories of an implacable rapacity, once more demanding that the Indians move on.

Shortly after this latest enactment of the native's dispossession, *The Redman's View* produces an early version of the cross-cutting that would become a hallmark of Griffith films. We see Minnewanna attempting to escape from the white men, followed by a cut to the band's laborious progress through the wilderness. As a new shot of Minnewanna shows her coming upon her people's trail, two lurking white men recapture her and drag her back to the camp, where a man orders her to resume her menial tasks.[44] The brief recapture scene accords with the perspectival shift by making possible the image of the *white man* as skulker, and because the young Indian maiden replaces the white woman as captive. The ethics implicated in the perspectival shift blame

44. When Silver Eagle later returns to the white man's camp to rescue Minnewanna, we see this man come out of the lodge right after Minnewanna does. The suggestion is clear enough: Minnewanna, however much against her will, shares the lodge with this white man. Surely this is the Indian woman's version of the "fate worse than death."

the Myth of Conquest both for Minnewanna's captivity and the death of the old chief. Yet these two events, metaphors of dispossession that they are, also suggest the underlying paradox whereby the Indian acquires his being in *time* for losing it in *space*. His expulsion defines his historicity.

Once the old chief dies and is buried, Silver Eagle leaves the band and slips into the white men's camp to rescue Minnewanna. Almost as soon as she comes out of the lodge and into Silver Eagle's arms, they try to make a run for it, but a white man appears before them. And now Minnewanna's young white master comes out of the lodge that she shares with him, and the other men in the camp rush out and surround the couple. Silver Eagle does not resist; instead, he pleads with Minnewanna's master to be allowed to leave with her, for she is now, after his father's death, all that he has. Unmoved, the young conqueror pulls out his pistol. Silver Eagle remains resolute, however, and he wraps Minnewanna in his blanket. The white master cocks his revolver, ready to shoot; but another of the conquerors, an older man, intervenes and, disarming the master, peremptorily orders him to let the couple go. Moved by pity for the poor Indians, this older conqueror points them in the direction they are to go. Minnewanna and Silver Eagle walk together out of the frame, yet awaiting them in the next shot is only the body of the old chief on the funeral scaffold. Standing before the lonely, windswept scaffold, their backs already to the camera, they perform a brief and restrained dance. Then, for the last time, Silver Eagle enfolds Minnewanna in his blanket, and together they bow their heads in sorrow.

The Indian had no "view" until the conqueror accorded him one. His freedom, too, was given him by a conqueror, a freedom every bit as derivative as the "view" itself. To witness the vanishment of the Indian and condemn it could hardly mean that such a perspective shared the Indian's view. To have shared this view so intimately would have meant sharing in the Indian's fate. It would have meant abandoning the view *of* the Vanishing American to join him *at* the vanishing point. Thus, the view that documents the "red man's" vanishment is also the view that condemns it, and the fiction that would claim to have transformed the conqueror's perspective into the Indian's own never explained how the "red man" could come by his "view" *after* his end. And what better proof that Conquest has done its work than the presence of the camera among the Indians, in the opening scene, already beginning the reenactment of their disappearance while pretending to behold them in the fullness of their native priority?

[124]

[3]

"When the Apaches Speak"

Revisionism's Discursive Dominance

Yo placiendo a Nuestro Señor llevaré de aquí al tiempo de mi partida seis a Vuestras Altezas para que aprendan a hablar. / I, please Our Lord, will carry off six of them at my departure to Your Highnesses, that they may learn to speak.

—Columbus, *Diario* (12 October 1492)

"We had proceeded to too great a distance to allow of our hearing his voice, before Wawatam had ceased to offer up his prayers." We never hear of him again.
—Thoreau, *A Week on the Concord and Merrimack Rivers* (1849),
quoting Alexander Henry, *Travels and Adventures* (1807)

Word by word by word these men were disposing of him in language, their language, and they were making a bad job of it.
—N. Scott Momaday, *House Made of Dawn* (1968)

The end of this story can only be written by you.
—Epilogue, *Run of the Arrow* (Fuller, 1957)

1

The Indian was no "American" until he vanished. The Vanishing American—as image, symbol, and idea—is roughly contemporaneous with the birth of the Republic. He was "ours" only after the land was—a part, however marginal or misconceived, of the American "heritage." However welcome at the time, his passing begot the nation's exceptional status, the privileged identity wrought in the crucible of the wilderness and wars with wild men. Thus he became, if intermittently, the fashionable revenant, and "playing Indian," to use the titular phrase of Philip

Deloria's fine book, became possible only because the real thing no longer haunted the very places where white men now so reverently invoked his image. Hence the Boston Tea Party and Tammany societies; hence the popularity of Indian costumes in the 1950s (even for those of us born in other countries); and hence the transformation of those little ersatz "braves" of the fifties into the "real" Edward S. Curtis Indians that adorned their college dorm rooms in the sixties and seventies. To be sure, the Indian also became, after his supposed disappearance, the cynosure of the American rebel: his name graces Thoreau's last breath, and his ways held the promise of a free and joyous alternative to Aunt Polly's "sivilizing" ways. The Indian remains the white man's source of the wisdom denied to him by American civilization.

Yet the new order of the ages could lament the Indian's passing without thereby relinquishing its implicit claim to a superior destiny. The conqueror had been meant for greater things than the conquered had, and the new dispensation reflected the providential design that the howling wilderness had so recently threatened. So blessed was the new order, so immense its embrace, that it could now pity in death those whom it had despised in life. The conqueror's own heirs thus became uncontested trustees of the Indian's image as well as of his "view," and they solemnly undertook the sacred task of remembering a noble and aggrieved Indian. And who knows but that in the instinctive arrogance begotten of triumph the conqueror's heirs bethought themselves able to produce an Indian more Indian than the Indian, somewhat after the fashion of the vainglorious bio-engineer of *Blade Runner*, Tyrrell, who claims that his "replicants" are "more human than human."

The many specific forms of the Vanishing American seem often to disclose not a more authentic Indian but a parable of Conquest. I am referring, for example, to those familiar white constructions in which the Indian claims the last toehold of Western land (as in Tomkins H. Matteson's painting, *The Last of the Race* [1847], an image re-created most famously by John Mix Stanley only a decade later, in *The Last of Their Race*); or rides slowly into the mists of oblivion (as in Edward S. Curtis's best known photograph, *The Vanishing Race* [1904]); or submits to his fate with bowed head (in James Earle Fraser's celebrated and ubiquitous, even parodied, sculpture depicting the Indian's banishment from the spaces of the Same, *The End of the Trail* [1915]); or denounces, with a single poignant tear held in close-up, the ruin that "progress" wrought upon the land (in the memorable pro-environmental commercial featuring Iron Eyes Cody); or stands, displaced and defeated, before the funeral scaffold of his father, as in the last shot of Griffith's *The Redman's View*.

Nowhere among these constructions do we find Indians in the plenitude of their cultural integrity. It is of course clear enough that these images of dejection and dispossession were never meant as trophies of Conquest, as images of a "proud race" vanquished by the white man. Neither, however, could they have been intended to contest and correct the Myth of Conquest. They were—or were meant to be looked upon as—the blazons of the conqueror's remorse, evocations of a past at once irrecoverable and disgraceful. The conqueror spun the pro-Indian ethos out of the sentiment of historical and cultural redress. By *revisionism* I mean to designate a near-doctrinal system of iconography and ideology, of narrative tropes and generic types, that articulates the *reaction against* the Myth of Conquest.

In the Hollywood Western, revisionism almost always unfolds through the agency of a loner or rebel, and this fact alone makes it tempting to construct a revisionist persona out of the shared ideological outlook that at times links protagonists and filmmakers. Yet, however unique or epoch-making, and no matter how deeply personal or insistently revolutionary, revisionism unfolds in almost predictable obedience to images and ideas, to conventions and structures that bind it to the Western in general and to the Indian Western in particular. Revisionism *requires* the Myth of Conquest; it presupposes an acquaintance with—almost to the point of explicitly invoking—the very issues and ideas that it means to contest. Revisionism does not so much break with the Indian Western as it engages it dialectically. Revisionism, then, is the Indian Western's *supplementary ideology*, and the solitary consciousness (and conscience) that labors for a figure of the true Indian is but one of its abidingly seductive illusions. Revisionism's implied motives and unanticipated consequences often obscure its stated claims and supersede, perhaps even subvert, both its apologia for the Indian and its polemic against the conqueror. Thus, a critique of the revisionist project ought to question postulates and premises that, however unconsciously held or indifferently deployed, support the ethical design of narrative strategies intended to transform the censured savage into the pitiable native.

Vanishment—irrevocable, complete, irreversible—is the first axiom of revisionism. The action almost always takes place in, or else rushes headlong toward, the last days of the Indian. Revisionism rescues these final moments and renders them full of moral insight into both the tragedy of the Indian and the crime of the conqueror. No matter how seemingly intent on rendering a genuine Indian, revisionism never returns him from his presumed absence, never presents him except by proxy. It is not that the Indian's past is irrevocable—that, of itself, fails to specify revisionism's Indian, since it designates a universal human condition; it is, rather, that, as revisionism would have it, *the Indian's past never passes*. Thus his "past" is as irrevocable as his destiny had been said to be by those who foresaw it even as they enforced it. "By the 1830s," writes Philip Deloria,

> American imaginings of the Indian had coalesced on a common theme: the past. The ongoing physical removal of Indian people from the eastern landscape proved to be the key prerequisite for this particular rethinking. For just as the Indian resistance of the 1790s had been accompanied by an emphasis on savagery, so actual Indian removal led to a friendlier, more nostalgic image.[1]

The rituals, beginning with the Boston Tea Party, whereby white men had donned Indian dress not only to disguise their identities but to express their freedom from the Old World, had within the space of four decades altered their purpose. Now, Deloria notes, "ritual had everything to do with custodial history—the preservation of a vital part of America's past. The Improved Order [of Red Men] painted itself as a gathering of historians, the worthy keepers of the nation's aboriginal roots."[2]

Alex Nemerov sees much the same relation between the Indian and the "past" still at work later in the nineteenth century: "At the turn of the century this privileged position [characterized by white condescension toward the Indian], in turn, informed attitudes toward Indians that indeed existed in the western present. Rather than people whose cultures (like all cultures) were constantly developing, adapting to changing historical circumstances, these Indians were regarded as remnants from a stopped or dead culture of the past."[3] The past is the Indian's immutable *place* in American history. Brian Dippie expresses as much when he writes that "the myth of the Vanishing American accounted for the Indians' future by denying them one."[4] Indian vanishment becomes the precondition of the revisionist's judgment of white culture. The lament for the Indian and the rebuke of the conqueror are as two sides of the revisionist coin.

The second principle of revisionism holds that the Indian himself

---

1. Philip J. Deloria, *Playing Indian* (New Haven: Yale University Press, 1998), p. 63.
2. Ibid., p. 65.
3. Alex Nemerov, " 'Doing the "Old America"': The Image of the American West, 1880–1920," in *The West as America: Reinterpreting Images of the Frontier, 1820–1920*, ed. William H. Truettner (Washington: Smithsonian Institution Press, 1991), p. 312.
4. *The Vanishing American*, p. xii.

never does the revising. He is, after all, presumed dead (or at least vanished), and his story always unfolds within the boundaries of his "past." Of course, revisionism requires the presence of its special Indian, an Indian whose heretofore unsuspected humanity transforms our preconceived ideas, even to astonishing and humbling us with his virtues. But no amount of nobility prevents the inevitable. Therefore, the Indian depends utterly not on *tribal* memory but on the white man's remembrance. No author outlives him except the conqueror—a conqueror as much chastened as enlightened, to be sure, but one, also, who alone can take the Indian's wisdom with him out of a vanished world. Accordingly, the revisionist is almost always a reformed conqueror, which means, then, that his mission is characterized by *self-othering*, by the *auto-alterity* implicit in the dialectical contest that compels him to reject his original race and culture. The white hero's self-othering originates almost always in his double and often simultaneous recognition of Indian worth and white perversity. Consider an instance of auto-alterity drawn from Kevin Costner's *Dances With Wolves* (1990). Once the Lakota leader Ten Bears (Floyd Red Crow Westerman) decides to move his people to the winter grounds, the hero, Lt. John J. Dunbar (now known to his Lakota friends as Dances With Wolves), rides furiously from the village to the abandoned Fort Sedgewick in order to retrieve his journal. But army troops now occupy the fort and, seeing Dances With Wolves in the distance, and taking him for an Indian, they fire on him, shooting his horse from under him. The soldiers then come upon Dances With Wolves and club him with the butts of their rifles. Now badly beaten and beset on all sides by his tormentors, Dances With Wolves refuses to answer their questions about Indian "hostiles" and then speaks to them in Lakota, which is of course as incomprehensible to them as is his Indianness itself. So we read in the subtitles: "I am Dances With Wolves. I have nothing to say to you. You are not worth talking to." He *others* himself before these irredeemable louts who, as we are asked to believe, fully represent the race and culture that the hero must renounce. His culture, his language, his very soul itself—all are thoroughly Lakota. We have his word on it; and his word, unintelligible as it is to these white fiends, not only confirms his Indianness but the vileness of the race from whose sins he now stands exempt.

"Self-othering," however, does not only designate the hero's own professions of Otherness, though revisionism relies heavily on the impassioned claims of his Indianness. Self-othering, then, takes the shape of a *narrative agency* that at once condemns the Myth of Conquest and isolates the hero, designating his Indianness as an enlightened condition, even as it would declare him an emissary of the white race's noblest virtues. Yet the hero's own othering reverberates in the frequent and no less vehement repudiations of white culture, especially in the various manifestations of the Myth of Conquest. To offer a vivid, though perhaps crude, example of revision's proffered censure of the white race: in the massacre of Cheyenne women and children at the end of *Soldier Blue* (Nelson, 1970) we see the white soldiers beat, mutilate, and rape the Cheyennes. Although the producers have duly warned us about the graphic detail of the climactic scene, they have also insisted that this is an accurate representation of the Sand Creek Massacre of November 29, 1864. History, perhaps. But our revulsion at the sight of whites behaving as Indians supposedly behaved will hardly let us watch with eyes safely shaded by historiographical detachment. The white hero's presence (as both eye witness and moral critic) in the massacre underscores its brutality, since he tries in vain to stop it before it begins; and then, even with barbarity at white heat, he carries a badly wounded child right up to the colonel leading the massacre and drops it on his lap. Images of white brutality thus set off the hero's own claims, both about his Indianness and about his exemption from complicity in Conquest.

Revisionism also requires a third component: the Indian, though he may not actively transform the white hero, nonetheless confirms and validates both the hero's own claims and the strategies and tropes of the supporting narrative agencies. "I was thinking," says Kicking Bird (Graham Greene) to his friend Dances With Wolves, "that of all the trails in this life there is one that matters most. It is the trail of a true human being. I think you are on this trail, and it is good to see." The certification of the white hero's Indianness is now complete. Yet we also note that the moment comes late in the action (though it is hardly the last such endorsement, so insecure does Costner seem in his hero's Indianness). The Indian's approbation, however needed, seems always a bit belated, maybe even superfluous. I will return to this feature of revisionism later.

The hero of the revisionist Indian Western seldom becomes Indian by coercion. Even the captive John Morgan (Richard Harris) in *A Man Called Horse* (Silverstein, 1970) learns to appreciate the Sioux culture, so much so that he becomes the tribe's chief. At first, Morgan/Horse undergoes great humiliations at the hands of his Sioux captors, and for a time he sinks to the very depths of dejection. Yet his abjectness intimates the greatness to come. Made to work in the field with the women, he courts Running Deer (Corinna Tsopei), the sister of Chief Yellow Hand (Manu Tupou). At first, he courts her only so that he can overcome his near-enslavement, but later he falls in love with her. He furthers his transformation when he comes to the aid of a Sioux boy who has run into two Shoshone warriors while hunting rabbits. Horse kills the two Shoshones and, in full view of a newly arrived party of Sioux warriors, he scalps one of the Shoshones (after registering the necessary revulsion). In time, he undergoes the torturing scene (*pohk-hong*) of the Okipa ceremony, the ancient *Mandan* ritual that the movie insouciantly mis-attributes to the Sioux.[5] He thereby proves his courage to the tribal elders and becomes a full-fledged warrior. The death of Yellow Hand in battle clears the way for Horse to become chief. Only when Running Deer dies does he return to England, only, of course, to return to the Sioux—to his true people—six years later in *Return of a Man Called Horse*.

If the conversion of the hero requires no coercion, however, neither does it depend on a process of *learning* from the native. It more properly consists of a series of moments that demonstrate his inherent fitness to be "Indian." He may enjoy his clear epiphanies about the Indian, but these tend to emerge from an uncorrupted moral center that the Indian can only mirror and confirm. The revisionist hero appears on the frontier as an integral and uncompromised being: his experiences there only disclose the timeless bond between his elemental soul and the Indian's. The Indian and the wilderness are as the midwives that usher it, unfettered and free, into the world. And yet, for all his complete and thoroughgoing Indianness, the white hero *never loses his individuality to tribal identity*. Indianness remains ever the token of his distinction *as a white man*, so that he wears his Indianness as a stamp of high privilege, of a moral aristocracy of one, not only among mere whites but among all the other Indians, who neither chose to be Indian nor ever seem to know fully the blessings they enjoy.

Revisionism may try to represent an authentic Indian, insisting that it narrates an unmediated native perspective, but the revisionist Indian Western solicits, above all, the *exemption* of its white hero, whose self-

---

5. *A Man Called Horse* presents this ritual as the Sioux Sun Vow. See George Catlin, *O-kee-pa, a Religious Ceremony and Other Customs of the Mandans*, ed. John C. Ewers (1867; New Haven: Yale University Press, 1967); see also Catlin, *Letters and Notes on the Manners, Customs, and Conditions of North American Indians* (1844; New York: Dover Publications, 1973), 1: 155–84; for the Sioux Sun Vow, see Catlin, *Letters and Notes*, 1: 232–33. On the Okipa, see also Alfred W. Bowers, *Mandan Social and Ceremonial Organization* (Chicago: University of Chicago Press, 1950).

proclaimed Otherness demands a compensatory dispensation from the guilt of Conquest. Specifically, then, revisionism solicits an exemption from the judgments of history, from that righteous condemnation of Conquest that has its source in the white hero's own *historical con-science.* In this way the revisionist dispensation requires the very Myth of Conquest that it would explicitly contest. The greatest benefit of his exemption, then, as in the case of prelapsarian Adam, is an exemption from history, which is to say, from time as well as guilt. In the end, the hero of the revisionist Indian Western stands before us *dehistoricized as at once the last Indian and the first Man,* however recent a witness to and participant in history he may have been.

Revisionism owes its existence as much to Conquest as to the Indian. The revisionist does not tell his tale from within the Indian's world but from within the conqueror's. If nothing else, revisionism must tell the story of the Indian to those of us who remain, and who, for remaining, are by implication Conquest's beneficiaries. We are the ones who must now come to terms with our past and see the Indian as the revisionist sees him. Though he will rebuke, the revisionist must engage in a dialogue with "us." He would *be* Indian, but his work of illumination returns him to "us." The revisionists may presume to occupy the Indian's place in the new order, but Conquest makes that place *available* to them. Where, for example, is Jack Crabb (Dustin Hoffman) at the beginning of *Little Big Man* (Penn, 1970) if not in the white man's institution being interviewed—and by an academic historian no less? Where exactly might Dances With Wolves be going at the end if not to tell the story of the Lakotas to "those who would listen"? The revisionist hero exists on Conquest's sufferance: that he bestrides the regions of civilization and savagery betokens not so much his courage or his open-mindedness as his ambivalence.

In the pro-Indian Western, that ambivalence reveals itself in the implicit failure of the white hero—male or female—to share the Indian's tragic fate.[6] The revisionist would thus be exempted from both the guilt with which he charges the conqueror and the fate that he attributes to

6. I can think of only one white revisionist *female* hero—Cresta Marybelle Lee, in *Soldier Blue.* Cresta is rude, lewd, and caustic, as frontier chronicles often portray long-time captives of the Indian. But *Soldier Blue* places Cresta's lusty and boisterous irreverence in the service of revisionist ideology. She has escaped from the Cheyennes because she has been unable to adapt to their way of life, but she repeatedly speaks on their behalf and, like the male hero, tries to save the Cheyennes during the climactic massacre.

When white women in other revisionist movies (in *Devil's Doorway,* for example, or *Sitting Bull*) take up the cause of the Indian, they do so primarily because of their romantic involvement with the hero.

the Indian. It therefore seems proper to ask whether revisionism really comes from outside Conquest. Might it not be, instead, that it narrates Conquest's own lament over its consequences, a jeremiad for atonement's sake, rather than—or at least in addition to—an invective against Conquest or an elegy for the Indian? In sum, the Indian's cultural inheritance is well-nigh irrecoverable, save for this white man poised to tell *his* story of life with the Indians as though it were not a jot different from the story that the bereft Lakotas themselves would tell of their origins, their history, their vision of the future. If Conquest claims that its righteousness and its wrath brought about the Indian's end, the revisionist's zeal takes that end for granted.

It can be no coincidence, then, that the revisionist protagonist so often claims the status of sole witness, as when we hear the following words over a dark screen that slowly fades in to the 121-year-old Jack Crabb: "I am, beyond a doubt, the last of the old timers. My name is Jack Crabb, and I am the sole white survivor of the Battle of [the] Little Bighorn, popularly known as Custer's Last Stand." Jack was there when the end came, and now, alone after it—an Ishmael of sorts—he remembers (or mythicizes) and tells. Having discounted the possibility of Indian cultural continuity, the revisionist presumes to provide the only connection between past and present, between "us" and the Indian. In constructing a past that so completely and finally circumscribes the Indian, revisionism produces one of its most glaring paradoxes; its emplacement of the Indian in history *dehistoricizes* him instead. In order to throw further light on the foregoing generalizations, I now turn to *Sitting Bull* (Salkow, 1954), a Mexican-produced Western (W. R. Frank and Tele Voz, S. A., released through United Artists) whose glaring yet unintended ironies bare the self-subverting ideology of the revisionist project.

2

As revisionist Westerns go, this one, however crude in the end, begins auspiciously enough: a slow panning long shot reveals the western vastness, and soon we hear Sitting Bull (J. Carroll Naish) introducing us to the land and to the Sioux in voiceover. Before we actually see Sitting Bull, there appears before us, in the distance below, what seems to be a westering wagon train. But this one consists not of pioneer families passing through (as in the Parkman and Sonntag tableaux that we discussed in chapter 2) but of gold prospectors invading the Black

[133]

Hills. Despite the image of the wagon train, the camera never moves in close to the white people, and Sitting Bull's voice continues over the pan shot: "And I have prayed that Dakota and its hills would be too rough for the white man and his flocks. But once again the white man comes. I watch their coming with a sad heart." Far from uttering the usual whoops and grunts, the Indian's voice speaks instead in measured and dignified tones; speaks, moreover, of the people's ancestral bond with the land; and it notes the white man's invasion not with unrestrained rage but with sadness and great foreboding. The camera now settles on a medium shot of Sitting Bull, alone on a white horse, though he is soon joined by many warriors, foremost among them Crazy Horse (Iron Eyes Cody). Though Crazy Horse would kill the prospectors, Sitting Bull means only to raid for their supplies: "We will kill if we must. Now, take what our women and children need for the journey to the Rosebud." Here, then, is an endearing Indian indeed—properly outraged yet mindful of his people's welfare; brave yet equable; able to inspire our hope that here at last may be an Indian to contravene the generic typology.

But the sudden appearance of the white protagonist, Major Robert Parrish (Dale Robertson), undermines the hopeful beginnings of *Sitting Bull*. In a cut from the Sioux raid on the prospectors' wagons, we see Parrish at the head of a column of cavalry. Even if the close-up serves the standard purpose of identifying the movie star, it also hints at the special relationship between this one white man and the Sioux leader. Yet the close-up of Parrish also initiates the predictable process whereby the white hero so appropriates the Indian's story as to displace the Indian entirely. Once Parrish appears, we never again hear Sitting Bull in voiceover, which suggests not only that Sitting Bull is powerless to influence the white man's history, but that the white hero has taken over the labor of presenting the Indian's case in that history. Despite the film's title, Parrish is its real protagonist.

Immediately after the raid, Parrish chastises the leader of the prospectors, a greedy villain by the name of O'Connor (William Tannen), and when one of the soldiers reports to Parrish that the warriors raided "for food," Parrish refuses to consider reprisals against the Sioux and orders the prospectors to follow him to the fort. If he does not yet enjoy complete dispensation from the white man's desecration of the Indian lands, he has at least already distinguished himself from this barbarous white invader. Early in the story, we learn that Parrish was a young colonel during the Civil War; when we first meet him, he is a major; following a heroic act of dubious legality, he is demoted to captain; and after his court martial we see him stripped of every in-signia, from the cross-sabers on his hat down to his belt and sash.[7] Yet the American rebel grows in moral stature in inverse proportion to his descent within the institution. Thus, Parrish's pro-Indianness ex-presses not a choice for a way of life but an unerring instinct for high-minded action. Once the column arrives back at the fort, Parrish stops just outside headquarters to speak with his fianceé, Kathy Howell (Mary Murphy), who happens to be the daughter of the commanding officer, General Howell (John Litel). Eavesdropping in the next room, Kathy hears Parrish's "report": "Those people [the prospectors] use this fort to buy their supplies in. Then they lie in their teeth about where they're going. They go into Sioux territory and slaughter their game, foul their water, and shoot every Indian they see, if he's old or harmless enough. Then the treaties—they don't mean anything to them. They're just words on paper." Although Parrish denounces the white prospectors, we sense that he does not thereby claim any moral or spiritual kinship with the Indian. As principal agent for revisionism, the white hero will invariably censure his race, but he acts fully and throughout *as a white man*, even if he is the only irreproachable member of his race. Even so, though he be but one of a kind, he fully represents his race—all of "us." His righteousness finds its source in his singularly exalted *whiteness*, and his sympathy for the Indian only expresses the very best impulses of that whiteness. No one but the white hero could have become Indian.

As part of its strategy of self-othering, the "report" scene includes none other than George Armstrong Custer (Douglas Kennedy). Mo-ments earlier, Custer chided Parrish for not showing "initiative" in the Sioux attack on the prospectors' wagons. Chiming in to General How-ell's reprimand ("We are all here to obey orders"), Custer adds: "And orders seem to be something of a stumbling block for you. Major, you have been a burr under my saddle ever since you came West. You were an aide to General Grant when I first knew you, a colonel. Now you seem to be traveling downward in rank." Still eavesdropping, Kathy takes it all in and, having determined that her father's reproof dims her fiancé's prospects, she immediately breaks her engagement to Parrish. Yet all throughout his ostracism Parrish remains noble: "Maybe," he says on his own behalf (and clearly referring to Custer), "I've got a few

7. I do not doubt that the filmmakers were thus, in part, alluding to the practice of brevetting, whereby an officer enjoys a higher rank without pay commensurate with that rank. I doubt, however, that the practice (which goes unexplained in the movie) would have been well known to the viewers of the fifties.

plans that don't suit these blue-bellied patriots who like to go around slaughtering Indians just to keep their name in print." Perhaps with more truth than she realizes, Kathy responds: "This Indian thing has become an obsession with you." Her scorn only validates his righteousness.

All our attention has been drawn away from Sitting Bull. It is as if, having met Parrish, we are to take it as an article of faith—if only of a faith begotten of generic convention—that the white hero can speak *for* the Indian—indeed even *as* the Indian—in ways that the Indian himself, even so eminent a one as the Hunkpapa Lakota, Tatanka Iyotanka, cannot match. The story that began with Sitting Bull's perspective, with his voice, with his image itself—that began with his very name—seems now to have turned into Parrish's story. The story that, vested in the historical person, purports to tell the tale of an entire nation and culture, seems now lapsed into the inconsequential tale of Parrish's personal tea-pot tempests. Self-othering pre-empts the Indian. In the narrative that replaces the Indian with the white hero, there is to be gleaned more than just another romantic adventure set against the breathtaking landscape and the thrill of the Indian fight. Revisionism would absolve the national conscience through its hero by presenting this hero as the definitive and irrecusable *American*, fully and uniquely so, because he has been somehow cleansed of sins committed against the Indian *in the name of America*. Beyond the artless evasions and the botched good intentions lies the yearning to emerge free from complicity in Conquest; and then more, for revisionism seldom conceals its double and self-enervating desire: to embrace the Indian—to live fully the *freedom* that white men called "savagery"—and yet be, unambiguously, American, that is to say, white.

How, then, since Parrish has taken over the story of the Indian, can *Sitting Bull* return to Sitting Bull? As Parrish and his column ride to their new post, they run into a starving escapee from the agency. He happens to be Young Buffalo (Félix González), the son of Sitting Bull. Parrish gives water and a sack of food to Young Buffalo, and when he learns the identity of Young Buffalo's father, he follows the advice of the interpreter and lets him return to Sitting Bull's village. Later, a dastardly Indian agent named Webber (Thomas Brown Henry) shoots Young Buffalo in the back during a Sioux outbreak (Parrish had ordered the fort gates thrown open). Sitting Bull's tragedy consecrates Parrish's privilege: in the very suffering of the Indians lies his self-justification. Sitting Bull laments: "Great Spirit, Father of my fathers, here lies the body of my son, killed without reason. Listen to the death chant of the women. Listen to the war cries of the chiefs. Give me your counsel, Mighty One. Must there be war? Is this land not big enough for all people? Guide me now, O God of my people. War or peace? War or peace?" We sense Sitting Bull's powerlessness before the historical imperatives that subvert his noble impulses. Once again he has spoken only to express doubt and to question; and the *Lakota* "Mighty One" offers neither reassurance nor answer.

But now the close-up of the praying Sitting Bull dissolves into a close-up of Parrish, who stands before President Grant (John Hamilton). Parrish's first words are, "We can have war or peace out there, Mr. President. It'll depend on how we treat the Indians." Though the repetition of the words "war" and "peace" reinforces the visual connection between Parrish and Sitting Bull, the white hero expresses none of Sitting Bull's doubt. More important, however, the moment illustrates revisionism's recourse to the white hero as a spokesman for the powerless Indian. A discursive agency substitutes a *counter-ideology* of the Same for the voice of the Other. The hero's agency instead usurps the Indian's own; he implicitly asserts the power of his race and culture *over* the Indian while explicitly pleading the Indian's cause. In this way the white hero's mediation at once posits and enforces the Indian's virtual absence. The hero's Indianness shall supplant the Indian's own. Hence revisionism's improbable transformations: the Great Spirit becomes the Great Father, and the Indian prays to his worst enemy for deliverance. The Indian's god, like the Indian himself, vanishes, and the Indian may well lament, as in Swinburne's "Hymn to Proserpine": "O Gods dethroned and deceased, cast forth, wiped out in a day!" Yet what greater compensation for such a loss than that the pagan god should yield to the President of the United States, or that the exempted and impeccable hero should replace the fallen Indian son? Such sublimations soothe the national conscience. For what are greedy prospectors and corrupt Indian agents to this authentic pair, Sitting Bull and Parrish, brothers in conscience, in whose unity of spirit the American character stands vindicated? Now Parrish must travel back west to Sitting Bull and convince him to go east to meet Grant.

He no sooner arrives at the fort from the White House than he runs into Kathy. Before she tells him that she is now engaged to a newspaper reporter from the East, Charles Wentworth (William Hopper), she informs him that more miners and prospectors are gathered at the fort, this time with their wives and children, ready to settle the Black Hills. But of all the sights that greet him at the fort, none affects him more than that of a cavalry column, led by Custer, in front of which walk three Sioux warriors, each bound to the other. A fourth man is bound to these three, a black man named Sam (Joel Fluellen), who has "been a friend of the great chief Sitting Bull for many years." No image of Custer could have been more economically specified as utterly villainous than this one that presents him as a slave master. And since we already know that Custer functions as Parrish's foil, the image of these four Others as slaves also *others* Parrish. Not in vain does Sam tell Kathy much later, just before the scheduled execution of Parrish: "Why they shoot Captain Parrish, Miss? Injun say 'cause white man hate Injuns, also hate Injun's friend."

Eventually, Sitting Bull agrees to speak with Grant, but only if Grant comes West. Back at the fort, following a tense wait, the telegram from Grant finally arrives: he will come West. The moral influence of the man Parrish proves great enough to enable the historical fiction that Grant traveled to the West in 1876 to meet with Sitting Bull. The same fabrication complicates the historical references through which *Sitting Bull* attempts to ground itself in actual events, most particularly in Custer's defeat at the Little Bighorn. As Custer is about to head out of the fort with the Seventh Cavalry (which includes Parrish in command of a column), Howell hands him sealed orders. We know what the orders say because we have just seen Howell and Parrish receive the telegram from Washington: Custer and the Seventh Cavalry are to serve as an advance guard for Grant, who is coming West for peace talks with Sitting Bull. But Custer never reads the orders. Though Wentworth and Parrish know that Custer plans to attack, they never tell him that Grant is on his way to talk with Sitting Bull. Of just such innocent oversights must revisionism construct its view of history.[8] More important, revisionism passes off the sins of a nation on the Indian-hating, glory-seeking Custer.[9] Yet—for revisionism will have it both ways—Custer's actions only reconfirm Parrish's status as the true representative of the national will.

8. The failure to tell Custer that Grant is coming out West seems all the more egregious because Parrish has already sent Sam to the Sioux village to tell Sitting Bull of the impending visit. Even the civilian scout Sam knows what Custer never knows. We are therefore to believe that as Custer approached the Sioux village on the afternoon of June 25, 1876, the Sioux, Cheyenne, and Arapaho were preparing a feast for the approaching white President and his army!

9. Brian W. Dippie writes: "Yet, for all its blatant absurdities, *Sitting Bull* had chosen wisely in making Custer its villain. It had singled out for opprobrium the man whom Indians themselves have since elevated to the status of supreme white anti-hero." *Custer's Last Stand: The Anatomy of an American Myth* (Missoula: University of Montana Publications in History), p. 110.

Before attacking the Indian village, Custer orders Parrish and his troops, including Sam, to ride to the miners' camp and lead them away from the immediate area of combat. Custer's men have not fired the first shot when the Indians attack Parrish's column; but the outcome of this battle remains uncertain for a good while because the movie cannot resist the allure of the Last Stand. The action now consists principally of cross-cutting between parallel "last stands," Parrish's and Custer's. The Indians overwhelm Parrish's troops and, for all we can see, only Parrish and Sam survive. They then ride to Custer's rescue, only to come upon the aftermath of the Last Stand. In the distance, they can hear the drums that celebrate the Indian victory, but Parrish remarks: "They are celebrating the biggest disaster they'll ever see. General Terry's army is only a day's ride from here." Ever the protector of the Sioux, Parrish, accompanied by Sam, rides into the Indian village, and after convincing Sitting Bull that "Yellow Hair [Custer] advanced without orders," he tells him about Terry's approaching army. Unable to decide on a route for the flight of his people, Sitting Bull turns to Parrish, who proposes that they go north to Canada. Sitting Bull makes Parrish lead them there; and when, Moses-like, Parrish brings the entire Sioux nation within sight of the vast northern back lot of the promised land, the process of Indian endorsement of the white hero seems complete: as Parrish takes his leave, Sitting Bull says, "Go, then. I will never forget you, my son."

"The Great White Chief," Parrish had assured Sitting Bull, "will understand what I have done." But when Parrish arrives at the fort, Grant himself cannot stay the execution that is to follow Parrish's cashiering. If the Great Father cannot save the nation's true "son," then Sitting Bull will save *his* white son—or so Kathy and Sam hope. For they ride to Sitting Bull and ask him to intercede on Parrish's behalf. As Parrish stands before the firing squad, Sitting Bull appears in the distance, magnificent astride a pinto pony, wearing a trailing feathered headdress. "Why," Sitting Bull asks Grant,

are you now going to kill this man for treason? This man has always risked his life to bring peace between us. He risked his life when he led my people north, so that there would be no more killings on both sides. For a long time the Indians will respect this man. When he left my side I called him my son. I feared for his return. I remember his last words to me: "The Great White Chief will understand what I have done," he said. Kill him, my Chief, and your nation will destroy a patriotic son, only to

Sitting Bull (1954, United Artists). The Indian chief's farewell to his white "son." Courtesy of United Artists/Museum of Modern Art Film Stills Archive.

> find their mistake too late. But let him live, and through him the Indian
> and the white man can sit again in peace council.

Every one of Sitting Bull's sentences concerns Parrish. So what has happened to the Indian's voice? Sitting Bull once voiced his love of the land, of his people; he voiced his outrage and his powerlessness; he voiced his hope for peace—all until the revisionist agent himself, the white hero, appropriated that voice, until there was no cause for the Indian to take up but that of the white hero.

Grant has no immediate response to Sitting Bull's plea, and rather unexplainably turns, downcast, away from him, prescient perhaps of the historical tragedy to come. He says farewell to Sitting Bull and shakes hands with him. As Sitting Bull rides out to join his warriors outside the fort, he is flanked by rows of troopers at attention. The camera pans left and cranes up, at once following Grant, who moves to foreground center, and watching Sitting Bull leave the fort. The movement of the camera takes on Grant's perspective, thus enacting a full reversal of the initial perspective, which was Sitting Bull's on the white prospectors. More important, the fort gate frames Sitting Bull almost in precise center, so that the Indian moves inexorably into the vanishing point. There is a cut to Sam, Kathy, and Parrish. They look on joyously, more confident it seems of their own well-being than of any peace to come. Kathy and Parrish kiss (which, incidentally, requires Parrish to turn his back to Sitting Bull). As Sitting Bull, his back to the camera, continues his ride out, a space opens up between the row of warriors that awaited his return. This space frames him, centers him, even as the fort's gate did, emphasizing yet again the point into which he continues to recede. As if to confirm the relation between the visually receding image and the Vanishing American, an iris-in shot suddenly closes in on Sitting Bull until he is nothing but a speck at the center of the screen. This shot is followed immediately by a complementary iris-out that ends in a close-up of Sitting Bull in a prayerful attitude. The shot is immediately frozen—and the Indian comes thereby to be detemporalized, ahistorical, forever uttering the prayer that will never be answered.

And Parrish? Once rescued by the improbable intercession of Sitting Bull, Parrish becomes empowered as the exalted Same. During the whole scene, he never exchanges a word with Sitting Bull. In the arms of his bride, and flanked by the faithful Sam, he stands poised to lord it over the ahistorical and guiltless American paradise. So the Vanishing American, if I may invert Leslie Fiedler, "returns" in the form of the white hero; and he lives in him alone who enjoys the supreme privilege of memorializing the vanished Indian while yet representing his own race's best.

3

Historians and cultural critics alike identify two sources of the Indian's "return" from oblivion—the white man's nostalgia and the white man's guilt. The desire to relive what had not quite happened and to exalt now the dead who had been degraded in life—these, it is often held, are the forces that continually bring back the Indian and accord him at last the dubious honorific, "American." The promulgation that guilt and nostalgia constitute the twin sources of the Indian's "return" reverberates so convincingly throughout the critical literature as to make needless even a small sample of the arguments. I contest only the virtually unanimous insistence of the critics on keeping each of the sources separate from the other, as if each were not only a distinct motive but also specified a different white response to the Indian. In the consideration of these two putative sources of revisionism, then, we must remember that Conquest's achievement, however decisive it may have seemed in its first moments, came in time to be constrained and qualified by a *judgment*—a judgment passed on the very purpose and vision that had driven Conquest ever onward. The instant of Conquest's triumph had produced uncertainty, and had thus thrown the national identity itself into doubt. Conquest had yielded to ambiguity: the nation that would be known for the daring exploits that settled the land and begot such unimagined abundance, is also the nation that rues the passing of the Indian, the disappearance of the wilderness. The same ambiguity could seem most damning when stated conversely: a nation insisting that its westering experiences had conferred upon it its exceptional status was also the nation that had so systematically destroyed the very sources of its identity, the Indian and the wilderness. The historical "place" to which it wished to return was also the site of its genocidal record. How, then, to distinguish between guilt and nostalgia? How, then, keep them apart?

The conqueror's remorse over the presumed disappearance of the Indian is almost always a strategy of cultural self-definition. Often, this sort of guilt appears before us as if meant to have a salutary effect—as if those who *suffer* from it are somehow *restored* by it. They seek it, they cultivate it, they proclaim it, and then they exempt themselves from it. *Guilt becomes a strategy of self-othering*: only those who are enlightened about the real Indians could indulge such an exquisite lament upon their passing. Remorse is therefore wisdom, and eulogy absolves. Guilt accordingly implies meliorism: it is the means whereby the perverse racio-cultural falling-out with the Indian will at last be remedied. But such meliorism in turn implicates the white man's conscience in the cant of progress: if guilt defines the *civilized* white man, then it paradoxically vindicates the ideology—the repudiation of "savagism" for the sake of a higher good—in whose name the Indian was destroyed.

Such a nicely self-subversive logic recasts the relation between guilt and nostalgia. Nostalgia becomes *guilt expiated*. That is to say, guilt over the forced disappearance of the Indian and the wilderness becomes a way to invoke the two again, to express the pain for the return (the literal meaning of *nostalgia*) by exalting them both to a status that they never quite enjoyed in historical actuality. Let us not fail to draw out the full significance of the all too obvious: the Indian has to have been declared disappeared, named Vanishing American, in order for nostalgia to be fully deployed as a means of returning him. The interplay between guilt and nostalgia generates a shadow-history. The Indian returns; yet he returns not as a living human being but as an icon of

American exceptionalism. His virtual absence betokens "our" special legacy as a nation, the inheritance forged in the crucible of racio-cultural wars. Indeed, it hardly matters that the returned Indian lack all humanity, that he be a shadow-Indian; for he was never more than a token of the mythic past. What, then, does he return *to*? Does his return—even his return as Noble Savage—alter the course of history? Does he ever—as Noble Savage or Vanishing American—enjoy a life independently of the white hero? Reintegrated though he may be in American history, even recast as he may be in heroic nobility, he is in truth nothing more than a lure for reimagining the *mythic* American past. It is not the Indian as such that matters most to nostalgia but the illusory "past" itself—a past that, when viewed through the prism of such dangerous desires, may yet reveal nostalgia's disastrous complicity with the Myth of Conquest. Revisionism may render the Indian noble where myth rendered him savage, but the one is no less a distillation of dubious origin and ambiguous motive than is the other.

As far as revisionism is concerned, then, guilt and nostalgia are neither clearly distinct from nor opposite to each other. Nostalgia and guilt emerge, as it were, contiguously out of the same revisionist time line. Their shared adjacency, moreover, presupposes the revisionist's own *presence* at the crucial moment and place that saw the last Indian vanish. The same time and place witnesses the birth of the revisionist as an agent for the transformation of triumph into shame, and of that shame into the longing for the Indian's return. But the revisionist invokes his authority as eye witness in order to authorize his own desires. The same presence that enabled him to witness the Indian's demise also allows him to view it wistfully. Thus, he can both tell the story of the last Indian and censure the imperial project that brought about his disappearance. Only thus could the nation so yearn to return where it had never been.

Revisionism proffers its authentic Indian not only as the culturally integral native but as a manifestation of our own original selves: the Indian is pattern and exemplum of all wherein we would recognize and reclaim our own inartificial best, *before* Conquest. The Indian is suffused with the Adamic godliness; he is humanity's own essence and, as such, proof and record of the happiness that had been ours as well in the time before the corrupting sophistications of progress. We, too, can be just such an "Indian." "As far as my travels have yet led me into the Indian country," writes Catlin in his fourth letter, "I have more than realized my former predictions that those Indians who could be found *most entirely in a state of nature*, with the least knowledge of civilized society, would be found to be the most cleanly in their persons, elegant in their dress and manners, and enjoying life to the greatest perfection" [italics mine].[10] Revisionism's "anthropological" claims invariably play handmaiden to an ethical project. We recognize the romantic logic that gladly equates the "state of nature"—that is to say, the "manners, customs, and conditions," *accurately rendered* in image and word—with "the greatest perfection" that the moral being can attain. Accordingly, it seems almost reasonable that revisionism should construct the story of the Indian in terms made familiar by the account of Eden before the Fall. In his real and uncorrupted self, the Indian lives his waning hours as the incarnation of our own long-since faded ideals, and thus as our last opportunity to recover, out of this evanescence itself, such imperishable values as may corroborate our own humanity. He is "us"—our (br)Other—bound to us, as we to him, by unyielding ties of ecumenical fellowship. Whether he acknowledges it or not, however, the revisionist hero benefits from the death of the Indian. The revisionist's elegy seeks to accord the Indian an identity that he did not have before his presumed vanishment; yet the revisionist exists—in opposition to Conquest, exempt from the guilt accruing to its barbarities—*only because the Indian has passed*. To the virtually absent Indian he owes his identity as revisionist hero; and in such an Indian—or more precisely, in his professed attachment to such an Indian—he accordingly finds his self-othering authenticated.

Although the Indian may endorse such a hero, it is the hero who most often supplies what I would like to call the *authenticating insight*, a term by which I designate the testimony that at once overturns the savage of the Myth of Conquest and confers on the hero the necessary dispensation. Early in *Broken Arrow*, the hero Tom Jeffords (James Stewart) is surprised to learn that Apache mothers cry for their missing children. In *Run of the Arrow* (Fuller, 1957), Yellow Moccasin (Sarita Montiel) saves O'Meara (Rod Steiger), an embittered ex-Confederate sergeant, from the deadly "run of the arrow," and moments later O'Meara declares before the entire tribe his seemingly sincere desire to be Sioux. When asked why, he responds: "Because I love your people. I've learned from Yellow Moccasin that a man can't live alone. He must have allegiance to a people, to a nation. In my heart, my nation is Sioux." In *Dances With Wolves*, Dunbar's first sojourn among the Lakota produces an explicit (in voiceover) protest against the general frontier belief (expressed earlier by the muleskinner Timmons [Robert Pas-

10. *Letters and Notes*, 1: 23.

torelli]) that Indians are "thieves and beggars": "Nothing I had been told about these people is correct" (I quote this refutation at greater length, below). Still, we easily recognize the hero's insight into the "Indian character" as a disclosure of *his own* essential whiteness. Once the hero produces the authenticating insight, he is well on his way to becoming his true self, a self no longer deluded by fantasies of race or extraordinary destinies, a hero in touch with his own primordial humanity. In this way, the hero's own self-othering functions as an affirmation of his racial origins and betokens the perfect stability of his "ethnicity."

If the once-contested regions saw the birth of the revisionist, they also witnessed the deeds of the conqueror. The revisionist often shares the space and the moment in which the conqueror confronts the Indian. Often, in fact, the revisionist is the erstwhile conqueror himself. Small wonder that those who presume to enlighten us about the noble Indian turn out so often to have been military men or else scouts in the service of the military—all, in any case, just recently Indian fighters. In *Legends of the Fall* (1994) Colonel Ludlow (Anthony Hopkins) begins his life of renunciation in Montana only after he kicks the last smoldering tepee to the ground and sends the last conquered Indians to the reservation. Most military revisionists, however, come in the person of career officers of lower rank (if of indisputably higher intelligence and finer sensibilities than those of their superior officers). Their authenticating insights, moreover, are clearly formulated in opposition to the views of officers who, though of higher rank, seem bent either by idiocy or bigotry on the extermination of the Indian. Lieutenant Dunbar, for example, seems all the wiser in contrast to the bigoted major who brands him a traitor. In *Geronimo: An American Legend* (Hill, 1993), Lts. Britton Davis (Matt Damon) and Charles Gatewood (Jason Patric) are positively enlightened about the Apaches, and all the more so by comparison to the benighted Brig. Gen. Nelson Miles (Kevin Tighe). Capt. Thomas Archer (Richard Widmark) in *Cheyenne Autumn* (Ford, 1964) fights not only the bureaucracy but the Teutonic arrogance of Oscar Wessels (Karl Malden), like Archer a captain, but in command of a Fort Robinson that Ford allusively offers as a World War II German concentration camp. And in *I Will Fight No More Forever* (Heffron, 1975) Capt. Charles Wood (Sam Elliott) seems forever pleading the cause of the Nez Percé against the well-meaning but duty-bound Gen. Oliver Otis Howard (James Whitmore):

> *Wood*: General, today we closed the door on any Indian hope of keeping their land, and I think it's wrong.
> *Howard*: It *is* wrong. God knows it's wrong. To make those Indians move out

of their own valley, it's wrong; to make them come down out of the mountains where their horses will cross rivers that are still at high water, it's wrong. Yes, it's wrong. And you know something, Captain? That's exactly what we're going to do, because we're soldiers and we have our orders.

Nonetheless, the central characteristic of the revisionist hero is not his rank but the fact that his moral mission emerges from *contact*. Contact presupposes the requisite authenticating insight, an insight that, in turn, specifies the regenerative and redemptive geography out of which the nation is said to derive its remarkable identity—*the frontier*.

As we saw in chapter 1, the white hero / conqueror tends to spurn the "fine good place to be," the ideal site at the end of the racio-cultural struggle. For its part, that culturally determined place excludes him almost immediately after he makes it possible; instead, his "place," the abiding focus of his dreams, remains the frontier—let it shift ever westward as it may. Thus as far as revisionism is concerned, nostalgia answers to much more than the innocent fantasy of the atemporal. For it is on the frontier that, ever and again, the Indian vanishes, only to return in due compliance with the conqueror's deepest desires—his yearning for absolution, certainly, but that yearning itself commingling with the contradictory longing to relive the time of danger and adventure in the undiluted confrontation between worthy enemies. In the fight itself the conqueror had found an antagonist whose contempt for civilization matched his own. The erstwhile Indian-hater becomes friend to the Indian. Seldom do we find more moving expressions of the passing of the frontier than those articulated by the voice of empire. Here the locus classicus may well be Parkman's 1892 preface to *The Oregon Trail*, which laments that, since the time of the previous edition (the fourth, in 1872), "change has grown into metamorphosis":

> For Indian tepees, with their trophies of bow, lance, shield, and dangling scalplocks, we have towns and cities, resorts of health and pleasure seekers, with an agreeable society, Paris fashions, the magazines, the latest poem, and the last new novel. . . . The buffalo is gone, and of all his millions nothing is left but bones. Tame cattle and fences of barbed wire have supplanted his vast herds and boundless grazing grounds. Those discordant serenaders, the wolves that howled at evening about the traveller's camp-fire[,] have succumbed to arsenic and hushed their savage music. The wild Indian is turned into an ugly caricature of his conqueror; and

that which made him romantic, terrible, and hateful, is in large measure scourged out of him. The slow cavalcade of horsemen armed to the teeth has disappeared before parlor cars and the effeminate comforts of modern travel.[11]

The American West is overrun with "irresistible commonplace," Parkman concludes. Yet here was a man who, in his brief sojourn out West in 1846, could complain of the "savage spectacle" that presented itself before him in the form of Indians eating a buffalo (see chapter 2); who also, at that earlier time, referred to them variously as possessing a "dark vindictive spirit," or as being "treacherous, cowardly banditti," or characterized by "fickleness and inconstancy"; here, also, the young man who contributed mightily to the silence of the wolves—"I dismounted, and amused myself with firing at the wolves"[12]—the silence so vehemently decried by the old man; here, moreover, the one whose lament for the passing of the buffalo in old age seems impossible to reconcile with the youthful and arrogant contempt of almost half a century before: "Except an elephant, I have seen no animal that can surpass a buffalo bull in size and strength, and the world may be searched in vain to find any thing of a more ugly and ferocious aspect. At first sight of him every feeling of sympathy vanishes; no man who has not experienced it, can understand with what keen relish one inflicts his death wound, with what profound contentment of mind he beholds him fall."[13]

But only a quarter of a century after that foray into the wilderness, already comfortably nestled in the afterglow of illusion with which we so stubbornly veil our past experiences, Parkman could recall (in the 1872 preface) riding with his friend Quincy Adams Shaw "by the foot of Pike's Peak," with only a dawning awareness of the great changes to come:

We knew that, more and more, year after year, the trains of emigrant wagons would creep in slow procession towards barbarous Oregon or wild and distant California; but we did not dream how Commerce and Gold would breed nations along the Pacific, the disenchanting screech of the locomotive break the spell of weird, mysterious mountains, woman's rights invade the fastnesses of the Arapahoes, and despairing savagery, assailed

11. Francis Parkman, *The Oregon Trail: Sketches of Prairie and Rocky-Mountain Life* (Boston: Little, Brown, 1892), pp. vii–viii.
12. *The Oregon Trail*, p. 68.
13. Ibid., p. 306.

in front and rear, vail its scalplocks and feathers before triumphant commonplace. We were no prophets to foresee all this; and, had we foreseen
it, perhaps some perverse regrets might have tempered the ardor of our
rejoicing.[14]

So could the Indian and the wilderness find favor at last in the eyes of
those who, like Parkman, had taken such pains to censure and scorn.
But better these—the savage native and the wild brutes—than commonplace triumphant and inexorable. Wildness, what Thoreau called
"the tonic of wilderness," was much preferable, if only in tranquil and
bedimmed recollections from far-away Boston. Revisionism often co-
opts the Indian as an ally in its battle against "irresistible commonplace," and this strategy, ever aimed at the unfeeling present, is as often
the conqueror's own.

The mythology that obscured the distinction between revisionist and
conqueror could make the nation yearn again for the time of rage and
retribution, especially now that it had discovered the antidote to guilt
in its derivative—its merely derivative—longing for the vanished Indian. Whose lament for the vanished Indian could be more plaintive,
whose avowals of brotherhood more sincere, whose declared fidelity to
the memory of the Indian more impassioned—whose tale, then, more
archetypally American—than that of *the Indian fighter*—out of whose
dangers and adventures in the wilderness the nation is said to have
been born? Who might better tell the story of the "last" Indian but this
white man who now outlives him? It was a sign, as unmistakable as it
was equivocal, of Conquest's triumph, that the Indian, having been
dispossessed by Conquest, could yet find himself enlisted in the cause
of America's quest for national identity.

The Indian cannot vanish and still represent himself, as the Cheshire
Cat can disappear and still somehow leave behind his grin for all to
see. The Indian's return depends entirely on the revisionist. And indeed the logic of revisionism not only *assumes* the passing of the Indian, it actually *insists* upon it. The good Indian will not be represented without a death certificate, and it is the revisionist himself who
more often than not signs it. Thereafter, the Indian can never return
but at the revisionist's behest. Hence the cruel irony that the Vanishing
American, presumably armed with his native and unique perspective,
should in the end be made to attest, if only implicitly, to the beneficent
effects of civilization. For civilization, which pursued him to the very
edges of oblivion, now purposes to rescue him by including him in an-

14. Preface to the 1872 edition, in the 1892 edition, p. xi.

other version of its story, in its ideal history, in its magnanimously pluralistic ethos. Revisionism indicted Conquest on behalf of the vanished Indian, and it in turn exacted from him not so much an absolution for the sin of complicity but an *immunity* from it. To honor the Indian in the aftermath of Conquest—and to do so, primarily, by disavowing Conquest—was somehow the same as not to have participated in Conquest at all. Thus did revision become one more form of Conquest. The revisionist's brotherhood with the dead Indian was a way of following him out of this world—a way, then, of renouncing progress, Caesar's gross and worldly things. Yet the revisionist also outlived the Indian, so that, exempt from guilt and having renounced the world, he still remained in its paradisal version, at once Indian and Adam.

4

I turn now to an analysis of revisionism by questioning the function and intent of a discursive strategy common to the pro-Indian Western—"voice." As a revisionist strategy, voice tends to take the form of voiceover narration; that is to say, speech that does not, as Gilberto Perez notes, "issue from the human body."[15] The revisionist Western usually presents the Indian's case as an ethical reflection on Conquest and its crimes against the Indian. At present, we need note nothing more specific about the function of voiceover narration than that its very nature implies the passing of the Indian: voiceover almost invariably adopts the past tense and thus already presupposes the Indian's disappearance. Yet voice functions not only as a strategy of authentication and censure but of exemption and self-othering as well. Already we can anticipate the aporia whereby revisionism collapses before the ironies and subversions embedded in its narrative strategies.

STILL BREATHLESS from their furious gallop to the remote army post, two scouts and Lieutenant Blanchard stand before Captain Sickels. After the first scout reports on Apache depredations, he points to the second scout and declares: "He had a brush with 'em last night; says they're being stirred up by Geronimo." Distraught, Sickels exclaims, "Geronimo!" but before asking for further details, he looks askance at

15. Gilberto Perez, *The Material Ghost: Films and Their Medium* (Baltimore: Johns Hopkins University Press, 1998), p. 83.

the second scout and asks the first one, "How do we know he isn't lying?" Cut to a close-up of the second scout, an Indian (Chief John Big Tree), his hair braided and feathered, gazing torpidly ahead. The lurid light that suffuses his face offers more than a hint of menace, but his stolid stare dominates the close-up, and, as much as the obligatory Indian accoutrements and Sickels's suspicions, identifies him as the racio-cultural Other of America's frontier mythology. Offscreen, over the close-up, the first—hereafter the *white*—scout responds: "No, he's a Cheyenne. They hate Apaches worse than we do." The scene ends shortly thereafter without so much as one word from the Cheyenne scout. We never see him again.

Even as it introduces us to the historical and dramatic context of the action, the first scene of John Ford's *Stagecoach* deploys a basic strategy through which the Western configures the American Indian—the unequal relation between the white man's *voice* and the Indian's *image*. As the white scout speaks *over* the close-up of the impassive Cheyenne, he implicitly claims the authority to present him. The Cheyenne scout has nothing of his own to say. Indeed, the close-up of him, defined principally by the vacant look, distinguishes the Cheyenne scout as the voiceless Other. The white scout identifies the Cheyenne by tribal affiliation, by the Cheyennes' enemy tribe, and by the proportion in which his hatred of the Apaches stands to "our" own. The Cheyenne may be an able scout, an ally, and trustworthy, but he is first and last a narrative dependent. Furthermore, both Sickels and the white scout speak about the Cheyenne in the third person, as if he were elsewhere. When Sickels asks if the Cheyenne can be trusted, he is addressing the white scout. Not only does Sickles distrust the Cheyenne, he implicitly declares the Cheyenne's *discursive absence*. The white scout, for his part, confirms this absence when he refers to the Cheyenne in the third person. Despite so decisively establishing the Cheyenne's virtual absence, however, the two white men also *present* him. The Cheyenne scout's identity has its source not in his own image but in the white man's voice.

The white man's voice, by whose authority the Indian comes to be virtually absent, claims nonetheless so complete an intimacy with the Indian as to declare itself in full possession of all that we can hope to know about him. No Indian ever seems to tender as thorough an account of himself as that which the white man offers. This third form of the relation between white voice and Indian image assures us that we know the Indian fully (or at least all that we need know about him) even as it enforces his narrative dependence. The Indian's *silence*

[150]

becomes therefore the central fact of his *story*. And yet, though such a white man may embrace all that is Indian, he remains distinctly white. By this paradox, indeed, nothing makes the white man so manifestly the hero of his own culture as does his knowledge of the Indian Other. Sickels's question—"How do we know he isn't lying?"—implicitly accords to the white scout the privilege to define the Cheyenne scout. The white scout, for his part, at once validates Sickels's trust and certifies his own authority by means of the nice discernment between Apache and Cheyenne; and the identification of the Cheyenne scout—of his difference, cultural and moral alike, from the Apache—serves principally to validate the white scout's unrivalled knowledge of both Cheyennes *and* Apaches—of *Indians*, therefore. The figuration of the white man, rather than the figuration of the Indian, describes this particular function of the relation between white voice and Indian image.

Before this short scene ends, *Stagecoach* will have confirmed the power of the word to make the Indian absent: just before the telegraph line goes dead, the army post receives an urgent message from Lordsburg. It contains only one word—"Geronimo." The near-panic that the name alone causes in Sickels's small group indicates with astonishing economy just how the Indian could acquire his identity as Other through the complex nexus of narrative agencies and modes given in so brief a moment. It is suggestive enough that the scene manages to define the Indian as absolute Other, making an irrelevance of his status as ally or foe. But the power for "othering" lies in the intricate modality of the references, all of which, in form as in content, can only render a dependent, a narratively abject, Indian. That the telegram, however incomplete, came through to the army post, suggests just how powerless the Indian was to stop the "talking wire," this form of voice that now generates a scene in a film. That scene in its turn articulates both the silent Indian image (of the Cheyenne ally) and the word that specifies the (himself silent) Indian foe, producing in their turn the close-ups of the unnerved white men and propelling that part of the plot in which the nation defines itself by that which it is not. In some respects, all the Indian needed in order to be cast as Conquest's Other was to appear in the movies: the *appearance* (to use the word in its double sense) guaranteed his Otherness.

White voice speaks for the Indian; it declares him absent, or at least virtually so; and it casts him as the white man's foil in a plot that recounts and reaffirms the creation mythos of the conquering hero and his culture. These three functions of the relation between

[151]

white voice and Indian image delineate a canonical model: the trope constitutes one way of identifying and studying other possible ways by which the Western perpetuated (perhaps even begot) the conquered image of the American Indian. That the relation between voice and image, as I have sketched above, should serve such aims in the *canonical* account of imperial America can hardly surprise us. Conquest is, after all, the theme here, and Conquest requires that its tropes render dominion's processes and purposes alike as both clear and blameless. That the relation between white voice and Indian image, long a trope of the canonical Western (and thus of Conquest) should play a prominent part in the *revisionist* Western, in which an overtly ethical critique of empire and a vehement insistence on the full and equal humanity of the Indian claim the thematic center, constitutes the fundamental irony to be elucidated in the remainder of this chapter.

The revisionist movies that I will examine are *Broken Arrow, Cheyenne Autumn, Little Big Man, Soldier Blue, Dances With Wolves,* and *Geronimo: An American Legend*.[16] As a list of pro-Indian Westerns, this one is hardly comprehensive, yet it would be nearly impossible to consider revisionism adequately without these titles.[17] In all of these Westerns a significant part of the action unfolds as a dramatic and ideological struggle to controvert the canonical Indian type, and in all of them (though obviously to various degrees) a white character's voice (often but not always as voiceover narration) assists the intent to refigure the Indian. Each of the chapter sections, below, examines how the white voice finds its counterpart in the three functions of voice in the canonical model drawn from *Stagecoach*: the Indian requires a white voice that will speak for him; the white voice presents an Indian that is "virtually absent"; and the white voice—despite its express intentions—exalts the

16. Throughout this chapter I refer to Walter Hill's movie simply as *Geronimo*. There are no textual references here to *Geronimo* (Laven, 1962) or to the Ted Turner / TNN *Geronimo* of the same year as Hill's.

17. An Indian Western with a voiceover narrator does not necessarily indicate revisionist intention. For example, the voiceover narrator of Sam Peckinpah's *Major Dundee* (1965), Corporal Tim Ryan, begins as an Indian hater. Many pro-Indian movies lack a voiceover narrator. Anthony Mann's *Devil's Doorway* (1950) is in many ways a more powerful indictment of Indian-hating America than is *Broken Arrow*, released the same year. Among the more important pro-Indian Westerns where there is no voiceover, I count *Apache* (Aldrich, 1954), *Run of the Arrow, Flaming Star* (Siegel, 1960), *Hombre* (Ritt, 1967), *Chato's Land* (Winner, 1971), *Ulzana's Raid* (Aldrich, 1972), and *The Last of the Mohicans* (Mann, 1992). *I Will Fight No More Forever* and *Son of the Morning Star* (Robe, 1991) are two made-for-TV Indian Westerns that make heavy use of the voiceover narrator.

white hero, so that in the end the Indian is made manifest in this white man.

5

As a trope in the service of revisionist dialectic, white voice both contests the stereotype and proffers the "true" Indian. Early in *Broken Arrow*, for example, the hero Tom Jeffords (James Stewart) sees buzzards circling over what he takes to be a dying animal. As he comes closer, however, Jeffords discovers, stumbling about in the draw below, a wounded Apache boy: "Not a rabbit, not a deer," Jeffords's voiceover now says, "but a wounded Apache boy. His kind was more dangerous than a snake. He was an Apache. For ten years we had been in a savage war with his people—a bloody no-give, no-take war." That which may seem to be gratuitous antipathy toward the Apaches is in fact a way of characterizing the canonical Indian—so to provide a proper context for the reversal, for the authenticating insight—even if there is a gross incongruity between Jeffords's epithets and the harmlessness of the wounded boy.

Predictably, Jeffords nurses the boy to health. Now recovered, the boy tells Jeffords that he shall be returning to his village because his mother "is crying for [him]." Jeffords's voiceover makes the first of several revisions—he tends to offer them more as epiphanies—about the Apaches: " 'My mother is crying,' he said. Funny, it never struck me that an Apache woman would cry over her son like any other woman." Jeffords has only now come by such an insight, yet he rushes to render the boy's simple longings as a disclosure of convergence at the highest levels of spiritual being. So be it. It is not the condescension that should concern us principally but the assumption—confident, even peremptory—that the Indian occupies a moral space where we may now recognize him as one of "our" own, no longer the Other but *like any other*—even, perhaps, "like" the Same. Yet we are to recognize Indian humanity only because it so faultlessly mirrors the hero's own. The Indian shall be most *real*, most *authentic*, when he most approximates our own *ideal* selves. Thus the intent to revise produces not a different Indian but a different *white perspective* on the Indian. "[I]t is ultimately to the history of White values and ideas," writes Robert Berkhofer, "that we must turn for the basic conceptual categories, classificatory schema, explanatory frameworks, and moral criteria by which past and present

Whites perceived, observed, evaluated, and interpreted Native Americans, whether as literary and artistic images, as subjects of scientific curiosity, or as objects of philanthropy and policy."[18]

Four decades after *Broken Arrow*, the voiceover narration of Lieutenant John J. Dunbar would invoke a similar dialectic. The first time that Dunbar fully voices his refigured Indian, he alludes to a remark made much earlier by the muleskinner Timmons as the two make their way to Fort Sedgewick. When Dunbar asks him how come they have not yet seen any Indians, Timmons replies: "Indians? God damn Indians! You'd just as soon not see 'em less'n the bastards are dead. They're nothing but thieves and beggars!" Costner lets this racist vitriol stand for universal white sentiment about the Indians. Then, much later, after his Lakota friends Kicking Bird and Wind In His Hair bring Dunbar a buffalo robe, the voiceover produces the requisite revision of Timmons's Indians: "Nothing I had been told about these people is correct. They're not beggars and thieves; they're not the bogeymen they have been made out to be. On the contrary, they are polite guests and have a familiar humor I enjoy." Could the Indian but speak about himself, he would surely say this much, and say it this eloquently (though he would hardly represent himself as "guest" in his own land and would be less likely to justify his taste by recourse to the first-person singular). Yet *Dances With Wolves*, for all that it endears us to its Lakotas, never produces an Indian so authoritative about his own virtues as this white hero who, alone though he may be among white men in his beliefs, yet incontrovertibly represents the full and ample measure of Indian humanity.[19]

When Jeffords characterizes the Apache youth as a "snake," he alludes, we saw, to a time before he knew the "true" Indian. The vilification, however, like Timmons's own in *Dances With Wolves*, functions primarily to enlist a traditional audience in the dialectics of revision. For Jeffords and Dunbar, we know, speak to us from the start as beings *already* enlightened. Furthermore, voiceover narration tends to be not only retrospective but comprehensive. Although it claims intimacy with the full range of Indian virtues, it implies the very opposite of that intimacy—*distance*: the hero's experiences with the Indians are not only over but *complete*: the narrator knows all, and all that *we* both need and hope to know, about the Indian. The hero/narrator—both Jeffords and

18. *The White Man's Indian*, p. xvi.
19. For a recent critique of *Dances With Wolves* along these lines, see Huhndorf, *Going Native*, pp. 1–5.

Dunbar, but also *Cheyenne Autumn*'s Thomas Archer, for example, or *Little Big Man*'s Jack Crabb, or *Geronimo*'s Britton Davis (though this last is not quite the protagonist)—*is never among the Indians when he tells the story*. Recall, for example, the first words of *Little Big Man* (spoken as a sort of voiceover, since the screen is still dark): "I am, beyond a doubt, the last of the old timers. [*FADE IN* to speaker] My name is Jack Crabb, and I am the sole white survivor of the Battle of [the] Little Bighorn, popularly known as Custer's Last Stand." In the nursing home, where the first scene is set, the 121-year-old Jack Crabb talks into the tape recorder of the Historian (William Hickey), who has come to interview him. Jack affirms: "I knowed General George Armstrong Custer for what he was, and I also knowed the Indians for what they was." His story of the Indian may be narrated only from this distance: across the spans of time the Indian appears already vestigial, ephemeral, vanished—the source at once of remorse and nostalgia, the embodied plea, therefore, as the revisionist voice understands it, for pity. Distance, accordingly, suggests *privilege*: it tends to subordinate the hero's experiences with the Indians, no less than the presumably re-figured Indians themselves, to an exclusive vantage. Nothing—not his experiences, not his own convictions, certainly not the Indian him-self—so validates the narrator's moral authority, as does this privi-leged perspective itself. His presence alone at the site of that perspec-tive evinces his privilege.

Many of the pro-Indian Westerns that deploy voiceover narration as a privileged perspective seem to require a *judgment* on whites. Here, the revisionist designs of voiceover narration find common ground with the assumption that the Indian's most eloquent voice belongs in fact to the outraged white man (or woman, in *Soldier Blue*). After white soldiers destroy the Cheyenne village in which Jack Crabb had hoped to find his captive white wife, Olga (but instead rescues his Cheyenne wife-to-be Sunshine), he returns to the village of his adoptive grandfa-ther, Old Lodge Skins (Chief Dan George). Old Lodge Skins names all the Cheyennes who have been "rubbed out" by the whites during Jack's absence. He names each victim slowly, deliberately, making their names stand for life and loss alike. As Jack registers the full force of the catastrophe, he cries out: "Do you hate them? Do you hate the white man now?" It is in part his censure of the white man that empowers Jack to become the voiceover narrator. But such denunciations also ex-onerate him from any possible blame for the actions of his race.

Ralph Nelson's *Soldier Blue* does not feature a voiceover narrator who is also the principal character. Instead, the voiceover speaks as

[155]

DBS Arts Library

Little Big Man (1970, National General Pictures). The white hero and his
Cheyenne mentor. Courtesy of National General Pictures/Museum of
Modern Art Film Stills Archive.

History itself, though of a decidedly revisionist sort. This revisionist
history is most evident in the opening, where folk-singer and Native
American activist Buffy Sainte-Marie sings over a long shot of a
Cheyenne village: "Tell you a story, it's a true one, / And I'll tell it like
you'll understand, / And I ain't gonna talk like some history man."

[156]

This is, shall be—dare we hope?—the Indian's own story. The Native American voice assures us of it. Yet even before we hear Buffy Sainte-Marie, Nelson has made us read:

> In 5,000 years of recorded civilization mankind has written his history in blood. Mankind's noblest achievements reveal a divine spark. But there is a dark side to man's soul that has festered since Cain slew his brother. The climax of "Soldier Blue" shows specifically and graphically the horrors of battle as blood lust overcomes reason. Brutal atrocities affect not only the warriors, but the innocent as well[—]the women and children. The greatest horror of all is that it is true.

The "native" voice derives its authority from—and is accordingly dependent upon—this impassioned exordium that recalls the ethical intertitles of silent revisionist Westerns, such as *The Redman's View* or *The Vanishing American* (Seitz, 1925). Following Buffy Sainte-Marie's song, *Soldier Blue* returns to the voiceover trope only at the end: over the shots of the endless graves of Cheyenne men, women, and children, a white male voice now identifies the historical event on which the action claims to be based—the Sand Creek Massacre of 1864. Clearly, however, Nelson presents Sand Creek as proto-Mylai: the age-old Manichaean struggle between "blood lust" and "reason" acquires its full force and import from this assumption that would have the four centuries of unremitting violence against native cultures in North America stand as an allegory for American military involvement overseas. The elegant historical reflections of scholars such as Richard Slotkin and Richard Drinnon have driven home the connection between Vietnam and the racio-cultural wars on the frontier; but *Soldier Blue*'s implied claim that the historical attempt to displace and annihilate a people can accurately reflect or explain America's presence in Vietnam is, to say the least, shamelessly self-serving.

Astonishingly, the voiceover concludes its grim account of Sand Creek by producing a quote from no less imperial a figure than General Nelson A. Miles (1839–1925), the most successful Indian fighter in the second half of the nineteenth century. Miles, the voiceover tells us, labeled Sand Creek "[p]erhaps the foulest and most unjust crime in the annals of America." Somewhere between Buffy Sainte-Marie and General Miles—between the *vox populi* and the *vox imperii*—Ralph Nelson locates the revisionist indignation of his white hero, Cresta Marybelle Lee.

When we first see her, Cresta is walking away from Spotted Wolf's

Cheyenne village (where she was a rather complaisant captive) and is trying to make her way back to Fort Reunion. Only one trooper, Corporal Honus Gant (Peter Strauss), survives the Cheyenne attack on the cavalry detachment that was escorting Cresta to the fort. Whenever Nelson is not conspiring to have Honus and Cresta fall in love, he has the hoyden Cresta enlightening Honus about the "plight" of the Indian. In the immediate aftermath of the Cheyenne attack on the cavalry escort, for example, Cresta and Honus stand on a hill looking down at the bodies of the twenty-one dead troopers. "A drop in the old bucket," Cresta remarks about the body count. Then she mocks the cause of westward expansion: "Our good, brave lads, coming out here to kill themselves a real live Injun, putting up their forts in a country they've got no claim to. So what the hell do you expect the Indians to do, sit back on their butts while the army takes over their land? . . . You ever see an Indian camp after the army's been there, huh? You ever see the women and what was done to them before they were killed? Ever see the little boys and girls stuck on the long knives? Stuck and dying? Well, I have." The judgment on a whole race—or at least on a generation of WASP males all too easily identified as the "Establishment"— aligns itself unequivocally with the "true story," with History beyond the ken of the "history man." Cresta has seen enough horror to declare herself enlightened, even if, in time, her censure implicitly seeks the endorsement of so central a figure in the history of Conquest as Nelson Miles.

For all the anger and the righteousness, however, no new figure of the Indian appears. Spotted Wolf (Jorge Rivero), an obscenely exoticized and muscle-bound Indian, is the lovelorn yet compliant warrior who, predictably, saves Honus's life. What better sanction of the white couple's exemption from racial guilt than that the doomed savage should die nobly for the white hero? The rest of the Indians are for the most part delivered from utter anonymity only by their ineradicable status as victims of this history inscribed in "blood." Perhaps it is the particular ghoulishness of the historical Sand Creek Massacre that causes these anonymous Indians to suffer the worst atrocities of any Indian in any Western. One wonders, however, if the images of these murdered and mutilated Indians do not, above all else, sanction the primal need of the white couple to extricate themselves from such a dark history, for only thus would they be likely to emerge—as they almost certainly do now that all the whites are damned and all the Indians are either dead or dependent—as the uncontested inheritors of the American Garden. That which might have sounded like the righteous

Soldier Blue (1970, AVCO Embassy). The exotic Indian and the submissive white woman. Courtesy of AVCO Embassy/Museum of Modern Art Film Stills Archive.

voice of the Indian is in fact the contentious debate of civilization's demons. The perspective that might have refigured the Indian begot instead only a flimsy refuge for a generation's conscience.

6

White voice renders the Indian voiceless, *absents* him for presenting him. Meaning to draw the Indian in from the margins of the great imperial tale, this voice ends up presiding over the story of the Vanishing American at the vanishing point. Of course, not all Indians in these Westerns are as voiceless as the Cheyenne scout in *Stagecoach*. For Indians here do speak. In *Little Big Man*, for instance, the Indian articulates the wisdom often associated with the Other, as when Old Lodge Skins tells Jack Crabb that white men killed the women and children of a Cheyenne village "Because they are *strange*. They do not seem to know where the center of the earth is." Also, the Indian in the revisionist Western often engages in compelling moral disputes with white au-

[159]

thorities. In *Geronimo*, Geronimo (Wes Studi) responds to the charges whereby General Crook (Gene Hackman) would identify him as the savage Other:

> *Crook*: A lot of White-Eye [*sic*] want to see Geronimo hanged for murder.
> *Geronimo*: Not murder, war. Many bad things happen in war.
> *Crook*: How many White-Eye did you kill since you left Turkey Creek?
> *Geronimo*: Maybe fifty! Maybe more! How many Apaches do you kill?
> *Crook*: You killed women and children.
> *Geronimo*: So did you.

These Indians speak most eloquently, however, which is to say most subversively, when they identify *white words themselves* as their enemy. "You were right to fight the White-Eye," Chato (Steve Reevis) says to Geronimo in the train that now takes the Apaches to their exile in Florida. "Everything they said to me was a lie."

Consider an elaboration on a similar moment in *Cheyenne Autumn*, a late exchange between the Cheyenne chiefs, Little Wolf (Ricardo Montalban) and Dull Knife (Gilbert Roland), and the white officials, Interior Secretary Carl Schurz (Edward G. Robinson) and Captain Archer before a cave where the Cheyenne remnant has made its stand against the pursuing troops. Here the *mise en scène* speaks as eloquently as the Indians could, for the council is held while hundreds of troops aim their rifles and cannons at the Cheyennes.

> *Schurz*: I know how many promises have been made to you and then broken, but I'm not here to make any promises; I'm asking you to take a gamble.
> *Little Wolf*: All *veho* words are the same.[20]
> *Dull Knife*: You keep us talking [*pointing to the massed troops some hundred yards behind Schurz and Archer*] . . . the soldiers.
> *Schurz*: Now please, listen to me, please. You've made one of the most heroic marches in history. You deserve to go back to your own homeland and stay there in peace. I'm sure that the people of this country will understand, and will agree when they hear the facts. Now, will you take the gamble?
> *Dull Knife*: The people—who will tell them? Who will tell the people about [the massacre at] Fort Robinson?
> *Schurz*: I will. I promise you. You call this Victory Cave. You can have an-

---

20. *Veho*, according to Mari Sandoz's source novel, is Cheyenne for "spider," but also for white man.

other greater victory here, right now. [*Little Wolf and Dull Knife look at Archer for reassurance*]
Archer: He speaks the truth.

Here, in the context of his expressed contempt for *veho* words—and more profoundly still, following his clear identification of words with weapons—the Indian must declare his narrative dependence on just such words. Schurz's pledge, more than any deed of the Cheyenne's heroic and tragic resistance, ensures *their* "victory." Never before did *veho* words frame so specious a tale: the Great Father guarantees the victory of the "hostiles" while demanding their surrender! That the Indian deserves this paternally decreed deliverance from enforced exile already suggests the violent abrogation of his cultural birthright. White words, white bullets: such warrants of justice and compassion as Schurz offers—and Archer underwrites—identify even these sympathetic white men as Conquest's own expedients, weapons no less effective or aggressive than the soldiers themselves. There is no "gamble" to be taken in surrender to such powers. The voice of the voiceless can speak only its resignation.

Thus, Indian speech, even the speech of resistance itself, already foretokens Indian absence. The white man will tell "the people"—will tell *us*, as Archer's voiceover does throughout—of the Indian's plight. But the telling presupposes the vanished Indian. In this way, *Cheyenne Autumn* unfolds as the keeping of a double promise, though perhaps more as the sustained enforcement of a duplicity: the white man speaks as apologist for the Indian, even as his voice assures us that the Indian is not free to speak for himself. Archer's voiceover shall in fact initiate the story of the Cheyenne flight to Montana, but if he has kept *his* promise, he has also *kept* (has appropriated) *their* words. *We hear their story only because they have no voice of their own.* Intending to tell the tragic and heroic story of the Cheyennes, Archer inevitably sings of Conquest. Elegy here is but the mask of Hollywood "epic."

Such a story of the Indian postulates his end. If distance and privilege suggest the voiceover's power to begin the story of the Indian, they also refer to a moment, just before or coeval with the constitution of the voiceover, when the narrator witnessed the end of the Indian. Of the revisionist Westerns under consideration, perhaps none so clearly establishes the affinity between the Indian's end and the voiceover's beginning as does *Geronimo*. Toward the end, General Miles banishes the hero, Lt. Charles Gatewood, to a remote outpost in Wyoming and orders all the Apache scouts that served the army in the so-called Geronimo Campaign disarmed and exiled to Florida, along with

Geronimo and his band. As the scouts are being disarmed outside, Lt. Britton Davis, who worships Gatewood, confronts Miles in his office. Indignantly (if ingenuously), Davis complains: "Sir, I thought the U.S. Army kept its word. I thought maybe we were the only ones left who did. What's going on out there is a disgrace." Miles's reply, though meaning to discredit Davis's idealism, in fact authorizes the moral stance of the Davis voiceover: "Lieutenant, you are more worried about keeping your word to a savage than you are [about] fulfilling your duty to the citizens of this country. We won. That's what matters. It's over, Lieutenant—Geronimo, the Apache, the whole history of the West, except being a farmer."

By declaring the end of the historical conflict between whites and Indians, Miles (who in *Soldier Blue* reviled Sand Creek) effectively delivers Davis from complicity in that history. Davis resigns from the army, and thus resigns himself to his role as the voiceover narrator of an ideal version of American history, of a *counter-history*. Davis shall tell the Indian's story less for the Indian's own sake than for the sake of dissociating himself from the shame of Conquest: "To the disappointment of family and friends, I had ended my military career. Over the years, the events surrounding the Geronimo Campaign have continued to haunt me. I carry the memory of those days, days of bravery and cruelty, of heroism and deceit. And I am still faced with an undeniable truth: a way of life that endured a thousand years is gone. This desert, this land that we look out on, would never be the same."

Over this repudiation of Manifest Destiny, we see an empty railroad track extending from the left foreground out and curving to the right at the middle ground; from the right background a train approaches. This train shall take the Apaches to an alien land. Now, in an *interior* shot of the train, Chato sanctions Geronimo's resistance ("You were right to fight the White-Eye."); and while Mangas (Rodney Grant) condemns Chato's allegiance to the army, Geronimo speaks of reconciliation: "There are so few of us left. We should not hate each other. . . . No one knows why the One God let the White-Eye take our land. Why did there have to be so many of them? Why did they have so many guns, so many horses? For many years the One God made me a warrior. No guns, no bullets, could ever kill me. That was my power. Now my time is over. Now, maybe, the time of our people is over." Geronimo drops his head, and Hill cuts to an *exterior* shot of the train, which now begins its slow certain movement to the far background, even as the end credits continue to roll. Geronimo's last words confirm him as a Vanishing

American. His speech heralds his presumed historical silence. The bowed head invokes none of the countless photographs of the historical Chiricahua leader, since so many show him, instead, by turns defiant and bemused; rather, it evokes images that we recall only under penalty of complicity in the construction of the canonical Indian—for example, Thomas Crawford's *The Dying Chief Contemplating the Progress of Civilization* (1855), Fraser's *The End of the Trail*, or Edward S. Curtis's famous photograph of the wizened Red Cloud.

And yet, as if to remind us that the Indian lacks authority even to declare himself vanished, Davis's voiceover emerges one last time, now over the long shot of the ever-receding train: "Geronimo lived for another 22 years, as a prisoner of war. Despite its promise, the federal government never let him return." There is a strange consistency here, for the voiceover, in order that it may take up the Indian's cause, must be present at the first moment of the Indian's absence. The voiceover locates the Indian at the vanishing point, and there, of course, it also *dis*locates him. As the train continues its inexorable movement, the voiceover locates the birth of its own dehistoricized perspective, a privileged perspective destined to tell the Indian's story mostly for the sake of declaring its own freedom from the burden of Conquest.

7

Cultural dominance requires a continual reinvention of strategies of self-flattery. As the intent to refigure never fails to present an Indian on the verge of extinction, so neither does it fail to imply his donation of the American Garden to the white hero. Revision can do no better by way of delivering the Indian from his character of Savage Reactionary than by casting the Indian in the role that Marsden and Nachbar identify as the "Noble Anachronism." In this type, of which Fenimore Cooper's Uncas is prototype, the Indian is "characterized by a high degree of natural virtue made more poignant by the audience's knowledge that his race and probably he himself are doomed."[21] Of the many images of the noble victim in the Westerns under consideration, perhaps there is none more moving than that of Wind In His Hair, alone on his horse, high up on a ridge, waving his lance exultantly as Dances

21. "The Indian in the Movies," pp. 607–16.

With Wolves and Stands With A Fist ride out of the Lakota village, and shouting (subtitled as): "Dances With Wolves, I am Wind In His Hair. Do you see that I am your friend? Can you see that you will always be my friend?" The warrior's farewell to his white friend takes on the tone and tenor of a death chant. Wind In His Hair's status as Noble Anachronism implies the Indian's acquiescence in the inevitability of his vanishment.

Just before he vanishes, the Indian friend comes to understand his role in a higher destiny and accordingly entrusts the white hero with the land—a land now miraculously cleansed of blood and greed. When the white voice speaks for the Indian, the white hero is already enjoying his Edenic blessings. In this, of course, there shall be no blame: white voice may define the "new" Indian, may commend him to us, may even exalt him above us, but it cannot keep him from disappearing. Even as the voice marks the moment of the Indian's absence, it announces its own presence in a land made vacant but for the white hero's own presence in it—a land the very vacancy of which portends the coming of the great white hordes. And if such an outcome to the hero's story should suggest his collusion with the work of Conquest, the voiceover may yet produce the Vanishing American himself—his "return"—to certify the white man's rightful and righteous inheritance.

Of the Westerns in question, none so audaciously transforms the story of the Indian into the tale of Adamic inheritance as does *Cheyenne Autumn*. Neither Archer nor Deborah Wright (Carroll Baker), the Quaker missionary and love interest—nor any characters like them—appear in the Mari Sandoz novel that "suggested" the Ford movie. Yet *Cheyenne Autumn* makes its Cheyennes utterly dependent on these two—on Archer who, as we have seen, comes to take up their cause and then to tell their story, and on Deborah, who plays madonna to the Cheyenne children, and especially to a wounded girl (whom the Cheyennes of the Sandoz novel call "Lame Girl") on whose inchoate literacy she invests the better part of her missionary fervor.[22] But Deborah's true life's work is to temper Archer's initial Indian-hating with her zealous vision of Indian assimilation. In an early scene, she tolls the reservation school bell summoning the Cheyenne children (even as the

22. There is enormous—undetected?—irony in the drawings, not so crude as Deborah's puzzlement would seem to make them, that "Lame Girl" makes on her slate. One of them clearly depicts a buffalo, emblematic of her yearning for the ancestral land. Later, she draws a locomotive, emblem of her acculturation, but also of her surrender to the forces of empire. "Lame Girl" thus announces her dependence by an allusion to Ford's own *The Iron Horse*, made four decades earlier.

[164]

bell rings in the imminent passing of their culture). Inside the school-house, the following exchange takes place:

> *Archer*: All you've seen is reservation Indians, looking pitiful as fish out of water. But give them a chance [and] they're the greatest fighters in the world. . . . It takes a blue coat to make a white man a soldier, but a Cheyenne is a soldier from the first slap on his bottom. War is his life. He's fierce, he's smart, and he's meaner than sin.
> *Deborah*: Possibly you can only think of their past, but I'm here to think about the future.

They may disagree about the Indian "character," and about the difference between wild Cheyennes and reservation Cheyennes, and about past and future; yet the scene also holds the promise of a fine romance between these two. Indeed, the difference of opinions about the Cheyennes brings them together romantically. We know, then, the relative position of the Indian in the context of Hollywood concerns. It is difficult to separate the development of the romance from the evolution of Archer's ideas about the Cheyenne, and as difficult to distinguish the change in Deborah's regard for Archer from her concern for the Apaches. In the end, of course, the Cheyennes have no future, and their fate seems somehow a direct consequence of the good intentions of the white couple.

Archer, like *Sitting Bull*'s Parrish before him, travels to Washington, thus making of the trip east something of a generic convention. Ever fond of invoking Abraham Lincoln, Ford turns Archer's appeal to Secretary Schurz into an appeal to "The People," by way of the presumed moral authority of the martyred Emancipator. The cultural icon that blessed westward expansion in Ford's *The Iron Horse* precisely four decades before, now (though in spirit only) underwrites Archer's humanitarian mission on behalf of the Cheyennes. Before such morally irreproachable power, what would it matter that the Cheyennes approved or denounced Archer's errand? Of itself Archer's errand to Washington exempts him from the guilt that accrues to Wessels for his atrocities against the Cheyennes (atrocities clearly intended to recall the Holocaust, especially given the German Wessel's self-exoneration for having followed "orders"; yet atrocities that, precisely for their strong allusive quality, deflect American blame for genocide against native populations). More important, perhaps, as a contribution to the unfolding story of white paradisal aspirations, Archer's mission succeeds in finding the Cheyennes a home—their own ancestral home, the

[165]

DBS Arts Library

one for the sake of which they undertook the long and arduous journey from Indian Territory—even as he succeeds in securing for himself and Deborah the promised Canaan in the very vastness of an American West itself rendered guiltless and ahistorical by his humanitarian fervor. Let the Cheyennes live happily in their ancestral home, be it ever so humbly a reservation, a wall-less prison, rather than sacred soil. Lincoln's own anointed will make certain that their millennial tenure in the land does not defile the Indian's memory.

The peace ceremony at Victory Cave now concluded, Ford gives us a medium shot of Archer, Deborah, and "Lame Girl" stopping their buggy before the land on which the Cheyennes shall, presumably, remain. Looking wistfully into the distance, Deborah now lifts "Lame Girl" out and, kneeling beside her says, "Home, H-O-M-E, home." Then "Lame Girl": "H-O-M-E." Heretofore virtually voiceless, she repeats the word that stands for the place made alien by the selfsame language that makes the place possible. She complies apishly not only with the decree of her narrative dependence—and thus unwittingly accepts her identity as a cultural cripple—but, above all, with the language that, because it is not her own and implies the enforced forgetting of her own, implacably assigns her to the site of her vanishment. The girl walks offscreen (her own helpless enactment of the Vanishing American) even as the camera stays with Archer and Deborah, now delivered of their "burden." By the power of language to mask Conquest as Indian triumph, Archer and Deborah release "Lame Girl" into a world that now "belongs" to her only by virtue of the white couple's power to bequeath it to her—the same power, that is, that took it away from them in the first place and sent them to Indian Territory. This meager plat that is now hers circumscribes the full allotment of the white man's remorse, but its boundaries also demarcate the spaces beyond, that vastness wherein the Indian *plot*—the white man's story of his Indian brethren—would be so soon forgotten in the consummate enjoyment of Edenic blessedness.

AFTER THE LAKOTAS rescue Dances With Wolves and he is reunited with his wife, he announces his intention to leave the village. "The soldiers hate me now," he explains to the warriors, "like they hate no other. They think I am a traitor, and they will hunt for me." He leaves to save the village from the vindictive soldiers. "I will be leaving," he now adds. "I must go and talk with those who would listen." This is a strange deliverance, since "those who would listen" can only be white, and Dances With Wolves has cast virtually all whites in the role of barbaric villains and crude bigots. In some transparent sense, of course, *we* are "those who would listen"—those who *have been listening*—and we

Cheyenne Autumn (1964, Warner Bros.). Farewell to "Lame Girl." Courtesy of
Warner Bros./Museum of Modern Art Film Stills Archive.

eagerly exempt ourselves from complicity in the demise of the Indian.
The very history that scrolls up over the last image (the hero and his
wife riding slowly out of the village) would seem to imply that no one
listened *then*, that Dances With Wolves's appeal, say, to some Carl
Schurz or to the spirit of Lincoln, failed completely to prevent the demise of the Lakotas. The voiceover therefore emerges as the memory of
that which was heretofore unremembered, and thus as the summons,
now, to our own exemption *from* history—that is to say, from historical
guilt—by the act of "listening." Ours, to be sure, is not a connivance
against the Indian, but neither is it a New Age transcultural coalition of
common humanity. Ours shall be, instead, the covenant only with the
white hero and his ethical voiceover, and this bond constitutes our
hope of inclusion in Eden's happy tenantry.

Still, the Indian must authorize, if only perfunctorily, such a bargain
as we ourselves have struck with revisionism—even when the authorization seals his doom. What Indian, then, shall boldly step forth to
guarantee this double bond of ahistorical renunciation and exculpatory
remembrance between the voiceover and "those who would listen"?
No moment in *Dances With Wolves* so decisively certifies this union be-

tween us and the hero as that when the boy Smiles A Lot (Nathan Lee Chasing His Horse) returns the hero's journal. The journal has functioned throughout as the voiceover's correlative, indeed, as its very source, inscribing the action's revisionist ethos, authorizing the white hero's voiced insights and judgments. Dunbar had left the journal behind, at Fort Sedgewick, and when he returned to the fort to get it (fearing that the journal would lead the army to the Lakota village), the evil Corporal Spivey had already found it and appropriated it. In the aftermath of the battle to rescue Dances With Wolves, we see the journal floating unnoticed in the river's current. Now that Dances With Wolves and Stands With A Fist have said all their farewells, Smiles A Lot, his eyes brimming with tears, tenders the journal to its owner, who had given it up for lost. The gesture that appears unambiguously to validate the hero's authority to speak on behalf of the Indian also identifies Smiles A Lot—and by extension the Indian generally—as an agent of the voiceover, and thus of his own conquest. (Smiles A Lot, of course, has recently killed the loathsome Sergeant Bauer [Larry Joshua], and to that extent he has become a man; but the child still rules in him, so that here again, as in *Cheyenne Autumn*, the infantilized native appears among our last views of the Indian.) The young Lakota may have rescued the chronicle of his own humanity, the archival source that makes it possible to remember his race, but the selfsame recovery of the writing also signals his end. As a trope in the service of revisionism, the voiceover prefigures the Noble Anachronism's last noble gesture—namely, his acquiescence in a historical destiny not of his own making. When he tenders the journal, Smiles A Lot seems to understand that his inscription in white history, though it may present itself as his salvation, as his deliverance from the ages of vilification, also spells his end. In this understanding all resistance dissolves.

JOHN A. PRICE reports that a serial of the mid-1930s, *Scouts to the Rescue*, gave the Indians their language "by running their normal English dialogue backwards." "By keeping them relatively motionless when they spoke," Price explains, "the picture could be printed in reverse and a perfect lipsync maintained."[23] Crude indeed, yet such a technique only echoed the centuries-old belief that the language of the Other—which was by both conception and definition his *linguistic*

23. John A. Price, "The Stereotyping of North American Indians in Motion Pictures," in *The Pretend Indians: Images of Native Americans in the Movies*, ed. Gretchen M. Bataille and Charles P. Silet (Ames: Iowa State University Press, 1980), p. 80.

lack—articulated only savagery's rash and doomed opposition to civilization, bespoke accordingly its own incoherence and so declared *non-language*, perhaps even silence, as the Indian's essential "language." Conquest's very first day—October 12, 1492—already declared that the Indian had *no language*: "I, please Our Lord, will carry off six of them at my departure to Your Highnesses, that they may learn to speak." [24] And thus, perhaps, did that first day already foretell the birth of that "language," itself concocted and supervised by Conquest, whereby the Indian could affirm only his narrative dependence. Power was the white man's not because of what the Indian said or failed to say, or because of how the Indian said it; neither was power the white man's merely because of what he himself said, in his uniquely eloquent way, about either himself or the Indian; power was his, rather, because it belonged to him to give it to or withhold it from the Indian—to present the Indian as a *mute*; to render his voice as a linguistic grotesquery; to reverse language itself (always "*The* Language," no less) thereby to produce a babbling commensurate with the savage himself; to deprive him, then, not only of language merely, or even of *lexis*, but of *logos* itself, so to account fully for his irrational resistance to civilization.

The revisionist Indian Western invokes no less absolute a possession of the Indian's speech. Language is the white man's no less absolutely for articulating the idea of Indian "humanity" than for promoting that of Indian "savagery." "According to Arnold Krupat," Susan Scheckel notes in *The Insistence of the Indian*,

> much of the writing about Indians produced in the East after 1830 was motivated, by a desire for "historical justice." However, Krupat maintains that those works about Indians written by a white man could not succeed in the textual redress of injustice since they "never went so far as to grant the Indian the right to speak for himself. Whatever the wrongs and injuries [the white author] protested, he was not yet able to protest in the actual form of his work what Gilles Deleuze has called the indignity of speaking for others." [25]

24. The translation from the Spanish that I quote here and in the epigraph is quite literal. See *The Diario*, p. 68. Todorov notes that the last clause, *para que aprendan a hablar* ("in order that they may learn to speak") so shocked Columbus's various French translators that all of them corrected the statement to: " 'so that they may learn our language.' " "The first, spontaneous reaction with regard to the stranger is to imagine him as inferior, since he is different from us: . . . if he does not speak our language, it is because he speaks none at all, *cannot* speak, as Columbus still believed." Tzvetan Todorov, *The Conquest of America: The Question of the Other*, trans. Richard Howard (New York: Harper and Row, 1984), pp. 30, 76.
25. Susan Scheckel, *The Insistence of the Indian: Race and Nationalism in Nineteenth-Century American Culture* (Princeton: Princeton University Press, 1998), p. 117.

At the very beginning of *Broken Arrow*, Tom Jeffords rides alone in the Arizona desert, about to meet the wounded Apache boy, but his *voice* already inhabits a different world, one where the historical struggle between civilization and savagery has ended, the Indian has "passed," and the white hero, though disavowing complicity in Conquest, now atones for the sins of his race by remembering the true Indian in the true course of events: "This is the story of a land, of the people who lived on it in the year 1870, and of a man whose name was Cochise. He was an Indian, leader of the Chiricahua Apache tribe. I was involved in the story, and what I have to tell happened exactly as you'll see it. The only change will be that, when the Apaches speak, they will speak in our language." "The only change" makes all the difference. For only by *appearing* to speak in their native language, while in fact speaking in the conqueror's own, and *seeming* to voice their impassioned resistance, while voicing their abject compliance instead, does such a reenvisioned Indian appear, in the end, to be more authentic than the savage of the canonical Western.

Part II
Typology, Identity,
and the Uses of Indianness

[4]

"Chartered in Two Worlds"

The Double Other

Finalmente nunca [se] pudo acabar con los indios creer que eramos de los otros christianos./ To the last we could not convince the Indians that we were the other sort of Christians.
—Alvar Núñez Cabeza de Vaca, *La Relación* (1542)

"I reckon right then I come pretty close to turning pure Indian." Little Big Man (on the occasion of the birth of his half-Cheyenne son).
—*Little Big Man* (Penn)

1

Ask the canonical Western to show you just how menacing and cruel its Indian can be, how complete an embodiment of civilization's most disquieting dread; or alternately, ask the revisionist Western to produce its noble Indian, an Indian as authentic in his wisdom as in his humanity, and in both cases you will more than likely see not the Western's *Indian*—that is, neither its bloodthirsty and befeathered savage nor its enlightened if melancholy native—but rather such an "Indian" as it produces through, and at last in, *the white hero himself*. To look for the savage Indian in the Western—to seek the full-formed enemy of civilization who is reputed to be as formidable as he is fierce—is to find him in that paradoxical figure, the Indian fighter. Alternatively, to seek the reconfigured Indian (at once typical and wise) in the revisionist Western is to discover him as a similarly paradoxical figure in the white protagonist. Everything else that claims to represent the *native* comes to us in the forms of appropriated voices or usurped perspectives, of that nexus of familiar yet specious tokens of cultural identity that present him as a virtual absence. I hardly mean to propose that Hollywood's white hero is unimpeachably authentic. But Hollywood, which has so undeviatingly followed the lead of the mythic legacy of representation, promotes and perpetuates the illusion—what I call below the "mystique"—that its white hero can fully articulate, represent, even embody, its native Other. Indeed, the white hero's Indianness is itself the mark of his greatness, though it be the Indian that he fights in the name of civilization. The present chapter explores the paradox whereby the Myth of Conquest would glorify its white hero for his capacity to become the very Indian whose savage abjectness justifies his defeat and disappearance. Representation presupposes appropriation: the figure itself of the Other already substantiates the dominance of the Same. Yet representation, precisely because it presumes arrogation, can exhibit its own inverse; it implicates the Same—the supposed unalterable—in a *process*, in an unintended and disconcerting metamorphosis: the Same becomes itself appropriated by its own invention, by its own creation of Otherness, of Indianness—of savagery, then.

Rightly, no doubt, have the native peoples themselves reviled Hollywood's Indian stereotypes, since these are the images that at once contain and project the five centuries of opprobrium that Conquest has heaped on the American Indian. And as rightly have they raised their voices against the purportedly revised Indian.[1] For even the Indian that Hollywood presents as noble and wise seems often to be so only on condition that he be also doomed. But the protest against Hollywood's Indian has seldom entertained the proposition, central to this chapter, that the Western presents its most complete Indian through the white hero.

Through the white Indian fighter (say, *The Searchers'* Ethan Edwards), as through the white friend of the Indian (perhaps in *Dances With Wolves'* Lieutenant Dunbar), we learn more about the Indian than we can from any Indian characters. The Indian fighter may, accordingly, know the Indians completely only to destroy them: hence Ethan Edwards. Or he may know them as completely so as to memorialize them: hence Lieutenant Dunbar. In either case, however, the white hero remains our preeminent authority on "all things pertaining to the Indian" (to generalize from a claim made in *Geronimo* by Lieutenant Davis). *Convention* has it so. How often does the Western bother with the details of the hero's apprenticeship among the Indians? And *con-*

---

1. Principally in Ward Churchill's essay on *Dances With Wolves* in *Fantasies of the Master Race: Literature, Cinema, and the Colonization of American Indians* (Monroe, Maine: Common Courage Press, 1992).

sent, "our" consent, has it so. *We* accept and endorse this intimacy of the hero's with the Indian, accept and endorse it, paradoxically, even as we agree that it belongs exclusively to the white hero. Moreover, the hero enlists—though more likely he enforces—the Indian's *own* consent. For example, in *The Searchers* Chief Scar confirms his vengeful nature when he tells Ethan and Martin how many white people he kills for each of his sons killed by the whites. In *Dances With Wolves* Kicking Bird authorizes Dunbar's power to "speak to those who would listen" when he (Kicking Bird) says to him, toward the end (and in English), "We've come far, you and me." Both convention and consent function as derivatives of the phenomenon that Richard Slotkin has called the "characteristic American gesture." In times of adversity, Slotkin writes, the American seeks "immersion in the native element, the wilderness, as the solution to all problems, the balm to all wounds of the soul, the restorative for failing fortunes. If the woods hold terrors, embrace them as signs of nature's power and God's. Do not flee from them, but master them, and make them your own powers. And if this requires that you become an Indian, then do so."[2]

Convention and consent become manifest in the various roles that the hero performs seamlessly and simultaneously, as if both the roles and the performances engaged him in no discernible inconsistency. As protagonist, he is, of course, the center of the action; yet he is also the *agent* of a specific ideology. Furthermore, he monopolizes discourse about the Indian, so that he is at once the focus of that discourse and the source of its dissemination. Whether as Indian fighter or as friend of the Indian, the hero, we might say, both *contains* and *denies* the Indian. The Indian that he claims to know so well is also an Indian made Other by and through just such a knowledge. So to know the Indian is to deny him any but a tributary presence. So to know him is to cast him, friend or foe, as an alien.

This chapter attempts to reconstruct the heroic type that at once contains and denies the Indian. Beyond the Indian's virtual absence as synecdoche, beyond the usurped perspective, beyond the Indian's dependence on the white man's discourse—in short, beyond all the stratagems and strategies that we examined in Part 1—there lies another, more subtle way of presenting him while dispensing with him. Yet this chapter is not so much about the sort of Indian that the white hero personifies (or is it impersonates?), but rather about the construction of a type out of the Myth of Conquest's unquestioned assumption that its

2. *Regeneration through Violence,* p. 267.

Dances With Wolves (1990, Orion Pictures). Stalking buffalo, becoming Lakota. Courtesy of Orion Pictures/Museum of Modern Art Film Stills Archive.

hero can in fact personify the Indian. Such an assumption—the assumption itself as much as its uncritical status—has its consequences, of course, even, as we shall see, its penalties. If the hero's intimacy with the Indian declares the Indian at once superfluous and alien, then the selfsame intimacy tends to subvert the hero's own identity as the anointed of the Myth of Conquest. Does the hero then lose his identity as hero for turning so thoroughly Indian—even when such a "turn" seems an essential constituent of his identity as hero? How are we to identify a hero whose supposedly faultless Indianness *others* him even as it certifies the Sameness that the Myth of Conquest requires of him in so exemplary a degree? Let us further elaborate upon the ambiguously heroic type under consideration by recourse to the possibilities for identity suggested by a claim made in a recent Indian Western.

Allow yourself for a moment to consider only the *propositional* value of the following statement: "I could be an Indian." Briefly suspend your curiosity about identities—the movie's, the speaker's, or even that of the various contexts in which the declaration might easily fit—dramatic, historical, cultural, and so on. Even when taken in near-isolation (it is of course impossible to dissociate it from all contexts), the proposition discloses a tension. Its *economy*, moreover, enables us to introduce a critique of the most stubborn assumption that the Indian Western de-

[176]

rives from the Myth of Conquest—namely, the uncontested conviction that it can produce a white hero who is authentically Indian in every respect, even as it presents the Indian—friend *or* foe—as an irredeemable Other.

Examined, then, as a plain proposition, the utterance announces the possibility of cultural conversion even as it tends to undermine it: if the speaker were in fact an Indian, the statement would be not only superfluous but downright absurd. To be such an Indian—an Indian *possibly*, perhaps *conditionally*—precludes one's being so at the moment of the utterance. If, however, the speaker *could be* an Indian, then such a likelihood itself would necessarily require a condition or a contingency for its realization—say, a specific temporal event when the transformation shall come about. Yet the declaration carries no stated condition or contingency that ensures its fulfillment. Accordingly, the eventuality of being Indian comes to be known, impossibly enough, by that which can never in fact occur. It is a prospect indefinitely deferred, and as such no prospect at all but rather an illusion (a wish?)—perhaps no more than a boast. The declaration itself tends to frustrate the identity that the speaker claims he can assume: the speaker's own conviction that he (and it is a "he") "could be" an Indian already articulates the impossibility that he shall *ever* be one: he "could be" an Indian *because he is irrevocably white*. Who the speaker is, I will reveal presently, after attending to a similar claim.

When he came to tell the tale of his adventures in the trans-Mississippi West, the young Francis Parkman explained his motive thus:

> I had come into the country almost exclusively with a view of observing the Indian character. Having from childhood felt a curiosity on this subject, and having failed completely to gratify it by reading, I resolved to have recourse to observation. I wished to satisfy myself with regard to the position of the Indians among the races of men; the vices and the virtues that have sprung from their innate character and from their modes of life, their government, their superstitions, and their domestic situation. To accomplish my purpose it was necessary to live in the midst of them, and become, as it were, one of them.[3]

Surely an inexhaustibly resourceful mythology assists at the birth of such claims and just as surely nurtures them. The belief in a racio-cultural metamorphosis becomes embedded in the dominant culture until at last it becomes an unchallenged premise of its foundation.

3. *The Oregon Trail*, p. 111.

Here Parkman entertains little doubt of his capacity to become Indian. Self-othering (auto-alterity) produces an unquestioned (though hardly unquestionable) authority; and the *as it were* that qualifies the purported alteration seems to function not—or at least not only—as an acknowledgement of the limits of cultural conversion, but as reassurance to his readers back East: the power *to become* Other must be balanced by the power to resist the *surrender* to Otherness. We may recall here that Parkman the racialist held fast to the idea that "the races of men" are ranked in predetermined positions. The Indian will never rise to the level of the white man, and certainly not to that of the Boston Brahmin. Accordingly, Parkman's Indianness implies a *descent* into savagery. Yet the *as it were* would assure us that his whiteness remains irreproachable, despite contact with the very Indians in the "midst" of whom he hopes to "accomplish his purpose." And so, the purpose more or less realized, it becomes necessary for Parkman to supply the needed reassurance. He did not become Indian, except *as it were*, and "observation" led him to his well known conclusion about the Indian: "For the most part, a civilized white man can discover but very few points of sympathy between his own nature and that of an Indian. With every disposition to do justice to their good qualities, he must be conscious that an impassable gulf lies between him and his red brethren of the prairie."[4]

If the illustrious Brahmin could venture into the spaces of savage spectacle and then confidently chart the geography of cultural difference, would the nation not be thereby emboldened to complete the work of Conquest? The conversion, moreover, could be accomplished in a trice, a simple cultural legerdemain to exhibit the power of the practitioner's art; and the trick would have no influence on the magician; it altered him not one jot. Whom, however, was Parkman reassuring, his readers or himself? Besides, was reassurance all that could be read into Parkman's conclusion about racial difference? Can we not find here, in the very effort to soothe white anxieties (or perhaps Parkman's own), an avowal of the *failure* of cultural conversion? Did Parkman become Indian and *then* take his position across the vast cultural spaces that divide him from the Indian; or does his remark on the "impassable gulf" belie the ready assumption that he could be an Indian, even if so much more modest a being as an Indian *as it were*? When we see Parkman, for example, as we did in our second chapter, a civilized man revolted by the spectacle of Lakotas devouring a freshly killed

---

4. Ibid., p. 242.

buffalo, do we not see him implicitly invoking the *as it were*? Did such a revulsion not contribute to compel Parkman's *construction* (rather than disinterested "observation") of the racio-cultural distance as "impassable"? More important, however, did the failure of cultural conversion, once acknowledged in the form of radical cultural difference, also indicate *the possible failure of the type itself*? That is to say, if we are to know the type by his unrestricted ability to become Indian, then what had we come to know when the type insisted on his absolute *difference* from the Indian? And did the possible failure of the type not suggest the limitations of the mythology that had so enthusiastically begotten, nurtured, and consecrated it?

The mythologies of national self-definition unfold in carefree ignorance of their own self-subverting tendencies. Thus the claim of identity with the Indian maps the irreducible, perhaps indeed the "impassable," distance between the Other and the Same. In the cultural spaces that separate the white subject-Same from the Indian object-Other, we find the persistent racio-cultural in-betweenness, the enduring flux between denial and affirmation, identity and difference, that characterizes the heroic figures of the Myth of Conquest. Yet we will do well to keep in mind that the declaration, "I could be an Indian," is no less compelling for being so thoroughly implausible, nor any less powerful for all its ironies.

2

"I could be an Indian." The speaker is none other than George Armstrong Custer, played by Gary Cole, in *Son of the Morning Star*, the TV miniseries based, for the most part, on the book by Evan S. Connell. The scene in which Custer claims that he "could be an Indian" compresses a series of events often documented in histories of the Sioux Wars. In the movie, Gen. Alfred H. Terry, who commands the army of Dakota Territory, relays to Custer orders from Washington that he, Custer, is to remain at Fort Abraham Lincoln when the Seventh Cavalry rides against Sitting Bull's "non-treaty" Sioux. Custer implores Terry: "Does anyone know what lies out there, beyond the cities and the newspapers? Does anyone know the thin line that separates the Indian from the soldier the way I do? I could be an Indian! I can find them! The President is crucifying me! [*Kneels before Terry, who is embarrassed by the unabashed emotion of the entreaty*] I appeal to you, as a soldier, to spare me the humiliation of seeing my regiment march to meet the enemy and I not share in its dangers."[5] Custer claims to know Indians so intimately as to be himself an Indian.[6] He will become an "Indian" so that he may find the Indians and destroy them. Thus, when Custer affirms that he "could be" an Indian, he means to cast himself as an Indian *fighter*. We must not doubt that Custer's claim has a simple, practical motive behind it: in order to defeat the Indian it is necessary to know him, to think like him, to act like him, at last to become him. A part, at least, of this process is surely ingrained in the prosecution of all wars. But we are interested chiefly not in the strategies whereby the white hero plans to defeat the enemy, but in the *identity* that is likely to emerge—that emerges already before the encounter—out of the confident avowal: "I could be an Indian." What does such a pronouncement assume about the Other and his culture? Or about what it means to *become* the Other? Indeed, what does it imply about being and becoming—or about "descent" and "consent"—as sources of cultural identity? How does the assurance of such a becoming produce, instead, uncertainty about the hero's identity, perhaps even about his allegiance? Does the claim not somehow contain its own countervailing (and all-too-disturbing) *Indian* claim: "I could be a white man"? Who, then, certifies the hero's Indianness, and by what authority? What ignorance of its attendant penalties does such a becoming betray?

The very impossibility that the hero should satisfy his claim of cultural alteration without sin or forfeiture—without irony, even—contributes as much to his identity as does his sanguine avowal of an uncomplicated cultural conversion. Hence his discontents, and those, also, of the Myth that promotes him. And hence, too, the complicated idea that drives and shapes the present chapter. Caught in such a play of racio-cultural forces—of ambiguous types and self-subverting claims—one is struck by the intricacies of this assurance whereby the

5. The historical event on which the scene from *Son of the Morning Star* is based took place in Saint Paul on May 6, 1876. Robert Utley writes that Terry "later confided to intimates [how] Custer, 'with tears in his eyes, begged my aid. How could I resist it?'" The words that the movie attributes to Custer, beginning, "I appeal to you . . ." and which he there directs to Terry, were in fact from a telegram to President Grant, composed (and endorsed) by *Terry* and signed by Custer. See Robert M. Utley, *Cavalier in Buckskin: George Armstrong Custer and the Western Military Frontier* (Norman: University of Oklahoma Press, 1988), p. 162.

6. The filmmakers may have derived Custer's claim from his book of 1874 (serialized two years earlier in *The Galaxy*): "If I were an Indian, I often think I would greatly prefer to cast my lot among those of my people who adhered to the free open plains rather than submit to the confined limits of a reservation, there to be the recipient of the blessed benefits of civilization, with its vices thrown in without stint or measure." George Armstrong Custer, *My Life on the Plains or, Personal Experiences with the Indians* (Norman: University of Oklahoma Press, 1962), p. 22. See also Utley, *Cavalier in Buckskin*, p. 149.

Indian fighter presents himself as an authentic Indian. The identities of protagonist and antagonist, so seemingly clear in a subgenre commonly considered heavy-handed and guileless, can nevertheless confound us with the vagueness of their boundaries. In the construction of such an identity, then, it is unwise to dodge complexity. The search for simplicity is a noble thing, but the distrust of it, though less often counseled, should be no less useful a habit of mind. "The prizes in the game of ethnic, moral, and cultural superiority," writes June Namias on the same issue and subject, "are more easily won than the understanding one might gain with a clearer but more complex vision."[7] As the Indian in the Western comes to be characterized by both virtual absence and imminent presence, so too does the white hero.[8]

As we saw in earlier chapters, the white man claims the authority to speak for and define the Indian. But the Myth of Conquest insists that such appropriations of Indianness, however much they may presume to be as thorough as they are valid, must not, in the end, produce a racio-cultural *crossover* on the hero's part. Instead, we are to interpret these appropriations as clear evidence of the hero's unimpeachable whiteness and not of a cultural backsliding: his power to become Other somehow confirms his Sameness. Somehow, he is one of "us" because he has become one of "them." Yet, as I hope to show in greater detail in the next chapter, the white hero's authority in matters concerning the Other invariably undermines his Sameness. Thus, the identity that I am trying to illuminate requires that the claim of the Indian fighter be in fact somehow fulfilled—that he become Indian—even as it also requires that such a fulfillment take the form of the claim's subversion—so that his purported Indianness upholds his whiteness. I am not referring now to the subversion of the hero's authority about things Indian; principally, I am referring to the subversion of his identity *by virtue of the authority that he does in fact possess.* The lance that kills Jorgensen's prize bull is indeed "Comanch'," as

---

7. June Namias, *White Captives: Gender and Ethnicity on the American Frontier* (Chapel Hill: University of North Carolina Press, 1993), p. 202.

8. Although I derive my model for a self-subverting heroic type from *Son of the Morning Star*, I note that this film, perhaps more than any other, authorizes both the Indian and the Indian voice in a compelling and rather novel way. The voiceover narration is shared by two women, Libbie Custer and Kate Bighead, just as the story itself brings balance to the history and drama of the Plains Indian Wars by attending alternately to Custer and Crazy Horse as the principals in whose respective persons the two cultures are vested. The technique is neither perfect nor evenhanded: clearly, for example, Libbie has more speaking parts and more scenes that Kate Bighead, and so similarly does Custer than Crazy Horse, who almost never speaks. Nonetheless, the technique makes of *Son of the Morning Star* a revisionist Western apart.

Ethan says it is; for Ethan knows things Indian. His knowledge of the Indian, indeed his virtual intimacy with him, somehow certifies Ethan's whiteness. Yet it also, and at the same time, invalidates it. Thus the white hero's Indianness as well as his whiteness, both, must be at once necessary and impossible.

If Custer's declaration inherently contests the possibility that he should become Indian, it does not quite *falsify* it. Custer's is an indelible racio-cultural *doubleness*, and this doubleness would be no such thing were it to be composed merely of a counterfeit Indian opposed by an authentic one. Instead, each of the components of his doubleness is engaged in both subverting and validating the other. To this general male type exemplified by this version of Custer I give the name *Double Other;* the indeterminate cultural quality that identifies the type I designate as *double Otherness.*[9] Double Otherness does not answer to the notion of a reconstituted Self—a Self, that is, in which the component yet contending cultural forces are now reconciled in a unity of identity. Nor does it refer to a cultural catholicity that points to the hero's open-mindedness and attests to his lofty status as citizen of the world. The forces that comprise him abide in continual contention, so that we can often detect, seething just beneath the heroic surface, a chaos of curses: his own against the Indian for compelling him, for good or ill, to become him; against himself for having betrayed his cultural inheritance; his own, yet this time as Indian, against the ethos of Conquest, so that his Indianness does not now afford him an Edenic foothold but becomes, instead, the source of his guilt; his own against his original culture, then, for propagating the seductive illusion that he can become Other and still be (and be known as) Same; and, in the end, against the mythology that sponsored his transformation only to condemn him, in the very instant of his triumph, for having effected it so successfully.

And yet I hold that, despite this at times bewildering mix of powers that contend for his soul, the Double Other is *integrally* himself, if only because his integrity affirms a devastating duality. *He realizes the heroic*

9. I came by these terms, *Double Other* and *double Otherness,* empirically, which is to say, during the natural course of my studies in the Indian Western and its mythic and historical contexts. So much said, however, I acknowledge the term "double other" in Gerald Vizenor's *Manifest Manners.* Vizenor identifies a different entity by his term—namely, the Native American who participates in both his tribal world and that of the conqueror's. When the Native American successfully negotiates the differences between the two worlds, he is a "postindian warrior of survivance." See, for example, pp. 45, 168, 169, 174.

*ideal of his culture and embodies its most exalted being by becoming his cul-
ture's very idea of savage Otherness.* To this fundamental paradox of white
male heroic identity we must quickly add a corollary: if we come to
know him as the opposite of that which he "could be," it is because, if
only by the ambiguous precepts of the mythology that he obeys, he did
in fact become just such a being. The continual fluctuations between
Sameness and Otherness reveal such stability as there is to the type. His
double Otherness itself distinguishes him from the mere "half-breed"
or the renegade—not only because these are their own types in the
Myth but because their identities as such hold neither mystery nor possibility nor resonance. The Double Other's is not an identity *fragmented*
(since that would posit an archaeology of recovery that can assemble
shards into a whole) but *composite.* He is, as the philosopher Babbal-
anja, in Melville's *Mardi,* might put it, "twain—yet indivisible; all
things—yet a poor unit at best."

Before continuing with this description of the Double Other, I note
that there are many variants of the basic type. For example, the "renegade" of the Simon Girty and Alexander McKee variety (exemplified
in the Western by the villain Deroux [named Bauman in foreign prints]
in Ford's *The Iron Horse*), shows certain affinities with the Double
Other, for he is originally white and has "become" Indian. Indeed, the
early history of Conquest suggests a primal division between the renegade and the Double Other. In 1519, when Cortés arrives in Cozumel,
he directs some of his men to investigate rumors of Spaniards living
among the Indians. One of them, Jerónimo de Aguilar, returns to the
Spaniards after eight years among the Indians and becomes an important agent of Conquest, principally by virtue of his talents as transla-
tor. The second, however, Gonzalo Guerrero, stays behind, explaining
to Aguilar: "I am married and have three children and the Indians look
on me as a Cacique and captain in wartime—You go, and God be with
you, but I have my face tattooed and my ears pierced, what would the
Spaniards say should they see me in this guise?"[10] Of course, the famous Alvar Núñez Cabeza de Vaca must have looked very little like
an *hidalgo* when he returned to Mexico after eight years of wandering
among the Indians. But double Otherness, even in its archetypal
forms, would emphasize the ability of the white man not only to become Indian, like Guerrero, but to defeat them for so having become.

10. Genaro García, ed., *The Discovery and Conquest of Mexico, 1517–1521,* by Bernal Díaz
del Castillo, trans. A. P. Maudslay (New York: Farrar, Straus and Cudahy, 1956), p. 43.

The Gentleman of Elvas, chronicler of DeSoto, tells of Juan Ortiz, living among the Indians in the town of Sancti Spiritus, in Cuba for 12 years. A ship

> sailing along the coast had in her a very sick man, who begged to be set on shore, which the captain directly ordered, and the vessel kept on her way. The inhabitants, finding him where he had been left, on that shore which had never yet been hunted up by Christians, carried him home, and took care of him until he was well. The chief of the town gave him a daughter; and being at war with the country round about, through the prowess and exertion of the Christian he subdued and reduced to his control all the people of Cuba.[11]

Here is the original of Capt. John Smith, perhaps of Daniel Boone, of the heroes of *A Man Called Horse*, of *Dances With Wolves*. The "fantasies of the master race" have historical foundations, however shaky and decayed.

There is a native Indian type in the Western that may well be, himself, Double Other: he is the usual companion of the white hero, and he labors in the service of civilization. This is, of course, the type of which Cooper's Chingachgook is prototype and of which Wind In His Hair (*Dances With Wolves*) is a worthy epigone, though my loose definition would certainly admit the witless and debased Poordevil (Hank Worden) of Hawks's *The Big Sky*, even as it inevitably invokes the Lone Ranger's own Tonto. The next chapter will take up the double Otherness of the white man—no longer clearly the hero—who becomes Indian; but in this chapter the Double Other identifies mostly a white hero who, however much he may have adopted Indian ways and even when he explicitly censures the dreams of a civilized West, acts as an agent of the Myth of Conquest. Sometimes despite his Indianness, sometimes through it, the type of Double Other under consideration validates and justifies the ideals and aspirations of white civilization.

This doubleness—this sort of typological evasiveness that yet indelibly stamps the hero—finds apt confirmation in the very concept itself of the *frontier*. The Double Other bestrides the line that is said to divide savagery from civilization. He becomes accordingly an incarnate national geography—himself, like his country, the battleground of con-

11. Theodore H. Lewis, ed., *The Narrative of the Expedition of Hernando de Soto by the Gentleman of Elvas*, trans. Buckingham Smith, in *Original Narratives of Early American History: Spanish Explorers in the Southern United States, 1528–1543* (New York: Charles Scribner's Sons, 1907), pp. 144–45.

flicting impulses, ideas, images. Friend or foe of the Indian, he is by his very nature lost to "civilization," to the idea that endorsed and promoted his errand into the wilderness—lost, then, even if the selfsame errand produces something that calls itself civilized, and even if the new order learns that it can call itself civilized only for having made an outcast of him whose savagery it abetted.

The frontier, Frederick Jackson Turner told us more than a century ago, produces the American. Begotten of the conflict between civilization and savagery, straddling the fine line between history and myth, the triumphant American hero stakes out his exceptional status and character. With this I have no real quarrel, or at least not one that is relevant here. Nor do I necessarily dispute the assertion that the dialectic between civilization and savagery produces the American—an American synthesis, so to say. For that synthesis corresponds to my own assertion, just now, that the white hero, though he may become savage for civilization's sake, is still himself integrally. I contest only the assumption, implicit throughout the famous "Thesis," that the American, in becoming just such a creature, resolves (perhaps dissolves) the opposing forces that fashion him, as if the old elements were lost in the new chemical. In other words, I hold that the concentration of the contending forces that design and construct him does not thereby constitute a resolution of the conflict, or a dissolution of the constituent elements (to stick to the chemical metaphor). He is an American, rather, because his identity *perpetuates* the two opposing tendencies that constitute him. Thus, while the type tends toward an equivocal identity, it consistently produces the image and idea in which America may readily recognize both itself and its Indian. And if such images and ideas reek with implausibility, they are not for that reason any less dear to a nation that continually calls upon them to reconfirm its sense of self. Custer's contention in *Son of the Morning Star* should stand as the first law of double Otherness, its maxim and its axiom alike, both its immediate identification and its own radical subversion.

In the next chapter I address the crisis of the Double Other by elaborating on the *ambivalence* to which the type is almost always doomed. Still, since this ambivalence is sufficiently grounded in double Otherness to be, indeed, its inevitable outcome, we would do well to provide a brief illustration, if only by way of anticipating the penalties of double Otherness. A scene from *Broken Arrow* will do, for the moment. Now that Jeffords and Sonseeahray tell Cochise that they plan to marry, Cochise advises:

[185]

It will not be easy for you. You're an American. Where will you live? Here? There will always be Apaches who have suffered from white men who will hate you for it. Tucson, maybe? Will there not always be whites who will hate your wife because of the color of her skin? You will go far away, maybe, to new places, but your eyes will never see anything. Always they will be turned backwards, toward home. And you, Sonseeahray, they will look at you as a strange animal, and make jokes. Hear me, Tall One, . . . is it not better to live with your own?

"Your own"? Just who would that be, now that Cochise has effectively determined that both the hero and his bride will be outcasts wherever they go? The placelessness itself that Cochise prophesies for the couple only replicates the couple's indistinct identity, an identity not so much inchoate or emergent or even uncertain as enduringly ambiguous. The Double Other, who would inherit the American Eden by his overcoming of the nation's racial history, seems instead doomed to isolation. Moreover, as J. Douglas Canfield brilliantly comments on the historical and cultural implications of the very passage that I cite above,

> [a] contemporary Arizona audience knows that the state antimiscegenation ordinance stayed on the books until the U.S. Supreme Court overturned it in 1977! Within the context of the film, the miscegenation will not overcome Jeffords's loneliness but simply compound it. He will not have completed a successful crossing [of cultures] over and back. He will not have completed even a full crossing over, a full going native. The children Sonseeahray envisions will ride no white horses. They will remain mavericks.[12]

Or Double Others. Perhaps, then, the Indian Western obeys more than convention when it casts both the Indian fighter Ethan and the friend of the Indian Jeffords alone in the desert at the end of the action. Overwhelmed by irreconcilable identities, they become outcasts, neither white nor Indian for being both at once.

The type to which I have given the name Double Other corresponds quite precisely to a version of the type that Richard Slotkin, in *Gunfighter Nation*, calls "the man who knows Indians": "As the 'man who knows Indians,' the frontier hero stands between the opposed worlds of savagery and civilization, acting sometimes as mediator or interpreter between races and cultures but more often as civilization's most effective instrument against savagery—a man who knows how to think and fight like an Indian, to turn their methods against

---

12. J. Douglas Canfield, *Mavericks on the Border: The Early Southwest in Historical Fiction and Film* (Lexington: University Press of Kentucky, 2001), p. 57.

Broken Arrow (1950, 20th Century Fox). Marrying into the tribe. Courtesy of 20th Century Fox/Museum of Modern Art Film Stills Archive.

them."[13] The constituent elements of this type, as I suggested earlier, appear readily enough in the claim that Custer makes in *Son of the Morning Star*. Thus, much later in *Gunfighter Nation*, Slotkin describes the basic form of action in which this version of the Double Other typically engages: "To defeat a savage enemy who will not fight by civilized rules or limit his ferocity to 'legitimate' objectives, civilization must discover and empower 'the man who knows Indians'—an agent of 'White' civilization who is so intimate with the enemy's way of thinking that he can destroy that enemy with his own weapons."[14] The Double Other, as I have so far sketched him, clearly answers to such a description, but the description does not quite exhaust his possible manifestations. Circumscribed by the requirements of Slotkin's typology, the Double Other could not encompass the friend of the Indian, or the white near-Indian—typological variants who deploy their knowledge of the Indian to *save* themselves from the "blessings of civilization." More important, the traits that define Slotkin's "man who

13. *Gunfighter Nation*, p. 16.
14. Ibid., p. 431.

[187]

knows Indians" leave out a quality that seems to me crucial, and which I find in equal evidence in both the Indian fighter and the friend of the Indian. The Double Other's knowledge of the Indians extends not only to a knowledge of how to defeat them; his knowledge is also of the sort that makes him an authority on the Indian. He is, accordingly, the principal source of most of what we can come to know about the Indian. Indeed, more than that the Indian is this or that sort of creature, the Double Other often teaches no more clear lesson than that *he* is our unchallenged authority on Indians, regardless of whether he kills them or befriends them. I now attend to the implied methodology whereby the Western authorizes the Double Other.

3

As the Indian Western continually avails itself of a respectable citizenry in order to point out the singular persistence, even the excesses, of the heroic Indian fighter, so does it require Indian-hating whites to highlight the virtues of the heroic friend of the Indian. In the revisionist *Broken Arrow*, for instance, an Indian hater by the name of Ben Slade (Will Geer) despises Tom Jeffords for his efforts to make peace with Cochise. Shortly after Jeffords enters the town, he tells a small gathering about his enlightening encounter with the wounded Apache boy, whom he has nursed back to full health. Then Slade remarks: "Maybe Captain Jeffords became too friendly with the Apaches. Maybe he doesn't know what side he's on. [*Jeffords, insulted, charges at Slade*] I'm not looking for trouble, but if you don't fight against them you're with them, and I've got a right to say that." More than four decades after *Broken Arrow*, Walter Hill's *Geronimo* would resort to a similar strategy in order to identify the Double Other as the heroic friend of the Indian. Al Sieber (Robert Duvall), angry at Lieutenant Gatewood's implicit trust of the army's Apache scouts, addresses him as follows: "No offense intended, Lieutenant, speaking off the record, sir. I just figure you're a real sad case: you don't love who you're fighting for, and you don't hate who you're fighting against." Characters such as Slade and Sieber (though the racist Slade much more than the redeemable Sieber) highlight the moral virtues of the hero because their hatred of the Indian tends to cast the hero as a soul expansive enough to contain all that we are meant to account best in both the Indian and the white man.

Double Otherness depends upon perspective and perception. That which we termed *self-othering* in a previous chapter constitutes only one of several possible perspectives on the Double Other. When (as we saw in chapter 3) Dances With Wolves, manacled and abused, despairs of the white officers asking him questions about "hostiles," he speaks to them defiantly in the Lakota he knows they will not understand: "I am Dances With Wolves. I have nothing to say to you. You are not worth talking to." Yet such moments of self-othering, like the many before it in Costner's movie, can seem somehow superfluous, self-serving to the point of narcissism, next to the moments when other characters, regardless of our sympathy toward them, define the hero's Indianness. Thus, for example, moments before Dunbar speaks in Lakota to the officers, the sadistic Sergeant Bauer, standing above the beaten hero, sneers knowingly, "You turned Injun, didn't you?" In the very effort to other Dances With Wolves, Bauer confirms the transformation that the action lures us into acknowledging. We, for our part, revel in the hero's exclusion from so vile a collection of white men, and affirm our own difference from those whites—declare something like an Indianness of our own, then, however provisional. No doubt history and culture, genre as well as drama, all play a part in the definition of the Double Other, and in the specification of its blessings as well as of its dangers.

In *The Searchers*, perhaps the most fully realized instance of the Indian-hating hero, the members of the posse riding with Ethan in search of the Edwards sisters repeatedly react to Ethan's singular extremism. In their first engagement with the Comanches, the Texas Rangers, led by the Rev. Capt. Samuel Johnson Clayton (Ward Bond), manage to cross a river ahead of the Comanches and safely ensconce themselves behind some rocks on the opposite shore. Scar and his warriors now charge across the river, but they retreat under heavy fire, wheeling their horses around in midstream. Even as the Indians retreat, Ethan continues to fire on them, intent on killing as many as possible, even if he has to shoot them in the back. Finally, Sam Clayton knocks Ethan's rifle down, calling on him, in the name of humanity, "Ethan, leave them carry out their hurt and dead"; and even then, as Ethan walks away from his position, he turns and lets off one more shot at the retreating Comanches.[15] Clayton prompts our common humanity. Placing Ethan thus beyond the moral pale, Clayton *others* him on our behalf, and thereby confirms his Indianness.

And yet, that very Indianness that Clayton's agency condemns on

15. There are several other moments in *The Searchers* that betray such hatred in Ethan, though perhaps none so much as when he fires indiscriminately on a herd of buffalo for the sole purpose of contributing to the starvation of the Comanches. It is to be noted, then, that here, too, someone (in this case Martin Pawley) interrupts the slaughter and condemns Ethan as vehemently as Sam Clayton did earlier by the river. Then of course

our behalf also designates the very quality whereby Ethan—and only Ethan—can fulfill our fondest hope that the Edwards sisters will be delivered from captivity. To be sure, the Double Other may not always be a native to his soul's very core. However, the desire itself to be Indian for good or ill already distinguishes him from white and Indian alike. Here, then, we should remember that the Indian hater himself devoutly wishes to be Indian, for in his Indianness lies his capacity to destroy the savage enemy. Whether we side with the characters who condemn Ethan's excesses or with Ethan's own efforts to return his niece to civilization, *The Searchers* casts us as ambiguous accomplices, attuned to the moral forces that pull us apart. The community's censure reverberates within us, but so does the celebration of the heroic persistence that returns Debbie to the "fine good place to be." To an extent greater than we might be willing to admit, the Hollywood Western plays upon—or should one say lays bare—our own double Otherness.

Often, the Myth of Conquest simply presupposes Indian-hating, and is content to postulate it as primal, immemorial, and vested utterly in racial difference. Accordingly, it tends to present the Indian-fighting Double Other not as the product of historical forces (or even of a specific narrative) but as the full-grown incarnation of a destined enmity. Yet the Myth of Conquest would also guarantee racio-cultural *triumph* by insisting on both the authenticity and thoroughness of the racio-cultural *metamorphosis* required from the hero for the achievement of that triumph. Of course the action will amply document the event that triggers a specific instance of Indian hating, the deed that releases fearful passions only so recently held in abeyance. To hear Major Rogers in *Northwest Passage*, the entire Anglo-American nation has suffered at the hands of the Indians as he himself has, so that the appeal to the persistence of such outrages becomes Rogers's rallying cry (seconded by a description of horrors against Rangers provided by one Lieutenant Crofton [Addison Richards]) just before the Rangers go into battle against the Abenaki:

> *Rogers*: I don't have to tell you who the Abenakis are. Most of you have lost folks and friends in Indian raids since '57. You'll find their scalps at St. Francis. Some of you men fought in the battle on Snowshoes. . . . They captured Lieutenants Crofton and Phillips, and twenty other Rangers. Lieutenant Crofton's brother is here. He can tell you what happened to them, if he'd like to speak up.

---

we remember that Ethan tries to shoot Debbie, and that again Martin Pawley rebukes him for it.

Crofton: Yes, Major, I can tell you. Phillips had a strip of skin torn upward from his stomach. They hung him from a tree by it while he was still alive. They chopped his men up with hatchets and threw the pieces into the pines so there wasn't any way of putting them together again. They tore my brother's arms out of him. They chopped the ends of his ribs away from his backbone and pried them out through his skin one by one.
Rogers: That's what happened to Crofton and Phillips, but they were soldiers; they had to take their chances. But your folks on the border farms, they weren't fighting anybody. They were clearing woods and plowing and raising children, trying to make a home of it. And then one night Abenaki tomahawks at the door. If it was over quick, they were lucky.[16]

As a source of double Otherness, Indian hating would seem to have been long since grafted upon the national consciousness, a vital part of the American genesis now lost in the generations. As Melville noted a century and a half ago, the frontiersman is weaned on tales of Indian savagery: according to Judge Hall in *The Confidence-Man*, the frontier youth hears

little from his schoolmasters, the old chroniclers of the forest, but histories of Indian lying, Indian theft, Indian double-dealing, Indian fraud and perfidy, Indian want of conscience, Indian blood-thirstiness, Indian diabolism—histories which, though of wild woods, are almost as full of things unangelic as the Newgate Calendar or the Annals of Europe. In these Indian narratives and traditions the lad is thoroughly grounded. "As the twig is bent the tree's inclined." The instinct of antipathy against an Indian grows in the backwoodsman with the sense of good and bad, right and wrong. In one breath he learns that a brother is to be loved, and an Indian to be hated.[17]

He but awaits the predictable outrage in order to set out to fulfill his type's destiny. An individual though he may be in the plot that contains him, he merely reenacts his cultural inheritance. He enters the site allotted to him by convention and consent and affirms once again the legacy that fashioned him long before.

When the double Other claims that the Indian endorses his transformation, he reenacts Conquest's oldest strategy of authorization—a central myth of the Myth. The effect and intent of the Indian's endorsement of the hero does not, however, authorize the Indian himself. That is to say, his endorsement of the white hero does not reveal the Indian's

---

16. Some of the dialogue, as transcribed, was made clearer by attending to the corresponding scenes in the source novel.

17. *The Confidence-Man: His Masquerade*, in *The Writings of Herman Melville*, ed. Harrison Hayford, Hershel Parker, and G. Thomas Tanselle (Evanston: Northwestern University Press, 1984), 10: 146.

own power. He does not create the hero's Indianness so much as he corroborates it; and he does not corroborate it because of a sense of identity with him, but because of the historical necessity that he almost always seems to understand so clearly. Indeed, the confirmation is often inevitable, marking at times the moment when the Indian despairs of survival by any means or agency save that of the white hero. Some such sponsorship empowered Faulkner's Ike McCaslin to be, so far as time and circumstance allowed, a claimant to the Indian inheritance. In "The Old People," the story that precedes "The Bear" in *Go Down, Moses*, Sam Fathers, the descendant of a Chickasaw chief, anoints the young Ike with the blood of the buck that the boy has just killed, his first: "Sam Fathers had marked him indeed, not as a mere hunter, but with something Sam had had in his turn of his vanished and forgotten people."[18] So, then, does the Indian himself hope, against time and circumstance, to endure in and through the race that defined itself by its opposition to him.

In the revisionist Western, the Indian's endorsement of the white hero licenses not only the hero's authority on Indian matters, it also (perhaps primarily) enfranchises him simply because he, alone of all white men, is worthy of such an endorsement. The circularity—that the hero should be proved worthy of the Indian's approbation because he is worthy of just such a thing—is part of such logic as the Myth of Conquest deploys on behalf of its hero. Recall, then, the parting benediction that Ten Bears bestows upon Dances With Wolves: "The man that the soldiers are looking for no longer exists. Now there is only a Sioux named Dances With Wolves." Such an authorization of the hero's Indianness functions not to establish the Indian's humanity, or to reveal something like the autochthonous wisdom that recognizes a common bond with this white man. Instead, it tends to announce the almost obligatory moment of perspicacity (conjoined perhaps with a touch of rueful self-interest) whereby the Indian, conceding his imminent doom, defers to this privileged white man. The deference, however, does more than tacitly acknowledge the Indian's own impending vanishment: it also and simultaneously validates this one exalted version of whiteness itself, anoints it as the only possible hope for the Indian, urging him to accept the unencumbered donation of this vestigial Indianness.

The white hero becomes thereby the repository, undiminished and

18. *Go Down, Moses* (New York: Modern Library, 1942), p. 182. For a beautiful reading of *Go Down, Moses*'s Ike McCaslin as an archetypal Double Other, see Canfield, *Mavericks on the Border*, pp. 11–25.

undiluted, of all things Indian. That purportedly consensual bond of surrender and appropriation—that racio-cultural transubstantiation—proclaims the embodiment of the Indian in the person of the double Other. The deference and the surrender become, indeed, the Indian's desperate entreaty not to the white hero alone but to an entire race as well, a plea to his agency on *our* behalf, the deathbed imploration that "we," too, can come to accept (with pride and humility) this white hero who is also the last Indian.

Dances With Wolves will speak to "those who would listen": *we* approve, *we* will listen—for so, as we are supposed to believe, would the Indian want it. We accept—and ourselves certify—the metamorphosis from Lieutenant Dunbar to Dances With Wolves. But we accept and certify it neither because we believe in the power of the Indian to transfer his Indianness without decrease nor because we trust to the special powers of the hero. Ours, rather, is the acquiescence *derived from* the presumed protean quality that allows the yet unformed American to become Indian. He embraces—and becomes—all that is Indian—all of it, without exception or condition; yet, somehow, his must never be the native's own authenticity. He must disclaim his whiteness, but he must never quite abrogate it. He is the double Other, authentic neither as Indian nor as white, yet the genuine *American*, and his Americanness—that identity that promotes his Indianness even as it belies it—always seems tragically linked to the power of the Myth of Conquest to enforce the disappearance of the Indian.

Such a benediction as Ten Bears bestows upon Dances With Wolves may thereafter serve the hero to talk to "those who would listen"; yet some such authorization may also empower the Indian-hating hero to destroy the Indian. It was an Indian, a dying Mingo shot by the young backwoodsman, who in *The Deerslayer* gave Natty Bumppo his *nom de guerre*—Hawkeye. As the newly baptized Hawkeye explains a bit later, the Mingo "thought I desarved to be known by the name of Hawkeye, and this because my sight happened to be quicker than his own, when it got to be life or death, atween us."[19] Chief Scar's remark that Ethan Edwards speaks "good Comanch'" tends to reinforce our belief that Ethan will, in the end, avenge the deaths of his family and the captivity of his niece Debbie. For we "know" that he who destroys the Indian shall have first become Indian. Somehow, then, these heroes share common ground, despite their divergent attitudes toward the Indian: their

19. *The Deerslayer or, The First Warpath. The Leatherstocking Tales* (New York: State University of New York; Library of America, 1985), 2: 721.

double Otherness, ambiguity and all, betokens an unmistakable Americanness. It is both heroic and American for Dunbar to leave his people that he may speak on behalf of the Lakotas. His righteousness and his sacrifice commend him, and his sense of justice proclaims an Americanness. It is no less heroic or American for Ethan to pursue and destroy the Indians that killed his family. His righteousness and his sacrifice commend him, and so on.

This determination of the hero's Indianness, however, functions as only one possible outcome of the encounter between white and Indian in the Hollywood Western. Another important consequence is that the Indian comes to be displaced, as much by the friend of the Indian as by the Indian fighter. In the classic Indian Western, the displacement of the Indian is indeed the very issue and result of the white hero's supposed appropriation of the Indian's "gifts": the Indian fighter, as we have seen, benefits from his knowledge because it enables him to destroy the Indian. In the revisionist movie, as we saw in chapter 3, the white hero appropriates the Indian's voice, the implication being that his speaking for the Indian *absents* the Indian, renders him no less voiceless or vanished than the Indian fighter renders him.

In the end, then, the strategies that would authenticate the Double Other—that would certify his Indianness and his whiteness alike—reveal the duality inherent in the Myth of Conquest itself. The double Other's *character* comes to be but an expression of an untenable cultural premise—a premise untenable not only in its relation to historical outlook or cultural claims, but to the very logic of national identity. The methodologies of authorization become themselves self-subversive: noble or savage, the Indian ratifies the white hero's fitness to be a native, but only to confirm, in the very instant, the mythic premise which holds that only this paragon of the conquering race can become Other. The white ethical conscience identifies the Indian fighter as a near-savage—vindictive, cruel, rancorous; yet it stakes the future of the nation—the nation itself as "fine good place to be"—on just such a "savage." Jill Lepore captures the essence of this dilemma of national identity with a pithy remark about the success of the actor Edwin Forrest (who embraced things Indian yet supported Indian Removal) in his portrayal of the eponymous hero in John Augustus Stone's *Metamora*: "ironically, Forrest was most American when he played an *Indian*."[20]

20. *The Name of War*, p. 200.

"THE CONQUEST of the earth," notes the narrator Marlow in Joseph Conrad's *Heart of Darkness*,

> which mostly means the taking it away from those who have a different complexion or slightly flatter noses than ourselves, is not a pretty thing when you look into it too much. What redeems it is the idea only. An idea at the back of it; not a sentimental pretence but an idea; and an unselfish belief in the idea—something you can set up, and bow down before, and offer a sacrifice to.[21]

More than a century ago, Conrad saw civilization's need for a presiding illusion, one that could generate unflagging conviction and unswerving commitment—even if belief and purpose were to be vested in such fables as that of the hero who becomes his race's best in the moment that he becomes his race's own enemy. He noted Conquest's dependence on a concept that might justify brutality and rapacity while vindicating, or at least masking, civilization's own "savagery." The Double Other is no mere instrument of the "idea at the back of" Conquest but inseparable, in the end, from sublime dispensations and manifest destinies, from millennial progress and the equivocal testimony of material prosperity. And the hero of revisionism, who does not so much repudiate Conquest as justify its ways to "us," benefits from both the ethos of empire and the postulated disappearance of the Indian. In body and spirit, both variants of the white hero appear before us at once savage and civilized, empowered by the imperatives of dominion to turn savage for civilization's sake yet at the same time renouncing that civilization—and risking its rebuke—by virtue of the freedom from social restraints implicit in his transformation. He is, himself, both the "idea at the back of it" *and* the immediate source of that idea's failure—at once its "redemption," to use Conrad's term, and the most abject form of its perversion; the consummation of the "ascent of man" (in Jacob Bronowski's inversion of Darwin's famous title) whose challenge to the Indian requires a descent into savagery.

Hence the Double Other: a hero in the end as alien to the Indians as to the civilization for whose sake he destroys them, the beau ideal of the American, yet ever denied participation in the new order of the ages. No wonder that his ambivalence would engender a kindred ambivalence in the America that he helped create, compelling it to engage in a form of collective double Otherness: for his great powers, powers

21. Joseph Conrad, *Heart of Darkness*, ed. Robert Kimbrough (New York: W. W. Norton, 1988), p. 10.

of sacrifice no less than of transformation, the hero would have to be apotheosized, enshrined that he may be appealed to in times of need; for the triumph begotten of so radical an alteration, he would have to be reproached, preferably forgotten.

4

Custer's dubious claim—"I could be an Indian"—requires the convergence of myth and history. The claim may be grounded in documented historical events, but the Western certifies its mythic lineage. The unlikely marriage of discourses traditionally held to have incompatible aims begets a type that reflects those discrepant ends, mirroring them in the form of a heroic identity that yet requires an improbable transformation. The seemingly irreconcilable difference between the Indian fighter and the friend of the Indian tends to dissolve in the Western's uncritically held assumptions about cultural transformation. Although we need to illustrate these assumptions in greater detail, we need not sort them out and classify them as much as we need to designate them; and our designation ought to be of the kind that acknowledges their operations, even as it doubts their implied claims. To this set of assumptions I give the name (with apologies to John Cawelti), *the mystique of cultural appropriation*. In the illustration of this mystique, it is impossible to ignore the attitude of specific Double Others toward the Indian. Nonetheless, our focus now falls on the premised capacity of the white hero to metamorphose into an Indian and still retain his identity as hero—the butterfly emergent yet still somehow chrysalid.

Seldom do we identify the hero of the Indian Western by the accoutrements and appurtenances that so readily identify the hero of the gunfighter Western. Shane, for example, wears his gunbelt as something of a lethal halo, a sign manifest and indelible that his power shall be deployed in the interest of an unequivocal good. But the hero that concerns us here carries no obvious, at least no consistently generic, outward mark of his mission. The mystique of cultural appropriation expresses itself not so much through icons as through the presumed power of the hero for cultural acquisition. As the classic gunfighter Western asks us to believe in the near-magic of the hero's six-gun, so the Indian Western asks us for unconditional acquiescence in the hero's capacity to appropriate the Indian's ways. We should not doubt that there are degrees of appropriation, that the different heroes' Indianness can be reckoned as a matter of more or less. Nor should we doubt that certain elements in the iconography of the Indian Western help to underscore the white hero's appropriation—for example, Ethan Edwards's fringed rifle scabbard or Dances With Wolves's hair feathers and eagle-bone breastplate. Regardless of degree or of supporting iconography, however, the mystique of cultural appropriation produces nothing more clear than a mystified heroic identity. In other words, the hero's Indianness all but dispenses with a *process of acquisition*: it is virtually ready-made; and in cases where the hero must *learn* his Indianness, he is far more likely to have come by its full measure in the cut between two scenes than through a gradual, measured, and therefore almost inevitably limited acculturation. Thus, the mystique of cultural appropriation is, or at least aspires to be, ahistorical. It is a sign manifest and unequivocal of Anglo-American genius that the race's hero can become not only like the Indian but, if need be, the very essence of Indianness. If nothing else, the hero could always count on the Myth's power of definition to present him in perfect and complete Indianness. Consider two examples of the mystique of cultural appropriation taken from *Broken Arrow* and *Run of the Arrow*. These two movies, after all, offer themselves up as exemplary representations of native authenticity. The process of cultural appropriation will accordingly take us through a series of discrete initiatory moments attesting the hero's power of cultural conversion even as they depict authentic events specific to a tribe.

From his early encounter with the wounded Apache boy, Tom Jeffords learns that Apaches have tender familial sentiments and a fine sense of justice. But it is only halfway through the action, after befriending Cochise and falling in love with Sonseeahray, that Jeffords yearns to be, as fully as possible, an Apache. He therefore enlists the services of an agency Apache by the name of Juan (Billy Wilkerson). "Juan," Jeffords proposes, "I've got some work for you. I want to hire you for maybe almost a moon. I want you to teach me to speak Apache good. I want to learn about Apache spirits; I want to learn about Apache ways, [*now bringing his hand to his heart*] Apache in here. Will you teach me?" To be, in one's heart of hearts, an Apache, takes slightly less than "a moon." One understands that Jeffords's proposed timetable mirrors his own urgency about things both private and public: Sonseeahray awaits seductively, and both white and Apache are counting on his efforts in the cause of peace. Also, it would make for poor filmmaking to chronicle Jeffords's struggles with Apache idioms and inflections. But his sense that he can be Apache to the core in "almost a moon" also discloses a persistent belief of the Myth of Con-

Geronimo: An American Legend (1993, Columbia Pictures). Indian and white hero fight the same enemy. Courtesy of Columbia Pictures/Museum of Modern Art Film Stills Archive.

quest—namely, not only does the white man possess an unlimited capacity to assimilate the culture of the Other, he can also do so fully and intimately, to the extent of becoming Other "here," in the heart itself—and all in a month.[22] The well-intentioned revisionist claims of the white hero's perfect Indianness diminish the native cultures—or else they undermine the hero's conversion itself, the *extent and thoroughness* of it, at any rate. No less than Parkman, Jeffords, too, becomes only a conditional Indian, an Indian "as it were." He is himself at once the full measure of such Indianness as the Myth of Conquest can ever reveal *and* the incarnate illusion that presents an Indian only to show, at the very heart of such a being, the white hero himself.

A Confederate private, O'Meara, the hero of *Run of the Arrow*, consumed by rancor toward Yankees and by shame over the defeat of the South, decides to go to the Far West and live among the Indians; for the "savages," he says, have "more pride" than southerners willing to accept the new post-war order. In the first scene out West, O'Meara rescues an old Lakota man, Walking Coyote (Jay C. Flippen), who wears a

22. When Jeffords's apprenticeship is over, Juan remarks: "You've learned to speak our language well. You do not yet think like an Apache, but you are not distant from it." Perhaps another moon will do the trick.

Union jacket and hat. We soon find out that Walking Coyote served the Union as a scout. He suffers from a bad heart and claims that his health will last only as long as his whiskey does. He is going home to die (though this implausibly postulates a home where whites have not yet introduced liquor). On their first night after their meeting, O'Meara expresses a wish to know about the Sioux—their language, their tribal divisions, the origin of the name "Sioux," and so on. Later, on what appears to be only the next day, O'Meara interprets a neat pile of three small rocks to mean that three more babies have been born to the Minneconjou branch of the Lakotas. Walking Coyote remarks: "[It's] surprising how quick you pick up our customs." O'Meara replies, "Well, it's not so difficult, you know."

Only moments later, the hero and his Lakota mentor find themselves tied to a large rock while their captors, a small band of Lakota led by Crazy Wolf (H. M. Wynant), help themselves to Walking Coyote's stock of whiskey and whoop in the fashion well known to the Western. Out of these whoops, generic though they may seem to all but the uninitiated, O'Meara constructs the following meaning: "They look like they're getting ready to hang you," he says to his fellow captive, who remarks: "You learned our lingo good." "I learned it good," O'Meara responds. "I learned it too good. Otherwise I wouldn't be sweating out the fact that they're gonna skin me." *Run of the Arrow* never tells us how much time has elapsed since O'Meara and Walking Coyote first met, but it would seem even less than the "moon" that Jeffords required. More important, however, we discover that generic yelping means much more than the animalistic sounds by which the Western has always designated an imminent peril at the hands of savages. Yet it is easy enough to learn the "lingo good"; if Otherness is a construction of the Same, then there can be no obstacle too great, neither linguistic nor cultural, for the hero to overcome.

I have not adduced these examples of cultural appropriation so that I can pronounce them implausible. If anything, perhaps, they produce quite the opposite of implausibility—not, of course, because they reflect a historical likelihood but because, prompted by convention and prodded by consent, we so readily acquiesce in the authentic Indianness of the hero. Such acquiescence, moreover, has only obliquely to do with a Coleridgean "willing suspension of disbelief": rather, it has its principal source in the tendency of the dominant culture to account the power of cultural appropriation as a sign of its manifestly exceptional character. We become accomplices of Conquest's seductive fantasies— inveigled by a mystique in the making of which we ourselves have had an active hand. For where is the myth that can survive without the participation of the people whom it exalts? When was a cultural leap of this sort made by those who broke faith with the master narrative? The need to establish the authority of the Indian fighter is so often dispensed with that we are to consider the hero's Indianness something of an axiom, another of the numberless mythic births that defy and deny process, historicity, even at times causality.

History, to be sure, hardly contests the white man's appropriation of the Indian's culture. Early in his biography of Daniel Boone, John Mack Faragher offers the following sketch of white males on the frontier:

> Like Indian men, American hunters let their hair grow long and dressed it with bear grease, plaiting it into braids or knots. In time of war or for ritual occasions, Indian warriors might shave or pluck their scalps, leaving only a lock of hair, which they greased to stand upright or to which they attached deerskin ornaments or feathers. They painted their bodies with vermilion. American backwoodsmen heading into battle frequently adopted a similar style of ornamentation. The frontier American was "proud of his Indian-like dress," wrote a preacher in western Pennsylvania. In breechclout and leggings, their thighs and hips exposed naked to the world, he had seen them strut down village streets and even into churches, which, he added, "did not add much to the devotion of the young ladies." Boone adopted these styles as a youth in Pennsylvania, and they remained his through the whole of his long life.[23]

The Myth of Conquest understands implicitly the dangers of so intimate a cultural appropriation, an appropriation that—as is all too evident in the drastically diminished "devotion of the young ladies"— does not so much betoken the superiority of the white male as it tends to blur the lines between the two races. It is such an understanding of frontier history that at once attracts and repels the Myth of Conquest to its own hero: on the one hand it finds confirmation of the hero's authenticity in the very image and manner of him handed down by history; on the other, it finds that the hero can become dangerously "authentic"—enough so that cultural appropriation can be no longer deemed a virtue, for now it attests to the dread of damnation in the wilderness rather than to the destined triumph of culture and race therein.

The Myth of Conquest negotiates the fine line between heroic appropriation and the threat of perdition in the wilderness by working out

23. John Mack Faragher, *Daniel Boone: The Life and Legend of an American Pioneer* (New York: Owl Books, 1993), 21.

what might be called a *code of cultural verisimilitude.* This code—itself an indication of the Myth's underlying ambiguity—answered to the dual requirement that the hero be capable of assimilating the Indian's culture yet remain unequivocally and essentially white. His being Indian was an expedient, a subterfuge, a dissemblance; however convincing an Indian he was, he would never lose his essential whiteness. Even, indeed, when he most eagerly praised the Indian, or when he most assiduously studied his language and his ways, he could testify to the genius and magnanimity of *his own race*—a race that could embrace the Other and yet remain fundamentally unaltered, serene and certain, unswerving in the pursuit of its high destiny. Cooper's *The Last of the Mohicans* can be seen as the first conscious and sustained effort of the Myth of Conquest to define the line that bifurcates the person and identity of the white hero. From the opening description of the three backwoodsmen in chapter 3—which distinguishes Hawkeye from Uncas and Chingachgook by the absence of the tomahawk worn by the two Indians—to the almost metaphysical status with which Cooper invests the notions of "white gifts" and "red gifts," to the unrelieved and near-pathological monotony of the hero's assurances that he is "a man without a cross"—all this suggests an effort to come to grips with the concerns and consequences of the white hero's Indianness. The codes of Indianness, not least of which are those that we treated in the first chapter as synecdoches, may exhibit the hero's power of cultural acquisition, as do also his knowledge of their language and their ways. These codes are in part a concession to history; they specify that the hero's Indianness is limited by mere verisimilitude. But these codes *must somehow* also betoken his superior nature. As outward signs of Indianness, then, these codes have their limits: if Ethan Edwards can tell a Comanche from a Kiowa lance, or if he wears moccasins or sheathes his rifle in a fringed scabbard or speaks "good Comanch'," none of these things must let us as much as suspect that he is Indian to the core. He is—and must remain—white; and like Hawkeye himself, we, too, take to the soothing mantra that insists on Ethan's being "a man without a cross"—until, perhaps, we recall how difficult it is to reconcile Ethan's "white gifts" with his taking of Scar's scalp, at the end.

I hardly mean to suggest that the white European (from whom the Myth of Conquest claims descent and in whom it fully vests the power of appropriation) did not in point of historical fact learn, both freely and of necessity, to assimilate the ways of the Indian. I mean, rather, that the Myth of Conquest *elides* the process of assimilation and adaptation—the *learning*, then: it abrogates historicity (or pretends to supersede history) in order that it may present appropriation not as the product of "contact" but as a sort of mythic license, a token of the hero's privileged station and rank among the citizens of the wilderness.[24]

The mystique of cultural appropriation holds, however implicitly, that the Double Other acts as the supreme authority on Indian matters—so much so, in fact, as to be, himself, Indian (if only Indian "as it were"). This mystique assumes, then, that the appropriation is thorough and thoroughly valid, and that it is also "natural," as if it required neither effort nor doubt. Furthermore, it takes our consent for granted: it assumes that we will not contest the hero's knowledge or, in the case of the revisionist variant, the soundness and thoroughness of the hero's transformation. Thus, the mystique of cultural appropriation is more convention than strategy, more a habit of representation deeply ingrained in culture and genre alike than a narrative trope. It is a formulation of cultural contact so ubiquitous in the ordinary grammar of American identity that even if we recognize it consistently we do not often think of questioning it. So ancient a thing it is, moreover, that it seems coeval with contact itself—present, as such, in the self-flattering interpretation that John Smith gave to the famous event: "[H]aving feasted him after their best barbarous manner they could, a long consultation was held, but the conclusion was, two great stones were brought before Powhatan: then as many as could

24. Native American belief would add a further irony to the mystique of cultural appropriation, since the indigenous peoples were far more likely than whites to accept the actual transformation of an Indian into a white man. John Mack Faragher has noted the genuine parental affection of the Shawnee chief Blackfish toward his famous captive, Daniel Boone, though less than a year before his captivity Boone had killed Blackfish's son during the rescue of his daughter Jemima and the two daughters of Richard Callaway:

> From the perspective of Americans, who tended to divide the world into immutable forces of "us" and "them," this custom [of adoption into the tribe] was inexplicable, but the Shawnees, like other Indians, believed in transmutation. With the application of the correct rituals an admired enemy might be made over into a beloved brother, actually thought to assume the identity of a deceased kinsman. During the eighteenth century hundreds of Europeans and Americans were captured and adopted into Indian tribes. . . . "We have taken as much care of these prisoners as if they were our own Flesh and Blood," the Shawnees told the British when returning several dozen captives after the Seven Years War. "They have been all tied to us by adoption, and we will always look upon them as our relations." *Daniel Boone*, p. 164.

In *Dances With Wolves*, Lieutenant Dunbar, the hero, first appears at the Lakota village shortly after the husband of Stands With A Fist, Dunbar's future wife, dies in a battle. This man was the best friend of the warrior Wind In His Hair. In a poignant moment toward the end of the film, Wind In His Hair makes a confession to Dunbar, who is now himself a dear friend: he understands now, he says, that his Lakota friend died because Dunbar was coming. From an indigenous perspective, such moments may confirm the belief in transmutation; yet these are also the events out of which the Myth of Conquest constructs the native's authorization of the white hero.

layd hands on him, dragged him to them, and thereon laid his head, and being ready with their clubs, to beate out his braines, Pocahontas the Kings dearest daughter, when no intreaty could prevaile, got his head in her armes, and laid her owne upon his to save him from death."[25] Thus transformed, as it were, instantly into an Indian, Captain Smith could become the Indians' worst enemy. Well might he have been first in North America to say, "I could be an Indian," and mean it in the same spirit in which Custer would mean it centuries later.

Cooper's Hawkeye was, indeed, as Leslie Fiedler has noted, the "first not-quite-White man of our literature, for all his boasts about having 'no cross in my blood.' "[26] And it was this not-quite-whiteness that enabled him to safeguard the future of the white race in America. He may have had no racial "cross," but he had tasted of savage ways too long to be entirely above the suspicion—ours, perhaps, quite likely Cooper's own—that he had crossed over into Indianness. Why else, but because he had in fact become Indian (even if not quite so), did Cooper have him invoke—in every other page, as it sometimes seems—this unavailing avowal meant to reassure us of his racial purity? What did the boast do for Hawkeye but affirm that only such a "man without a cross" is also the one eminently suited to cross over into Otherness? Such are the curses, yet also the blessings, of the Double Other—the destiny, at once exalted and degraded, awaiting a man appointed, by fate more than by circumstance, to serve as "a link between them [the Indians] and civilized life."[27] That virtue which was meant to vouchsafe the hero's unadulterated inheritance, to attest to his uncompounded "blood," did not relieve his racial anxieties but instead bound him, in helpless compliance with Conquest's fancies, to accept and embrace his Otherness. And then the same fancies affirmed that the racially pure white hero, having become Indian and therefore doubly Other, had thereby become a singularly true American, himself prototype and model of a nation whose cultural integrity showed forth nothing more clear than that it had been, itself, "chartered in two worlds."[28] For what

---

25. *Captain John Smith: A Select Edition of His Writings*, ed. Karen Ordahl Kupperman (Chapel Hill: University of North Carolina Press, 1988), p. 64.

26. *Return of the Vanishing American*, p. 25.

27. *Last of the Mohicans*, p. 875.

28. I use the phrase in the title of the chapter with the gracious consent of its author, John Demos, who uses it to designate the dual initiation of Eunice Williams's children in both Christian and Kahnawake cultures. See *The Unredeemed Captive*, p. 159.

would become of the Double Other if the nation itself should withhold its consent, if it should at last renounce its complicity?

So much for a sketch of the mystique of cultural appropriation. Let us now consider two instances of this mystique, one as exemplified by an Indian fighter, the other by a white man adopted by the Indians.

5

An early reference to Major Robert Rogers, the hero of *Northwest Passage*, provides a useful elaboration of the Custer claim in *Son of the Morning Star*. A certain Sergeant McNott (Donald McBride) explains to Langdon Towne and Hunk Marriner how Major Roberts once tracked a drunken Indian scout who ran away: "That Indian got drunk and went over the hill. Now, if you let one Indian get away like that, they'll all go over the hill. So Major Rogers went out after that Indian hisself. Knew right where to look for him. Yes, sir, the smartest Indian alive can't think half as much like an Indian as Major Rogers can." The "smartest Indian alive" should be flattered that he is almost half as much an *Indian* as Major Rogers, the Indian *fighter*, can be. Indeed, the "more" *white* Major Roberts accounts himself—that is, the more clearly heroic his mission on behalf of his race and culture—the more necessary it seems for us to accept his Indianness without question.

In relation to Rogers's Indianness, the movie seems to mirror the actual man who, as Richard Slotkin tells us, "attempted in the 1760s to dramatize himself to the British court and public as the American hero par excellence."[29] Rogers was leader of his own company of rangers, the doubly alliterative "Rogers's Rangers." During the French and Indian War, Slotkin notes, Rogers exemplified the development of the mythic frontier hero of the first century or so of white colonial presence in North America. He represents "an intellectual movement toward secularization, a tendency to imitate Indian ways of fighting in the wilderness, and a somewhat clearer image of Americans' concept of themselves and their land as embodiments of a new and promising order, derived from the conditions of life in the American wilderness."[30]

In Vidor's movie, the destruction of the Abenakis at St. Francis and a

29. *Regeneration through Violence*, p. 187. Slotkin's somewhat odd phrase, "dramatize himself," makes more sense when we recall that he is referring to Roger's play of 1766, *Ponteach, or the Savages of America*. See also *Regeneration through Violence*, pp. 235–41.
30. Ibid., p. 188.

harrowing trip back to Portsmouth hardly quench Rogers's thirst for adventure—or for Indian blood. Following a little rest, the intrepid Rogers is ready to lead his Rangers in search of the Northwest Passage, and as ready to mow down such Indians as may foolishly stand in his way. Rogers's idea of the Northwest Passage is not a chimerical concept of the fabled route to the Pacific Ocean but a vision of Manifest Destiny. In the historical moment of the action, then, Rogers becomes a prophet, foreseeing Thomas Jefferson and Lewis and Clark, Texas in 1836, California in 1850, maybe Cuba and the Philippines in 1898 (and who knows but Vietnam, however ironically, in 1972)—prophesying, perhaps even, the time when the movies themselves would celebrate just such a vision. So now, refusing to read to his men from the stilted wording of the King's commission, he invests his enterprise with the aura of a sacred trust, a divine appointment, and thus appeals to his men through the rhetoric of Conquest (as "My Country 'Tis of Thee" plays softly):

> I'll tell you where we're going in plain language, so you'll know where we are when we get there. . . . We're taking a walk first, for our appetites— about a thousand miles, to a little fort called Detroit. But that's just the jumping off place. Why, you Rangers haven't seen any Indians yet. You're going to see the Plains Indians. You're going to see the red men of the Shining Mountains, and those men along the mighty river Oregon—red men [whom] white men haven't seen before, because we're going to end up by the great Western Ocean itself. You're going to find a way across this Continent, a Northwest Passage. You'll see hardwood groves like cathedrals, cornstalks as tall as elms, rivers packed with salmon, trout, and grass so high the cows stand knee-deep in it and give nothing but cream. . . . All you have to do is just walk along, through Ottawas, Wyandots, Chippewas, Miamis, Sauk, Shawnees, Sioux. Well, I'll sort them all out to you when we get to them.

The great American destiny, manifest and alluring, beckons; and all it will take for this particular Moses to set foot in the land of milk and honey is to "sort out" a few Indian tribes. For the Indians, as ever, stand in the way, stubbornly and futilely resisting the compelling vision—the sacred revelation of America's unchallenged greatness among the nations of the world. Seeing the Indians and sorting them out will not bring them into view as members of a new America, much less initiate Rogers's white proto-Americans into community with the indigenous peoples. Rather, to see them, since here past is always prologue, is to know them, and to know them is to kill them. Seeing becomes an ironic metaphor for virtual absence, for rendering the Indian, at last, invisible. And Rogers, if not as the historical figure then as prototype, will be the first to engage in the centuries-old process. For, as the historical figure tells us in his *Journals*, even from the time of his youth,

> my manner of life was such as led me to a general acquaintance with the British and French settlements in North America and especially with the uncultivated wilderness, the mountains, valleys, rivers, lakes, and several passes that lay between and contiguous to the said settlements. Nor did I content myself with the . . . information of hunters but travelled over large tracts of the country myself, which tended not more to gratify my curiosity than to inure me to hardships and, without vanity I may say, to qualify me for the very service I have been employed in.[31]

Conquest makes poor distinctions between the specific forms of such "service" as the likes of Major Rogers are "employed in": for Conquest may now call for the massacre of the St. Francis Indians, now for the arduous trek back to the settlements, only to demand—in quiet and self-assured compliance with the great westering imperative—at once a fresh assault on the wilderness and on the Indian. Though he has not yet seen them, he will still sort these new Indians out—no great task for one who knows them so intimately as to know, in the end, that there is no difference between the tribes. After all, "the smartest Indian alive," East or West, Abenaki or Sioux, "can't think half as much like an Indian as Major Rogers can." Happy the Indian who would meet his fate at the hands of so superior a version of himself.

American culture long ago foresaw the dilemma of cultural appropriation: double Otherness has almost always evoked the fear that whites will become too much like the savage enemy. "Perhaps," Jill Lepore writes in *The Name of War*, "the English New Englanders worried, they themselves were becoming Indianized, contaminated by the influence of America's wilderness and its wild people."[32] So much so, indeed, that, as she convincingly argues, the New England Puritans may have gone to war against the Indians not so much for land or access to commerce as to preserve their Englishness. Accordingly, it became necessary to invoke the deities of exclusion, the ready powers of cultural self-definition, in order to bring about the needed separation: "By telling about the war, and most especially by writing about it, the

---

31. Quoted in *Regeneration through Violence*, pp. 188–89.
32. *The Name of War*, p. 7.

colonists could reclaim civility, could clothe their naked war with words. The writing itself would 'dress' the English back up; it would undo the damage of the war by making clear once again who was English and who Indian, and what made a massacre and what a victory."[33] It was possible for the white man to be Indian, and therefore Other, in war (just as, in time, it would be possible for him to be as noble as the Indian during times of moral and spiritual crisis), as long as he could reclaim his Sameness—all in stubborn defiance of history, not to mention of a memory held, for good or ill, in common with the Indian. But let us turn to the much more problematic *Hombre* (Ritt, 1967), there perhaps to see, through its tangle of motives and prepossessions, whether the revisionist Western can represent its white hero's Indianness as more than an expediency.

What *Hombre* would consciously illuminate is not necessarily what we would find illuminating about it. The action gives us a misunderstood and despised man—white by descent and later by adoption, but Apache by upbringing and consent—who at a crucial if predictable moment obeys the impulse and call to a sacrifice that all but one of the white characters resist. Yet we must wonder whether, in the end, our own acceptance of his sacrifice—that is, not merely our approval of it but our understanding of it as culturally plausible, our identification, therefore, of its moral source—derives really from a new insight into the Indian's superior humanity or from an Indianness that but thinly masks primitive, homiletic, uncorrupted Christianity.

More than the illumination of the transcultural nature of virtuous sacrifice, *identity itself* is *Hombre*'s proper theme. The hero (played by Paul Newman), whose Anglo name is John Russell, was captured by the White Mountain Apaches as a child, "raised among red devils to be a red devil," as one character puts it. Russell has remained among them, or more precisely, has returned to them after some time in the settlements, where he had lived with his adoptive Anglo father, from whom he received his name. Yet in spite of his seemingly clear choice, Russell hardly enjoys an uncompromised ethnic identity. The introductory shot at once designates and foreshadows his embattled doubleness: he wears long hair and the traditional Apache headband; yet the Indianness so instantaneously betokened by this synecdochical headband is at once complicated by another feature that the close-up makes equally salient—namely, his pellucid blue eyes (which are also the

33. Ibid., p. 94.

most famous pair of blue eyes in all of male moviedom).³⁴ "'He doesn't look Apache, does he?'"³⁵ remarks a character in the Elmore Leonard source novel. Similarly the film, like the novel itself, would secure and certify the authenticity of this "Apache" by appealing to his *whiteness*—that is, to his capacity to act in accord with an indeterminate idea of Indianness.³⁶

Still in the first scene, while the hero and his two Apache partners try to lure a herd of wild horses into a trap, a young white man, Billy Lee Blake (Peter Lazer), approaches the site of the trap in order to tell Russell that the stage line is closing and will need no more horses from him. Unable at first to find Russell, he addresses the two Apaches: "I'm looking for John Russell [*the two men are silent*]. Tres Hombres [*silence still*]. Ish-kay-nay. Whatever you call him."³⁷ And only moments later, as Russell appears before him, Billy Lee again: "I guess you're Mr. John Russell, unless one of them [Russell's Apache partners] is. I can hardly tell you apart." In both instances, Billy Lee's tone is unmistakably contemptuous; he is thus the first of several characters whose racism functions, as in so many revisionist films, to identify the Indianness of the white hero. Only a couple of scenes later, Mendez (Martin Balsam), who runs the station at Sweet Mary, greets Russell in a tone only slightly less sardonic than Billy Lee's:

Mendez: Hombre. Which name today? Which do you want?
Russell: Anything but bastard will do.

34. The movie opens with sepia-toned photographs of native peoples, photographs quite likely by Edward S. Curtis, or else in his style. At the end, the close-up of the dead Russell transforms into the face of a *white* boy, and as the camera pulls away from the boy, we find him among Apache boys. The photograph quite clearly establishes the connection with the action proper, as if indeed the white boy were the John Russell whom we have met, a boy at home in his "natural" habitat. Of course, the photograph also historicizes the action, lending to it an aura of plausibility, even of authenticity, perhaps even insisting that Russell could not have learned to be a Christian except in such a traditionally un-Christian setting. Yet the photograph also insists that, though the man's skin be white, he is not for that reason any less Apache than the rest of the Apaches are. The photograph is actual, and the white boy is Santiago (Jimmy) McKinn, a famous white captive of the Apaches.

35. Elmore Leonard, *Hombre* (New York: Ballantine Books, 1961), p. 68.

36. As if meaning to elaborate at once on the conflicted double Otherness of the opening close-up, *Hombre* now introduces us to Russell's livelihood, an enterprise of ambiguous cultural purpose, if ever there was one: he captures wild horses to sell to the stagecoach company. The proud and free stallion, no mean cinematic metaphor for the wild and free Indian (as in *Wild Horse Mesa*, for instance), shall be harnessed in the service of westward expansion.

37. The spelling of the Apache name is from the source novel.

Hombre (1967, 20th Century Fox). Blue-eyed Apache and his Apache friends. Courtesy of 20th Century Fox/Museum of Modern Art Film Stills Archive.

Mendez: We use John Russell. No Apache names, no single names, all right?

Perhaps these early scenes announce that the hero is *un hombre, a* man common and ordinary, an Everyman of sorts, whose sacrifice in the end redeems the *human* race[38]—a man therefore singularly virtuous despite the burden of his polyonymy. And perhaps he is *el hombre, the* man, heroic regardless of racio-cultural designation. Yet he is also Russell *and* Ish-kay-nay, and (therefore) Tres Hombres—three men: white, Indian, and the integral yet dual identity given in his double Otherness. Three men, then: the white, the Indian, and neither of the two precisely for being the two at once—something of a cultural "bastard," then, though hardly for that reason base. It therefore makes sense that his actions, often without apparent motive and as often subjected to gross misinterpretations on the part of the other characters, should soon

38. Hence perhaps the double irony when the crooked Indian agent, having had his first encounter with Russell's pro-Indian sentiments, says: "Mr. Russell obviously feels sympathy for the Indians' plight. If you're a *humane* man, you do" (my italics).

[209]

come to reflect his several names. Perhaps principally, however, such a complex identity seems calculated to release the hero's actions from the tyranny of ethnicity, to declare him, in a word, a transethnic individual: he shall act in accordance with no concept of race or culture; he will baffle our efforts, and those of the other characters in the story, to attribute his actions to race or culture. Indeed, then, Russell is already that most endearing of American types—the rebel. For certainly the long hair and the headband evoke the sixties' hippie, cast him as a dropout of sorts who would find common ground with the heroes of the two landmark movies of that year, *The Graduate* and *Bonnie and Clyde*. Yet it is not difficult to foresee, given his first encounter with Billy Lee, that the other characters will cast Russell in the role of that most contemptible of all frontier figures, the renegade.

When Russell arrives in Sweet Mary, Mendez tells him that his (Russell's) adoptive white father died and bequeathed him a watch and a house. For some years now, a woman named Jessie (Diane Cilento) has been running the place as a boarding house, with the profits going to Russell's father. But almost immediately after Jessie shows Russell the ledgers, which he peruses only perfunctorily, he tells her that he has decided to trade the house for a herd of horses.[39] His decision results in the dispossession of the four tenants—Billy Lee, his disaffected wife Doris (Margaret Blye), Jessie, and Jessie's live-in lover, the freeloader Sheriff Braden (Cameron Mitchell), who later refuses to marry Jessie. All but Braden choose to leave Sweet Mary in a stagecoach bound for Contention and Bisbee. Mendez drives.

Joining this suddenly dispossessed assortment are the dastardly (if all too respectable) Indian agent, ironically surnamed Favor (Fredric March), and his much younger yet just as hardhearted wife, Audra (Barbara Rush). The Favors are in a great hurry to reach the border. Although the stage has stopped running out of Sweet Mary, they insist on hiring a conveyance to the border. We soon discover that they have cheated the Apache reservation and the U.S. government out of a fortune and that, now on the run, they hope to make it as far as Vera Cruz, possibly to catch a Europe-bound steamer. A trooper recently discharged from the Army and off to Bisbee to get married joins the group as the stagecoach is about to leave, but then the outlaw Cicero Grimes

---

39. Since *Hombre*, in so many ways like *Stagecoach*, develops the action by assembling a motley group in close quarters, the sale of the house, causing as it does the immediate dispossession of its tenants, would seem only an expedient for bringing the group together. But Russell's trade of the house for the herd of horses also specifies his repudiation of the fruits of Conquest.

(Richard Boone) arrives in the station and bullies the trooper out of his seat in the stagecoach. Grimes, we eventually discover, knows about the money that the Favors have stolen. His gang (which includes Sheriff Braden, now turned outlaw) waits in a remote part of the route, ready to rob the thieves.

Inevitably, the stagecoach interior becomes the dramatic stage where the characters put forth their views on race and ethnicity and history. It begins with Doris's expressed fear of an Apache raid on the stagecoach. Moments later, Audra offers a racist vignette of life as the wife of the Indian agent—racist yet, not surprisingly, also lascivious, adulterous: "I've lived among the Apaches on a reservation—the women grinding corn and rubbing skins, the men almost naked, some of them quite striking. And just when you begin to find them almost beautiful, they squat and pick at themselves with the dog sniffing at them. I can't imagine eating a dog and not thinking anything of it." Throughout most of the exchange, Russell has been silent, almost quiescent. Now, though he remains serene, he voices his outrage, and thus generates the following exchange:

> *Russell*: You ever been hungry, lady? Not just ready for supper [but] hungry enough so that your belly swells up?
> *Audra*: I wouldn't care how hungry I got. I know I wouldn't eat one of those camp dogs.
> *Russell*: You'd eat it and you'd fight for the bones, too.
> *Audra*: Have you ever eaten a dog, Mr. Russell?
> *Russell*: [*Ironically*] Eaten one and lived like one.
> *Audra*: [*Not so much scandalized as disdainful*] Dear me!

Such candor immediately earns Russell the contempt of the Favors. At the next stop, Alex Favor insists that Russell ride on top, "shotgun," with Mendez.

The exchange all but guarantees our acceptance of Russell's Indianness, for Indianness is now grounded on his sympathy for the downtrodden Apaches—sympathy not as condescension but as the shared suffering implicit in the root sense of the word. We are made ashamed of our own squeamishness, of our own snobbery which, like Audra's, distances us from both the Indian and our own humanity. Hence the ethical basis of cultural appropriation as well as of our own acquiescence in it: however much the two may derive from our unacknowledged recognition of culturally specific sources, we will embrace Russell's Indianness because of its patently Christian extraction. Moreover, the Favors' insistence that Russell ride on top identifies the hero's

[211]

DBS Arts Library

virtues—and grounds them even more firmly in a putative Otherness—as decisively as Russell's outrage itself does. Their contempt for Russell, itself made contemptible by their heinous crimes against the reservation Apaches, highlights his own self-isolating censure of them, even as it cues our approbation of his Indianness as the source of a superior ethic.

Surely, then, *separation* underscores the mystique of cultural appropriation. It wraps the hero gently in the nimbus of a glorious and exalted martyrdom even as it already lures us all to join him in his righteous sojourn in the desert. His separateness identifies him as alone able to embrace, indeed to incarnate, that noble Otherness, that ethic of patient and irrevocable sacrifice that, however mystified and exoticized, still derives recognizably from a cultural orthodoxy, though it would yet shame the selfsame orthodoxy's pretenses to moral preeminence. Even if only in death, separation guarantees the Double Other's eventual triumph over contumely. Thus, cultural appropriation is made possible, in part, by a slight yet crucial recasting of the received ethos. The Indianness of the white hero is above reproach because his ethical impulses are so familiarly white. In the revisionist Western, then, culture is no less a guarantor of moral ascendancy than it is in the Indian-fighting Western; only here it is the culture of the *Other* (however persistently and self-subversively he may appear in the form of the Same) that underwrites the virtuous life. So now that he rides on top with only the lowly Mexican for his companion—two outcast Others now that the evicted tenants have found a consolatory Sameness in the company of thieves—Russell already appears before us in his true moral essence.

Yet Russell, for all his vocal and pointedly didactic rebukes of the whites, ends up sacrificing his life in order to save, of all people, Audra Favor. *Hombre*, to be sure, follows a rather twisted path to this climactic moment, and perhaps for this reason it is worth sketching the events leading to it.

Having found the money that Favor stole and loaded it in Braden's saddlebags, the gang is ready to ride away; but before they do, Grimes takes Audra hostage. The gang rides away driving all the stagecoach horses before it, thus leaving the passengers to make their way to Bisbee (which includes the crossing of a desert) on foot. As if taking the horses did not sufficiently handicap the passengers—none of whom, least of all Favor himself, has any intention of rescuing Audra—one of the robbers, Lamar Dean (David Canary), shoots several of the passengers' water bags, leaving them with precious little water. Also, Grimes takes care to disarm the passengers, though he fails to notice Russell's rifle, wrapped in a blanket on the stagecoach roof rack. After Russell kills Dean and Braden with his rifle, the passengers recover their guns, yet they never prove a match for the outlaws (Mendez, for instance, loses his nerve at a crucial moment and fails to fire when he has the Mexican bandit [Frank Silvera] in his shotgun's sights). Clearly, then, the abduction of Audra Favor sets up, however implausibly, the climactic rescue attempt—and thus the coarsely preceptive moment of immolation and atonement, as much as of recognition, and even penance.

Although Favor is first to get to the saddlebags on Braden's dead horse, Russell demands the money as a condition of leading the passengers to safety. Now that Russell has led the passengers to a shack atop a hill in an abandoned silver mine, the outlaws demand the money, and when Russell refuses, they tie Audra to a rail halfway up the hill. Exposure to the blazing sun and lack of food and water are the instruments of torture. She calls out piteously to her husband, "Alex, Alex," but Favor seems unmoved. Jessie, the sole conscience among the white passengers, challenges Russell: "You have to give them that money. I think you know that." Russell, however, maintains that the passengers, himself included, could choose *not* to help Audra.

Jessie: You mean you'd sacrifice her life for that money? Is that what you're saying?
Russell: You go down there and you ask that lady what she thinks of life. Ask her what she thinks life is worth to those Indians in San Carlos when they run out of meat.
Jessie: But she didn't take the money. Favor did.
Russell: She said, "Those dirty Indians eat dog," [and] that she couldn't eat dog no matter how hungry she got. Go down there and ask her if she'd eat dog now.
Jessie: I don't know what your gripe is against the world. Maybe you've got a real one.
Russell: Lady, up there in those mountains there's a whole people who've lost everything. They don't have a place left to spread their blankets. They've been insulted, diseased, made drunk and foolish. Now you call the men who did that Christians, and you trust them. I know 'em as white men, and I don't.
Jessie: Russell, if nobody ever lifted a finger until people were deserving, the whole world would go to hell. We better deal with each other out of need and forget merit, because none of us have too much of that—not me, not you, not anybody.

Long-winded, no doubt. And inelegant: for we could dispense with so raw a reminder that Audra would gladly eat a camp dog, "and fight for the bones, too." Nor did we need so sanctimonious an identification of Christianity as the religious mask of empire, and therefore of its hypocritical invocations in the name of race. Yet the exchange (whether consciously or not) hints already at an alternative Christianity, one that, though in the guise of Indianness, is still and recognizably "true," undogmatic, and uncompromised, a universal Christianity: the Christianity, presumably, of Christ himself and of his legion meek, including Indians and white heroes.

As if to prove that all these so-called Christians are moved only by self-interest, Russell now throws the saddlebags down in the middle of the floor and addresses each of the passengers, Favor first.

> That's your wife down there. You gonna cut her loose? Mendez, you gonna save her? Billy Lee, what's your last name? You gonna go down there? [*Pointing to Favor*] This one won't. That's his woman, but he won't do it. He doesn't care enough about his own woman, but maybe somebody else does. [*Now to Jessie*] All right, you, lady. You worry about his wife more than he does. Go on down there. Cut her loose, start back up again, get shot in the back, or in the front if the Mexican by the trough does it.

Moved by Audra's plight and stung by Russell's scorn, Jessie decides that she will take the money to Grimes, who waits at the bottom of the hill. Russell himself may not have suspected her capable of such selflessness; and so, sensing that there is, after all, one righteous soul among them, he decides that he will take the money to Grimes himself—only it is not the money he will take in the saddlebags, but empty canvas sacks. The money he entrusts to Billy Lee, who will supposedly deliver all of it to the Apaches if Russell should die in the rescue attempt. Having further instructed the young man on when and how to shoot the outlaws, Russell (allegorically enough, no doubt) ventures below. But only moments after he frees Audra, he gets killed. Indeed, his death is all that much more a sacrifice because, as Audra makes her way laboriously up the steps to the shack above, she blocks Billy Lee's line of sight on the Mexican bandit. Thus Russell dies for the woman who insulted him, while the woman herself, however unwittingly, thwarts any possible effort to save Russell. As he dies, she has her back to him, still making her way up the steps with Doris's help, for all we know unaware, and who knows but uncaring, of the sacrifice below.

Hombre, I hold, compels us to weigh Russell's deed of sacrifice in the balance not of contending ethnicities but of competing ideas and perceptions of Christian action. Yearn as we might for a sign that would

[214]

unequivocally render Russell's deed both authentically and exclusively native, we have no other Indian in *Hombre* but this self-sacrificing white man. Nor have we any other Indian who will affirm that Russell's actions are consistent with those of an ethnicity—that his sacrifice on behalf of these contemptible whites merely exemplifies the course of action that any other Apache might take under similar circumstances.[40] Is it any more so, however, in the case of the whites? Does their ethic reflect their ethnicity in greater measure than does that of the "Indian" Russell? To the extent that whiteness here specifies self-interest, then to that extent will the association of race and moral doctrine produce a glaring discrepancy. Thus, by exposing the *un*-Christian sentiments of these "Christians," *Hombre* produces a hero whose pure and complete Christian act seems to be almost exclusively grounded in his Otherness.

But what sort of *Indian* is this whose death and sacrifice conform so precisely to a supposedly ideal Christianity? To be sure, the Indian may well be the Christian primitive, as artless as he is zealous, eyes fastened on heaven, unconcerned with social respectability or cultural compliance. But we are not asking what sort of Christian he is but what sort of Indian—if any. If his deed embraces so pure a Christianity, is he, then, still Indian? Has his sacrifice in the end affirmed the whiteness that he thought he had renounced? Did the Christian act itself claim him—as if by an unwilled pentecost, "unimplor'd, unsought," as Milton's angel describes divine grace itself—despite his avowed and seemingly unshakable Indianness? Did he at the last yield to race and culture, as if these were themselves overpowering moral forces? Of course, we can never know the answer to these questions with any certainty. Yet it seems not so much curious as consistent that a question about Indianness should generate questions about the possible whiteness behind it. Still before us lies the perplexing problem of Russell's whiteness—though this is quite likely the very problem that *Hombre* would have us ignore.

Let us consider it further from two distinct, if in the end inevitably related, perspectives, the one dramatic, the other cultural. First, the dramatic. Favor, we recall, has made his way through the desert alone (so condemned by Russell for trying to steal the money yet a third time). When Favor reaches the abandoned mine, half-dead with thirst,

---

40. Russell's two Apache partners, present only in the early scenes, never so much as utter one syllable (in Apache or English) between the two of them, not even when Lamar Dean deliberately splashes mescal in the face of one of them. Their insignificance is also exemplified by their namelessness and by their absence from the credits.

Jessie calls out to him and points to the water bag. Jessie has no love for Favor, to be sure, but she justifies her act as a necessary and disinterested mercy. Now that he comes up to the shack, however, Favor gives Jessie's act a decidedly racial construction. He addresses Russell: "You'll learn something about white people: they stick together." The remark, of course, redounds to his damnation only moments later, when he fails to lift a finger to help his very white wife. But can this racist maxim of Favor's explain, however subversively, Russell's sacrifice? Could it be that, in the end, we are to believe that Russell acts out of a sense of racial kinship with Audra Favor? If so, *Hombre* may be asking us to accept Russell's final sacrifice as a deed inspired by an intuitive and irresistible *agape*, by a sort of evangelical *caritas* that stands as the hallmark of civilization. If so, then Russell's martyrdom validates neither a common humanity nor a transcultural Christianity, but the superior "humanity" of the white race.

If the mystique of cultural appropriation charms us, reassures us, could it be because it empowers and confirms our repudiation of racist hypocrisy, even as it exempts us from oneness with the Other? We will be consenting Double Others ourselves: each of us Indian enough to escape the judgments of history on "our" culture, yet white enough to know that we need not be, after all, fully Indian to be righteous. Do we not, then, acquiesce in the proposition that our white heroes can become Others only because we stand to know, in the end, that their *ethic* confirms their ineffaceable whiteness? But what then of the requisite oblivion that would make such reassurance possible? Consider now the *cultural* perspective on Russell's whiteness.

I suggested, above, that the Indianness of the hero in *Northwest Passage* functions as Conquest's expedient. So, too, as an expedient (though surely for other ends) does Indianness function in the revisionist ethos: it provides a moral sanctuary—the hero's as well as "ours"—from the perversion of our dearest values. Then, at the foreseeable and irrevocable moment of racio-cultural reaffirmation—in the requisite casting off of that Otherness that had been so piously appropriated—Indianness would vanish; or rather it would be revealed as but a necessary phase in the fulfillment of Conquest's promise. The influence of civilization would prove to be so irresistible that it would overcome the pull of the wilderness. Or so it was hoped, often vainly so. Thus Cooper, reflecting in 1850 upon the genesis of his great white hero Natty Bumppo, more than a quarter century before, considered the question of whether his hero had been based on actual backwoodsmen known to the author. To some extent, it was so, Cooper answered,

> but in a moral sense this man of the forest is purely a creation. The idea of delineating a character that possessed *little of civilization but its highest principles* as they are exhibited in the uneducated, *and all of savage life that is not incompatible with these great rules of conduct*, is perhaps natural to the situation in which Natty was placed. . . . In a moral point of view it was the intention to illustrate the effect of seed scattered by the way side. To use his own language, his "gifts" were "white gifts," and he was not disposed to bring on them discredit. On the other hand, removed from nearly all the temptations of civilized life, placed in the best associations of that which is deemed savage, and favorably disposed by nature to improve such advantages, it appeared to the writer that his hero was a fit subject to represent *the better qualities of both conditions*, without pushing either to extremes.[41] (Italics mine.)

The American experience on the frontier had yielded a new moral calculus: civilization's corruptions found their precise counterpart in the excesses of savagery to which the white man could sink in the wilderness. Cooper could not, in the end, reconcile these extremes except by doling out both civilization and savagery in safely measured drams. Having been exposed to "little of civilization but its highest principles" while yet "placed in the best associations of that which is deemed savage," the American hero became naturally a Double Other, "a fit subject to represent the better qualities of both conditions." Yet, though both—and both at once—the hero complied with the austere imperative that his gifts, begotten though they may have been of the union of the two "conditions," were first, last, and exclusively *white* gifts. Indeed, heroism was to be predicated upon action recognizably originating in and obedient to just such "white gifts." What does the quantum of civilization do for the hero, then? Does it not assure us that, at once despite and because of his all-but-complete yet altogether provisional immersion in the savage wilderness, the best of the hero's racio-cultural inheritance shall compel him to act in perfect harmony with "our" values?

Russell, I hold, is of this type first fleshed out by Cooper. Consistent with the archetype, he affirms the national ethos by presuming to condemn it. He wears his Indianness as a sign of his censure of Conquest. Historically, the American hero affirmed his identity by a process of *de-*

---

41. *The Leatherstocking Tales,* 2:490–91.

civilization, by that stepping outside his culture that characterizes Natty Bumppo or Huck Finn, both alike (and whatever Twain's opinion of Cooper) seeking *both* regeneration *and* identity, both renewal and reassurance, through the Indian and in the Indian's domain. So, then, *Hombre* might have sought similar benefits for its hero, but also (and no less) for the postulated "us"—the shaken and divided "we-the-people," beset by Vietnam and assassinations and race riots and political processes gone awry, outraged and dismayed witnesses to the failure of the American promise. So Russell's baby-blues—like Iron Eyes Cody's iron eyes, which in the same year as *Hombre* first cried for the devastation of the environment—shed figurative tears for America's moral wasteland; but we should not doubt that his sacrifice exempts him from all complicity in the nation's moral decline, nor that it is made possible by his unapportioned access to a distillation of moral resource that *Hombre* would have us identify as uniquely Indian. But the selfsame Indianness that defines the hero must yet reflect that Sameness in which the nation would hold itself redeemed. Let Russell be as Indian as need be, so long as in his martyrdom the nation comes to recognize, and inevitably to vindicate, its own identity as well as its own "history." So (*mis*)appropriated, Indianness becomes primarily a strategy not so much of national self-definition as of national self-censure, if not national *self-vindication*. Indeed, Indianness itself, so conceived, becomes a ruse whereby to bring about national regeneration.

Russell now dead, *Hombre* gives us one last close-up of him, thereby framing the action by drawing attention to his face. In the opening shot, we remarked above, Russell appeared in long hair and Apache headband, tokens both of the hero's postulated, perhaps even hypostatized, Indianness. He has long since cropped his hair and, but for the Apache leggings that he dons after the holdup (the better to walk through the desert), his outfit may well have been that of any movie gunfighter. Hatless now, eyes closed, the hero is indistinguishable from any tragic hero of the classic Western. It is in the context of this transfigured Russell that the dying Mexican bandit asks Mendez (who has come down from the shack after the shootout), "I would like at least to know his name." "He was called John Russell," Mendez replies. Mendez, recall, had earlier refused to address Russell by any but his Anglo name ("no Apache names, no single names, all right?"). Mendez's insistence on the Anglo name consecrates the hero even as it tends to specify the cultural derivation of the hero's sacrifice. Mostly, however, Mendez's insistence on Russell's Anglo name complements the close-up of Russell, the visually verifiable transformation of the hero. Perhaps, then, the change of looks (the clothing, the hair) prefigured the restoration of the hero's cultural outlook, augured his eventual and timely consent to an ethic that supposedly belongs to him by racial descent. So Russell's immolation functions as a racio-cultural homecoming of sorts. With no Indian in sight for a long time now in the action, and with the humble Mexican Mendez both to acknowledge and bless the hero's Anglo soul, Russell dies among white Americans, their reluctant deliverer, yet inescapably their kin—whiteness both incarnate and assimilated, reassuring yet unsettling avatar of Favor's racist adage, that white people "stick together."

Of course, we may believe that Russell's sacrifice has more in common with Jessie's deed of mercy toward Favor than with any unthinking obedience to racial kinship. At least from the time of Owen Wister, the Western tended to base its moral conflicts on the clash between unavoidable violence and the irreproachably tender sentiments of the woman who counsels against it. The trick, from *The Virginian* on, was to have the hero have his way twice over: he would engage in violence *and* he would get the girl. Say, then, that Russell's martyrdom is in fact inspired by Jessie's rescue of Favor and by her willingness to rescue Audra. Say, moreover, that the continually intimated sexual attraction between Jessie and Russell can only be consummated through the hero's sacrifice not for Audra, perhaps even not for Jessie alone, but for a thoroughly generic concept of white womanhood—one that would include Audra, but also Jessie, and even Doris (Billy Lee's languorous and peevish wife), just as Ringo's sacrifice, in *Stagecoach*, benefits not only Dallas but also Lucy Mallory. Would we not recognize here as well the cultural origins of Russell's sacrifice? Can we not easily enough flatter ourselves, if only by the very act of seeming to recognize those origins, that Russell has vindicated not only white American womanhood but white American masculinity as well?

And yet what dies—in face and name and inheritance—is the Indian—dies as if in fit yet self-refuted representation of that old rallying cry of philanthropic arrogance which would kill the Indian to save "the man." The man, *el hombre*, Man, turns out to be, as if by essence and definition, white. Perhaps Russell had to die in order that the white woman (however unmaidenly *Hombre*'s Jessie) might be spared the inevitability of intercourse with the Indian. Indeed, perhaps Russell's sacrifice itself (Russell leaves his rifle behind when he goes down to take the money) at once substitutes for and consummates the forbidden sexual encounter between white and Indian, as if the deed consisted not so much of dying nobly as of a self-emasculation that fulfills desire by ab-

[219]

rogating it. Perhaps. Much more certain, however, is that all traces of savagery disappear—from the man himself and from "America"—with Russell's death. He enacts the fictive tragedy of the Vanishing American, just as he reaffirms the values of white American manhood. Here then we note that Russell's sacrifice hardly begets the new America that the Indian Western often declares established, or at least hints at, upon the defeat and disappearance of the Indian. He may have reaffirmed white American values, but his death, though his Indianness may have all but required it, exacts a penalty of its own on the presumed post-Indian order of white America. There is no unifying and restorative birth, as at the end of *Fort Apache;* no "fine good place to be," as at the end of *The Searchers;* no promise of Americas yet to be conquered, as at the end of *Northwest Passage.* Bandits aplenty have died, including Grimes and the Mexican; but the nastiest of all bandits, Favor, yet lives; and it is difficult to believe that the naive Billy Lee, for all his earlier assurances to Russell, or the dull and subservient Mendez, will long keep the money from Favor. The movie's remaining Other (Mendez), the three women, and Billy Lee, form but an inchoate America at the mercy of the merciless Favor—somewhat as if Ford's *Stagecoach,* revisited in the late sixties, would have allowed the embezzler Gatewood to remain at large after Ringo and Dallas leave Lordsburg.

Yet what more salutary context for the evocation of nostalgia and self-exemption than this? Here, indeed, nostalgia for the Indian merely masks a renunciation of America, of what we used to call, in more tumultuous times, the Establishment. We will be Indians, even dead Indians. Guilty ourselves of surrender to the mystique of cultural appropriation, we turn Other for the sake of affirming our own dearest values. We shall be Double Others, then; and the siren song of Indianness shall soothe the fevered conscience, shall reaffirm the hopeful outlook for redemption at the very core of white America's soul. As defeated as it is martyred—martyred if only because it is defeated—Indianness rescues, redeems, restores—even if, in the end, it should rescue no more than white America's racio-cultural vanity; redeem only the conscience of a nation begotten of Conquest and much too at ease with such dubious blessings as it confers; and restore the white nation's generative bent and impulse to claim the Indian as its brother. Yet no Indian could so exactly delineate or so fully incarnate his own native virtues and values as does the white hero who appropriates him and, appropriating him, destroys him.

It makes, perhaps, for a harsh indictment of revisionism that, just as in the case of the canonical Western, it can so persistently produce, at the end, the separation of the white hero from the Indians. No Indian witnesses Russell's death, and for a long time before his death we have seen nothing of his two nameless Apache partners. But then, of course, Jeffords rides alone through the desert in the end, and Dances With Wolves, though more fortunate for riding off with his wife, still leaves the Lakota village behind. So, too, with only slight variations, the white heroes of *Cheyenne Autumn*, of *Soldier Blue*, of *Little Big Man*, of *The Last of the Mohicans* (Mann): by choice or by compulsion, by historical necessity or by mythic license, they leave behind what is left of the Indians and find themselves either well ensconced in or at least headed to the paradisal inheritance. And if the filmmakers of *Run of the Arrow* do in fact leave to us the "writing" of that story's ending, those of us who have learned something of the genre's conventions may have no choice but to send O'Meara back whence he came, even if he must forsake the lovely Yellow Moccasin in the bargain.

The canonical Western attempts to make the separation from the Indian, at the end, less problematic than the revisionist Western does. Closure, the canonical Western would have it, implies the closing of the frontier and the concomitant opening of the Edenic gates. *The Massacre, The Covered Wagon, The Iron Horse, Stagecoach, Arrowhead, The Indian Fighter, The Stalking Moon, The Unforgiven,* perhaps also, among Ford's cavalry trilogy, *Rio Grande*—these and many more posit the end, imminent or accomplished, of the Indian, and thus the beginning of the heroic claim of the paradisal homeplace. (I have deliberately avoided classifying the ending of *The Searchers* because of its great complexity. I attend to it late in the next chapter.)

But the canonical Western cultivated a second kind of ending, one that seems to stand in implicit refutation of the more frequent type. In this variant, the Indian fighter, although he may have wiped out the Indians on this latest westernmost version of the frontier, fixes his deadly eyes on yet other frontiers, on yet other Indians to wipe out. At the end of *The Last of the Mohicans* (Seitz, 1936), *Northwest Passage, Fort Apache,* and *She Wore a Yellow Ribbon* (to cite four well-known examples)—the hero enjoys no respite from the work of Conquest. For there are yet more Indians to fight. There are, indeed—*there always must be*—more Indians to fight. The persistent (and persistently needed) warring against the Indians, precisely because its ending can appear so indefinite even if its outcome is much less so, raises the possibility that the hero will never enter the promised paradise. His life's calling condemns him to everlasting estrangement from civilization. For that same calling compelled him, in due measure and token of his sacrifice on behalf of his race and culture, to assimilate the ways of the Indian. It may well be, accordingly, that his Indianness abrogates his claim to the American Eden as much as does his commitment to duty. Thus it can hardly surprise us that, at the end of these four movies, the heroes—Hawkeye, Major Rogers, Captain York, and Captain Brittles—lack a living woman in their lives. As he goes off to fight for the British, Hawkeye (Randolph Scott) is hopeful of a future union with Alice (Binnie Barnes), but Rogers and York are much too busy for romance, and Brittles's wife has been dead a good while when the action opens. By contrast, the heroes of all the other canonical movies that I cited above end up with a woman, Indian or white, virginal or former captive or erstwhile whore—it hardly matters, since the eradication of the Indian somehow yet surely transforms her into a millennial madonna.

The endings of Westerns such as *The Last of the Mohicans* (Seitz), *Northwest Passage*, *Fort Apache*, and *She Wore a Yellow Ribbon* project American life as an enduring heroic adventure and invest duty to country and culture with all the allure of the high-minded and selfless quest. Yet such endings, I suggest, hint at an anxiety about the outcome of the fight against wild men in the wilderness; they but thinly veil an uneasiness about the hero's *identity* in the aftermath of his victory. For he demonstrated his devotion to the cause of Conquest by becoming an Indian, and the transformation, that it might warrant his success, had to dispense with niceties such as Parkman's precautionary "as it were." Such endings, then, point out the Sisyphean nature of the quest for American identity in the Indian's domain—a quest that continually shapes that identity even as it continually defers it, that dislocates it from the promised Edenic home for locating it in the shifting frontier. The elimination of savagery requires the continual appeal to it. That which sustains the heroic effort is also that which subverts it. These Double Others do not return home; neither do they occupy a new home. Or, if they "return," it is only to the new frontier; and such homes as they "occupy" show them ever on the move. At home only in the wilderness, they would be outcasts in the very social order that they made possible. The frontier does not beckon; it compels. It is not so much a future as a destiny, not home but exile.

I draw attention to the endings of these four Westerns because, of all the others (both revisionist and canonical) that I mentioned above, they most clearly prompt an investigation of another uncritically held assumption of the Western—the capacity of the white hero to shed his Indianness once he has either killed the last Indian or witnessed the Indian's passing. In general, however, virtually all Indian Westerns avoid an encounter with the Indianness of the white hero in the new order. Most of these endings gloss over the important issue of identity, and without a doubt the glossing-over implies just how discomfiting the issue can be. So most Westerns, canonical or revisionist, will wrap the end of the Indian in the romance of the Edenic couple, a romance that excuses every excess (even the excess of its own importance in the invoked historical context of the action), a romance that allows virtually any variant closure save that which would show the hero, his Indianness, so to say, still fresh upon him, knocking with bloody knuckles at civilization's newly painted door.

Consider, then, that which the Indian Western implicitly asks of its hero as a precondition for entrance into the Western paradise: though his experiences in the wilderness constitute the very measure of his life, those selfsame experiences shall have altered him neither jot nor whit. These, then, are some of the questions that the next chapter asks of the Double Other. What if the sojourn among the Indians brought about a more thorough transformation than whites had bargained for? What if the white hero became Indian without anything like a qualifying "as it were"; or what if, to echo a passage from Demos's *The Unredeemed Captive* cited fully in chapter 1, instead of his civilizing the wilderness, the wilderness were to "*un*civilize" him? What if the alchemy of Conquest went awry and irrecoverably transmuted white to Indian? In such cases, which I discuss in the next chapter, the mystique of cultural appropriation would have to be reconceived, in both method and purpose, in order that it might explain this new identity, this American who was not quite white, not quite Indian—this new and unexpected "essence" that revealed nothing more certainly than the equivocal identity of hero and nation alike. In such cases, Conquest's alchemy would have to *invalidate* the transmutation of the hero. Or to put it less metaphorically, it would have to acknowledge temporality, historicity, in the process that had converted the white hero into an Indian, even as it would have to arrest that process, to rescind it, somehow. It would thereupon have to engage in the specious and tortuous exercise of presupposing the mystique of cultural appropriation even as it negated it, of deploying it as an expedient only to disclaim the hero who had come to embody Otherness. What, then, was it to be distinctly American when the appropriating powers had been co-opted by their own representations of savage Otherness?

[223]

[5]

"Not Enemies, Not Friends"

Racio-Cultural Ambivalence and
Mythology's Ahistorical Imperatives

But it is a curious fact, that the more ignorant and degraded men are, the more contemptuously they look upon those whom they deem their inferiors.

—Herman Melville, *Omoo*

"He looked like any other Indian on Army pay."
"Then he is Apache?"
"Well, maybe you can't answer that yes or no."

—Elmore Leonard, *Hombre*

"In the world of white men there are men who are not enemies, not friends."

—Buffalo Horn, *Flaming Star* (Siegel, 1960)

The risk of playing Indian to become American was playing Indian too convincingly.

—Jill Lepore, *The Name of War*

1

The erasure of Otherness marks America's birth, and the young nation, privileged and long-awaited, revels in the self-transacted justification of its ancient animus against the Indian. In this eradication of the Indian, the winner of the West had found his vindication, the manifest proof of his destined glory. Defeated savagery would henceforth blazon the nation's greatness. Here, then, were heritage and fulfillment all at once, a birth so far fabulous as to have amply contained all of the nation's glorious past even as it forecast its illustrious future. So goes, ever more hopeful than certain, the tale told by the Myth of Conquest.

To a continually westering folk—a people ever finding and fighting Indians on the Continent's ever-receding western limit—each war against "savagery" signaled some such finality: each victory, achieved and consecrated on the site of each successive frontier line of westward advance, amounted to a luminous and decisive disclosure of the millennial mandate. And perhaps it had always been so between Indian and white: triumph would forever vouchsafe the nation its uncontested and inalienable dominion over unregenerate Otherness, and the "winning of the West" would become the national apotheosis. So unequivocal a sanctification of American identity clearly cautioned against anything less than the utter extirpation of Otherness from the character of the new-born people. As Conquest's alchemy had fulfilled the need to transform the white American into an Indian, so now it would satisfy the resulting need to purge the last traces of the Indian in the American.

A scene late in *Son of the Morning Star* clearly illuminates the cultural significance of victory over the Indian. In Washington, D.C., following a massacre of miners in the Black Hills, Generals Sherman (George Dickerson) and Sheridan (Dean Stockwell) hand President Grant a draft of an ultimatum directed against the Sioux and Cheyenne. The so-called non-treaty Indians, this document reads, "must report to their agencies by January 31st" 1876 or "be considered hostile." The generals behave as Conquest's own harpies in accosting Grant, deriding his doubts, importuning him to restore Custer's command of the Seventh Cavalry. They place their trust in Custer because his dash and his courage will guarantee victory in the Plains Indian Wars. Then Sherman, coming closer to Grant, as if to unravel for him alone a riddle's meaning, divulges the essential mytho-historical imperative. "We've been killing Indians for hundreds of years," he murmurs with demonic vehemence. "Let's get the business over with. I want Custer to head the expedition. We need one great, bloody battle." What deadly paradoxes would not beset a nation compelled to destroy the Indian in the name of atonement, to seek, in Richard Slotkin's inspired formula, "regeneration through violence"? Sherman's sentiment of apocalyptic righteousness echoes Fergus Bordewich's observation that in America killing Indians "became not merely warfare but the cleansing of sin itself."[1] The violent end of the Indian, Sherman's speech implies, will not only win the

1. Fergus Bordewich, *Killing the White Man's Indian: Reinventing Native Americans at the End of the Twentieth Century* (New York: Random House, 1996; Anchor Books, 1997), p. 35.

West, it will also somehow redeem white America's sins against the Indian, as if the atonement, too, were manifestly destined. Triumph had implied an unamalgamated national character, a unity of outlook, a clarity of purpose; its very prospect had fostered the comfortable illusion of a common ancestry, and these promises had in turn stood for an apotheosis of ethno-cultural homogeneity.

Once won, the West itself would attest to the singular genius of a people united by race and language, a people sharing one past and one destiny. In this way it was possible for Theodore Roosevelt to begin *The Winning of the West* by praising the heroic deeds of the English-speaking peoples (a term with which he would have happily excluded any native English speaker not of Anglo-Saxon descent): "During the past three centuries the spread of the English-speaking peoples over the world's waste spaces has been not only the most striking feature in the world's history, but also the event of all others most far-reaching in its effects and its importance."[2] Having thus calmly assumed that which he should have instead proved, Roosevelt could deduce the privileges and perquisites owed to a people already blessed by race and language. "England's insular position . . . permitted it to work out its own fate comparatively unhampered by the presence of outside powers; so that it developed a type of nationality totally distinct from the types of the European mainland. All this is not foreign to American history."[3]

Not so, indeed. Yet neither is the Indian "foreign," no matter that American history may have persistently cast him as such. For America could not have so intimately identified itself with the frontier without having at the same time appealed, however covertly or reluctantly, to the Indian for its own identity. Perhaps, then, the "exceptionalism" that Roosevelt claims for America by virtue of its English inheritance could just as well be invoked in consequence of America's *Indian* heritage. Thus, the very instant that would reveal a triumphant America would also reveal the compromised—perhaps even the tragic—methodology of American self-definition in terms of an exclusively Anglo-Saxon derivation. No doubt Indianness persisted despite the aims of Conquest: the perceived national destiny had required the westering nation to embrace Indianness. This was to be merely an expedient, to be attained through some quick and easy alchemy whereby civilization's heroic agent might temporarily appropriate the savage "character" that he supposed the Indian to have. The white hero had been but an *ad hoc* Indian—Parkman's Indian-as-it-were. And had not Cooper's Hawkeye

2. *The Winning of the West*, 1:1.
3. Ibid., 1:7.

The Last of the Mohicans (1992, Morgan Creek Productions). The white hero as Indian warrior. Courtesy of Morgan Creek Productions/Museum of Modern Art Film Stills Archive.

himself counseled the tenderfoot Duncan Heyward that "Whoever comes into the woods to deal with the natives, must use Indian fashions, if he would wish to prosper in his undertakings"?[4] Now, the white hero might have assumed, his victory empowered him to perform (as quickly and as easily) the alchemical reversal, to transmute himself back, without trace or taint, into a being at once fully formed and elemental, the result of a centuries-old struggle yet somehow impervious to the influences and operations of historical change. Cultural appropriation had had an urgency about it. That which had been purportedly the Indian's, in the form of attributed character traits, had become the white hero's property, an instrumental possession for the sake of the promised dispossessing. And now, at the end, the hero's Indianness could be easily enough cast off. But the triumph of the presumed raciocultural One produced only an uncertain national identity, begot *the ineradicable persistence of Otherness in the Same*. In this chapter I question and explore the assumption that Otherness, though it may have been completely appropriated, can nonetheless be easily and completely enough sloughed off in the moment of the great national coming-to-be.

Mythology, however awkwardly, aspires to the condition of history. Yet mythology not only appeals to historical events but narrates its account of the events in terms of the values by which a nation *already* defines itself. It *promotes* those values while pretending to *explain* their origin. It *dramatizes* them as if it were *inaugurating* them. Mythology's explanations and justifications, no less than its codes and indices of Otherness, may accordingly make for poor history and even poorer historiography, but they have nonetheless had all-too-palpable cultural, and therefore also historical, consequences. Such efficacy can well sustain an illusion, even (within a certain "universe of discourse") to predicating its reality—or at least its usefulness as a soothingly suasive teleology, as comfortable when defining the emergence of the nation as when projecting its undiminished greatness throughout the ages. Since the deed of racio-cultural transformation had been performed in the name of the enduring and unalterable Same, it then became necessary to deny it, or to evade it, as a way of transforming that very Same back to its (presumed) original form. Upon the first moment of triumph (and upon the ruins of native cultures), the nation could resume its "first form," could recover, as if intact, its own "essential" identity as easily as it had appropriated the Indian's. More than two decades ago, Richard Drinnon clearly saw the fundamental moral difficulty of the millennial nation. His understanding of the problem of

---

4. *Last of the Mohicans*, p. 514.

post-apocalyptic America illuminates the dilemma that I address in this chapter: "How could a system of justice in the clearings be built upon a record of injustice in the wilderness?"[5] Drinnon, to his everlasting honor, cast his vision in terms of the historical injustice done to the Indian, while I have chosen to cast mine less boldly, merely in terms of the complex national identity that follows the last war with the Indians. Still, as the injustice abides—ineradicable, haunting, demonic—so, too, does the Otherness to which the white hero resorted in order not only to bring justice to the "clearings" but also to "prosper in his undertakings." I now consider the irony inherent in the Indian Western's assumption that cultural appropriation brings about no enduring change in the hero or in the emergent nation.

2

The *illusion of cultural divestment*: this is the term by which I would like to identify the belief, coeval with the nation's mystified birth, that hero and nation alike could cast off the Indianness that had been necessary for triumph. It must be kept in mind throughout that cultural divestment exists primarily as a *tacit claim* of the Myth of Conquest. This presumably complete purge of Otherness functions as a postulate, suffering neither doubt nor interrogation, brooking neither corollary nor condition. Cultural divestment is to come effortlessly and naturally and completely at its appointed place in Conquest's mythic timeline, and makes possible the undisturbed condition of national selfhood. All this, of course, is chimerical, a vital part of the "fantasies of the master race." Yet who will say with complete assurance that a nation's power for self-deception must not be accounted a part of its identity, or that an illusory identity can never be a source of power—however blind that power may be?

Cultural appropriation yields a *new*—and, because new, then potentially ironic—Sameness. I call this "new" identity the *Othered Same*.[6] The type reveals a new identity, but it also functions as an unfailing index of cultural ambivalence. As a tacit claim, therefore, cultural di-

5. Richard Drinnon, *Facing West: The Metaphysics of Indian Hating and Empire Building* (New York: Schocken Books, 1980), p. 162.

6. There are, however, Indian Westerns that might be said to *begin* with an Othered Same, usually in the form of a Double Other who tends to be identified as Indian. In *Flaming Star* (Siegel, 1960), based on the novel by Clair Huffaker (going by both titles, *Flaming Lance* and *Flaming Star*), the Othered Same, Pacer Burton, is the son of a white father and a Kiowa mother. Cultural and racial doubts overwhelm him—and in the end kill him. Another important movie of this sort is *Broken Lance* (Dmytryk, 1954). The parentage of the Indian Double Other, Joe Devereaux, is similar to that of Pacer Burton.

vestment, at least in the canonical Western, belies the Othered Same, and the Othered Same subverts cultural divestment, making of it an "illusion." They thus stand, each to the other, as ironic reciprocals. We need not elaborate on the Othered Same in abstraction from the details that suggest the concept and urge its study. Still, it seems useful briefly to differentiate the Othered Same from the Double Other. Double Other and Double Otherness refer to the *activity* of the heroic type—the appropriation, implicitly or explicitly narrated, of cultural difference and the specific deployment of that appropriation for or against the cause of Conquest. The Othered Same, however, refers to the same type, but as *product* or *consequence* of his agency. He emerges "Othered," I suggest, at the *end* of the action, and his Othered condition suggests both the success of his appropriation of Indianness and the unlikely prospect that he should divest himself of that cultural "property."

I begin the characterization of the Othered Same and the inquiry into the illusion of cultural divestment with a look at the ending of *Hondo* (Farrow, 1953).[7] The ending of *Hondo* substantiates the difficulties of the illusion that the hero emerges unaltered by the requisite cultural appropriation. Here are the bare facts leading to the ending: Hondo Lane (John Wayne), an army scout and dispatch rider who is also part Indian, leaves Arizona and heads for his ranch in California. Joining him—in a covered wagon, no less, so that they complete the image of westward expansion—are Angie Lowe (Geraldine Page), a white woman whose shiftless husband, Ed (Leo Gordon), has died earlier in a shootout with Hondo, and her six-year-old son Johnny (Lee Aaker), for whom Hondo readily becomes a surrogate father. Hondo, so lately our Double Other, so thoroughly at home in the wilderness and among wild men, metamorphoses into a white pioneer headed to his American garden spot. His last words (and the movie's) are "Wagons forward, ho!" the rallying cry of Manifest Destiny.

The action establishes Hondo's heroic status by insisting on his unimpeachable Indianness. Hondo is "part Indian." Unlike Cooper's Natty Bumppo, he is a man *with* a cross. Yet it seems ludicrous to relegate him

7. John Tuska writes that, during the shooting of *Hondo*, "John Ford acted as an unofficial adviser on the picture, wanting to do what he could to make [John] Wayne's venture into film production a success." *A Variable Harvest: Essays and Reviews of Film and Literature* (Jefferson, N.C.: McFarland, 1990), p. 331. In the annotated filmography at the end of his book, Tag Gallagher writes the following of John Ford's hand in *Hondo*: "Two shots, only, were directed by Ford—of a troop of cavalry that Wayne sees when he visits an army post—but they stand out in this film like Delacroixes in a gallery of *TV Guide* covers." *John Ford*, p. 535. Perhaps; yet *Hondo's* first image of Wayne (afoot, rifle in his right hand, saddlebags in the left, flanked by the mean but loyal cur Sam), however indebted it may be to Ford's *Stagecoach* and its own first image of Wayne, has provided the single most reproduced image of Wayne.

to the type of the "half-breed." Indeed, the part that is Indian is so principally because so much of Hondo's unassailable *whiteness* hinges on the possibility that he may convincingly appropriate the Indian's own *Indianness*. Grant, then, that Hondo has Indian parentage. Even so, Indianness here is hardly a racial claim—hardly, we might say, an avowal of biogenetic kinship. Instead, it is a claim of Hondo's *fitness as white hero*, an attestation of the Western's persistent need to identify the champion of civilization by exalting his capacity for savagery. A brief exchange from the L'Amour novel dramatizes this recurrent paradox (even if L'Amour, as I suspect, remained unaware of it as such). Vittoro (so spelled in the novel), the Apache chief who has adopted Angie's son Johnny, notes the extended absence of her husband from the ranch and asks her to choose a new husband from among his Apache warriors. Angie responds by invoking race: the Apache warriors, she says, "'follow a strong leader, . . . but an Apache woman for an Apache man—a white woman for a white man.'"[8] And when Vittoro insists, Angie, implicitly claiming the absent Hondo as her man, replies: "My son . . . is born to this land. I would have him know it as the Apache knows it. The man I choose will teach him to know the ways of the Apache" (85). Who better, then, than the *white* hero (and what better white hero than Wayne) to incarnate the strange yet seductive logic whereby we come to believe that an irreproachable Indianness both originates in and guarantees his preeminent whiteness? But once we have acquiesced in this power of cultural appropriation are we not also obligated to hope that some sort of cultural divestment will accompany closure? In these hopes, no less than in these acquiesences and attributions, we may already identify the hero by his racio-cultural *ambivalence*.

The chronicling itself of Hondo's Indianness falsifies the implied claim of divestment at the end. So heavily, even monotonously, does *Hondo* attest its hero's Indianness, that it can actually make such declarations and depositions serve other purposes as well—foreplay, for example. In the long opening sequence, Hondo, alone with Angie, makes a dubious analogy: as dogs can "smell Indians," so "Indians can smell white people." To Angie's skepticism, Hondo replies, "Well, it's true. I'm part Indian, and I can smell you when I'm downwind of you. . . .

8. Louis L'Amour, *Hondo* (1953; New York: Bantam Books, 1983), p. 84. It should be noted that the novel *followed* the release of the movie. "The film," writes Lee Clark Mitchell, "was developed from L'Amour's short story 'The Gift of Cochise,' (1952)," and recast by James Edward Grant as a screenplay with a significantly different plot and newly named hero. See *Westerns: Making the Man in Fiction and Film* (Chicago: University of Chicago Press, 1996), p. 198. "The Gift of Cochise" appeared in *Collier's* (5 July 1952).

You baked today. I can smell fresh bread on you. Some time today you cooked with salt pork. . . . You smell all over like soap. You took a bath, and on top of that you smell all over like a woman. I could find you in the dark, and I'm only part Indian." Also, *Hondo* deploys a strategy that we have already encountered, the Indian's own endorsement of the hero's Indianness. Late in the story, Hondo easily detects a young Apache warrior sneaking up on him and Angie. Victorio (Michael Pate), who had allowed the young warrior to lead the way into the clearing, now appears out of the bushes and smiles approvingly at Hondo: "You are Apache," he resolutely declares. If a young Apache warrior should somehow fail at being an Apache, then the great Victorio himself shall offer the white hero as a model. It suffices for our purposes to adduce one more example of this insistence on Hondo's Indianness—an early exchange between Hondo and Angie about Apaches.

At the opening, Hondo, having lost his horse trying to escape from the Apaches, approaches the Lowe ranch hoping to buy a horse so that he can carry his report on Apache war preparations back to General Crook. Ed, Angie's husband, is absent from the ranch. As we will discover later, Ed is a rancorous churl who tries to shoot Hondo in the back just before Hondo kills him. The exchange below, late in the long opening scene, shows how the need to establish Hondo's Indianness tyrannizes the action. Once Angie confesses that she lied about her long-absent husband's whereabouts, Hondo tries to convince her that she and Johnny should leave the ranch and seek safety with the army:

> *Hondo*: Mrs. Lowe, if you've got good sense you'll pack you and that boy of yours and come out with me. There's trouble brewing in the Apache lodges. Victorio, their main chief, has called a war council. A full report of it is in that dispatch I'm carrying.
> *Angie*: But you don't know. We've always gotten along splendidly with the Apache. They drink and bring their horses to our spring on their way north to the buffalo hunt. I've never seen the great Victorio, but there have always been plenty of Apache here.
> *Hondo*: I've seen the great Victorio, before the treaty. His horse had forty scalps on its mane.
> *Angie*: That was before the treaty.
> *Hondo*: We broke that treaty—us whites. There is no word in the Apache language for *lie*, and they've been lied to. And if they rise there won't be a white left in the Territory.
> *Angie*: They won't bother me—us, I mean. We always got along very well.

The exchange defies generic convention in several respects, not least of which is Angie's unconcern at the Indians' imminent presence. As

[232]

we saw in chapters 1 and 2, the white woman is most often ignorant of the Indians; and her response to their presence, potential or actual, tends to take the form of shock or panic. More important, however, the exchange deprives the hero of that easy authority through which he can usually compel the white woman to dread the "fate worse than death" (and therefore quickly learn to depend on him). Instead, the dialogue turns into a contest between *degrees* of knowing Apaches. If we never doubt which of the contestants will prove to know the Apaches in the highest degree, it is in part because we recognize the stakes in the contest: the different degrees of their knowledge of the Apaches ultimately affirms culturally prescribed gender roles. What kind of man would Hondo be if this unprotected woman turned out to be right about the Apaches? How would Hondo, not needing to rescue the woman from the Indians, prove himself worthy of her?

If the hero's manhood is at stake in the contest, however, so also is the Western's own credibility as a mirror of American values. Not surprisingly, the contest is rigged in Hondo's favor: if distance and mere habit characterize Angie's relation with the Indians, testimony and intimacy mark Hondo's own (and this, especially the intimacy, even before we learn that Hondo has had an Apache wife). Angie affirms that "we are at peace with the Apaches," but Hondo knows, and seemingly at first-hand, that "Victorio . . . has called a war council." Angie protests that the Lowes and the Apaches have always been at peace, though she "has never seen the great Victorio." But Hondo *has* seen him. Moreover, Angie, who is thoroughly domestic for all her professed Western independence, remains bound to place (until the hero carries her off, at the end). The long absence of her husband from the ranch makes of it a place that fairly trumpets her vulnerability. Hondo, by contrast, freely roams the spaces of savage spectacle. He is the eye witness, and the specific image that Victorio presented to him at the time—this vision of savagery palpable and overwhelming via the scalps that adorn the chief's pony—aims to convince us that Hondo's is indeed the deeper, or at least the more necessary, knowledge of the Apaches.

Still, this same knowledge—the very thoroughness of it, however presumptuously affirmed—only highlights Hondo's ambivalence. Even when he appears to be demonstrating his knowledge of the Apaches, he betrays his own whiteness. Though he may know that the Apache language lacks the word *lie*, he prefaces the bit of lexical lore by identifying himself not only *as* a white man but also *with* the treaty-breaking white men. Indianness and whiteness, mingling as they do in the one moment, undermine the presumed stability of a heroic white identity. In the effort to explain the narrative and cultural maneuvers through which the hero simultaneously avows and evades historical complicity in the disappearance of the Indian, we come upon an instance of the ambivalence that characterizes the Double Other: he invokes his heroic *whiteness* in order that it may sanction his Indianness, while still counting on his *Indianness* to absolve him of his whiteness.

In the movie's final scene, just before he swings the wagons westward, Hondo expresses regret at the passing of the Indian: "[The] end of a way of life. Too bad, it was a good way." In a post-apocalyptic America, such an endorsement shall have cast the white hero as the sole repository of the Indian, his memorializer. In him the Indian endures. Yet, if he now stands alone as America's "last" Indian, it is only because his whiteness somehow allows it; and it is this selfsame whiteness on which he must count, in order that he may divest himself of even the last trace of his Indianness; for only thus may he enter the paradise that his racial inheritance has reserved for its exalted own. Yet again, his Indianness would exonerate him, anoint him, separate him from the rest of "us whites."

So then, must Hondo not *retain* his Indianness, if only as one more token of his Adamic fitness? Where, however, in the implicit if tenuous compact between the hero and his *ethnos* was a paradise promised to him who betrayed his "gifts"? If the hero has indeed become the Indian, then is he not a stain on the very civilization that urged and sanctioned the transformation? And will the paradisal bliss not be threatened correspondingly if, as Hondo contends, the Indian had been noble, if only because the hero's work for civilization implicates him in crimes against such nobility? Does it not then seem as necessary that he should divest himself of guilt as that he should shed all vestiges of his Indianness? Is he then white? Indian? And if he should be neither for being, now, *American*, is he really identified by anything more precisely demarcated than his cultural ambivalence? Could he, paradoxically, enter the national paradise only as a man without a country?

We thus find ambivalences within the basic ambivalence that stamps the Double Other—an identity subverted not merely by a fundamental opposition of Other to Same but one thoroughly splintered, self-contested by the insistent traces of opposing cultures and ethnicities each of which must be affirmed and denied, avowed and denounced, each with equal force, each with utmost vehemence. The Indian "part" of him is itself divided, since the "red gift" that declares him supremely fit to participate in the destruction of the Indian is also the "gift" that would keep him free of remorse once the Indian vanishes. So, too, however, is his whiteness itself divided: the whiteness that endorses his Indianness prods him to destroy the Indian, yet it also compels him to demand his share of the blessings of civilization. And who shall say with confidence that the mythic American identity is anything but this continual affirmation and denial of these fragments, fragments various and, as one might say, yet unshored against the ruins?

In a mythology that presumes to have resolved all tensions between Other and Same in the instant following triumph, the hero, as does the nation that he represents, comes instead to embody those tensions. The necessity of cultural divestment becomes clear, and as clear a national imperative—yet never so much so that the Othered Same, even as he leads the wagons westward, cannot reveal it to be a mere illusion, his own and the nation's alike. The Same has become irreclaimably Othered. The necessity itself of cultural divestment determines its impossibility. In this way, the aporia of cultural divestment becomes the aporia of the *ahistorical*. Hondo's move from Arizona to California suggests a form of the illusion of cultural divestment: for Hondo, Arizona has become the site not only of bloody combat against the very Indians that he admires but of a sort of homicidal contest with Angie's husband; and for Angie herself Arizona evokes not only a failed marriage but also the adulterous impulses that the movie would have us sweep aside by making a reprobate of her husband Ed. We learn only late in the story that Hondo owns a ranch in California, when his friend Buffalo Baker (Ward Bond) remarks that the Lowe ranch greatly resembles Hondo's own. Like the Arizona ranch, yet free of the great elemental guilt, the California ranch defines and circumscribes the hero's very own Edenic future.

The half-century since *Hondo* has seen significant variants of the illusion of cultural divestment, several of which we will examine below. The genre, after all, endures to a large extent by virtue of its modifications. Yet the frequent lapses of our generic memory, abetted perhaps by the importunate allures of the Myth of Conquest (say, in the guise of more technically accomplished movies, of the latest cultural icons, even of more accurate historical reenactments), often enable the return of the illusion in its oldest and most familiar form. A look at *The Patriot* (Emmerich, 2000) will not only bring our inquiry closer to date but also will allow us to explore how the cultural comforts of an illusion account for its obstinate recurrence.

The Patriot begins with the opening of a mahogany chest, its lid trimmed with fancy Chippendale brass fittings. A close-up shot of the contents takes in papers, coins, a beribboned star-like bijou (which the hero later gives to his daughter-in-law), a pocket watch, a well-worn sword. Over somber music, the chest still open, we see a tomahawk (followed by a powder horn) gently deposited over these other items. The camera lingers for a while on the tomahawk, which is quite ornate: its head of steel, with the hero's rank and initials etched in fancy scroll; the whole length of its wooden handle carved with an acanthus motif; the tip fitted with metal, perhaps silver—in short, the delicate art of the lethal weapon. For all its ornateness, however, it, too, like the sword, has seen active service. Over the close-up of the tomahawk now comes the hero's voiceover—plaintive, remorseful, full of foreboding: "I have long feared that my sins would return to visit me; and the cost is more than I can bear." These, *The Patriot*'s first words, will find a confirming context much later, when the hero repeats them over the dead body of his oldest son, Gabriel (Heath Ledger), and renounces, though only for a while, further participation in the Revolutionary War.[9] The chest lid closes, and the action cuts to a brightly lit close-up of a basketful of corn ears—the bounty of the American harvest begotten of secret and dismal deeds.

The fearful man of the opening voiceover is the once fearless hero of the French and Indian War, Capt. Benjamin Martin (Mel Gibson) "whose fury," as a member of the South Carolina Assembly puts it in a later scene, "was so famous during the Wilderness campaign." The opening of *The Patriot* also makes it clear that the hero's "fury," and therefore his "sins," connect unambiguously with the tomahawk—that is, with the Indian and with savage warfare. Not until much later, however, following a terrible defeat of the rag-tag revolutionary militiamen under Martin's command, do we learn the particulars of these sins. The remaining militiamen have taken refuge in a swamp hideout. Father and son are beyond the hearing of the other men, yet all these men seem to know what only the son does not:

9. *The Patriot* narrates the thinly veiled story of Francis Marion, the renowned "Swamp Fox," South Carolinian of Huguenot parents and hero of the Revolutionary War. After Tories captured, tortured, and cruelly killed Marion's nephew, Gabriel (a lieutenant in the militia), we are told that Marion "grieved for his nephew as for an only son." Robert Duncan Bass, *Swamp Fox: The Life and Campaigns of General Francis Marion* (New York: Henry Holt, 1959, 1972), p. 90.

Gabriel: Father, wherever you go, men buy you drinks because of what happened at Fort Wilderness. Strangers know more about you than I do. Tell me what happened.

Martin: Your mother asked me that question around about the time you were born. I was drunk and foolish enough to answer it. [*Gabriel, taking this as his father's refusal to tell the story of Fort Wilderness, gets up to leave, but now Martin, his back to Gabriel, begins to talk, as if to himself*] The French and the Cherokee had raided along the Blue Ridge. The English settlers had sought refuge at Fort Charles. By the time we got there, the fort was abandoned. They'd left about a week before, but what we found was [*hesitates, does not finish the sentence*].

Gabriel: Go on.

Martin: They'd killed all the settlers, the men. With the women and some of the children, they had [*again, recalling the horror, hesitates and cannot finish the sentence*]. We buried them all—what was left of them. We caught up with them at Fort Wilderness. We took our time. We cut them apart slowly, piece by piece. I can see their faces. I can still hear their screams. All but two—we let *them* leave. We placed the heads on a pallet and sent them back with the two that lived back to Fort Ambercon. And the eyes, tongues, fingers we put in baskets, sent them down the Asheulot to the Cherokees. Soon after, the Cherokees broke their treaty with the French. That's how we justified it. We were [*long pause, resumes with great irony*] heroes.

Gabriel: And men bought you drinks.

Martin: And not a day goes by when I don't ask God's forgiveness for what I did.[10]

In the wilderness, then, this future hero of the American Revolution went "native." The sins that he accumulated there plague not only him and his progeny but the very character and soul of the young nation itself. In the memory of the horror lies already the remorse; yet the selfsame memory, painful though it may be, shall yet serve as a mighty resource—the savage wherewithal solicitously attendant upon the birth of the nation. It may be worth noting that *The Patriot*, for all that it identifies the Indian as the source of savagery, shows only two Indians in

10. The atrocities in the fictional Fort Wilderness allude to the historical devastation wreaked upon the Cherokees by Lieutenant Colonel James Grant in the summer of 1761. Marion was one of 1200 or so provincials who joined Grant's 1200 soldiers. Grant, writes Robert Duncan Bass, "swept the Little Tennessee and the Tuckaseegee Valleys with fire until Chief Attakullakulla [Little Carpenter] came to him at Keowee and sued for peace" (*Swamp Fox*, p. 9). See also Peter Horry and Mason Locke Weems, *The Life of Gen'l Francis Marion, a Celebrated Partisan Officer in the Revolutionary War against the British and Tories in South Carolina and Georgia* (New York: John W. Lovell, n.d.); Hugh F. Rankin, *Francis Marion: The Swamp Fox* (New York: Thomas Y. Crowell, 1973), pp. 4–6; Fred Anderson, *Crucible of War: The Seven Years' War and the Fate of Empire in British North America, 1754–1766* (New York: Alfred A. Knopf, 2000), pp. 457–71.

one brief scene. Following Martin's battle with the British troops that are escorting the captive Gabriel, a long shot of the British camp shows two Indians—long black hair, breechcloth, leggings—their backs to the camera, at the edges of the camp. The whole shot of these tiny and faceless Indians lasts about five seconds. But then, who needs Indians? No better source of Indianness and of savagery than the white hero himself.

In an earlier chapter I made passing reference to the way in which, in *The Last of the Mohicans*, Cooper distinguishes Hawkeye from Chingachgook when he introduces us to the two friends. Here is that difference again, now in detail:

> [Hawkeye] wore a hunting-shirt of forest-green, fringed with faded yellow, and a summer cap, of skins which had been shorn of their fur. He also bore a knife in a girdle of wampum, like that which confined the scanty garments of the Indian, but no tomahawk. His moccasins were ornamented after the gay fashion of the natives, while the only part of his under dress which appeared below the hunting-frock, was a pair of buckskin leggings, that laced at the sides, and which were gartered above the knees, with the sinews of a deer. A pouch and horn completed his personal accoutrements, though a rifle of great length, which the theory of the more ingenious whites had taught them, was the most dangerous of all fire-arms, leaned against a neighboring sapling.[11]

Only two objects distinguish the white hero from the Indian: one of these we know by its absence—the tomahawk—the other because only the white hero possesses it—the long rifle. So goes the mythology that would distinguish white from Indian, even when the historical record of white colonial practices during the French and Indian War would seem to confute it.[12] Indeed, there seems to be no reason for the white wilderness warrior not to carry a tomahawk, even one, like Chingachgook's or Benjamin Martin's, "of English manufacture," unless this reason be thoroughly typological—and to that extent, of course, racist and mythic—rather than military or historical. To discover, then, even at the beginning, that Martin has known the use of the tomahawk and that he fears for his soul is to suspect him already of the sin of savagery. For

---

11. *Last of the Mohicans*, pp. 500–01.

12. Colonial males between the ages of 16 and 60 called to muster in the French and Indian War would be "required to keep a firearm, ammunition, gunpowder, and hatchet ready for instant use." William R. Nester, *The Great Frontier War: Britain, France, and the Imperial Struggle for North America, 1607–1755* (Westport: Praeger, 2000), p. 152.

Martin has fought in the wilderness, which means that he has fought Indian style—deaf to the implied entreaties of his own "white gifts."

Yet, if his savage deeds beget certain retribution, so, too, do they distinguish and empower him for victory in the Revolutionary War. At the beginning, Martin declares himself a pacifist. The burying of the hatchet, so to say, finds its proper complement in his persistent (and as persistently failed) effort to make impossibly light Windsor rocking chairs: the synecdoches of war yield to those that evoke the pastimes and idle obsessions of peace. (Even so, our first glimpse of Martin's rage occurs when he smashes the latest broken chair against a pile of previous failures.) Martin, though a widower, lives in the southern colonial version of the "fine good place to be"—a stately mansion, a gaggle of handsome children, freed slaves who lovingly stay on the land, and (not to forget the romantic interest) a beautiful and single sister-in-law, Charlotte (Joely Richardson), who lives close to the Martin plantation. Martin, it seems, counts on this domestic bliss to help him forget that he is an Othered Same.

On the eve of the Revolution, Martin, precisely because he has known war's horror, argues against the levy in the Assembly. When the aforementioned assemblyman expresses doubt that such counsel should come from the warrior famous for his "fury," Martin simply acknowledges: "I was intemperate in my youth." And later, when asked to weigh his decision in terms of his principles, he responds, rather disarmingly yet to the shame of his two oldest sons, who are present at the Assembly: "I'm a parent. I haven't got the luxury of principles." But children proverbially fail to heed the counsel of their parents, and Gabriel enlists immediately after the levy passes.

Later, even as the British are taking Gabriel to be hanged as a spy, Martin, intending to protect the remaining six children from the evil Colonel Tavington (Jason Isaacs), still refuses to act. Not so, however, his son Thomas (Gregory Smith), who rushes to the aid of his shackled brother only to be shot in the back by Tavington, who now orders the Martin mansion fired. No sooner does Thomas die in his father's arms than Martin rushes into the burning house, retrieves the instruments of war—rifles, powder horn, knife, and, most prominently visible in the shot, the tomahawk—and musters his two next oldest boys, Nathan (Trevor Morgan) and Samuel (Bryan Chafin), both well short of adolescence, to Gabriel's rescue. Twenty-one British soldiers escort Gabriel through the woods, and twenty fall to Martin and his boys (the one survivor left to testify to Martin's mythic powers).

Skulking behind trees, looking down at the soldiers on the trail below, and ably supported by his two boys, Martin kills many with his rifles. But then, when there are but a handful of soldiers left, he descends upon them with only a knife and the tomahawk. Fighting *mano a mano*, he kills four with the tomahawk, then turns from the last of these only to find a soldier holding a knife to Gabriel's throat. Only a moment's hesitation and Martin, though a good distance away, hurls the tomahawk and sinks it in the soldier's forehead, killing him instantly. Recovering his tomahawk, he rushes at a soldier who is running away. He hurls the tomahawk at him, burying it in his back, and now, though the soldier appears to be dead from the single blow, Martin leans over him and strikes him repeatedly, maniacally, grunting as he strikes, howling, crying. Already at the end of the brutal assault against the last soldier, Martin looks heavenward, perhaps uttering a prayer for forgiveness now that his fury seems spent, perhaps pleading that this grisly commingling of paternal grief and savage cruelty should be the extent of the "cost" that he shall have paid for this latest form of his "sins." Now Martin, exhausted, turns to look at his children. The reverse shot shows them looking at him aghast: his face drips everywhere with the soldier's blood and brains, and his expression reflects a soul gone mad, lusting after even more blood, though longing for forgiveness from God and children alike.

Martin's *Indianness* accounts therefore for the necessary and justifying *difference* between the stiff and stale Anglo-Saxons and the young and mobile Anglo-Americans, between tyranny and freedom—between a decaying empire and the promised greatness of the new one. No more than in Cooper's *The Pioneers*, the struggle here has little to do with Indians. As Susan Scheckel has noted about the first Leatherstocking Tale, "[t]he crucial event underlying the conflict has nothing at all to do with Indians but is strictly a matter among whites: as Cooper ingeniously constructs the plot, the American Revolution (fighting between the Indians' 'English and . . . American fathers') becomes the ultimate source of the conflict over who has the right to own and inherit American land."[13] By *The Patriot's* logic of American national identity, then, wilderness warfare is the Indian's contribution to American independence—the brawn and the sweat, the cunning and the craft that enforce the high-minded principles of the Declaration. Yet the Indianness that so often wins the day in *The Patriot* is hardly all strategy: at least to the extent of its investment in the tomahawk, Indianness iden-

13. *Insistence of the Indian*, p. 23.

tifies not so much the Indian *culturally* considered as it does savagery *morally* considered. Indianness is not, therefore, a token of colonial cultural appropriation but an index of the dark soul. Thus, we might extend the logic of Scheckel's fine argument by suggesting that if Martin needs to shed his Indianness, he somehow needs to appropriate—perhaps merely to recall—the mystical love of liberty that characterized the ancient Anglo-Saxon paragons.

The implied premise that the dark soul is "Indian" makes for a fine illusion indeed, since such a premise also projects the eventual elimination of things "Indian"—and thus, presumably, of American ambivalence—from the soul of both the white hero and the new nation. In other words, the illusion of cultural divestment comes fully into play almost as soon as Martin emerges from the depths of his enraged and tormented soul, after he tomahawks the last soldier. His son Samuel, the youngest of the two with him in the rescue raid, turns away from Martin later that night (safe at Aunt Charlotte's), as if horrified by this ghastly sight—this unimagined side—of his father, awash in blood and brains. And Gabriel understands that Martin acted not out of sympathy for the Cause but (like an Indian) out of revenge for the murder of Thomas. From this point on, *The Patriot* seems as if self-ordained to bring all of Martin's savage power into the Revolutionary War without thereby staining the Cause with his "Indian" savagery. To this project of cultural divestment the disappearance of the synecdochical tomahawk is central.

The Patriot deploys all the filters that would distill pure patriotic sacrifice from the contagion of savage rage: the family in general, of course, but in particular the declared love of Martin's youngest girl Susan (Skye McCole Bartusiak), who had heretofore refused to speak to her father in punishment for his long absences; the love of the comely, courageous, and devoted Charlotte; the new-found devotion to the dream of the new nation, as vested in the American flag that Gabriel had been mending and which Martin (following Gabriel's death) now carries with him into the Battle of Cowpens; and finally, the love of Martin's men (a love representative of a nation's reverence for its hero) who, immediately after the war, appear before the ruins of the Martin home to help rebuild it. No such filter seems more effective, however, or more appropriate for the dubious enterprise of cultural divestment, than the actual loss of the tomahawk in the climactic *mano a mano* between Martin and Tavington. After all, Martin had once before enjoyed the blessings of friends, of loving children, and of a wife whose tender mercies had led him to suppress the demon of youthful violence. Yet the demon had reappeared, unappeased, implacable. Tempered by re-morse though the demonic fury may have been in the years between the two wars, Martin had failed to exorcise it (else why just put the tomahawk safely away in the mahogany chest rather than renounce it entirely by discarding it)?

When the line held jointly by the Continental Army and the militia falters, Martin, though he has already spotted Tavington in the fray, chooses rather to exhort his men to hold the line than to confront his mortal foe. He takes the colors from a retreating soldier and charges, alone, the onrushing British soldiers. He reaches high ground and waves the flag, rallying the troops. Inevitably, however, Martin and Tavington fight each other. As Tavington charges on his horse, Martin steps aside at the last moment and drives the flagstaff's spearhead into the horse's chest, knocking Tavington off his mount. He then shoots at the disoriented Tavington, using the last of the bullets cast from Thomas's lead toy soldiers; but a cannon shot exploding behind him throws off his aim, and he only wounds Tavington. They then fight man-to-man, Tavington causing the more serious wounds with his sword. Already badly wounded and on his knees, Martin raises the tomahawk in defense against the onrushing Tavington, but the villain's swing of the sword knocks it out of his hand. And now the camera ac-tually leaves the hand-to-hand fight to look at the tomahawk as it flies off (in slow motion, lest we miss the moment's importance). It never again appears.

Still on his knees, his back to Tavington, Martin's death seems in-evitable. Yet suddenly the screen seems unusually bright, shouts of tri-umph drown out the din of battle, and the Stars and Stripes wave proudly everywhere as the Americans, inspired by Martin's one-man charge, chase the British, who run away even before the proud Corn-wallis (Tom Wilkinson) gives the order to retreat. Martin, from whose point of view we see some of these shots, seems newly nerved by the sight of the flags and the advancing Americans. But Tavington, made overbold by the sight of his prostrate enemy, mocks a threat that Martin made in an earlier encounter: "Kill me before the war is over, will you. It appears that you are not the better man." He rushes at Martin from behind, sword aloft. Though still on his knees, Martin has already picked up a rifle fitted with a bayonet. As Tavington approaches, Mar-tin ducks, turns, and thrusts the bayonet all the way into his abdomen, paralyzing him instantly, but not knocking him over. "You're right," Martin responds, though still on his knees; but then he rises and looks

Tavington in the eye: "My sons were better men." He drives an uncoupled bayonet through the villain's gullet.

Presumably, then, the final act of violence constitutes an act not of vengeance—an act such as one might have expected from the white man's Indian or even from a Double Other—but of vindication: Martin, his savage rage not so much spent or even diluted as converted into patriotic zeal, can—indeed, must—kill Tavington in what amounts to an apotheosis of his two dead boys. For their martyrdom, unlike his original heroism, is innocent of savage warfare; and to have killed their vile murderer by recourse to savage methods—thus again incurring the "sins" that have long since revisited Martin—would have stained the sacrifice of the two pure sons. So that we may acquiesce in the conversion, the transformation of blind and vengeful "fury" into redemptive violence, Hollywood casts the flag(staff) as a weapon that is as allegorical as it is lethal, and then follows this transmutation with the bayonet. Let the new *American* ferocity—now as distinct from Indian savagery as the new war is distant from the old—assert itself at the point of a properly civilized weapon—the newly born nation begotten of the repudiation of savagery yet every bit as capable of the "Indian's" fury.

The Patriot had to Indianize its hero in order that it might thereby distinguish him from the British conqueror. It had called upon the Euro-American's experience in wilderness warfare so as to make clear the difference between British Empire and free nation—to *justify*, indeed, the difference between England and Anglo-America, even as it thereby also *explained* the historical outcome of the Revolutionary War, and thus the origins of a new world order. The hero's Indianness, his (supposedly) appropriated savagery, accounted for his triumph, even as it certified his new identity. The American was an American because he had been, at a crucial moment in the formation of his character, "Indian," unrestrained and merciless in his cruelty to his enemies. Yet, having so thoroughly convinced us of Martin's capacity for savagery, *The Patriot* now needed, toward the end, to *de*-Indianize him—to remove all doubt that an enraged and deliberate cruelty could ultimately claim to be an integral component of the emergent American *ethnos*, a part of that which made it "exceptional." It became necessary to repudiate this defining trait, this link of the national soul with *its own*—not the Indian's—dark side, by repudiating the Indian entirely, if only in the form of that persistent synecdoche, the tomahawk, that never betokened anything so palpable as the utter absence of the historical Indian from the mythic action.

[243]

Giambattista Vico, Edward Said writes (endorsing the conclusions of the Italian philosopher), "having rethought beginnings, . . . saw that no one could really be first, neither the savage man nor the reflective philosopher, because each made a beginning and hence was always *being first*."[14] No doubt so. But mythology, having generated a process of its own, now purposes to abrogate it by rescinding its own temporal schema of the nation's emergence for no more ironic purpose than to locate and authorize an absolute origin—an origin to be understood in the impossibly unrelated way that Aristotle defines it: as "that which is not itself necessarily after anything else (*Poetics* 1450b 27)." Somehow, then, the Myth of Conquest must deploy a *mythos* (both a plot and a myth) that will distinguish between origin and beginnings, that will sunder that which would be first from that which begets. Hence the illusion of cultural divestment becomes but a special case of the illusion—so dear to all mythologies—of timelessness, of an *archē* that is simultaneously immutable and generative—the Myth of Conquest as American *logos*. The hoped-for eradication of the Indian as a component of the national identity finds an apt correlative in the very nature of the mythic itself: the discourse that culminates in the victory of Sameness must deny *alteration* as fervently as it denies *alterity*.

Conquest's impossibly delicate task had been *to make power innocent*. Whenever Conquest, compelled by the vicissitudes of its own self-perpetuation, operates without a justifying idea, without a purpose that can be held up and bowed down before, then, like the famous and powerful Oz, naked without his curtains and contraptions, it beholds only its own pitiless truculence—civilization as but an arbitrary exercise of force, power without vision. It must then reinvent itself by inventing a new version of the old sustaining ideas: Civilization, Progress, Destiny, Humanity, the latest New World Order. Nothing about Conquest is therefore to be more distrusted than its self-examinations, its "revisions" in the name of "history." Hollywood's "revisions," so radical at first glance, would reveal little more than the persistence of the Adamic myth in American culture. I discuss the major revisions of the nineties, below, but it seems appropriate to introduce them by a brief look at the Western that may well be at once the most

14. Edward Said, *Beginnings: Intention and Method* (New York: Columbia University Press, 1985), p. 350.

artless of these and the most preposterous, *Quigley Down Under* (Wincer, 1990).

Matthew Quigley (Tom Selleck) travels from Wyoming to the Australian Outback at the behest of Elliott Marston (Alan Rickman), a wealthy cattle baron. Quigley answers Marston's advertisement for the world's best marksman, and he shows up in the ranch ready (as he supposes) to rid Marston's ranch of an infestation of dingoes. Alone with Marston at a lavish dinner for two, Quigley soon learns that Marston has hired him to exterminate not dingoes but aborigines. The aborigines, whom Marston holds in utter contempt—and whose cultural backwardness he pointedly explains by drawing a parallel with that of the American Indian—killed his parents. Marston also notes that the aborigines, for all their presumed stupidity, have learned to stay beyond the range of most firearms: hence the need for Quigley and his Sharps rifle, deadly at over 900 yards. Suddenly there is a cut from the dinner scene to the exterior of the ranch house, and we see Marston flying out the window. Quigley, outraged by the proposition, has tossed the villain out of his own house.

Quigley becomes, not surprisingly, the great deliverer of the aborigines. Yet this privilege, by itself, though implausible—if not, indeed, offensive—hardly describes the extent and reach of the Myth of Conquest in the action. *Quigley Down Under* complicates its plot by making Marston, the villain, a lover of the American "Wild West," and it does this specifically by making him the full repository of the Wild West's most naive, if persistent illusion, the "mystique," as John Cawelti might call it, of "the six-gun." He accounts himself, as he says just before the shootout with Quigley, a man born not in the wrong century but on the wrong continent. Indeed, Marston has mastered the Colt's revolver, and has throughout made much of his preference for that weapon over Quigley's Sharps (Quigley having noted earlier that he never had much use for a six-gun). Thus, Marston's fascination with the West functions as a component of his villainy. Once Marston's men bring in the battered and bruised Quigley (having captured him, they drag him behind a horse over a long distance), Marston decides to give Quigley the chance to beat him in a shootout and has one of his men shove a six-shooter in his belt. Of course, Quigley wins, noting sardonically the difference between having no use for a six-gun and not knowing how to use it. The plot complication, then—if complication it is—hinges on the need to have Quigley, on the one hand, denounce American history by condemning Marston's genocidal plan and, on the other, affirm his legitimacy as a Western hero through his undisputed dexterity with the six-shooter.

Here, then, is the impulse, in crude form, to be sure, yet so typical of the Myth of Conquest's revisions, to *de*historicize the conqueror's relation with the conquered while ensuring that his power to conquer remains undiminished: for power must be somehow innocent. Quigley's travel to Australia is accordingly a journey toward a place presumed to be without history; the trip in space merely masks the voyage in time—in a *pre*time, really, when guilt over the dispossession of the native has not yet haunted the white hero. Yet the very presumption of Quigley's *ahistorical* presence in Australia implies his own all too keen awareness of American history: the genocidal proposition so offends and outrages Quigley because he recognizes it as both immoral and *historical*—because he takes it as an incitement, on Marston's part, to repeat America's genocidal history against the Indian.

Quigley, who enjoys the reverence of the aborigines, stands fully absolved of any such guilt. Yet we must wonder about his past, though we would be seduced into believing that he has none. Whence his fancy western gear? Whence, perhaps especially, the Sharps rifle? Why were we never once told that the Sharps rifle was, because of its power and accuracy, crucial in the devastation of the buffalo herds? Is it mere coincidence, moreover, that Quigley is made to look so much like the historical Buffalo Bill Cody—the goatee, the mustache, the long hair, but also the splendor of his outfit, which clearly evokes those worn by the great showman? And did the filmmakers know that Cody is reputed to have earned his nickname in a contest with another "Buffalo Bill," a contest in which the one who could kill the most buffalo would get to keep the coveted sobriquet? Or that Cody took "the first scalp for Custer" in a one-on-one fight with Yellow Hair? Perhaps. Wincer, after all, gave us, only a year before, the sublime *Lonesome Dove* (1989) based on Larry McMurtry's rich fictionalization of the historical Goodnight-Loving partnership. Australia, in any case, functions as a guilty nation's second chance, its chance at redemption—and thus, much too ironically, as yet another Western frontier wherein to repeat the genocidal deeds against the *American* aborigine. If Quigley in fact escapes genocidal guilt in Australia, it is because he cannot escape it in America. Yet more: for in the end he leaves Australia—with Cora (Laura San Giacomo), herself redeemed of her American sins—for America. The deliverance of the Australian aborigines from the evil Marston somehow cleanses the sins of Conquest in the back-home Eden where there are, still, no Indians. With all this in mind, I now turn to a further exploration of the ahistorical in three revisionist Westerns—*Dances With Wolves, Geronimo: An American Legend,* and *The Last of the Mohicans* (Mann).

5

At the end of these three Westerns, the reinvented Indian, in apparent full exercise of his cultural integrity, endorses the old mythological decree that the white hero have *an ahistorical beginning,* an *archē* entirely without cultural or historical precedent. All three Westerns would have it that the Indian, in the end, disappears; in this, of course, they are hardly revisionist, since such is also the ending prescribed by the Hollywood canon. But at the end of these Westerns the Indians, just before they vanish, perform a crucial errand: they validate—and by validating proclaim uncontested and foreordained—the Edenic inheritance of the white hero. They identify, anoint, and then yield to this one white man, as if in confirmation of his exalted status as hero of a redeemed Western civilization in the New World. They accordingly attest to the emergent preeminence of that other "authentic American," the one that R. W. B. Lewis has described "as a figure of heroic innocence and vast potentialities, poised at the start of a new history."[15] To the extent that such an Indian authorizes the Edenic birthright of the hero—endorses, then, the non-history of his own epoch in American history—he can hardly be called new or accounted free of the white man's influence. These three Westerns, I hold, produce not so much a new Indian as an updated version of what I would like to call *mythological historicism*: the Indian, whom revision would present as an authentic historical person, still complies with the demands of the Myth of Conquest.

Uniquely Indian though he may be at the end, the white hero is also principally the American Adam. Alone of all white men he stands, at the end, exempted from history—so exempted not only by his claims of innocence, but by his having so thoroughly identified with the Indian as himself a being *outside history.* Alone in his Indianness, now that the Indian vanishes, he is not so much the last Indian as *the first American.* America can begin in him—not again or anew but *absolutely,* as if without a past. Revision's mythological historicism then gives us an Indian who, at the instant before his vanishing, understands, complies with,

15. R. W. B. Lewis, *The American Adam: Innocence, Tragedy, and Tradition in the Nineteenth Century* (1955; Chicago: University of Chicago Press, 1984), p. 1.

and sanctions these paradoxical temporalities, these transposed chronologies. According to this history, the white hero does not only outlast the Indian, he *outfirsts* him. The Indian's impending disappearance, coupled with his endorsement of the white hero's ascendancy, guarantees the precedence of the American Adam—what we might call, in a homely neology, *firstness*.

It would seem as if the white hero, having so successfully attained to full Indianness, should easily dispense with the urge to cultural divestment. For Indianness, as he knows it and embodies it, shows him at his best. Why then should he feel implicitly compelled, as do the Indian fighters, say, Hondo or *Arrowhead*'s Bannon, to shed the mark and stamp of so lofty a distinction? Of course he does not: he wears his Indianness as a badge of merit, a sign indelible and conspicuous of that privileged humanity that the Indian himself acknowledged. Is it, however, Indianness that he so proudly boasts at the end? Is he in truth radically *Other* to the nation that has come into being with the passing of the last Indian? Is the white hero the last Indian, and is he, unlike the presumed last *native*—unlike Kicking Bird or Geronimo or Chingachgook—exempt from passing? In the delicate difference between the last Indian and the first American, in that fine interstitial gap that separates the narrated ending from the implied mytho-historical origin, the revisionist insistence on the white hero's Indianness yields an ironic version of the illusion of cultural divestment: his unimpeachable Indianness, which he enjoys alone now that the last native has passed, renders him the first man in American history. Thus the white hero of the revisionist Western exists under an ironic illusion, believing as he does that he has divested himself of his whiteness when in fact it is his Indianness that he sheds. His lastness as Indian ensures his firstness as American.

Certainly this "firstness" of the white hero's is no invention of these three Westerns. Firstness answers to the basic premise that D. H. Lawrence identified as "the true myth of America": America "starts old, old, wrinkled and writhing in an old skin. And there is a gradual sloughing of the old skin, towards a new youth."[16] Firstness, therefore, refers not so much to importance or rank but to *origins*, to the initial state itself of unprecedented youth and perfect innocence, even if—though perhaps *because*—all this comes into being only in the wake of

16. D. H. Lawrence, *Studies in Classic American Culture* (1923; New York: Penguin Books, 1977), p. 60.

the disappearance of savagery. America belongs to the white hero of the revisionist Western by a self-evident teleology. At the *end* of history there is the original man, young, ever innocent—without so much as a genealogy yet somehow the culmination and apotheosis of all human endeavor.

Does the Indian, in his last moments, endorse only the *transfer* of his own firstness to the white hero, or does he endorse a *conflicting* claim, one shaped by the Edenic mythology of the Old World? Here revision fudges and equivocates. For it counts on our *recognition* (however dim or misinformed) of the Adamic type and his timeless paradisal hope, yet it presents him, at the end, as if he were the Indian's own legatee, Indian therefore by both descent and consent. I offer no direct answer to the question whether revision is manifestly disingenuous or merely the dupe of a mythology to which it must perforce appeal, even as it means to contest it. Yet irony does function here as a principle of inquiry (how else to be discussing "firstness" in a last chapter?), and can perhaps make clearer the necessary inferences for those concerned chiefly with such questions.

These three Westerns exhibit a tension between historical consciousness and what might be called the *mythic postulates*—the unquestioned assumptions of the Myth of Conquest, often present as generic convention—that guide and frame the story of the supposedly historical Indian. Revision, as they propose it, consists of an appeal to historical accuracy: to follow the lives of these Indians is to document in poignant detail the tragic and all too actual march of the native peoples toward cultural extinction. It is, moreover, to be deeply moved by the irrecoverable loss of such fine forms of humanity. Consider the following reflection of the voiceover narrator, Lieutenant Davis, toward the end of *Geronimo*: "I carry the memory of those days, days of bravery and cruelty, of heroism and deceit. And I am still faced with an undeniable truth: a way of life that endured a thousand years is gone. This desert, this land that we look out on, would never be the same." Here history appeals to our consciences: we are to take it as settled that the narrative action has rendered the Apaches and their destiny faithfully. And now the same narrative action closes the thousand-year chapter of that history. This all has passed, and to the extent that "our" history involves theirs, we are at once the richer for having their ideal humanity before us and the poorer for "our" complicity in their extinction.

Yet the ending of *Geronimo*—the fact itself of *closure*, as much as its assumption that the Indian's story can be brought to a definitive end

[249]

by the white perspective on history—already discloses a postulate of the Myth of Conquest—namely, that the Indian ceases to have a history, or at least a story worth telling, following the triumph of white civilization. It hardly matters, then, that Davis sympathizes with Geronimo, or that he is outraged by the army's treatment of Chato and the rest of the Chiricahua scouts (whom General Miles has ordered disarmed and exiled to Florida with Geronimo and his band).[17] We understand, even in the expression itself of outrage, that Davis has a life and a future that the Apaches do not have. His authorship seems curiously, even suspiciously, independent from their story, itself a form of firstness. This independent authorship becomes even more detached from the Indian because the presiding spirit of Davis's tale is not the titular Geronimo but First Lt. Charles B. Gatewood. For it is Gatewood whom Davis reveres, Gatewood whose "fascinating" virtue (as the Davis voiceover tells us) is "his sympathy and knowledge of all things pertaining to the Apache." He will cast Gatewood as a victim of white civilization, as no less a victim of Conquest than the Apaches themselves.

Mythological historicism takes it on faith that the last necessary victory of civilization over savagery specifies the moment in which the Indian finds his properly paradoxical *place* in "history" by somehow *disappearing* from it. History, as these Westerns understand it, is itself the source of our vision of the unchanging Indian. The two related ideas that I wish to develop further on the topic of "firstness" can be expressed in the following proposition: while the mythological historicism of these three revisionist Westerns holds the Indian in virtual timelessness, it releases the white hero—Indian though he may yet be—into a separate *yet equally timeless* region. In his own ahistorical region, the Indian seems to be forever fading, but not so the white hero in his own, emerging now as America's authentic beginning. At the moment when his oblivion appears imminent, the Indian authorizes the Adamic status of the white hero. What now follows is a brief look at the Indian of these recent Westerns at the instant just before he is supposed to vanish. Another brief look at the ending of *Dances With Wolves* may provide a clear example of this idea.

17. The historical Davis condemned the army for its treatment of the Apaches, but he reserves his most vituperative tone for his description of the ill-treatment of the Indian fighters, especially Lt. Charles B. Gatewood, who died, a broken man, in May, 1895. Britton Davis, *The Truth about Geronimo*, ed. M. M. Quaife (New Haven: Yale University Press, 1929), pp. 31, 235.

Soon after his return to the Lakota village from his captivity among the white soldiers, the hero Dances With Wolves decides to leave forever. Earlier, in the rescue raid, he and his Lakota friends killed all the white soldiers, and he now reasons that the army hates him "like they hate no other." The white hero and his wife, Stands With A Fist, begin their long ride out of the village. Then the following words scroll up: "Thirteen years later, their homes destroyed, their buffalo gone, the last band of free Sioux submitted to white authority at Fort Robinson, Nebraska. The great horse culture of the Plains was gone and the American frontier was soon to pass into history." What can it mean that the Indian is "gone," that he now passes, along with the American frontier, "into history"? As such an account would have it, the Indian passes into history because his moment in the mytho-historical conflict has come to an end. Unlike the white man's, the Indian's story suggests no possible extension beyond that end. Not only is "the great horse culture of the Plains" gone, no distinctly native culture replaces it. No less than the canonical Indian Western, then, revisionism posits an Indian who finds his sole historical justification in his predestined doom. Despite the revisionist ethos of these Westerns, the "new" Indian stays behind, stuck in "exoticism" or "savagism" or fashionable "Vanishing Americanism"—condemned in any case to the assigned "Otherness" that presumably ennobles him even as it continually foretells his extinction.

Yet the specific type that the new mythological historicism assigns to even this supposedly refigured Indian is not as important to our present purposes as is the *condition itself of historical conclusion*, the Indian's (en)closure, in an *ahistorical region* (or "ahistorical zone") from which white civilization now moves on in the full and unencumbered enjoyment of its triumph. The emplacement of the Indian in an atemporal space is, of course, no casual metaphor, as the reservation system proves. Berkhofer has noted the "curious timelessness" that whites invoke "in defining the Indian proper": "In spite of centuries of contact and the changed conditions of Native American lives, Whites picture the 'real' Indian as the one before contact or during the early period of that contact. . . . [M]ost Whites still conceive of the 'real' Indian as the aborigine he once was, *or as they imagine he once was*, rather than as he is now"[18] (my italics). The Indian is all past, and his past decrees the im-

18. *White Man's Indian*, pp. 28–29.

possibility of any genuine future. The Indian lacks a future because he vanishes from *white* history. To "pass into history" is to lag hopelessly as the course and star of empire track their destined and irrepressible ways. It is, accordingly, to have no part in "American" history—to be ever Other to "our" American history. To "pass into history" is to be forgotten.

But even as he fades, the Indian performs his vital role in the mytho-historical scheme: he testifies to the white hero's status as first American. Consider, then, the ending of Michael Mann's *The Last of the Mohicans*. Magua (Wes Studi) has killed Uncas (Eric Schweig) in a hand-to-hand fight where the winner was to take Alice Munro (Jodhi May). But as Magua offers his hand to Alice, she jumps off a cliff. Chingachgook (Russell Means) arrives too late to save his son Uncas, but he battles Magua and kills him. Now Hawkeye (Daniel Day-Lewis) and Cora Munro (Madeleine Stowe) join Chingachgook atop a mountain, where the camera pans over the vast surrounding landscape and returns to a medium shot of Chingachgook and Hawkeye. Then follows Chingachgook's poignant prayer: "Great Spirit and maker of all life, a warrior goes to you swift and straight as an arrow shot into the sun. Welcome him, and let him take his place at the council fire of my people. He is Uncas, my son. Tell them to be patient, and ask death for speed [*Hawkeye looks surprised that Chingachgook should pray for death*], for they are all there but one—I, Chingachgook, last of the Mohicans."[19]

There are no more spoken words in the film. Chingachgook turns to look lovingly, plaintively, at Hawkeye, who places a comforting arm on his shoulder. As he turns from Hawkeye to face the vast expanse of land before them, Cora enters the frame, and with Chingachgook *out* of the frame, the lovers kiss, then hold their embrace in a series of close-ups. During one such close-up, Cora gives Hawkeye a nod of assent, perhaps a response to the implied offer that she remain with him in this limitless America that now stretches before them. Then Chingachgook reappears in the frame with Hawkeye and Cora; but the essential American destiny has been decided without him—and yet with his blessing—for the previous series of close-ups, and of course his own last speech, anticipated his impending absence. He performs for the mythic birth of the nation a function similar to that which the historical

---

19. The speech owes more to the George B. Seitz–Philip Dunne version of *Mohicans* (1936) than it does to Cooper's novel. In that movie, Chingachgook prays: "Great Spirit, a warrior goes to you swift, straight, and unseen like arrow shot into sun. Let him sit at council fire of my tribe, for he is Uncas, my son. My fire is ashes, your fire is bright. Now, all my tribe is there but one—I, Chingachgook, last of the Mohicans."

Black Hawk performed for America after his defeat: "As a representative of an era that had passed," writes Susan Scheckel, "Black Hawk helped Americans to situate themselves within a historical framework that defined the present as a triumph over the past."[20] The camera then leaves all three and pans over the pine-covered mountains.

Chingachgook fades into his ahistorical region at the precise moment that the hero emerges into an ahistorical world of his own. Mythological historicism exacts from the Indian the surrender of his own historical status as "first American," for only thus, by this mythically postulated elision of the Indian's historical presence, can the Adamic hero inhabit the American Paradise—innocent not so much because he is guiltless as because he is *enduringly first*, himself the inhabitant of a region beyond the grasp of time, and thus (or so he must ever hope) of remorse. Then, in the midst of that tenuous illusion, it might yet occur to the American Adam that the patrimony he has received and the bequest he enjoys imply, after all, a history—the doings, deedings, and dyings—and his firstness shall be ever troubled by the reflection. He shall be, like the Indian hater himself, merely an Othered Same, an Adam compromised by his own (pre)history, a being, then, whose very Otherness contests his paradisal legacy and implicates him in the very Conquest that he so vehemently denounced.

7

That the vanishing Indian endorses the white hero's inheritance of the American Eden must not be taken to mean that he sanctions that version of American history that begins as a result of Conquest. Nor must we think that the history now about to begin has the white hero for its principal character. The three Westerns in question identify an America unworthy of both the Indian and the white hero. In these Westerns, accordingly, this other America is vested exclusively in white men—men vicious, cruel, and arrogant—who are as much the antagonists of the white hero as they are of the Indian. Because the revisionist Western tends to "other" such white men as the canonical Western "others" the Indian, we might call them *White Others*. They embody the revisionists' unequivocal condemnation of the predacious pursuit of happiness and the frenzied cult of progress in which all white America, with the exception of the white hero, presumably engages. When the White Others

---

20. *Insistence of the Indian*, p. 111.

are not themselves engaged in the most corrupt form of the winning of the West, they are clearing the way for those who will soon be. Thus, the revisionist Western assigns to them a curiously historical role: evil and stereotyped as they are, and represented though they are in the absence of all cultural or socio-economic motive, they are still engaged in the historical process of Conquest. In some respects, they borrow from the savage Indian of the canonical Western, for they, too, serve as mere foils to the white hero. Just as important, they embody the very history from which the white hero must learn to dissociate himself.

Geronimo's General Nelson Miles makes for a more imposing White Other than any such out of *Dances With Wolves* or *The Last of the Mohicans*. For Miles presides at the "disappearance" of the Indian and thus unveils "American" history. Toward the end, as we have seen, when Lieutenant Davis confronts him about the injustice done to Geronimo's band and the Chiricahua scouts, Miles responds: "Lieutenant, you are more worried about keeping your word to a savage than you are fulfilling your duty to the citizens of this country. We won. That's what matters. It's over, Lieutenant—Geronimo, the Apache, the whole history of the West, except being a farmer." In declaring the completion of Conquest's work, Miles defines, apportions, as it were, the Indian's ahistorical region; then he severs it from the history—the now official American history—that unfolds, all without the Indian, beyond that region. As all that is past portends the advent of the yeoman farmer, so does it justify the end of the Indian. Thus the Indian has been the victim of a cruel teleology: having resisted the conqueror, the Indian has played savage to the white hope of triumphant civilization, has lived only that he may be forgotten.

For his part, Lieutenant Davis now tells us that Miles has betrayed not only the Apaches but Gatewood as well. At this moment we see Gatewood looking at the cavalry column that escorts the Apaches to the railhead. Over this shot, the Davis voiceover tells us that Gatewood should have been "rewarded with a medal for his heroic effort." Instead, he "was sentenced to obscurity." Now Gatewood, still in long shot, turns his horse and rides away, presumably, to a "remote garrison in Wyoming." Alone and separate as we see him, we yet know him to be destined for far greater things than "obscurity." The same "obscurity" to which history consigns Gatewood betokens his deliverance from this history's sins and compromises; it prefigures his destined instauration as Adamic hero, though Adamic not because he is about to enjoy a paradisal bliss, but because his innocence distinguishes him from all the other soldiers who have participated in Conquest's work of

[254]

dispossession and genocide.[21] His destined "obscurity" shields him from censure.

A man apart, he bears with him the mark of freedom from American history, the timeless and inviolate aura itself of that special, mythically conferred sanctity that vouchsafes, even to a guilty nation, the promise of a redemptive glory. Thus the Indian and the white hero share this much, at least in *Geronimo*: both are exiles from American history, except that the Indian is all past, while the white hero belongs to a future as insistently real as it is continually deferred. That Miles's version of history "wins," then, can hardly mean that *Geronimo* endorses his triumph. Neither are we to think that the movie entrusts Miles with the task of articulating a historical inevitability. On the contrary, *Geronimo* patently assigns such historical authority to Miles (as White Other) only for the sake of disengaging the white hero from the ambivalence of American history. Lewis has noted that "the valid rite of initiation for the individual in the new world is not an initiation *into* society, but, given the character of society, an initiation *away from it*: something I wish it were legitimate to call '*de*nitiation.'"[22] Gatewood may escape history but not his own sort of ambivalence: his status as a "*de*nitiate," as an outcast from historicity, identifies him as the one remaining American *innocent,* even as the same status necessarily remands him to that history, since he played such a crucial role in its inception. His, accordingly, is but the innocence that closes, the *un*narrated and *un*narratable innocence beyond history and culture. His is a divestment as thorough as it is thoroughly ironic, since the enjoyment of its blessings requires his complete renunciation of the world and of time, if only because it was his Indianness that so thoroughly involved him in history.

Revisionism holds that the Indian can overcome oblivion only because the white hero emerges as his last hope. Yet the white hero, so considered, is hardly the remnant of the splendid Indian; he is—as revision fashions him—the very source and principle of that "Indianness," himself the *ab-original* man. The hero of the revisionist Western may resist cultural divestment, preferring to be the world's last Indian to his last day, but the Myth of Conquest, which after all gave life to the very notion of the last Indian, insists upon this Indian's Adamic status. The white hero's vestigial and yet essential final connection with the Indian affirms the bond not of cultural affinity but of firstness. That

21. I do not mean to suggest that the historical Gatewood benefited personally from this "obscurity." He died a broken man (see note 17). But even the martyrdom with which the Davis book invests him releases him from complicity in the work of Conquest.

22. *American Adam*, p. 115.

[255]

DBS Arts Library

which the white hero shall keep of the Indian's is his historical first-ness. The white hero's firstness thus discloses the revisionist version of the illusion of cultural divestment, for it at once presumes and enforces the elimination of the Indian, both as last and as first.

8

When savagery was a virtue—however fearful a virtue, as it is for the Indian-fighting Benjamin Martin or Jeremiah Johnson—then it was the conqueror's to possess in the greatest degree. The Indian is the Myth of Conquest's necessary demon, not only because the Myth needs to rep-resent him as evil, but because it needs to appropriate the demon's sup-posed savage qualities in order that it may defeat him. Indeed, one may wonder whether this necessary Indian, for all his savage Otherness, is not the very same being as the Vanishing American, and thus whether the eternal elegy for the disappearing native is not in reality a lament for the passing of the Spartan virtues that are said to have founded the nation—a yearning, then, albeit masked, for one more demonic chal-lenge to the heroic virtues of the young nation, one more opportunity to testify on behalf of the spirit of savage freedom that yet seethes be-neath the frail foundations of the American Canaan. What else besides this yearning might explain, for example, Francis Coppola's Kurtz (Marlon Brando) in *Apocalypse Now* (1979), the genius who has gone "native" but who might have won the war if "they"—not only the mil-itary but his own tortured soul as well—would only let his savage free-dom be? What explains the part-Indian John Rambo (Sylvester Stal-lone) in *Rambo: First Blood, Part Two* (1985), who is released from prison only so that he can locate MIAs but who, against orders, launches a one-man redemption of the U.S. defeat in Vietnam? And when Rambo fastens his "Indian" headband tight around his head and shoots his ex-plosive arrows out of his high-tech bow, who is winning the war "this time," the American soldier or the Indian?[23] Hence, in any case, another paradox: his annihilation at the hands of the conqueror invests the In-dian himself with a righteousness much like that of the hero, for only as a formidable foe could the Indian validate the virtues of the new na-

23. See Gregory A. Waller, "*Rambo*: Getting to Win this Time," in *From Hanoi to Holly-wood: The Vietnam War in American Film*, ed. Linda Dittmar and Gene Michaud (New Brunswick: Rutgers University Press, 1990), pp. 113–28. See also H. Bruce Franklin, *M.I.A. or Mythmaking in America: How and Why Belief in Live POWs Has Possessed a Nation*, rev. ed. (New Brunswick: Rutgers University Press, 1993), pp. 150–63.

Jeremiah Johnson (1972, Sanford Productions). Fighting "Indian style." Courtesy of Sanford Productions/Museum of Modern Art Film Stills Archive.

tion. If he found his way into art and coins and bogus speeches and the shifting masks of false shamans, was it not because honoring him was a way of exalting not a different way of life or the way of life that had been, but the formidable enemy whose very defeat would de facto enshrine the American virtues? But how, then, would the American really come to be distinguishable from the Indian?

Ever more attuned to public approval than to its own unexplored paradoxes, and eminently aware of the profit potential of cultural self-flattery, Hollywood's Indian Western, like the master Myth itself, all but ignored the dark side of Conquest. If the Western's white men took scalps or mutilated Indians, Hollywood (like, say, Cooper in *The Deerslayer* or Robert Montgomery Bird in *Nick of the Woods*) would make certain that we saw them as irreclaimable freaks of the race. On the rare occasions that such characters appear in the Western, then, they are so utterly (yet uniquely) degraded as to be at once beneath contempt and easily disposed of. For instance, in Ford's *Cheyenne Autumn* we meet a small group of ragged cowboys, just outside Dodge City, who come across two starving Cheyennes on the run from the pursuing U.S.

[257]

Army. A cowboy named Homer (Ken Curtis), remarking to his companions that he always wanted "to kill myself a' Injun," pursues and kills one of the hapless Cheyennes. He brings the Cheyenne's scalp with him into the saloon in Dodge City, and an outraged Wyatt Earp (James Stewart) makes him pay dearly for displaying it. We never see this Homer again. Far more ghastly, likely figures out of Cormac McCarthy's *Blood Meridian*, are the scalp-hunters in *Geronimo: An American Legend;* and although not all of them are white, a white man seems to be their leader. In a brief scene, this one also in a saloon, the noble Lieutenant Gatewood and his small group—which consists of the Apache scout Chato, the white scout Al Sieber, and Lieutenant Davis—shoot and kill all the scalp-hunters. In this way, Apache and American, civilian and soldier, come together in this one righteous act that erases the frontier's most easily identifiable evil. With white savagery thus easily disposed of, Conquest could fully trumpet its millennialist pieties; or, at its most demure, it could present itself as an inevitability, a dialectical decree to be obeyed by winners and losers alike.

So the wilderness had catalyzed the white hero's noblest impulse into a fearful identity with the heartless enemy. But what happened when both Indian and white somehow lost their assigned "gifts," when the *crossover* implied neither heroic sacrifice nor historical justification? How, then, does the Myth of Conquest respond to the tale of a "crossover" that proves, in the end, to be no cross-*over* at all? How would it present the "man without a cross in his blood" should such a man prove to be no less savage than the "red-gifted" Other?

Hollywood, ever cautious, produced only one major movie about the Vietnam War during the time of great domestic upheaval—the army-bankrolled pro-war *The Green Berets* (Kellogg/Wayne, 1968), starring John Wayne.[24] The Western, however, provided a ready, if all too transparent, mask for the nation's concerns with the war—for its anxieties not only about the prosecution of the war but about the crisis of national identity that the war had provoked. One of these Western-based Vietnam allegories was *Chato's Land* (Winner, 1971), another one *Ulzana's Raid* (Aldrich, 1972). (I have already attended to two others in chapter 3: *Little Big Man*, which draws a parallel with American brutality in Vietnam by reenacting Custer's massacre of a defenseless Cheyenne village in the Battle of the Washita [1868], and *Soldier Blue,*

---

24. According to Dittmar and Michaud, the first fiction movie to show "images of the American war in Vietnam" is *The Quiet American* (1958). See Appendix B in *From Hanoi to Hollywood*, p. 351. For a thorough analysis of *The Green Berets* in the context of the Myth of the Frontier and the Vietnam War, see Slotkin, *Gunfighter Nation*, pp. 520–33.

which, as we saw in chapter 3, presents its cyclical idea of history by way of an analogy between the massacres at Sand Creek in 1864 and Mylai in 1968.)[25] I do not propose to look at *Chato's Land* and *Ulzana's Raid* as mere Vietnam allegories or parables. It is impossible, however, to ignore that these two Westerns reflect the national disquiet over the faraway war. More important, Vietnam—the epoch as much as the war itself—*authenticates* the representation of these Indians as *radical* Others. Like the elusive and enigmatic enemy in Vietnam, the Indian appears before us not as the derivative of the Same but as a mystery both cultural and racial. In their analysis of a particularly gruesome scene in *Ulzana's Raid*, which I will discuss further below, Arnold and Miller write: "This is a shocking scene, not only because of its explicit violence, but because it so suddenly defies—even mocks—our smug preconceptions. We simply do not expect this to happen, and when it does, we realize that *anything* can follow. We can no longer rely on the comfortable formulas which dictate how such films should develop; our sense of security is shattered."[26]

To some extent, of course, this radical Otherness remains forever challenged by the very claim that the American Indian can substitute for the Vietnamese enemy, by that which would insist on the incomprehensibility of the Other in Vietnam while presuming to render the enemy in familiar terms (the Indian). Yet this allegorizing could also suggest that our ignorance of the enemy in Vietnam mirrored our historical ignorance of the Indian. Moreover, these two Westerns could cast whites themselves as radical Others, as would-be heroes who commit the sort of crimes that the Myth of Conquest charges exclusively to the Indian. Mylai became the source of this possibility: suddenly we had to confront the historical actuality that we, ourselves, behaved as we had thought only Indians did. The movies made it possible for the righteous "us" to cast those white men "there," on the screen or in Vietnam, as radical Others, to affix on them the mark of Cain. (Why else but because they were reentering the land of the "righteous" would returning Vietnam veterans have been greeted with chants of "Baby killers"?)

25. For the connections (however generalized) between *Ulzana's Raid* and Vietnam, see Edwin T. Arnold and Eugene L. Miller, *The Films and Career of Robert Aldrich* (Knoxville: University of Tennessee Press, 1986), p. 173; Donald Lyons, "Dances with Aldrich," *Film Comment* 27, no. 2 (March–April 1991), 72–76; Phillip Drummond, "*Ulzana's Raid*," in *The BFI Companion to the Western*, p. 307; Tom Milne, "Robert Aldrich (1962 to 1978)," in *Robert Aldrich*, ed. Richard Combs (London: British Film Institute, 1978), pp. 23–36.

26. *Films and Career of Robert Aldrich*, p. 167.

In these scantily veiled allegories, we meet Indians so formidably empowered as to offer themselves, simultaneously, both as representations of the cunning enemy in Vietnam and as models, clearly derived from American mytho-historical sources, of the kind of fighting that would win the war. (The titles themselves of the two films, each with the Indian's name in its possessive form, suggest not only a shift of perspective but the empowerment of the Indian.) This Indian was at once the radical Other of the distant jungle and our very own Indian. Yet these two Vietnam parables also show "white men behaving like Indians," as the central white character of *Ulzana's Raid* puts it at a crucial moment in that movie, when white troopers mutilate a fallen Apache warrior. What greater sense of ambivalence could we derive from even such a brief sketch of these two movies than that the Indian should appear before us both and at once as a being to be imitated and repudiated? Hollywood summoned the Indian as a representation through which Americans might disown the nation's own dark deeds in Southeast Asia. Yet it also encouraged the nation to rediscover the Indian—its *own* Indian—as a source of victory, if not, indeed, of regeneration. Censuring the Indian again was as dangerous for the national soul as becoming him. Becoming the Indian again was as necessary for the national soul as censuring him.

Even as Americans fought against these "Indians" in the remote "Indian Country," who would get to play Indian, who cavalry? No simple answer offers itself to this seemingly simple question. If the defeat of the Indian on the American frontier had depended on the white hero's exceptional gift of cultural appropriation—on his becoming, himself, "more Indian than the Indian"—why were we not winning? Could it be because the nation as a whole had long since successfully exorcised the demons of Otherness, had performed a perfect feat of cultural divestment? If the "quagmire" indicated a failure of "resolve"—could this failure have been remedied, the blame and the guilt assuaged, even purged, by a renewed appeal to the mystique of cultural appropriation? Had Hollywood and the nation alike not, after all, insisted that the American hero could in fact seize, at will and again, the savage soul of its (invented) Other? That he could thereby come to believe that he fought not his own demonic soul but an enemy utterly real in his utter Otherness? Consider the national dilemma through a famous movie meditation, his last, of Coppola's Col. Walter E. Kurtz. It may well constitute a lament for America's failure to appropriate such a savage freedom, yet it also amounts to a confession—Captain Willard (Martin

Sheen) is his principal auditor—the desperate plea of the long lost soul for deliverance.

> I remember when I was with Special Forces—it seems a thousand centuries ago—we went into a camp to inoculate some children. We'd left the camp, after we had inoculated the children for polio, and this old man came running after us and he was crying; he couldn't say [what was wrong]. We went back there, and they had come and hacked off every inoculated arm. There they were, in a pile, a pile of little arms. And I remember I cried; I wept like some grandmother. I wanted to tear my teeth out. I didn't know what I wanted to do. And I want to remember it. I never want to forget it; I never want to forget. And then I realized, like I was shot with a diamond bullet right through my forehead. And I thought, "My God, the genius of that! The genius! The will to do that—perfect, genuine, complete, crystalline, and pure." And then I realized that they [the enemy in general] were stronger than we, because they could stand that these [men who assaulted the children] were not monsters. These were men, trained cadres. These men fought with their hearts. [They are men] who have families, who have children, who are filled with love. But they had the strength to do that. If I had ten divisions of those men, then our troubles here would be over very quickly. You have to have men who are moral and at the same time who are able to utilize their primordial instincts to kill without feeling, without passion, without judgment, without judgment. Because it's judgment that defeats us.

But for the "horror" that has long since overwhelmed his soul, Kurtz himself might well have been one of these men who kill "without judgment," who revel in savage freedom's last excess, and thus in the freedom that, by its very nature, inhibits "judgment."

Yet Kurtz himself has not been above a crippling *self*-judgment. How else but through self-judgment was he to know "the horror," to counsel Willard, as he does in preface to his meditation, above, that "you must make a friend of horror"? For "horror and moral terror are your friends. If they are not, then they are enemies to be feared. They are truly enemies." In a rebellion against the institutional powers of the army, he had reclaimed the savage freedom of the Indian fighter, only to succumb to his own self-judgment, to the sentiment—somewhere between disabling doubt and crushing remorse—that follows an act that may have been, in the absolute integrity of its moment, "perfect, genuine, complete, crystalline, and pure." Thus Kurtz articulates both the horror of savagery and the horror of ambivalence, leaving it not to Willard but to us to imagine which of the two *we* might have chosen for the lesser evil—we who might yet believe that there had ever been a choice, who yet fail to suspect that each horror was implicated in the other, each begotten of the other, each misbegotten.

"He broke from them [the people back home]," the Willard voiceover tells us before Kurtz begins his last meditation, "and then he broke from himself. I've never seen a man so broken up and ripped apart." Kurtz, who was second in his class at Harvard, who completed Special Forces training at the advanced age of 38, the golden boy of the U.S. General Command, the "warrior poet" who reads his Eliot and keeps Jessie Weston and James George Frazer by his bedside, who, like his Conrad epitome, had been "a universal genius" and "an emissary of light"—this Kurtz is yet the selfsame one who (this, too, like the Conrad prototype) "had kicked himself loose of the earth." "His mind is clear," the harlequin photographer (Dennis Hopper) desperately explains to Willard, "but his soul is mad." Like that of his archetypes on the mythic frontier, Kurtz's own "horror" can be cured only by the great illusion of the ahistorical: when the action "perfect, genuine, complete, crystalline, and pure" passes beyond the bounds of its duration, then it becomes adjudged "savage," "horror." "Judgment"—the judgment that "defeats us"—originates contiguous with yet clearly beyond the limits of the integral act. It implies reflection, certainly, but even more fundamentally it implies *temporality*, since it inherently attests to the "pastness" of the event.

But Conquest would concoct other nostrums—simpler, less ambitious—wherewith to cure the hero's ambivalence. One of these would be the reversal of roles. In *Chato's Land* (Winner, 1971), the Indian is, if not "good," then at least right, and the whites—*all* the whites, without exception, though certainly in different degrees of cruelty and stridency—are savages. Taken merely as artless allegorizing, this role reversal encourages the easy moral identity of the Indian and the enemy in Vietnam. Just as the Indian, aggrieved by the Anglo-American invasion of his land, had righteously sought to turn back the tide of westward expansion, so, too, were the Vietnamese "insurgents" now justified in their fierce aggression against imperialism. In the defense of culture and home and family, no act of war was too "savage," and savagery, thus righteously meted out, approximated the highest form of patriotism. For their part, in their savage debauchery, the white racists in *Chato's Land*, would now be embodied corruptions of humanity, as the Indians of old had been.

Taken at a slightly more sophisticated level—taken didactically—this role reversal could suggest that America was losing in Vietnam because it had forgotten lessons learned from its Indian-fighting days. Yet the Vietnam allegory, taken didactically or as role reversal, can easily enough double in on itself. When we see, as we do in *Chato's Land*, a single Apache warrior demoralize and defeat a heavily armed posse of some twelve white men, are we to take Chato as a guileless emblem of the tiny Asian nation that was embarrassing the great superpower, or are we to take him as an intimation that "our own" Indian held the key to our victory in Vietnam? Was Chato, in short, "them" or "us," Other or Same? As "our" Indian, moreover, Chato summoned us to a virtuous return to savage war, exhorted us to revel in the savage freedom that had long since been ours by the great gift of cultural appropriation—the freedom before the time of "judgment." Even so, this implied "us" in *Chato's Land* had to be somehow separate from the repulsive whites of the posse. Neither, however, could that "us" be Indian, for the Indian—the one on screen no less than the one in Vietnam—had been (was) the enemy, the Other. Even a brief look at *Chato's Land* reveals the ambiguities that beset the national identity's transactions with its mythic history, both distant and recent.

Goaded by the racist sheriff Eli Saunders (uncredited?) into a deadly saloon shootout, his wife later gang-raped by half of the possemen (the other half too intimidated to intervene), his friend tortured and killed, his village set ablaze, Chato (Charles Bronson) wages a one-man war against white racists from an Arizona desert community. In the opening scene, Saunders's taunt predisposes us in Chato's favor: "This is a white man's saloon," he says, "and it sells white man's liquor, and I'm telling you to crawl yourself out of here, 'breed. Do you hear, you redskin nigger?" After Saunders draws his gun and seems ready to shoot him in the back, Chato draws and shoots. Some time later, a white man who refuses to join the posse, Ezra Mead (Peter Dyneley), refers to Saunders as "a redneck with a loud mouth and a gun," and well might he be describing most of the white men who ride after Chato. Following the sheriff's death, most of the white pursuers will give vent to a similar racism: "I'll ride any place to see a dead Injun," says one of the milder white characters as the posse begins to assemble. Others, less restrained, give us lines such as: "God knows what God was thinking when he made Apaches"; or the less meditative: "They ain't men, they're animals." Much later, after Chato kills Earl Hooker (Richard Jordan), who had instigated the rape of Chato's wife, all that his brother Jubal (Simon Oakland) can say by way of elegy is: "I need to see that 'breed dead. I can't step past that!" Perhaps, however, the cynical Nye Buell (Richard Basehart) sums up the animus that presses the white men onward: "We've got Indian fever. . . . [It] drives [a man] blind in the eye and not quite right in the head."

This persistent and coarse-grained hatred functions not only to identify the white characters (the way it does in most revisionist Indian Westerns, which need to distinguish such men from the white hero) but to produce a substantially uniform perception of *all* the white men as the real—and only—savages. The best that can be said of the *least* racist characters in *Chato's Land*—for example, the Irishman Gavin Malachi (Roddie McMillan) or his Scottish brother-in-law Brady Logan (Paul Young), or of the ineffective leader of the group Quincy Whitmore (Jack Palance)—is that they are too weak to resist the ruthless racism of those like sheriff Saunders and the Hooker clan. Here, then, *race hatred licenses white savagery*. That is to say, savagery reveals itself to be not a cultural attribute or an index of Otherness but a willing surrender—prompted, fostered, even justified, by race hatred—to the dark soul. The white men's insistence on the degradation of the Indian—that insistence that, to their way of thinking (if thinking it is), confirms their implicit claim to the status of superior beings—becomes indistinguishable from the impulse that drives them to savage deeds. The supremacy of their race manifests itself fully in the savagery that their hatred authorizes. With such a corrupt citizenry entrusted to the execution of justice, it is no wonder that the Indian wins, or that his triumph is no less moral than military. Perhaps more important, this race hatred, its boisterousness no less than its virulence—its transparency, then—ensures *our own disengagement* from these contemptible specimens of "our" race. *Their* race hatred licenses *our* censure of their savagery. We acquiesce in the image and idea of Chato, magnificent in the plenitude of his native freedom, as he attains the status of uncontested hero. The very forces that the white man had been manifestly destined to tame, the native and the land, falsify at last his fantasies and his fictions.

But the Indian did not win the West, so that his triumph in *Chato's Land* carries no final historical authority. *Chato's Land* may well have contradicted both history and the Myth of Conquest simply for the sake of indulging an imperfect allegory. Neither, however, does *Chato's Land* discourage us from asking whether such a magnificent warrior as Chato lies really beyond reclamation by the nation's dominant mythology. Could we not find comfort, perhaps even hope, in this latest transmutation whereby a white actor (of Polish descent: Charles Bushinski) had become the Indian—and all the more so because he had become

[264]

the Indian of the white hero's own worst nightmares—the Indian, then, who could be loosed upon the enemy in the far-off war?

ULZANA'S RAID authorizes its "hostile" Indian by empowering him in the form of the Apache army scout Ke-Ni-Tay (Jorge Luke).[27] Ke-Ni-Tay's intimacy with Ulzana (Joaquín Martínez) gives utterance to radical Otherness—to a difference the construction of which does not *of necessity* reveal its origin in Sameness, to a difference, accordingly, that can resonate with Sameness, that admits of relatedness, without thereby ceasing to remain fundamentally and inherently itself. Ke-Ni-Tay's voice obtrudes upon the virtual silence to which the Indian Western holds radical Otherness; it articulates the great disquiet provoked by the possibility, unthinkable as it may be, that "savagery" reveals not the corruption of culture but an integral part of it—that savagery, then, so-called, is but "civilization's" scorn for that which the native knows as *the overflowing passion of cultural resistance*. In this way, Otherness discloses a cultural ontology, unequivocally affirms cultural integrity. Though he may speak in halting English, indeed, though he may be in the conqueror's employ, Ke-Ni-Tay shall prove to be articulate enough—perhaps even disturbingly eloquent—in the elucidation of such an Otherness.

Of course, *Ulzana's Raid* also features a white Indian-fighter, the crusty McIntosh (Burt Lancaster). Endearingly irreverent toward the military, McIntosh lives comfortably among the Apaches at Fort Lowell, and he has an Apache wife. Yet McIntosh, for all his frontier experience, functions more as a competent tracker and mentor to young Lieutenant DeBuin than as an unimpeachable authority on Indians. McIntosh's knowledge of *Otherness*, in other words, falls short of the native's own, and it can appear considerable, even formidable, only to those, like the major in charge at Fort Lowell, who hold the Indian to be an enigma. We will call on McIntosh later, but let us now return to Ke-Ni-Tay.

I am not proposing that Ke-Ni-Tay's insights and explanations illuminate the historical and cultural life of the actual people known to

27. The titular character is based on the historical Ulzana, more frequently known as Josanie or Jolsanny. See Dan L. Thrapp, *The Conquest of Apacheria* (Norman: University of Oklahoma Press, 1967), pp. 335, 339. See also Angie Debo, *Geronimo: The Man, His Time, His Place* (Norman: University of Oklahoma Press, 1976), pp. 247–63. In the film, Ke-Ni-Tay is not only a Chiricahua Apache, like Ulzana, but is actually related to him, since the two men's wives are sisters (though Ke-Ni-Tay insists that his wife is the prettier of the two). For possible connections between Ke-Ni-Tay and historical Apache scouts, see Thrapp, *Conquest*, pp. 343, 353.

Ulzana's Raid (1972, Universal). The young lieutenant and his frontier
mentors. Courtesy of Universal/Museum of Modern Art Film Stills Archive.

themselves as the N'dé, Indé, or Diné. He does, however, articulate
something very much like an idea of radical Otherness—as much, I
think, as any Indian is able to in the Western—and does so the more effectively because his explications and illustrations tend to baffle him
for whose benefit (and on whose demand) he offers them—Lt. Garnett

[266]

DeBuin (Bruce Davison). DeBuin, just out of West Point—and all too firm in his belief, which he shares with his father, a Philadelphia minister, "that it's a lack of Christian feeling toward the Indian that's at the root of our problems with them"—is cast in the mold of the eastern innocent through whom, in time, the harsh frontier experience reaffirms the national civilizing mission.[28] The colloquy on radical Otherness appears most complete—and most completely inaccessible to DeBuin—in Ke-Ni-Tay's response to the young lieutenant's interrogation concerning the Rukeyser family's fate, which I now sketch.

An outrider, Sergeant Horowitz (Dean Smith) warns the Rukeysers of Ulzana's uprising. Mr. Rukeyser (Karl Swenson), however, refuses to leave his farm. He sends his wife and adolescent son, Billy, to Fort Lowell and stays behind (with only the dog Jeff for company) to defend the homestead against the "drunk fellows," as he refers to the Apaches. With only Horowitz as an escort, wife and son are, of course, doomed. DeBuin's cavalry column is too late to see the gruesome sequence that we witness: Horowitz shoots Mrs. Rukeyser (Gladys Holland), so to spare her the "fate worse than death"; moments later, his horse shot from under him and Billy (who was riding in back), he unhesitatingly shoots himself in the mouth. Three Apaches stab his corpse repeatedly, take out his heart, and play catch with it. They spare Billy because his youth makes him an unworthy enemy, as Ke-Ni-Tay eventually explains. Later, the cavalry column finds Rukeyser outside his farmhouse, dead. He sits on the ground, his back to a tree; he is strapped to the tree by the waist and head; his legs are spread apart, each tied by the ankle to stakes in the ground. A fire still smolders between his legs, and one at each foot. His shirt is burned off, and he is, from head to waist, one raw lump of flesh. There is something stuck in his mouth, but DeBuin cannot tell what it is. "It's the dog's tail," McIntosh explains.

That night DeBuin, as baffled by the torture of Rukeyser and Horowitz as he is revolted by it, demands an explanation from Ke-Ni-Tay.

> *DeBuin*: Ke-Ni-Tay, I want to ask you something. Why are your people like that? Why are they so cruel? What is the reason?
> *Ke-Ni-Tay*: Is how they are.
> *DeBuin*: But why?

28. Arnold and Miller show convincingly how thoroughly and relentlessly *Ulzana's Raid* explodes DeBuin's belief in the efficacy of Christianity in the wilderness. See *Films and Career of Robert Aldrich*, p. 167. The authors might have also mentioned that at one point early in the action the Arizona of the setting is explicitly referred to as "hell."

Ke-Ni-Tay: Is how they are. They have always be like that.
DeBuin: Are you like that? Would you kill a man like that?
Ke-Ni-Tay: Yes.
DeBuin: Why?
Ke-Ni-Tay: To take the Power.[29] Each man that die, the man who kill him take his Power. Man give up his Power when he die, like fire give heat. Fire that burn long time, many can have heat.
DeBuin: You mean you torture a man for hours, and you get "power" from watching some poor creature suffering? What kind of "power" is that?
Ke-Ni-Tay: Here in this land, man must have Power. You not know about Power.
DeBuin: I want to know. I want to understand.
Ke-Ni-Tay: Ulzana is long time in the agency. His Power very thin. Smell in his nose are all smell of the agency, old smell—smell of woman, smell of dog, smell of children. Man with old smell in the nose is old man. Ulzana came for new smell—the pony running, the smell of burning, the smell of bullet. For Power! Soldier [the suicide Horowitz] back with the wagon—no Power. Woman [Mrs. Rukeyser, shot by Horowitz]—no Power, no pleasure.
DeBuin: Why didn't they kill the boy?
Ke-Ni-Tay: Man cannot take Power from boy, only from man.

The exchange renders DeBuin powerless to insist that savagery is the characteristic trait of Otherness. If power, so conceived of—which is to say, so culturally specified—consecrates violence, then it stands outside the censuring ethos of "civilization." It lies outside "reason" and "knowing" and "understanding," which are DeBuin's—and Euro-American civilization's—modes of apprehending and judging Otherness. Commenting on the same exchange, above, between DeBuin and Ke-Ni-Tay, Tom Milne writes: "Lucid, coherent, absolutely convincing, Ke-Ni-Tay's ideological exposé is yet totally alien to the Western mind."[30] Aldrich himself seems to have seen it thus when he asserted that the film reveals, "on many levels," the harmful effects of "ignorance of other people's cultures."[31]

Ke-Ni-Tay *theologizes* Power, accords it its ontology ("Is how they are."). Thus, Power incorporates the savage into the human, indeed, into the relation between humanity and divinity. "Most Chiricahua ceremonialism," writes Morris E. Opler, "centered upon the individual acquisition and manipulation of supernatural power. It was believed that the universe was pervaded by diffuse supernatural power that was

29. When Ke-Ni-Tay uses the term, I capitalize it, as does Debo in her *Geronimo*.
30. "Robert Aldrich (1962–1978)," p. 33.
31. Harry Ringel, "Up to Date with Robert Aldrich" [interview], *Sight and Sound* 43, no. 3 (summer 1974): 166–69.

eager to be of service to the pious but that could approach an individual (either a man or a woman) and teach him what he must do only through the medium of familiar beings and objects."[32] Opler also writes that the Mescalero Apaches "believed that their world was flooded with undifferentiated supernatural power (*dighi*) which was more than willing to help man if it was properly approached. Power had to reach man through some 'channel.' . . . Sometimes individuals who were very religious believed that they had received power grants from more than one source and were said to be 'loaded up' with power."[33]

Thus, for example, the declaration of the historical Geronimo, that "war is a solemn religious matter,"[34] might baffle DeBuin, if only because DeBuin, as a "Christian soldier," can never find full and unambiguous cultural sanction for the integral union of his two professions, the long and illustrious company of Christian soldier-saints notwithstanding. For Ulzana, for Ke-Ni-Tay, for the historical Geronimo, war and religion are sanctified each in the other, mutually consummated and justified, as if in a hypostasis (theologically understood). The very destructiveness of war becomes an act of both cultural and spiritual affirmation, a sustained act, to recall Coppola's Kurtz, "perfect, genuine, complete, crystalline, and pure"—and therefore as perfectly and completely beyond the reach and grasp of Conquest's "judgment." To censure such acts as savage, to relegate them to an indeterminate moral Otherness—to assert, then, that herein precisely lies the distinction between "them" and "us"—only deploys difference as a defense against *the overflowing passion of cultural resistance*. It is to co-opt difference and transmute it into "savagery" by a purposeful, perhaps even necessary, act of misunderstanding.

For all that Ke-Ni-Tay's discourse on Power resonates with actual ethnological reports of Apache belief, the exchange, above, measures radical Otherness mostly by DeBuin's incomprehension. From his perspective, the idea of Power may but confirm the Apache in his Otherness, yet the same perspective, for failing to "understand" Power, affirms the *integrity* of that Otherness, that indefeasible wholeness that specifies it as a principle of moral action even as it places it beyond judgment: "Is how they are." In the scene that immediately follows De-

---

32. Morris E. Opler, "Chiricahua Apache," *The Handbook of North American Indians: Southwest*, ed. Alfonso Ortiz (Washington, D.C.: Smithsonian Institute, 1983), 10: 401–18.

33. Morris E. Opler, "Mescalero Apache," pp. 419–39. Opler's opening essay on the Apaches in the same volume suggests that Chiricahua rites differed little from those of the Mescalero. See "The Apachean Culture Pattern and Its Origins,"ibid., pp. 368–92.

34. Quoted in Debo, *Geronimo*, p. 30.

Buin's exchange with Ke-Ni-Tay, the young lieutenant enters the ruins of the Rukeyser home to find McIntosh in a rocking chair, calmly reading from a massive family Bible. "Do you hate Apaches, Mr. McIntosh?" DeBuin abruptly asks.

> *McIntosh*: No.
> *DeBuin*: Well, I do.
> *McIntosh*: Well, it might not make you happy, Lieutenant, but it sure won't make you lonesome. Most white folks hereabouts feel the same as you do.
> *DeBuin*: Why don't you feel that way?
> *McIntosh*: It'd be like hating the desert 'cause there ain't no water on it. For now I can get by just being plenty scared of them.

The Myth of Conquest had always manipulated Otherness to its own advantage because Otherness had always been a thing of its own making. The forms of virtual absence had testified as much to the power of the Myth of Conquest as to the presumed human inconsequence of the Indian. An Indian of one's own making could be easily enough suppressed because he had been so easily invented, and cultural divestment had been a feat easily enough achieved. Here, however, Ke-Ni-Tay's speeches, as much as the mutilation of Horowitz and the torture of Rukeyser, force upon DeBuin the need to hate; and of just that need is a different sort of Otherness begotten in the mind of the Same. What I find especially compelling about this moment in *Ulzana's Raid* is that DeBuin, *in and through his hatred*, attains to an insight into radical Otherness. In the very failure to understand the proffered idea of Power, he hits, though no doubt ironically, upon the *alienness* of the Indian. In a way, therefore, he hates the Apaches because he *does in fact understand them*—understands them enough, that is, to repudiate them utterly, if only in the name of understanding's *failure*. Such irony may confirm only what the ages have often taught us: our hatreds are proportionate to our fears, and our fears commensurate with the limits of our grasp. Even so, DeBuin's hatred of the Apache amounts to an implicit (and all too reluctant) acquiescence in the integrity of radical Otherness. It functions as an endorsement, as disturbing as it is unintended, of the desert's inalienable right to be itself rather than a waterless place; as the acknowledgement that the Indian is much more and much different than non-white. In its very radicalness, Otherness ceases to be Otherness at all: it is how and what it is; "is how they are." Such an Otherness transcends difference, stands outside judgment. It has no other name, unless it be the Same's very own name for hatred.

Ke-Ni-Tay's explanation of the Apache idea of Power endows the *Indian's* purported savagery with a context, refers it to a cultural, indeed a spiritual, place central to the Apache cosmos. Yet, predictably enough, none of this justifies "savagery" to the white soldiers. Late in the action, just before a desperate ride to intercept Ulzana's ponies (see below), DeBuin has the following exchange with a longtime veteran of the Apache wars, Sergeant Burns (Richard Jaeckel):

Burns: Is that the Bible you're reading, sir?
DeBuin: Yes. It was a gift from my father my last trip home. My father's a minister.
Burns: So I heard tell, sir.
DeBuin: I wish I could ask him about the Apache.
Burns: What about them, sir?
DeBuin: Why do they do these terrible things? I mean, after all, they are men, made in God's image, like ourselves.
Burns: Lieutenant, seems to me the place in there [the Bible] that tells you about an eye for an eye and a tooth for a tooth is the only fix you're going to get on the Apache. That's the way we ought to treat them.
DeBuin: Well, Christ taught us another way, Sergeant.
Burns: Yes, he did, sir. But Christ never fetched no infant child out of a cactus tree and then waited around for two hours till it died so he could bury it, did he, sir, huh?
DeBuin: No.
Burns: I did. Ain't nobody gonna tell me to turn the other cheek to no Apache, sir [*Walks away, offended*].

Whether in spite of his harsh introduction to frontier violence or because of it, DeBuin remains, at least so far, beguiled by a persistent white fantasy about the Other, by that illusion which, in the name of a bountiful benevolence, only masks a deep-seated cultural arrogance—namely, that the Indian's *humanity* must perforce be "like" ours, derived from ours, perfected through ours. He is human only to the extent that he is human *like us*; and without us to perceive and endorse his humanity, to develop it and bring it forth into the world as if by some wondrous Socratic midwifery, he would remain forever the benighted brute, forever impaling white infants on cactus trees, hacking off little inoculated arms. The Indian's resistance, then, the passion of it, at once defines, explains, and justifies his savagery, for it constitutes his defiant repudiation of civilization's purported blessings.

Soon enough DeBuin faces the white man's own act of savagery. It is late in the action, and Ulzana makes a bold attempt to trap the cavalry column. He ties all his warrior's ponies together, halters to tails, and they ride in this way, single file, through a desert. As the horses pass by some large rocks, each of the riders but the first and last dismounts and steps on the rocks. The warriors thus leave no footprints on the sandy ground. Ke-Ni-Tay, however, notices that the middle horses leave a lighter print. Ulzana, McIntosh explains to DeBuin, intends "to stretch us out into them hills, make us keep coming while he circles 'round behind. His ponies are going to be a lot fresher than ours by the time they get to him. And if we go chasin' after him there's a good chance of becoming infantry. But if we don't [chase him], he gets ahead of us. Either way, he's smiling." McIntosh then proposes to "outfox" Ulzana by "getting to [Ulzana's] horses before he does." He suggests that DeBuin send out four outriders—McIntosh and a trooper, Ke-Ni-Tay and another trooper—to intercept Ulzana's ponies and leave him and his warriors on foot. Although the Apache riders and the ponies cross behind McIntosh, he soon catches up with them and chases them at a gallop. He dismounts and shoots the lead horse first, then the trailer. The Apache on the lead horse recovers and shoots McIntosh off his horse, and then both Apaches rush him. From behind his dead horse, McIntosh shoots the rider of the lead horse first, then the rider of the trailer. The first of these, though badly wounded, manages to get away on foot. The second is dead: he is a boy, about the same age as Billy Rukeyser. He is, as we will shortly discover, Ulzana's son.

Later, while the soldiers, casually assembled in small groups, rest on the open prairie, near where McIntosh fought with the Apaches, four troopers stand over the body of the dead boy. When DeBuin is not looking, they fall upon the body, knives in hand, shouting maniacally, "Cut it!" "Cut it out of him!" "Cut it clean out!" "Dirty Apache dog!" DeBuin rushes to intervene, and the men explain the mutilation by pointing out that the boy "had a trooper's side gun," that "they cut Horowitz [who died trying to rescue Mrs. Rukeyser and Billy] up pretty bad," and that "Apaches don't like it when you do this to their dead. It spooks them." One of them also tells the enraged DeBuin what all but he seem to know: the boy is Ulzana's son.[35] Shocked by this display of white savagery, DeBuin returns to his lonely place on the prairie. McIntosh approaches him, and the following exchange ensues:

---

35. When Ulzana's warriors lay siege to Rukeyser's cabin, this boy, who carries a bugle with him, plays the cavalry charge, thus making Rukeyser believe that he was being rescued (and thus subverting the old *Stagecoach* rescue ploy). McIntosh shoots the rushing boy through the bugle, and a cut to Ulzana and his men suggests that Ulzana hears not only the shots but the clang of the bullet striking the bugle.

McIntosh: What's bothering you, Lieutenant?

DeBuin: Is that Ulzana's son?

McIntosh: So I believe.

DeBuin: So you believe. [*Pause*] Why wasn't I told that Ulzana's son was one of them?

McIntosh: Would it have made any difference to anything if you had known?

DeBuin: Well, it might have made me feel that I was the officer in command.

McIntosh: That's fair enough, Lieutenant. I was wrong not to mention it.

DeBuin: Killing I expect, Mr. McIntosh, but mutilation and torture—I cannot accept that as readily as you seem to be able to.

McIntosh: What bothers you, Lieutenant, is you don't like to think of white men behaving like Indians. It kind of confuses the issue, don't it?

DeBuin falls silent. A close-up of him registers his "confusion." If white men do that which the Apache do, should he hate *them* as he hates the Apache? If he had heretofore been so convinced that savagery was only the Indian's, should he, now that he knows otherwise, hate *himself*? It seems pointedly ironic, moreover, that Ulzana's son is about as old as Billy Rukeyser. Recall that the Apaches had not harmed Billy because "Man cannot take Power from boy." What happens then to the Christianizing mission that DeBuin brings with him from Philadelphia? "White men behaving like Indians" may indeed "confuse the issue," yet it clearly establishes the extent to which the Same has become *Other to himself* as well as to his own idea of Otherness. The *Indian* Other was, then, at once a denial and a projection of this dark side, its name rather than its embodiment. Sameness *denied* it because it implicitly understood the extent to which it had failed to attribute it to its proper source; it *projected* it because its horror called for the invention of an Other upon whom that dark side could be completely and exclusively foisted and to whom it could yet be attributed as source and origin.

That racial *difference* should evoke not Otherness but *Sameness* should certainly confuse "the issue" enough. Having witnessed his troopers mutilating the body of Ulzana's son, DeBuin can no longer hold that his *racial* equals are for that reason alone his *moral* equals. Ke-Ni-Tay and Ulzana and his warriors are far truer to their professed cultural ethic than are DeBuin's troopers. Yet the aporia of racial difference could complicate "the issue" even further: for the Myth of Conquest would blindly continue to insist on "judgment"—and therefore on its right to censure—even when it implicitly understood that it could no

[273]

longer do so in terms of race or of culture. The "issue" had once been clear enough, and the Myth of Conquest had easily transformed the "ocular proof" of racio-cultural difference into the source of *moral* difference. Spectacle had nourished idea, and it was the idea—what Conrad's Marlow calls "the idea at the back" of Conquest—that exalted the otherwise loathsome task even as it sustained it. Now, however, the "savage spectacle" of "white men behaving like Indians" deals the Myth of Conquest a convulsive blow: Conquest's agent, DeBuin, learns that it lies within the range and prospect of white men to act not only *like* Indians but to act in such a way as to utterly break faith with the very beings that they claimed to be, with the values, then, that had seemed to justify Conquest. The frontier has forced DeBuin to look within the soul of his race, and he has seen, as if in "darkness visible," a soul more cruel and benighted than any he had imagined the Indian to have. The "savage spectacle," such as the one that had revolted Parkman and, most recently DeBuin, has been transformed into *the spectacle of degraded Sameness*. Perspective becomes that which it beholds, and exterior and interior collapse each upon the other.

Following his encounter with the white men who behave "like Indians," DeBuin intensifies his campaign to "Other" Ke-Ni-Tay (spitefully ordering him to surrender his horse to McIntosh and follow on foot, referring to him in the third person when Ke-Ni-Tay is within arm's reach, and so on). Earlier, when the cavalry troop had ridden into the Riordan ranch, intending to water the horses, they had found, instead, a ruined place: house and stables burned; Mr. Riordan hanging upside down by the back of his knees from the top rail of a fence, a fire still smoldering where his head meets the ground; Mrs. Riordan barely alive, raped many times yet left to live (so that escorting her to the fort will divide the cavalry force). McIntosh and Sergeant Burns rush to untie Mr. Riordan's body, but DeBuin, still mounted, demands that they leave the body alone.

> *McIntosh*: It needs burying.
> *DeBuin*: I want the Apache scout to do that.
> *McIntosh*: Damn it, Lieutenant, you're not making any sense.
> *DeBuin*: [*Beside himself with rage*] Now look, Mr. McIntosh, that used to be a white man—like yourself, a white man! Now it seems to me that you're the one that's not making any sense.

His racism is now at its most virulent, his own ethnicity at its most defensive. Appearing to make the Apache scout confront the "sins" of his race, DeBuin's order in fact betrays the desperation with which he holds to his shattered idea of race. Somehow, if Ke-Ni-Tay buries Riordan (so this racist logic goes) he thereby acknowledges savagery as the characteristic and exclusive feature of the Indian. And somehow, if Ke-Ni-Tay buries Riordan, DeBuin's guiltless whiteness will be reaffirmed. It is, no doubt condignly, in the context of this latest encounter with Apache forms of Power, that McIntosh reprimands DeBuin: "You'd be well advised to stop hating and start thinking, Lieutenant, because you ain't doing too well up to now."

Suddenly, DeBuin's racism subsides. Perhaps McIntosh shames De-Buin by pointing out to him the palpable irony that a zealous Christian should so enthusiastically surrender to hatred. Perhaps the alteration has only to do with the young lieutenant's realization of the urgency with which he had better "start thinking." At any rate, DeBuin imme-diately summons Ke-Ni-Tay again, not, however, to importune and re-buke but to ask him, as one soldier to another, what he thinks Ulzana's next move will be. This time, when Ke-Ni-Tay talks of Power ("Ulzana must give [his warriors] good Power—many horses—or the raid is fin-ished"), DeBuin listens attentively and ends up acting on the advice of Ke-Ni-Tay and McIntosh. Later, he trusts Ke-Ni-Tay to kill the lone Apache vedette, and he even relinquishes his field glasses to Ke-Ni-Tay on demand. After the main firefight, he orders the corporal (John Pearce) to bury the Apache warriors, that is to say, to honor the enemy and not to leave the bodies to rot. When Ke-Ni-Tay at last shows up with the body of Ulzana, whom he has killed, DeBuin orders the cor-poral to bury the warrior. When the corporal remonstrates, arguing that the men back at the fort will want to see the body, "or at least the head," DeBuin says, "They'll see my report." And when Ke-Ni-Tay peremptorily insists that he, not the corporal, will bury Ulzana, DeBuin allows it. If he meant to punish Ke-Ni-Tay by ordering him to bury Ri-ordan, he now acknowledges the scout's right to bury his kinsman, who is also his "kill." After he says good-bye to McIntosh, who is mor-tally wounded and insists on being left out in the desert to die, DeBuin turns and salutes Ke-Ni-Tay, who respectfully nods in return.

But what did DeBuin learn, which is to ask, how convincing is the conversion (even if this last is hardly more than an accommodation)? When the wounded McIntosh refuses a burial party to stay behind until he dies, DeBuin, imagining the man dying and dead, alone in the desert, says, "It's not Christian." McIntosh responds, "That's right, Lieutenant, it's not." Though his faith be shaken, DeBuin continues to believe in the moral relevance of Christianity on the frontier, and as

[275]

clearly does McIntosh continue to teach him, even *in extremis*, that "it's not." What becomes of the justifying principles of the Myth of Conquest? Was the civilizing force of Christianity on the Western frontier limited to providing, no doubt all too ironically, *a principle and origin of hatred* precisely for functioning as a *principle of difference*? That is, did Christianity not serve as the measure and standard of difference, thereby allowing the conqueror to hate in the name of the religion that yet enjoined him to love his enemy? Perhaps DeBuin escapes the censure that he himself heaps on the white men who behave "like Indians," but if so, he does only to the extent that he learns, in McIntosh's terms, to "think" rather than to "hate." Military efficiency would never hold it against the desert that it lacked water. Perhaps, then, this separation of the military from the ideological specified the Vietnam lesson in *Ulzana's Raid*, the all-too-limited extent of its allegorical reach: if we wanted to win, we had to *demystify* the war, to abandon our own pretenses of a *grande mission civilisatrice*. We had to repudiate the mandate to win "hearts and minds" and simply win.

But what then would have been the "purpose"—the moral purpose, I mean—of being there in the first place? If we had to "behave like Indians" to win, was winning worth it? And what was the prize to be won? And how was the "winning" of it to prove us in the right, when "winning" had compelled us to become the very being over whom we had to triumph?

The wars for identity impressed upon the nation the indelible stamp of ambivalence. Such Vietnam analogies as could be framed out of *Ulzana's Raid* had been in fact disturbingly precise. Only superficially, of course, could it be said that Apaches in 1885 were much like the Vietnamese enemies of 1972. And only superficially could guerrilla warfare in the Arizona and New Mexico deserts resemble that in the jungles and rice paddies of South Vietnam and Cambodia. Yet the analogy held true in this one fundamental sense: the principles of difference, delimited by the illusion of a unified and self-evidently superior cultural will, had collapsed. The force of Conquest had itself produced the guilt of Conquest, and a double guilt at that: the dark deeds against the Other had betrayed the exalted vision of the Same. All credit, then, to *Ulzana's Raid* for resisting the temptation to recast DeBuin as a friend of the Indian, or worse, as a white man "gone native." Even if his "epiphany" seems unwarranted, he has reached an accommodation with the desert, with the Indian: the desert is not merely waterless, and the Indian is much more than a soul eagerly awaiting "the blessings of civilization."

[276]

If DeBuin's experiences do not quite render him wise, they at least sober him: the wilderness and the fight against wild men displace Christianity and declare race irrelevant: white men behave "like Indians," and the Indian (Ke-Ni-Tay), though very much in possession of his cultural inheritance, still honors his duty to the army. But is DeBuin's new-found trust of Ke-Ni-Tay merely a way of claiming the old Indian "sidekick" of generic convention? Is his having an ally in the loyal Ke-Ni-Tay only a measure of his newly acquired status as "the man who knows Indians"? Moreover, is the sidekick a strategy of divestment—the Indian, let us say, cast as both repository and vehicle of the needful savagery that the white hero must ever confront in the wilderness even as he must keep from being tainted by it? I suppose that the answers to such questions depend on the degree of influence that we accord to generic convention over a Western that proposes to revise the genre; and on our inclination to ignore the dignity with which Ke-Ni-Tay asserts his loyalty to both the army and his own culture. Still, we should note two more separations that tend to underscore DeBuin's exemption (if not divestment) from the Indianness of the conventional white hero—from the troopers under his command, from McIntosh. We can account for the first of these in terms of class, though also in terms of that regional origin that in the Western so often suggests class: DeBuin comes to the West as an easterner of privileged upbringing, whereas the troopers that assault the body of Ulzana's son can easily be held to belong to a rabble of unenlightened emigrants. Savagery, then, may cross racial but never class boundaries. Yet the third such separation seems most important: McIntosh dies and DeBuin now has to carry on without him.

The Indian Western knows well the tradition of the Bildungsroman, as Ford's cavalry trilogy readily reminds us; and convention most often has it that the young initiate's mentor, however much he may know about Indians and about savage ways, often becomes part of his charge's world. Here, however, he dies. McIntosh refuses even a burial party, dying alone in the wilderness, the shade of a wagon and a cigarette his only comforts. Such deeds as may have incriminated him in savagery—he does, after all, kill Ulzana's son—remain thus with him in the wilderness, while DeBuin, who never kills any Indians, returns to the outpost of civilization. In thus separating the white mentor from the white initiate—indeed, in thus dividing the character of the Indian fighter—*Ulzana's Raid* performs its own deed of cultural divestment on DeBuin's behalf. Savagery can be left safely behind now, or foisted on society's scum, or assigned to the noble sidekick, but the hero's projected homecoming seems all but assured, and his anticipated attestation of the marvels and miracles of his frontier experiences also functions as a categorical disavowal of surrender to its horrors and its heartaches. Thus, as Donald Lyons writes, "Debuin [*sic*] judges but does not know the Apache; McIntosh knows (in fact, he lives with an Apache woman) but does not judge. And Ke-ni-tay [*sic*] . . . *is* Apache, but has committed himself to a career as an Army Scout."[36] Ambivalence could be avoided only by denying experience. But let us now turn to an ending that does not separate its "McIntosh" (or its "Ke-Ni-Tay") from its "DeBuin" but that instead presents "them" as integral, if ever-contending, components of the same being. I end this entire study with one last look at *The Searchers,* for it seems to me that no Indian Western so exacts the need for cultural divestment even as it presents it, at the end, as a near impossibility. It may be of some consequence that Alan Sharp, who wrote the screenplay for *Ulzana's Raid,* compared his McIntosh "to Ethan Edwards. . . . (Sharp intended *Ulzana's Raid* to be 'my sincere homage to Ford.') Of the two men, Sharp thought McIntosh 'a more stoical, more pessimistic, yet more humane figure, whose rage against the gods has cooled into a weary antagonism.' "[37] All Indian fighters will share traits, of course, but of all these that might surely bind McIntosh to Ethan, none may seem more relevant to the rest of our study than that both fail to find a welcoming home in the "fine good place to be."[38]

9

The Searchers affirms nothing more clearly than the ambivalence of the heroic character, undermining its own celebration of Ethan Edwards's heroic persistence by its continual reminder that his surrender to savage freedom can find no redemption in the "fine good place to be." Scott Eyman has recently summed up this ambivalence: "Ethan hates Indians for their savagery *and* takes their scalps for killing his relatives; he despises Martin Pawley's Cherokee blood *and* makes him his heir; he wants to kill his niece for becoming a squaw *and* he embraces her and takes her safely home. Ethan is a monster *and* he is John Wayne."[39]

36. "Dances with Aldrich," p. 74.
37. *Films and Career of Robert Aldrich,* p. 171.
38. Arthur M. Eckstein oversimplifies Ethan's exclusion by assigning it to a directorial decision. See "After the Rescue: *The Searchers,* the Audience and *Prime Cut* (1972)," *Journal of Popular Culture* 28, no. 3 (winter 1994): 33–53.
39. *Print the Legend,* p. 449.

Ethan's predicament, brought about by his Double Otherness, parallels that which Susan Scheckel articulates in her treatment of the famous captive Mary Jemison. "If Jemison were seen as locating her loyalties and identity entirely in the Indian world, she would be considered either an outlaw . . . or an outsider. . . . On the other hand, if she actually tried to reintegrate herself into American society, her experiences among the Indians . . . might create difficulties."[40]

Late in our examination of the representational codes of virtual absence and imminent presence, in chapter 1, I haltingly offered an argument—more like a suggestion, really—intended to account, at least in part, for the reversal of Ethan Edwards's earlier intention to kill his niece Debbie, who has been a captive of the Comanche chief Scar for some five years. Ethan, I proposed, having taken Scar's scalp, now aligns himself disturbingly with those "gifts" said both by cultural tradition and generic convention to belong only to the savage. Thus, only by embracing Debbie's own savagery can Ethan rescue her. Such savagery as had been hers by taint of miscegenation is now also Ethan's because he has scalped Scar. If his Indianness lay heretofore hidden under the mask of Indian hating, it emerges now into its visible and palpable form. At the end of the "search," Ethan has discovered that he is savage to the core.

Thus, at the end of *The Searchers*, Indianness itself suffers alteration, for Ethan's Indianness as an Indian *fighter* now becomes an Indianness that identifies him as America's last savage. This once-submerged yet handy Indianness that had so efficaciously assisted and abetted his Indian-hating now yields to an Indianness openly defined as unremitting savagery. Knowing, as of old, damns: Ethan, knowing Indians, becomes Indian. Ethan now stands accursed by his knowledge of the Indian, which is now also—though perhaps it has been throughout—his self-knowledge. Thus, the instant that renders him triumphantly heroic reveals him also tragically so—that consecrates the deliverance of the white victim damns him to accursed savagery. At once savage and savagery's formidable enemy, he embodies the Double Other's ambivalence, becomes both agent and exhibit of Roy Harvey Pearce's axiom of cultural appropriation: "Americans would vindicate savage character even as they destroyed it."[41] Let us now look more closely at the details of the last moments in their relation to the illusion of cultural divestment.

After he helps Debbie off the horse they have shared on the way from

40. *Insistence of the Indian*, p. 82.
41. *Savagism and Civilization*, p. 78.

the devastated Comanche village, Ethan carries her the rest of the way to the Jorgensen porch, where both Lars and Mrs. Jorgensen hold out their arms to her.⁴² She crosses into the "fine good place to be," while Ethan remains just outside its outer boundary. Standing on the ground just before the porch and framed by its massive scroll-bracketed posts, Ethan watches (it seems contentedly) a timorous yet compliant Debbie enter the house in Mrs. Jorgensen's maternal embrace, these two followed in by a doting Lars. The camera, still inside the house, tracks back to see the threesome enter, and when these three leave its field of view, the doorway (and part of the porch posts) frames Ethan. Now Ethan steps up to the porch, as if he is himself about to enter; but having caught a glance of Marty and Laurie, who approach from behind, he steps aside for them to enter. After Marty and Laurie enter the house (they also come to the foreground and exit screen right), Ethan, still framed by the doorway, remains standing on the porch, still looking in, awkwardly holding his right elbow in his left hand, as if uncertain what to do now, the wind blowing strong against his hat, pushing the brim up against the crown. Then he turns around and begins to walk away.⁴³ Though none of those who have entered the Jorgensen home could have physically closed the door, it now closes, as if by itself, on Ethan's solitary and wind-swept form. Already when Ethan helped Debbie off the horse, the chorus sang on the soundtrack:

A man will search his heart and soul,

42. Six people (five horses) ride into the Jorgensen place. Of these we clearly see only Debbie, Ethan, and Martin. One of the others is almost certainly Sam Clayton, the other, perhaps, Charlie McCorry. As Ethan carries Debbie to the house, the figure that I identify as Sam Clayton leads the horses off to screen right, in the background. We never see these two characters again, though it is not difficult to surmise that they would be welcome into the Jorgensen place in a way that Ethan may not be.

43. This isolation was prefigured early, in two contrasting instances—one concerning Martin, the other Ethan, the first invested with racist overtones, the second one with sexual innuendo. Immediately after the dinner scene, in which Ethan, upon first seeing Martin after many years, says to him, "A fellow could mistake you for a half-breed," we see Martin on the porch steps of the Edwards home. The front door is open, and the light from within streams out on the porch. Martin stands up, walks in, and bids goodnight to all, thus boldly asserting his right to membership in this family. Once all the young ones—including Martin—have retired to bed, Ethan empties his saddlebags of all the "Yankee" money ($3600 in "fresh-minted" gold coins) and hands them to Aaron. Then, after he hands Martha the lamp from the top of the mantle, she goes off to her bedroom, and Ethan goes outside, sitting on the porch, empty saddlebags in hand, in the precise spot that Martin sat just moments before. But when Ethan looks over his shoulder and past the open front door, he sees not the warm and welcoming light that Martin saw but Aaron entering the bedroom where Martha—Ethan's own beloved Martha—awaits. Chris, the family dog, joins Ethan outside, thus underscoring his isolation. For a similar look at these two scenes, see Clauss, "Descent into Hell."

Go searching way out there.
His peace of mind he knows he'll find,
But where, O Lord? Lord, where?
Ride away, ride away, ride away.

"The only certainty," writes Geoffrey O'Brien, "is that he will be alone."[44]

In *The Searchers*, both the hero's knowledge of the Indian and his Indian hating originate in his whiteness. Whiteness both empowers and justifies the necessary cultural appropriation, the mythically mandated descent into savagery. Yet the same whiteness demands the eventual dissolution of this double (and doubly conflicted) Indianness of Ethan's, the resolution of the racio-cultural instability that throws into question not only Ethan's own identity but the identity of the newly established nation as well. The question before us is, then, whether Ethan's Indian hating comes to be so exhausted at the end of the action as to leave only an unambiguously *white* hero. Is there a moment at the end of *The Searchers* where we might see so perfect and reciprocal a consummation of his hatred of Indians and his knowledge of them—each spent utterly on the satisfaction of the other—as to erase all traces of Otherness? Is Ethan any less Indian, or any less hateful, at the end, after having scalped Scar? Or does *The Searchers* say of Ethan, as Ethan of the white captives at the fort, that he ain't white, anymore; he's "Comanch' "? By way of a response to these questions, I appeal to the visual subtlety of the ending. The responses are of course—like the film itself—hardly simple, hardly unequivocal, hardly answers, then. The last moments, silent but for the reemergence of the choral music with which the movie opened, consist of two basic events: Debbie, the Jorgensens, and Martin enter the house; Ethan remains outside. The significance of the last scene unfolds as a play between these two events. I have already described how the participants in the scene enter the house—their grouping, the order of their entering, their visual and spatial relation to Ethan, the mode of their exit, and so on. I now attend to the events that immediately precede these entrances and exits. I apologize for the repetition of some of the details.

Moments before the arrival of the riders, Lars, Laurie, and Mrs. Jorgensen stand on the porch (Mose Harper rocks in his chair) and recognize the riders in the distance (so that the moment unfailingly recalls the opening scene, when the Edwardses first saw Ethan approaching

44. "Movie of the Century."

[281]

DBS Arts Library

The Searchers (1956, Warner Bros.). Bringing Debbie to the "fine good place to be." Courtesy of Warner Bros./Museum of Modern Art Film Stills Archive.

their place). The Jorgensen couple remain on the porch, but Laurie rushes off to Martin. Mrs. Jorgensen, overcome with emotion, moves closer to Lars, who fairly beams at the sight of the returned captive. He points outward to the riders, as if to remind his wife that he knew all along that Ethan would return with Debbie. With the camera already inside the house, as if posted at the door itself, Ethan, Debbie in his arms, walks right up to the edge of the porch and sets her down on it, though he remains standing on the bare ground just at the edge. As all four come to be framed by the heavy posts of the porch, Ethan and Debbie stand between Lars and Mrs. Jorgensen. All eyes are on Debbie, while her own timid gaze falls first on Ethan, then (following a hug from Mrs. Jorgensen) alternately on each of the Jorgensens, even as they lead her into the house. When Ethan set Debbie down on the porch, Mrs. Jorgensen briefly put an appreciative hand on his shoulder, but all throughout this poignant moment *neither Lars nor Mrs. Jorgensen ever looked at Ethan*. Now they walk in, the camera tracks back to see them inside the house, and then they exit screen right. Then Martin and Laurie come up behind Ethan, who is framed by the doorway; yet as

[282]

they approach, and even now that they pass him as he steps aside for them, *they themselves never look at him.* They, too, enter the house and exit screen right. Indeed, when Laurie dashed out of the porch to greet the riders, she ran right past Debbie and Ethan, as if they were not there at all. Mose Harper has been absent from the frame a good while, and the other riders have long since vacated the background, leaving it a scene of the desolation that will shortly become Ethan's only home.

Ethan has become almost invisible, virtually absent, to the community of the "fine good place to be," almost as if he is now the object of their censure. They enforce their censure—and avoid, therefore, their own complicity in his crime—by not looking at him. In this way, Ethan recapitulates Natty Bumppo, "the mourner," as Susan Scheckel writes, "who himself cannot be mourned and laid to rest, [who] becomes a national hero for providing the means to confront and defer the national guilt that cannot be resolved."[45] His visual absence, the presence now unacknowledged by the gaze that only moments before (when these same people saw him in the distance) reveled in the man's achievement, suggests already something crucial about Ethan's post-apocalyptic identity—namely, his ironic kinship with the very Indian whose absence his hatred has made possible. This virtual absence that so suddenly comes to be his links him, at least in the perspective of the new community, with the absent Indian. Indeed, it is impossible not to suggest, further, that if the Jorgensens look so adoringly on Debbie yet manage to avoid looking at Ethan, then Debbie, at least by the dynamics of the moment, has been cleansed of her Indianness in a way that Ethan has not. Such a suggestion, moreover, seems consistent with the equivocal function of Mrs. Jorgensen's hand on Ethan's shoulder: is it only appreciative, or does it also evoke a gesture of detainment, of determent—an indication that the "fine good place to be" is now proscribed space, that deeds both heroic and savage committed beyond the margins of this place are to remain there, in the spaces occupied by the solitary and ostracized Othered Same. The gesture betokens appreciation and arrest, both, and thus the incertitude in which the new nation holds the hero-savage.

This withheld gaze seems to contain (at least) one more possible meaning: it suggests Ethan's passage into *history*, into a history of the making—the "winning"—of the "fine good place to be." Yet it is a history that has become suddenly and terrifyingly irrelevant to the very being of the place. For the past of that place only reminds it of the du-

45. *Insistence of the Indian*, p. 40.

bious way that it came into being. In that willfully unacknowledged history, Ethan remains both hero and Indian. His very duality defines the Othered Same, and thus presents a challenge far greater than the Indian Debbie or the eighth-Cherokee Martin to the illusion of cultural divestment. The heroic Indian-hating white man has come to incarnate the history of the *Othered nation*, and like that history itself, he had best remain unrecognized, disavowed, ever at the margins, lest his claims on that nation unravel its illusions. He has actually stepped on the porch, as if to enter the Jorgensen home, and thus in a sense has dared to bring his past, savagery and all, into this place that must know no history, that must continually remember not to recall. He has crossed the border from savagery to civilization, has in a way reenacted the supposed process whereby America itself is born out of the selfsame crossing. But then, perhaps heeding the choral refrain ("Ride away, ride away . . ."), he turns and steps back down into his own native ground, still irredeemably Othered, still unimpeachably heroic.

We have so far considered the last moments of *The Searchers* as if the community alone determined the hero's fate in the post-apocalyptic America. Yet Ethan turns from the Jorgensen home *before the door begins to close on him*. It is a moment, like so many others in *The Searchers*, clearly stamped with the mark of indeterminacy. Does Ethan, having made a half-hearted attempt to enter the "fine good place to be," accept now his virtual absence, his invisibility, his historical irrelevance? Or does the turn reveal a repudiation of the new order? Consider: if America has to be composed of immigrants (Lars Jorgensen), people of mixed races (Martin and, to some extent, now Debbie), half-wits and dimwits (Mose Harper, Charlie McCorry, Lieutenant Greenhill) and lapsed Confederates (since Sam Clayton, according to Ethan, reneged on his oath to the Confederacy)—if this is the cast of the promised nation, could someone as empowered by the hatred of Otherness as Ethan is suddenly become a full-fledged member of such a community? Does he scorn the new order because he sees it as itself irrecoverably Othered?

The *Indian* Ethan invites similar, even parallel, questions. If, for example, the "fine good place to be" is indeed the millennial hope fulfilled, would not the one remaining savage repudiate it, since the fulfillment has come at his expense? And does he not then, as "Indian," turn from this place only to enact his virtual absence, which is to say, the proper form of his presence in the Myth of Conquest? Could he be, as Indian, any less historically irrelevant than as the white hero who has accomplished his mission? The Indian Ethan and the heroic Ethan

[284]

The Searchers (1956, Warner Bros.). "And turn his back on home." Courtesy of Warner Bros./Museum of Modern Art Film Stills Archive.

converge into a single type: yet ambivalence and paradox and irony can find resolution only at the vertex of these two typologies, at that point where both—and both as one—become an *anachronism*—not a throwback merely, or a relic, but *extra-temporal*, and thus *mythic*. They live as one (though hardly in harmony) only *out* of history, at once condemned to oblivion and resigned to it, both ostracized and self-exiled.

Whatever its function as a narrative device, the closing of the door in *The Searchers* resonates with the moment meant to specify an identifying moment in American history—the closing of the frontier. And in those open spaces *beyond* the closed door of the American Canaan there is only the dreadful intimacy, the self-haunting presence, of the Indian and his hater. In that composite being that is never whole, we find always the essential American anachronism. What forms of anxiety might the suppression of such a being produce in the new nation? Are closing and closure only futile evasions of that anxiety? Does the nation close its door, does it close the frontier, more as a hope than as an accomplishment? Where does such a nation turn for an account of its coming-to-be, now that it has found it necessary to renounce its hero? Or does it live (as often seems to be the case) in blissful oblivion, as if under the unbroken spell of the illusion of cultural divestment—as if

amnesia were redemption? Does the nation deploy its appointed an-
gels at the border, at the "frontier," in order that such a compromised
being as Ethan may never challenge its own fragile identity?

If the hero has become the American anachronism, he has also become the very source and embodiment of American "history"—of that
mythic version of the past that distills, out of the complex currents of
passion, power, and contingency, the one elemental extract—the contest between savagery and civilization. In the millennial time, when the
pursuit ceases and happiness is said to abound, the nation also becomes vulnerable. And this, too, becomes a source of anxiety: for if one
anxiety would suppress the return of the hero, another one would welcome him back, however compromised he may be by dark deeds in the
wilderness. Does the nation allow the hero into the "fine good place to
be" only when it sees him as we do Ethan at the beginning—a hero, as
it seems, not yet compromised by savage dealings? But does the opening of the door itself not presuppose a *previous* closing of it—the demon
of the Frontier Thesis—and thus the reemergence of the Double Other
who is always and already an Othered Same? At times, guilt and nostalgia seem but pat responses to the question of why America keeps
representing its Indian and its Indian fighter: anxiety often seems the
more plausible, if less welcome, answer. Suddenly, then, now that the
Indian is no longer a threat, it becomes necessary to invoke him—
though not so much as savage or as noble but as index of the time of
righteousness in the very race that destroyed him.

Even as revisionism of the *Dances With Wolves* type was but repeating
the claims made decades earlier by *Broken Arrow* and *Devil's Doorway*, a
new way of representing the Indian was emerging—a radical revisionism—"radical" because it seemed to dispense with the need to invoke
the canonical Western even as it pretended to revise it. *Black Robe*
(Beresford, 1991), *Cabeza de Vaca* (Echevarría, 1991), *Dead Man* (Jarmusch, 1995), *Smoke Signals* (Eyre, 1998) all differ each from the other,
but they share their radical difference from the Western, canonical or
revisionist. Yet it would seem naive to consider these productions as
evidence that the Myth of Conquest in Hollywood has run its course. If
native cultures persist, so, too, does the conqueror's own, revised and
reviled though it be. The native forever confronts the fragility of his culture because he constantly faces the overwhelming power of the conqueror's own, most imposingly, perhaps, in the images that do mythology's work of national self-identification. To be sure, the Myth of
Conquest can hardly change its spots. Its hero will forever be the one
on whose ability to become Other the Same pinned its millennial

hopes, and mythology will long continue to cast America as a nation that had to appropriate—and by appropriating destroy—another culture in order to acquire its own identity. The Western performs the curiously ambivalent role of reminding the nation of its encounter with the Indian even as it endeavors to present the resolution of that conflict as the origin of the nation. Perhaps the America in which we ourselves live will learn to think of cultures in their inviolable integrity, to imagine an Other without thereby rendering him—and her—absent. Until some such dispensation comes to pass, however, the Indian Western, as a response to cultural history and national identity, shall continue to suggest nothing more strongly than that a nation so rapturously enamored of its mythology will make many tragic appeals to its past.

Filmography

Title (Year of Release, Production Company, Distributor). D: Director. S: Screenplay. PP: Principal Players (including players cast in the major Indian roles).

America (1924, D. W. Griffith Productions, United Artists). D: D. W. Griffith. S: Robert W. Chambers. PP: Neil Hamilton, Carol Dempster, Erville Alderson.

Apache (1954, Hecht-Lancaster Productions, United Artists). D: Robert Aldrich. S: James R. Webb. From the novel *Bronco Apache* by Paul Wellman. PP: Burt Lancaster, Jean Peters, John McIntire.

Apocalypse Now (1979, Zoetrope Studios, United Artists). D: Francis Ford Coppola. S: Francis Coppola, John Milius, Michael Herr. Adapted from *Heart of Darkness* by Joseph Conrad. PP: Marlon Brando, Martin Sheen, Robert Duvall, Dennis Hopper, Frederic Forrest, Laurence Fishburne.

Arrowhead (1953, Paramount). D and S: Charles Marquis Warren. From the novel by W. R. Burnett. PP: Charlton Heston, Jack Palance, Katy Jurado.

The Battle at Elderbush Gulch (1914, Biograph). D and S: D. W. Griffith. PP: Lillian Gish, Robert Harron, Mae Marsh, Alfred Paget.

The Big Sky (1952, Winchester Pictures, RKO). D: Howard Hawks. S: Dudley Nichols. From the novel by A. B. Guthrie, Jr. PP: Kirk Douglas, Dewey Martin, Elizabeth Threatt, Hank Worden, Arthur Hunnicut.

The Birth of a Nation (1915, David W. Griffith Corp. and Epoch Producing). D: D. W. Griffith. S:—, Frank E. Woods. From the novels *The Clansman* and *The Leopard's Spots* by Thomas F. Dixon, Jr. PP: Lillian Gish, Mae Marsh, Henry B. Walthall.

Black Robe (1991, Alliance Communications and others, Samuel Goldwyn). D: Bruce Beresford. S: Brian Moore, III. PP: Lothaire Bluteau, Aden Young, Sandrine Holt, August Schellenberg, Tantoo Cardinal.

Blade Runner (theatrical and director's cut, 1982, The Ladd Co. and Blade Runner Partnership, Embassy Pictures and Warner Brothers). D: Ridley Scott. S: Hampton Fancher, David Peoples. From the novel *Do Androids Dream of Electric Sheep?* by Philip K. Dick. PP: Harrison Ford, Rutger Hauer, Sean Young.

Broken Arrow (1950, 20th Century Fox). D: Delmer Daves. S: Elliott Arnold, Albert Maltz, Michael Blankfort. From the novel *Blood Brother* by Elliott Arnold. PP: James Stewart, Jeff Chandler, Debra Paget.

Broken Blossoms (1919, D. W. Griffith Productions, United Artists). D and S: D. W. Griffith. From the story by Thomas Burke. PP: Lillian Gish, Richard Barthelmess, Donald Crisp.

Broken Lance (1954, 20th Century Fox). D: Edward Dmytryk. S: Richard Murphy. From the story by Philip Yordan. PP: Spencer Tracy, Robert Wagner, Jean Peters, Katy Jurado.

The Call of the Wild (1908, Biograph). D and S: D. W. Griffith. PP: Charles Gorman, Charles Inslee, Florence Lawrence, Mack Sennett.

Cabeza de Vaca (1991, Fondo de Fomento a la Calidad Cinematográfica and others, Concorde) D: Nicolás Echevarría. S:—, Guillermo Sheridan. From the narrative *La Relación, o Naufragios* by Alvar Núñez Cabeza de Vaca. PP: Juan Diego, Daniel Giménez Cacho, Roberto Sosa, Carlos Castañón, Geraldo Villareal, José Flores, Eli "Chupadera" Machuca.

Chato's Land (1971, Scimitar Films, United Artists). D: Michael Winner. S: Gerald Wilson. PP: Charles Bronson, Jack Palance, Simon Oakland.

Cheyenne Autumn (1964, Warner Bros.). D: John Ford. S: James R. Webb. From the novels *The Last Frontier* by Howard Fast and *Cheyenne Autumn* by Mari Sandoz. PP: Richard Widmark, Carroll Baker, Karl Malden, Ricardo Montalbán, Gilbert Roland.

Cheyenne Warrior (1994, Libra Pictures). D: Mark Griffiths. S: Michael B. Druxman. PP: Kelly Preston, Bo Hopkins, Pato Hoffman, Nick Winterhawk.

Comata, the Sioux (1909, Biograph). D: D. W. Griffith. S: Stanner E. V. Taylor. PP: Linda Arvidson, Vernon Clarges, Arthur V. Johnson.

The Covered Wagon (1923, Paramount). D: James Cruze. S: Jack Cunningham, Emerson Hough. PP: J. Warren Kerrigan, Lois Wilson, Alan Hale.

Custer's Last Fight (1912, Thomas H. Ince, Quality Amusement). D: Francis Ford. S: Richard V. Spencer. PP: Francis Ford, Grace Cunard, Charles K. French, William Eagle Shirt.

Dead Man (1995, Miramax). D and S: Jim Jarmusch. PP: Johnny Depp, Gary Farmer, Robert Mitchum, Billy Bob Thornton.

Dances With Wolves (1990, Tig Productions, Orion Pictures). D: Kevin Costner. S: Michael Blake. PP: Kevin Costner, Mary McDonnell, Graham Greene, Rodney A. Grant, Floyd Red Crow Westerman, Tantoo Cardinal, Jimmy Herman, Nathan Lee Chasing Horse, Wes Studi.

Devil's Doorway (1950, MGM). D: Anthony Mann. S: Guy Trosper. PP: Robert Taylor, Louis Calhern, Paula Raymond, Harry Antrim, Chief John Big Tree.

Distant Drums (1951, Warner Bros.). D: Raoul Walsh. S: Niven Busch, Martin Rackin. From the story by Niven Busch. PP: Gary Cooper, Mari Aldon, Richard Webb, Ray Teal.

Drums Along the Mohawk (1939, 20th Century Fox). D: John Ford. S: William Faulkner, Sonya Levien, Lamar Trotti. From the novel by Walter D. Edmonds. PP: Claudette Colbert, Henry Fonda, Edna May Oliver, John Carradine, Chief John Big Tree.

Duel in the Sun (1946, Vanguard Films, Selznick Releasing). D: King Vidor. S: Oliver H. P. Garrett, Ben Hecht, David O. Selznick. From the novel by Niven Busch. PP: Jennifer Jones, Joseph Cotten, Gregory Peck, Lionel Barrymore, Herbert Marshall, Lillian Gish, Walter Huston.

Firing the Cabin (1903). D: McCutcheon.

Flaming Star (1960, 20th Century Fox). D: Don Siegel. S: Clair Huffaker, Nunnally Johnson. From the novel by Clair Huffaker. PP: Elvis Presley, Steve Forrest, Barbara Eden, Dolores del Rio, John McIntire.

Fort Apache (1948, Argosy, RKO). D: John Ford. S: Frank S. Nugent. From the story by James Warner Bellah. PP: John Wayne, Henry Fonda, Shirley Temple, Pedro Armendariz, Victor McLaglen, Ward Bond, Miguel Inclán.

Geronimo (1962, United Artists). D: Arnold Laven. S: Pat Fielder. PP: Chuck Connors, Kamala Devi, Pat Conway.

Geronimo: An American Legend (1993, Columbia Pictures). D: Walter Hill. S: Larry Gross, John Milius. PP: Jason Patric, Gene Hackman, Robert Duvall, Wes Studi, Matt Damon, Rodney A. Grant, Kevin Tighe, Steve Reevis, Carlos Palomino, Victor Aaron, Stuart Proud Eagle Grant.

Grayeagle (1978, American International Pictures). D and S: Charles B. Pierce. PP: Ben Johnson, Alex Cord, Lana Wood, Iron Eyes Cody, Jack Elam, Paul Fix.

The Great Train Robbery (1903, Edison Manufacturing). D and S: Edwin S. Porter. PP: A. C. Abadie, Gilbert M. "Broncho Billy" Anderson, Justus D. Barnes, Walter Cameron.

The Green Berets (1968, Batjac Productions, Warner-Seven Arts). D: Ray Kellogg, John Wayne. S: James Lee Barrett, Col. Kenneth B. Facey. PP: John Wayne, David Janssen, Jim Hutton, Jack Soo, Irene Tsu, Craig Jue.

Hombre (1967, Hombre Productions, 20th Century Fox). D: Martin Ritt. S: Irving Ravetch, Harriet Frank, Jr. From the novel by Elmore Leonard. PP: Paul Newman, Frederic March, Richard Boone, Diane Cilento, Barbara Rush, Martin Balsam.

Hondo (1953, Wayne-Fellows Productions, Warner Bros.). D: John Farrow. S: James Edward Grant. From the story by Louis L'Amour. PP: John Wayne, Geraldine Page, Ward Bond, Michael Pate, James Arness, Rodolfo Acosta.

Incident at Oglala (1992, Spanish Fork Motion Pictures, Miramax). D: Michael Apted.

The Indian Fighter (1955, Bryna Productions, United Artists). D: Andre De Toth. S: Frank Davis, Ben Hecht. PP: Kirk Douglas, Elsa Martinelli, Walter Matthau, Lon Chaney, Jr., Alan Hale, Jr.

The Invaders (1912, Kay-Bee, Mutual Film). D: Thomas H. Ince. S: Richard V. Spencer. PP: Art Acord, Carlyle Blackwell, Sr., Francis Ford, Ethel Grandin, Ann Little, William Eagle Shirt.

Iola's Promise (1912, Biograph). D: D. W. Griffith. S: Belle Taylor. PP: Dorothy Bernard, William J. Butler, Arthur V. Johnson, Charles Hill Mailes, Mary Pickford.

The Iron Horse (1924, Fox). D: John Ford. S: Charles Darnton, Charles Kenyon, John Russell. From the story by Charles Kenyon. PP: George O'Brien, Madge Bellamy, Cyril Chadwick, Fred Kohler.

I Will Fight No More Forever (1975, David Wolper, ABC). D: Richard T. Heffron. S: Jeb Rosebrook, Theodore Strauss. PP: Sam Elliott, Ned Romero, James Whitmore.

Jeremiah Johnson (1972, Sanford Productions, Warner Bros.). D: Sydney Pollack. S: John Milius, Edward Anhalt, David Rayfiel. From the novel *Mountain Man* by Vardis Fisher and the book *Crow Killer* by Raymond W. Thorp and Robert Bunker. PP: Robert Redford, Will Geer, Delle Bolton, Josh Albee, Stefan Gierasch, Joaquín Martínez.

The Last of the Mohicans (1920, Maurice Tourneur Productions, Associated Producers). D: Clarence Brown, Maurice Tourneur. S: Robert Dillon. From the novel by James Fenimore Cooper. PP: Wallace Beery, Barbara Bedford, Alan Roscoe, Lillian Hall, Henry Woodward, James Gordon, Harry Lorraine.

The Last of the Mohicans (1936, Reliance Productions, United Artists). D: George B. Seitz. S: Philip Dunne. From the novel by James Fenimore Cooper. PP: Randolph Scott, Binne Barnes, Henry Wilcoxon, Bruce Cabot, Heather Angel, Philip Reed.

The Last of the Mohicans (1992, Morgan Creek Productions, 20th Century Fox). D: Michael Mann. S: Christopher Crowe, Michael Mann. From the novel by James Fenimore Cooper. PP: Daniel Day-Lewis, Madeleine Stowe, Russell Means, Eric Schweig, Jodhi May, Wes Studi.

Leatherstocking (1924, Pathé Exchange). D: George B. Seitz. PP: David Dunbar, Frank Lackteen, Harold Miller, Edna Murphy, Tom Tyler, Whitehorse.

Legends of the Fall (1994, TriStar Pictures). D: Edward Zwick. S: Susan Shilliday, William D. Wittliff. From the story by Jim Harrison. PP: Brad Pitt, Anthony Hopkins, Aidan Quinn, Julia Ormond, Gordon Tootoosis, Tantoo Cardinal, Karina Lombard.

Little Big Man (1970, Cinema Center 100, National General Pictures). D: Arthur Penn. S: Calder Willingham. From the novel by Thomas Berger. PP: Dustin Hoffman, Faye Dunaway, Chief Dan George, Martin Balsam, Richard Mulligan, Aimee Eccles, Robert Little Star.

Lone Star (1996, Castle Rock Entertainment and Columbia, Columbia TriStar). D and S: John Sayles. PP: Kris Kristofferson, Stephen Mendillo, Stephen J. Lang, Chris Cooper, Elizabeth Peña, Joe Morton, Ron Canada, Miriam Colon, Clifton James, Matthew McConaughey, Frances McDormand, Gordon Tootoosis.

Lonesome Dove (1989, Motown Productions, Quintex Entertainment, and RHI Entertainment, Cabin Fever Entertainment). D: Simon Wincer. S: William D. Wittliff. From the novel by Larry McMurtry. PP: Robert Duvall, Tommy Lee Jones, Danny Glover, Anjelica Huston, Diane Lane, Rick Schroder, Frederic Forrest, Robert Urich.

Major Dundee (1965, Columbia). D: Sam Peckinpah. S:—, Harry Julian Fink, Oscar Saul. PP: Charlton Heston, Richard Harris, Jim Hutton, James Coburn, Michael Anderson, Jr., Senta Berger, Michael Pate, Warren Oates, Ben Johnson, R. G. Armstrong, L. Q. Jones, Slim Pickens.

A Man Called Horse (1970, Cinema Center 100, National General Pictures). D: Elliot Silverstein. S: Jack DeWitt. From the story by Dorothy M. Johnson. PP: Richard Harris, Judith Anderson, Manu Tupou, Corinna Tsopei, Dub Taylor, Eddie Little Sky.

The Massacre (1912, Biograph). D and S: D. W. Griffith. PP: Lionel Barrymore, Robert Harron, Blanche Sweet.

Maverick (1994, Donner/Schuller-Donner Productions, Warner Bros.). D: Richard Donner. S: William Goldman. From the television series "Maverick," by Roy Huggins. PP: Mel Gibson, Jodie Foster, James Garner, Graham Greene, Alfred Molina, James Coburn.

The Mended Lute (1909, Biograph). D: D. W. Griffith. S: Stanner E. V. Taylor. PP: Arthur V. Johnson, James Kirkwood, Florence Lawrence, Owen Moore, Mack Sennett, Red Wing.

Northwest Passage (1940, MGM). D: King Vidor. S: Talbot Jennings, Laurence Stallings. From the novel by Kenneth Roberts. PP: Spencer Tracy, Robert Young, Walter Brennan.

The Outlaw Josey Wales (1976, Malpaso, Warner Bros.). D: Clint Eastwood. S: Sonia Chernus, Philip Kaufman. From the novel *Gone to Texas* by Forrest Carter. PP: Clint Eastwood, Chief Dan George, Sondra Locke, Bill McKinney, Sam Bottoms, Geraldine Keams.

The Patriot (2000, Centropolis Entertainment and Mutual Films, Columbia). D: Roland Emmerich. S: Robert Rodat. PP: Mel Gibson, Heath Ledger, Joely Richardson, Jason Isaacs, Chris Cooper.

Quigley Down Under (1990, Pathé Entertainment, MGM). D: Simon Wincer. S: John Hill. PP: Tom Selleck, Laura San Giacomo, Alan Rickman, Steve Dodd, Nosepeg, Billy Stockman.

Rambo, First Blood, Part II (1985, Carolco Entertainment, TriStar Pictures). D: George P. Cosmatos. S: Kevin Jarre, Sylvester Stallone, James Cameron. PP: Sylvester Stallone, Richard Crenna, Charles Napier, Julia Nickson-Soul.

Ramona (1910, Biograph). D: D. W. Griffith. S:—, Stanner E. V. Taylor. From the novel by Helen Hunt Jackson. PP: Mary Pickford, Henry B. Walthall, Kate Bruce.

The Red Man and the Child (1908, Biograph). D and S: D. W. Griffith. PP: Linda Arvidson, George Gebhardt, Charles Inslee.

The Redman's View (1909, Biograph). D: D. W. Griffith. S: Frank E. Woods. PP: Arthur V. Johnson, James Kirkwood, Owen Moore, Alfred Paget, Lottie Pickford.

Red River (1948, Charles K. Feldman Group and Monterey Productions, United Artists). D: Howard Hawks. S: Borden Chase, Charles Schnee. From the story "The Chisholm Trail" by Borden Chase. PP: John Wayne, Montgomery Clift, Joanne Dru, Walter Brennan, Coleen Gray, John Ireland, Noah

Beery, Jr., Chief Yowlachie, Harry Carey, Harry Carey, Jr., Paul Fix, Hank Worden.

The Return of a Man Called Horse (1976, Sandy Howard Productions, United Artists). D: Irvin Kershner. S: Jack DeWitt. From the story by Dorothy M. Johnson. PP: Richard Harris, Gale Sondergaard, Geoffrey Lewis, William Lucking, Jorge Luke.

Rio Grande (1950, Argosy Pictures and Republic Pictures, Republic). D: John Ford. S: James Kevin McGuinness. From the story by James Warner Bellah. PP: John Wayne, Maureen O'Hara, Ben Johnson, Claude Jarman, Jr.

Run of the Arrow (1957, Globe Enterprises and RKO, RKO). D and S: Samuel Fuller. PP: Rod Steiger, Sara Montiel, Brian Keith, Ralph Meeker, Jay C. Flippen, Charles Bronson.

The Searchers (1956, C. V. Whitney Pictures and Warner Bros., Warner Bros.). D: John Ford. S: Frank S. Nugent. From the novel by Alan LeMay. PP: John Wayne, Jeffrey Hunter, Vera Miles, Ward Bond, Natalie Wood, Lana Wood, Beulah Archuletta, Henry Brandon, John Qualen, Olive Carey, Harry Carey, Jr., Ken Curtis, Hank Worden, Dorothy Jordan.

Shanghai Noon (2000, Jackie Chan Films and others, Buena Vista Pictures). D: Tom Dey. S: Miles Millar and Alfred Gough. PP: Jackie Chan, Owen Wilson, Lucy Liu, Simon Baker.

She Wore a Yellow Ribbon (1949, Argosy Pictures and RKO, RKO). D: John Ford. S: Frank S. Nugent, Laurence Stallings. From the stories "War Party" and "The Big Hunt" by James Warner Bellah. PP: John Wayne, Joanne Dru, John Agar, Ben Johnson, Harry Carey, Jr., Victor McLaglen, George O'Brien, Chief John Big Tree, Noble Johnson, Tom Tyler.

Sitting Bull (1954, Tele-Voz and W. R. Frank Productions, United Artists). D: Rene Cardona, Sidney Salkow. S: Jack DeWitt, Sidney Salkow. PP: Dale Robertson, Mary Murphy, J. Carrol Naish, Joel Fluellen, Iron Eyes Cody.

Smoke Signals (1998, Shadow Catcher Entertainment, Miramax). D: Chris Eyre. S: Sherman Alexie. From the book *The Lone Ranger and Tonto Fistfight in Heaven* by Sherman Alexie. PP: Adam Beach, Evan Adams, Irene Bedard, Gary Farmer, Tantoo Cardinal.

Soldier Blue (1970, AVCO Embassy Pictures). D: Ralph Nelson. S: John Gay. From the novel by Theodore V. Olsen. PP: Candice Bergen, Peter Strauss, Donald Pleasence, John Anderson, Jorge Rivero.

Son of the Morning Star (1991, Republic Pictures). D: Mike Robe. S: Evan S. Connell. PP: Gary Cole, Rosanna Arquette, Rodney A. Grant, Kimberly Norris, Floyd Red Crow Westerman.

The Squaw Man (1931, MGM). D: Cecil B. DeMille. S: Lenore J. Coffee, Lucien Hubbard, Elsie Janis. From the play by Edwin Milton Royle. PP: Warner Baxter, Lupe Velez, Eleanor Boardman, Charles Bickford, Mitchell Lewis.

Stagecoach (1939, Walter Wanger Productions, United Artists). D: John Ford. S: Dudley Nichols, Ben Hecht. From the story "Stage to Lordsburg" by Ernest Haycox. PP: Claire Trevor, John Wayne, John Carradine, Thomas Mitchell, Louise Platt, Chief John Big Tree.

The Stalking Moon (1969, National General Productions and The Stalking Moon

Co., National General Productions). D: Robert Mulligan. S: Wendell Mayes, Alvin Sargent. From the novel by Theodore V. Olsen. PP: Gregory Peck, Eva Marie Saint, Robert Forster, Noland Clay, Nathaniel Narcisco.

Stolen Women, Captured Hearts (1997, CBS Productions). D: Jerry London. S: Richard Fielder. PP: Janine Turner, Jean Louisa Kelly, William Shockley, Michael Greyeyes, Rodney A. Grant, Saginaw Grant.

Tell Them Willie Boy Is Here (1969, Universal). D and S: Abraham Polonsky. From the story by Harry Lawton. PP: Robert Redford, Katharine Ross, Robert Blake.

They Died With Their Boots On (1941, Warner Bros.). D: Raoul Walsh. S: Wally Kline, Æneas MacKenzie. PP: Errol Flynn, Olivia de Havilland, Arthur Kennedy, Anthony Quinn.

Thunderheart (1992, Tribeca Productions, TriStar Pictures). D: Michael Apted. S: John Fusco. PP: Val Kilmer, Sam Shepard, Graham Greene, Fred Ward.

Two Rode Together (1961, Columbia). D: John Ford. S: Frank S. Nugent. From the novel by Will Cook. PP: James Stewart, Richard Widmark, Shirley Jones, Linda Cristal, Woody Strode, Henry Brandon.

Ulzana's Raid (1972, Universal). D: Robert Aldrich. S: Alan Sharp. PP: Burt Lancaster, Bruce Davison, Jorge Luke, Richard Jaeckel, Joaquín Martínez.

The Unforgiven (1960, United Artists). D: John Huston. S: Ben Maddow. From the novel by Alan LeMay. PP: Burt Lancaster, Audrey Hepburn, Audie Murphy, John Saxon, Charles Bickford, Lillian Gish, Carlos Rivas, Joseph Wiseman.

The Vanishing American (1925, Famous Players-Lasky Corp., Paramount). D: George B. Seitz. S: Ethel Doherty, Lucien Hubbard. From the novel by Zane Grey. PP: Richard Dix, Lois Wilson, Noah Beery, Nocki, Bernard Siegel.

War Arrow (1953, Universal International). D: George Sherman. S: John Michael Hayes. PP: Maureen O'Hara, Jeff Chandler, John McIntire, Noah Beery, Jr., Henry Brandon.

Wild Horse Mesa (1925, Famous Players-Lasky Corp., Paramount). D: George B. Seitz. S: Lucien Hubbard. From the novel by Zane Grey. PP: Jack Holt, Noah Beery, Billie Dove, Douglas Fairbanks, Jr., George Magrill, George Irving, Edith Yorke, Bernard Siegel, Margaret Morris.

Winterhawk (1976, Charles B. Pierce Film Productions, Howco International Pictures). D and S: Charles B. Pierce. PP: Leif Erickson, Michael Dante, Woody Strode, Dawn Wells, Sacheen Littlefeather, Gilbert Lucero.

The Yaqui Cur (1913, Biograph). D: D. W. Griffith. S: Stanner E. V. Taylor. PP: Lionel Barrymore, Kate Bruce, Christy Cabanne, Victoria Forde.

Bibliography

Alberti, Leon Battista. *Della pittura* [*On Painting*]. Translated by John R. Spencer. New Haven: Yale University Press, 1966.

Anderson, Benedict. *Imagined Communities: Reflections on the Origin and Spread of Nationalism.* Rev. ed. London: Verso, 1991.

Anderson, Fred. *Crucible of War: The Seven Years' War and the Fate of Empire in British North America, 1754–1766.* New York: Alfred A. Knopf, 2000.

Aristotle. *Poetics.* Translated by Ingram Bywater. In *The Basic Works of Aristotle,* edited by Richard McKeon. New York: Random House, 1941.

Arnold, Edwin T., and Eugene L. Miller. *The Films and Career of Robert Aldrich.* Knoxville: University of Tennessee Press, 1986.

Aros, Andrew A. *An Actor Guide to the Talkies, 1965–1974.* Metuchen, N. J.: Scarecrow, 1977.

Awiakta, Marilou. "Red Alert! A Meditation on *Dances With Wolves.*" *MS.* (March–April 1991): 70–71.

Bass, Robert Duncan. *Swamp Fox: The Life and Campaigns of General Francis Marion.* New York: Henry Holt, 1959; Columbia, S.C.: Sandlapper, 1972.

Beaver, Frank E. *Dictionary of Film Terms.* New York: McGraw-Hill, 1983.

Berkhofer, Robert F., Jr. *The White Man's Indian: Images of the American Indian from Columbus to the Present.* New York: Vintage, 1979.

Bird, Robert Montgomery. *Nick of the Woods, or The Jibbenainosay: A Tale of Kentucky.* 1837. Edited by Cecil B. Williams. New York: American Book, 1939.

Bordewich, Fergus M. *Killing the White Man's Indian: Reinventing Native Americans at the End of the Twentieth Century.* New York: Random House, 1996.

Bowers, Alfred W. *Mandan Social and Ceremonial Organization.* Chicago: University of Chicago Press, 1950.

Bradford, William. *Of Plymouth Plantation.* Edited by Samuel Eliot Morison. New York: Modern Library, 1981.

Brisbane, Arthur. *Moving Picture World* 72, no. 2 (10 January 1925): 109.

Browne, Nick. "Griffith's Family Discourse: Griffith and Freud." *Quarterly Review of Film Studies* 6, no. 1 (winter 1981): 67–80.

Brownlow, Kevin. *The War, the West, and the Wilderness.* New York: Alfred A. Knopf, 1979.

Buscombe, Edward, ed. *The BFI Companion to the Western.* New York: Atheneum, 1988.

———. *Stagecoach.* London: British Film Institute, 1992.

Cabeza de Vaca, Alvar Núñez. *La Relación, o Naufragios* [*Cabeza de Vaca's Adventures in the Unknown Interior of America*]. 1542. Translated and annotated by Cyclone Covey. Albuquerque: University of New Mexico Press, 1983.

———. *La Relación, o Naufragios.* Edited by Martin A. Favata and José B. Fernández. Potomac, Md.: Scripta Humanistica, 1986.

Canfield, J. Douglas. *Mavericks on the Border: The Early Southwest in Historical Fiction and Film.* Lexington: University Press of Kentucky, 2001.

Catlin, George. *Letters and Notes on the Manners, Customs, and Conditions of North American Indians.* 1844. 2 vols. Reprint, New York: Dover, 1973.

———. *O-kee-pa, a Religious Ceremony and Other Customs of the Mandans.* 1867. Edited by John C. Ewers. New Haven: Yale University Press, 1967.

Caughie, John. "Teaching through Authorship." *Screen Education,* no. 17 (winter 1975/76): 3–13.

Cawelti, John G. *The Six-Gun Mystique Sequel.* Bowling Green: Bowling Green State University Popular Press, 1999.

Churchill, Ward. *Fantasies of the Master Race: Literature, Cinema, and the Colonization of American Indians.* Monroe, Me.: Common Courage, 1992.

Clauss, James J. "Descent into Hell: Mythic Paradigms in *The Searchers.*" *Journal of Popular Film and Television* 27, no. 3 (fall 1999): 2–17.

Columbus, Christopher. *The Diario of Christopher Columbus's First Voyage to America, 1492–1493. Abstracted by Fray Bartolomé de Las Casas.* Translated by Oliver Dunn and James E. Kelley, Jr. Norman: University of Oklahoma Press, 1989.

Connell, Evan S. *Son of the Morning Star: Custer and the Little Bighorn.* New York: Harper Collins, 1984.

Conrad, Joseph. *Heart of Darkness.* Edited by Robert Kimbrough. New York: W. W. Norton, 1988.

Cooper, James Fenimore. *The Deerslayer; or, The First War-Path.* 1841. Vol. 2 of *The Leatherstocking Tales.* Reprint. New York: Library of America, 1985.

———. *The Last of the Mohicans: A Tale of 1757.* 1826. Reprint. New York: Library of America, 1985.

Costner, Kevin, Michael Blake, and Jim Wilson. *Dances With Wolves: The Illustrated Story of the Epic Film.* Edited by Diana Landau. New York: Newmarket, 1990.

Cronon, William. "Telling Tales on Canvas: Landscapes of Frontier Change." In *Discovered Lands, Invented Pasts: Transforming Visions of the American West.* Edited by Jules David Prown. New Haven: Yale University Press, 1992.

Custer, George Armstrong. *My Life on the Plains or, Personal Experiences with the Indians.* Norman: University of Oklahoma Press, 1962.

Davis, Britton. *The Truth about Geronimo*. Edited by M. M. Quaife. New Haven: Yale University Press, 1929.

Debo, Angie. *Geronimo: The Man, His Time, His Place*. Vol. 142 of *The Civilization of the American Indian Series*. Norman: University of Oklahoma Press, 1976.

Deloria, Philip J. *Playing Indian*. New Haven: Yale University Press, 1998.

Demos, John. *The Unredeemed Captive: A Family Story from Early America*. New York: Random House, Vintage, 1994.

Denig, Lynde. "More Griffith Pictures." *Moving Picture World* 24, no. 13 (26 June 1915): 2110.

DeVoto, Bernard. *The Course of Empire*. Boston: Houghton Mifflin, 1952.

Díaz del Castillo, Bernal. *The Discovery and Conquest of Mexico* [*Historia verdadera de la conquista de la Nueva España*]. Edited by Genaro García. Translated by A. P. Maudslay. New York: Farrar, Straus and Cudahy, 1956.

Dippie, Brian W. *Custer's Last Stand: The Anatomy of an American Myth*. Missoula: University of Montana Publications in History, 1976.

——. *The Vanishing American: White Attitudes and U.S. Indian Policy*. Lawrence: University of Kansas Press, 1982.

Dittmar, Linda, and Gene Michaud, ed. *From Hanoi to Hollywood: The Vietnam War in American Film*. New Brunswick: Rutgers University Press, 1990.

Drinnon, Richard. *Facing West: The Metaphysics of Indian Hating and Empire Building*. New York: Schocken Books, 1980.

Drummond, Phillip. "Ulzana's Raid." In *The BFI Companion to the Western*. Edited by Edward Buscombe. New York: Atheneum, 1988.

Durgnat, Raymond. *King Vidor, American*. Berkeley: University of California Press, 1988.

Eckstein, Arthur M. "After the Rescue: *The Searchers*, the Audience and *Prime Cut* (1972)." *Journal of Popular Culture* 28, no. 3 (winter 1994): 33–53.

Ellis, Edward S. *Seth Jones; or, The Captives of the Frontier*. In *Reading the West: An Anthology of Dime Westerns*. Edited by Bill Brown. Boston: Bedford, 1997.

Eyman, Scott. *Print the Legend: The Life and Times of John Ford*. New York: Simon and Schuster, 1999.

Faragher, John Mack. *Daniel Boone: The Life and Legend of an American Pioneer*. New York: Henry Holt, 1992; New York: Owl Books, 1993.

Faulkner, William. *Go Down, Moses*. New York: Modern Library, 1942.

Fiedler, Leslie. *The Return of the Vanishing American*. New York: Stein and Day, 1969.

Filson, John. *Kentucke and the Adventures of Col. Daniel Boone*. 1784. With an introduction by Willard Rouse Jillson. Reprint. Louisville: John P. Morton, 1934.

Fisher, Vardis. *Mountain Man*. New York: Simon and Schuster, 1965.

Foucault, Michel. *Madness and Civilization: A History of Insanity in the Age of Reason*. Translated by Richard Howard. New York: Random House, Vintage, 1965.

Franklin, H. Bruce. *M.I.A. or Mythmaking in America: How and Why Belief in Live POWs Has Possessed a Nation*. Rev. ed. New Brunswick, N.J.: Rutgers University Press, 1993.

Friar, Ralph E. and Natasha Friar. *The Only Good Indian: The Hollywood Gospel.* New York: Drama Book Specialists, 1972.

Gallagher, Tag. *John Ford: The Man and His Films.* Berkeley: University of California Press, 1986.

Gish, Lillian. *Dorothy and Lillian Gish.* Edited by James E. Frasher. London: Macmillan, 1973.

Gish, Lillian, with Ann Pinchot. *The Movies, Mr. Griffith, and Me.* Englewood Cliffs, N.J.: Prentice-Hall, 1969.

Graham, Cooper C., et al. *D. W. Griffith and the Biograph Company.* Metuchen, N.J.: Scarecrow, 1985.

Greenberg, Joel. "War, Wheat, and Steel." *Sight and Sound* 37, no. 4 (autumn 1968): 192–198.

Gunning, Tom. "The Voice of Whiteness: D. W. Griffith's Biograph Films (1908–1913)." In *The Birth of Whiteness: Race and the Emergence of U.S. Cinema.* Edited by Daniel Bernardi. New Brunswick, N.J.: Rutgers University Press, 1996.

Guthrie, A. B. *The Big Sky.* New York: William Sloane, 1947.

——. *The Way West.* New York: William Sloane, 1949.

Hall, James. *Sketches of History, Life, and Manners in the West.* 2 vols. Philadelphia: Harrison Hall, 1835.

Hawkridge, John. "*The Battle at Elderbush Gulch.*" In *The BFI Companion to the Western.* Edited by Edward Buscombe. New York: Atheneum, 1988.

Hawthorne, Nathaniel. "The Duston Family." In *The Complete Writings of Nathaniel Hawthorne.* 22 vols. New York: Houghton Mifflin, 1903.

Hilger, Michael. *The American Indian in Film.* Metuchen, N.J.: Scarecrow, 1986.

——. *From Savage to Nobleman: Images of Native Americans in Film.* Lanham, Md.: Scarecrow, 1995.

Hogue, Alexander. *Erosion No. 2. Mother Earth Laid Bare.* [Painting.] 1938.

Horry, Peter and Mason Locke ["Parson"] Weems. *The Life of Gen'l Francis Marion, a Celebrated Partisan Officer in the Revolutionary War against the British and Tories in South Carolina and Georgia.* New York: John W. Lovell, n.d.

Horsman, Reginald. *Race and Manifest Destiny: The Origins of American Racial Anglo-Saxonism.* Cambridge: Harvard University Press, 1981.

Hubbard, William. *The History of the Indian Wars in New England: From the First Settlement to the Termination of the War with King Philip in 1677.* 2 vols. Revised by Samuel G. Drake. Facsimile reprint in one volume. Bowie, Md.: Heritage Books, 1990.

Huhndorf, Shari M. *Going Native: Indians in the American Cultural Imagination.* Ithaca: Cornell University Press, 2001.

Huston, John. *An Open Book.* New York: Knopf, 1980.

Hutton, Paul A. "Correct in Every Detail: General Custer in Hollywood." In *The Custer Reader.* Edited by Paul A. Hutton. Lincoln: University of Nebraska Press, 1992.

——. *Phil Sheridan and His Army.* Lincoln: University of Nebraska Press, 1985.

Internet Movie Database. http://www.us.imdb.com.

Irving, Washington. *A Tour on the Prairies.* Edited by John Francis McDermott. Norman: University of Oklahoma Press, 1956.

Jackson, Helen Hunt. *A Century of Dishonor: The Early Crusade for Indian Reform.* 1881. Edited by Andrew F. Rolle. New York: Harper Torchbooks, 1965.

———. *Ramona.* 1884. Reprint. New York: New American Library, Signet Classic, 1988.

Jennings, Francis. *The Invasion of America: Indians, Colonialism, and the Cant of Conquest.* New York: W. W. Norton, 1976.

Jones, Howard Mumford. *O Strange New World: American Culture: The Formative Years.* New York: Viking, 1964.

Kaminsky, Stuart M. *John Huston: Maker of Magic.* Boston: Houghton Mifflin, 1978.

Kelly, Fanny. *Narrative of My Captivity among the Sioux Indians.* Edited by Clark C. Spence and Mary Lee Spence. Stamford: Longmeadow, 1994.

Kilpatrick, Jacquelyn. *Celluloid Indians: Native Americans and Film.* Lincoln: University of Nebraska Press, 1999.

Kolodny, Annette. *The Lay of the Land: Metaphor as Experience and History in American Life and Letters.* Chapel Hill: University of North Carolina Press, 1975.

L'Amour, Louis. *Hondo.* 1953. Reprint. New York: Bantam, 1983.

Las Casas, Bartolomé de. *Brevísima relación de la destruición de las indias.* Edited by Consuelo Varela. Madrid: Editorial Castalia, 1999.

Lawrence, D. H. *Studies in Classic American Literature.* 1923. Reprint. New York: Penguin, 1977.

Lehman, Peter. "John Ford and the Auteur Theory." Ph.D. diss. University of Wisconsin-Madison, 1978.

———. "Texas 1868/America 1956: *The Searchers.*" In *Close Viewings: An Anthology of New Film Criticism.* Edited by Peter Lehman. Tallahassee: Florida State University Press, 1990.

LeMay, Alan. *The Unforgiven.* 1957. Reprint. New York: Berkeley, 1992.

Leonard, Elmore. *Hombre.* New York: Ballantine, 1961.

Leonardo, Da Vinci, . *The Notebooks of Leonardo da Vinci.* 2 vols. Compiled and edited by Jean Paul Richter. New York: Dover, 1970.

Lepore, Jill. *The Name of War: King Philip's War and the Origins of American Identity.* New York: Random House; New York: Vintage, 1998.

Lewis, Meriwether, and William Clark. *The Journals of Lewis and Clark.* Edited by Frank Bergon. New York: Penguin, 1989.

Lewis, R. W. B. *The American Adam: Innocence, Tragedy, and Tradition in the Nineteenth Century.* 1955. Reprint. Chicago: University of Chicago Press, 1984.

Lewis, Theodor H., ed. *Narrative of the Expedition of Hernando de Soto by the Gentleman of Elvas.* Translated by Buckingham Smith. In *Original Narratives of Early American History: Spanish Explorers in the Southern United States.* New York: Charles Scribner's Sons, 1907.

Limerick, Patricia Nelson. *The Legacy of Conquest: The Unbroken Past of the American West.* New York: Norton, 1987.

Lovell, Alan. "*The Searchers* and the Pleasure Principle." *Screen Education,* no. 17 (winter 1975/76): 53–57.

DBS Arts Library

Lyons, Donald. "Dances with Aldrich." *Film Comment* 27, no. 2 (March–April 1991): 72–76.

Maltby, Richard. "A Better Sense of History: John Ford and the Indians." In *The Book of Westerns*. Edited by Ian Cameron and Douglas Pye. New York: Continuum, 1996.

Marsden, Michael T., and Jack Nachbar. "The Indian in the Movies." In *History of Indian-White Relations*. Edited by Wilcomb E. Washburn. Vol. 4 of *Handbook of North American Indians*. Edited by William C. Sturtevant. Washington, D.C.: Smithsonian Institution, 1988.

Mather, Cotton. "A Narrative of Hannah Dustan's Notable Deliverance from Captivity." In *Puritans among the Indians: Accounts of Captivity and Redemption, 1676–1724*. Edited by Alden T. Vaughn and Edward W. Clark. Cambridge: Harvard University Press, Belknap Press, 1981.

McBride, Joseph, and Michael Wilmington. *John Ford*. New York: Da Capo, 1975.

McCarthy, Cormac. *Blood Meridian*. New York: Vintage, 1992.

Melville, Herman. *The Confidence-Man: His Masquerade*. Vol. 10 of *The Writings of Herman Melville*. Edited by Harrison Hayford, Hershel Parker, and G. Thomas Tanselle. Evanston, Ill.: Northwestern University Press, 1984.

———. *Omoo*. 1847. Mineola, New York: Dover, 2000.

———. *Typee*. 1846. New York: Penguin, 1996.

Miller, Angela. *The Empire of the Eye: Landscape Representations and American Cultural Politics, 1825–1875*. Ithaca: Cornell University Press, 1993.

Milne, Tom. "Robert Aldrich (1962 to 1978)." In *Robert Aldrich*. Edited by Richard Combs. London: British Film Institute, 1978.

Mitchell, Lee Clark. *Westerns: Making the Man in Fiction and Film*. Chicago: University of Chicago Press, 1996.

Moffitt, John F., and Santiago Sebastián. *O Brave New People: The European Invention of the American Indian*. Albuquerque: University of New Mexico Press, 1996.

Momaday, N. Scott. *House Made of Dawn*. New York: Harper and Row, 1968.

Moses, L. G. *Wild West Shows and the Images of American Indians, 1883–1933*. Albuquerque: University of New Mexico Press, 1996.

Murfin, Ross, and Supryia M. Ray. *The Bedford Glossary of Critical and Literary Terms*. Boston: Bedford, 1997.

Namias, June. *White Captives: Gender and Ethnicity on the American Frontier*. Chapel Hill: University of North Carolina Press, 1983.

Neal, Steve. "'The Story of Custer in Everything but Name'? Colonel Thursday and *Fort Apache*." *Journal of Film and Video* 47, nos. 1–3 (spring-fall 1995): 26–32.

Nelson, Dana D. *National Manhood: Capitalist Citizenship and the Imagined Fraternity of White Men*. Durham: Duke University Press, 1998.

Nemerov, Alex. "'Doing the "Old America"': The Image of the American West, 1880–1920." In *The West as America: Reinterpreting Images of the Frontier, 1820–1920*. Edited by William H. Truettner. Washington, D.C.: Smithsonian Institution, 1991.

Nester, William R. *The Great Frontier War: Britain, France, and the Imperial Struggle for North America, 1607–1755*. Westport: Praeger, 2000.

Nevins, Allan. Introduction to *Ponteach or the Savages of America: A Tragedy* by Robert Rogers. New York: Lenox Hill, 1914.

Nims, John Frederick. *Western Wind: An Introduction to Poetry*. 3d ed. New York: McGraw-Hill, 1992.

O'Brien, Geoffrey. "The Movie of the Century." *American Heritage* 47, no. 7 (November 1998): 16–22.

Olsen, T. V. *The Stalking Moon*. 1967. Reprint. New York: Leisure, 1997.

Opler, Morris E. "The Apachean Culture Pattern and Its Origins." In *Southwest*. Edited by Alfonso Ortiz. Vol. 10 of *Handbook of North American Indians*. Edited by William C. Sturtevant. Washington, D.C.: Smithsonian Institution, 1983.

——. "Chiricahua Apache."

——. "Mescalero Apache."

Paris, Barry. *Audrey Hepburn*. New York: G. P. Putnam's Sons, 1996.

Parkman, Francis. *The Conspiracy of Pontiac and the Indian War After the Conquest of Canada*. 6th ed. 1870. Reprint. New York: Library of America, 1991.

——. *The Oregon Trail: Sketches of Prairie and Rocky-Mountain Life*. 1849. Reprint. New York: Library of America, 1991.

——. *The Oregon Trail: Sketches of Prairie and Rocky-Mountain Life*. Boston: Little, Brown, 1892.

Pearce, Roy Harvey. *Savagism and Civilization: A Study of the Indian and the American Mind*. Berkeley: University of California Press, 1988.

Perez, Gilberto. *The Material Ghost: Films and their Medium*. Baltimore: Johns Hopkins University Press, 1998.

Plato. *Sophist*. In *The Dialogues of Plato*. 2 vols. Translated by Benjamin Jowett. New York: Random House, 1937.

Prats, Armando José. "His Master's Voice(over): Revisionist Ethos and Narrative Dependence from *Broken Arrow* (1950) to *Geronimo: An American Legend*." *ANQ* 9, no. 3 (summer 1996): 15–29.

——. "The Image of the Other and the Other *Dances With Wolves*." *Journal of Film and Video*, no. 50 (spring 1998): 3–20.

——. "'Outfirsting' the First American: 'History,' the American Adam, and the Hollywood Indian in Three Recent Westerns." In *Proceedings of the Society for the Interdisciplinary Study of Social Imagery*. Colorado Springs: Colorado State University Press, 1996.

Pratt, Mary Louise. *Imperial Eyes: Travel Writing and Transculturation*. London: Routledge, 1992.

Price, John A. "The Stereotyping of North American Indians in Motion Pictures." In *The Pretend Indians: Images of Native Americans in the Movies*. Edited by Gretchen M. Bataille and Charles P. Silet. Ames: Iowa University Press, 1980.

Pye, Douglas. "*The Searchers* and Teaching the Industry." *Screen Education*, no. 17 (winter 1975/76): 34–48.

Rankin, Hugh F. *Francis Marion: The Swamp Fox*. New York: Thomas Y. Crowell, 1973.

Remington, Frederic. *The Collected Writings of Frederic Remington*. Edited by Peggy Samuels and Harold Samuels. Garden City: Doubleday, 1979.

Ringel, Harry. "Up to Date with Robert Aldrich" [interview]. *Sight and Sound* 43, no. 3 (summer 1974): 166–69.

Roberts, Kenneth. *Northwest Passage*. Garden City: Doubleday, 1937.

Rogers, Robert. *Journals of Major Robert Rogers*. Dublin: J. Sheppard and J. Milliken, 1759.

Roosevelt, Theodore. *From the Alleghanies to the Mississippi, 1769–1776*. Vol. 1 of *The Winning of the West*. Lincoln: University of Nebraska Press, 1995.

Rowlandson, Mary White. *The Sovereignty and Goodness of God*. In *Puritans among the Indians: Accounts of Captivity and Redemption, 1676–1724*. Edited by Alden T. Vaughn and Edward W. Clark. Cambridge: Harvard University Press, Belknap Press, 1981.

Russell, Don. *The Lives and Legends of Buffalo Bill*. Norman: University of Oklahoma Press, 1960.

Said, Edward. *Beginnings: Intention and Method*. New York: Columbia University Press, 1985.

———. *Orientalism*. New York: Random House, 1978.

Sale, Kirkpatrick. *The Conquest of Paradise: Christopher Columbus and the Columbian Legacy*. New York: Penguin, 1990.

Sarris, Andrew. *The John Ford Movie Mystery*. Bloomington: Indiana University Press, 1975.

Scheckel, Susan. *The Insistence of the Indian: Race and Nationalism in Nineteenth-Century American Culture*. Princeton: Princeton University Press, 1998.

Schimmel, Julie. "Inventing 'the Indian.'" In *The West as America: Reinterpreting Images of the Frontier, 1820–1920*. Edited by William H. Truettner. Washington, D.C.: Smithsonian Institution, 1991.

Seaver, James E. *A Narrative of the Life of Mrs. Mary Jemison*. Edited by June Namias. 1824. Reprint. Norman: University of Oklahoma Press, 1992.

Sedgwick, Catharine Maria. *Hope Leslie; or, Early Times in the Massachusetts*. 1827. Edited by Mary Kelley. Reprint. New Brunswick, N.J.: Rutgers University Press, 1987.

Sewall, Samuel. *The Diary of Samuel Sewall*. 2 vols. Edited by M. Halsey Thomas. New York: Farrar, Straus and Giroux, 1973.

Sheehan, Bernard W. *Seeds of Extinction: Jeffersonian Philanthropy and the American Indian*. New York: Norton, 1974.

Slotkin, Richard. *The Fatal Environment: The Myth of the Frontier in the Age of Industrialization, 1800–1890*. Middletown: Wesleyan University Press, 1985.

———. *Gunfighter Nation: The Myth of the Frontier in Twentieth-Century America*. New York: Atheneum, 1992.

———. *Regeneration through Violence: The Mythology of the American Frontier 1600–1860*. Middletown: Wesleyan University Press, 1973.

Smith, Captain John. *Captain John Smith: A Select Edition of his Writings*. Edited by Karen Ordahl Kupperman. Chapel Hill: University of North Carolina Press, 1988.

Sollors, Werner. *Beyond Ethnicity: Consent and Descent in American Culture*. New York: Oxford University Press, 1986.

Thomson, David. "Open and Shut: A Fresh Look at *The Searchers*." *Film Comment* 33, no. 4 (July–August 1997): 29–31.

Thoreau, Henry David. *Walking*. 1862. Boston: Applewood, 1987.

———. *A Week on the Concord and Merrimack Rivers*. 1849. New York: Library of America, 1985.

Thorp, Raymond W., and Robert Bunker. *Crow Killer: The Saga of Liver-Eating Johnson*. Bloomington: Indiana University Press, Midland Books, 1983.

Thrapp, Dan L. "Cochise (Apache)." In vol. 1 of *Encyclopedia of the American West*. Edited by Charles Phillips and Alan Axelrod. New York: Simon and Schuster, 1996.

———. *The Conquest of Apacheria*. Norman: University of Oklahoma Press, 1967.

Todorov, Tzvetan. *The Conquest of America: The Question of the Other*. Translated by Richard Howard. New York: Harper and Row, 1984.

Tompkins, Jane. *West of Everything: The Inner Life of Westerns*. New York: Oxford University Press, 1992.

Turner, Frederick Jackson. "The Significance of the Frontier in American History." 1893. In *The Turner Thesis Concerning the Role of the Frontier in American History*. Edited by George Rogers Taylor. 3d ed. Lexington, Mass.: D. C. Heath, 1972.

Tuska, John. *A Variable Harvest: Essays and Reviews of Film and Literature*. Jefferson, N.C.: McFarland, 1990.

Twain, Mark. *Roughing It*. Edited by Hamlin Hill. New York: Penguin Books, 1981.

———. *Roughing It*. 1872. Vol. 2 of *The Works of Mark Twain*, edited by Paul Baender. Reprint. Berkeley: University of California Press for the Iowa Center for Textual Studies, 1972.

Utley, Robert M. *Cavalier in Buckskin: George Armstrong Custer and the Western Military Frontier*. Norman: University of Oklahoma Press, 1988.

———. *The Indian Frontier of the American West, 1846–1890*. Albuquerque: University of New Mexico Press, 1984.

Unruh, John D. Jr. *The Plains Across: The Overland Emigrants and the Trans-Mississippi West, 1840–60*. Urbana: University of Illinois Press, 1979.

Vaughn, Alden T. *New England Frontier: Puritans and Indians, 1620–1675*. 3d ed. Norman: University of Oklahoma Press, 1995.

Vidor, King. *King Vidor on Film Directing*. New York: David McKay, 1972.

Vizenor, Gerald. *Manifest Manners: Postindian Warriors of Survivance*. Hanover: Wesleyan University Press, 1994.

Wagenknecht, Edward, and Anthony Slide. *The Films of D. W. Griffith*. New York: Crown, 1975.

Waller, Gregory. "*Rambo*: Getting to Win This Time." In *From Hanoi to Hollywood: The Vietnam War in American Film*. Edited by Linda Dittmar and Gene Michaud. New Brunswick, N.J.: Rutgers University Press, 1990.

Washburn, Wilcomb E. "The Clash of Morality in the American Forest." In *First

Images of America: The Impact of the New World on the Old, vol. 1. Edited by Fredi Chiapelli. Berkeley: University of California Press, 1976.

Webb, Walter Prescott. *The Great Plains*. 1931. Lincoln: University of Nebraska Press, 1959.

West, Elliott. *The Way to the West: Essays on the Central Plains*. Albuquerque: University of New Mexico Press, 1995.

Wexman, Virginia Wright. "The Family on the Land: Race and Nationhood in Silent Westerns." In *The Birth of Whiteness: Race and the Emergence of U.S. Cinema*. Edited by Daniel Bernardi. New Brunswick, N.J.: Rutgers University Press, 1996.

Wister, Owen. *The Virginian, a Horseman of the Plains*. New York: Grosset and Dunlap, 1902.

Index

Page numbers given in *italics* indicate illustrations. Films are followed by date or director's name. Titles of books or works of art are followed by author's or artist's name.